A Thousand Tears Falling

For Bob Silano
In the spirit of peace

Lubbock, Texas
15 March 08

A Thousand Tears Falling

The True Story of a Vietnamese Family

Torn Apart by War, Communism, and the CIA

Yung Krall

LONGSTREET PRESS
Atlanta, Georgia

Published by
LONGSTREET PRESS, INC.
A subsidiary of Cox Newspapers,
A subsidiary of Cox Enterprises, Inc.
2140 Newmarket Parkway
Suite 118
Marietta, GA   30067

Printed in the United States of America

1st printing 1995

Library of Congress Catalog Card Number: 95-77247

ISBN 1-56352-231-4

This book was printed by Quebecor Printing, Martinsburg, W. Va.
Film Preparation by Holland Graphics, Inc., Mableton, GA
Jacket photograph courtesy Indochina Archive, University of California–Berkeley
Jacket design by Jeff and Leslie Cohen
Book typeset by Laura McDonald

To my grandparents, who gave me roots,
and my parents, who gave me wings.

In memories of my brother Hai Van,
and my dear friends Sergeant Nguyen van Phan, ARVN,
and Captain Robert Eugene Spiegel, U.S. Army.

P.O.W. Lieutenant Colonel Charles R. Connor, U.S. Marine Corps.
You are not forgotten.

"To those who fight for it, life has a flavor the protected never know."

FOREWORD
BY GRIFFIN B. BELL
Former United States Attorney General

More than twenty years after the United States withdrew its forces from Viet Nam, Americans still wrestle with the pain and loss that resulted from this divisive war. Huge crowds gather daily at The Wall in Washington, D.C., to remember the nearly sixty thousand Americans who died in the conflict; popular movies like *Forrest Gump* remind us of the physical and emotional carnage that resulted; remains of some American MIA's are slowly, painfully returned, bringing closure for a few families, while others still wait and wonder; national debate and even protests are sparked anew by Robert McNamara's reassessment of America's military involvement in Southeast Asia; and impassioned speeches ring from the floor of the U.S. Congress as the president authorizes the resumption of diplomatic relations with Viet Nam.

This national catharsis is further complicated by our growing compassion for the people who were not "the enemy." Images of Vietnamese families running from burning villages, bombs raining fire on the rice fields, and families being divided by the civil war are forever fresh in our minds. From this horrific and nightmarish backdrop now emerges an individual's true story of honor and courage that is a testament to the human spirit.

In *A Thousand Tears Falling*, Yung Krall — a daughter of the Vietnamese Communist ambassador to the Soviet Union who was loyal to Ho Chi Minh, and a granddaughter of a South Vietnamese patriot who was reared to believe in democracy — gives her personal account of life in the cross fire.

Yung grew up in the midst of war, and, in the absence of her father, she embraced the ideals of democracy and freedom. She married a U.S. naval officer and came to the States, bringing with her the many lessons she had learned from her extraordinary family. During my tenure as attorney general of the

United States, I came to know of her as a valuable asset in our intelligence community, where she was an operative for the Central Intelligence Agency. Her love for America led her to become the key witness in the prosecution of the "Magic Dragon" espionage case, knowingly placing herself and her young son at great risk.

Yung Krall is truly a great American. I appreciate her service to our country, and I am delighted that this remarkable woman's story is finally available for others to read and know. My hope is that it will contribute to the healing process that continues in this country and in Viet Nam.

ACKNOWLEDGMENTS

Words are not enough to thank my mother for living a life of unconditional love for my father, and for her total devotion for us, her children. I thank her for allowing me to share our family's story with other families.

Thanks also to Lance, my son, who lived part of this story, and at his young age brought brief moments of happiness into his grandfather's heart. Lance's childhood was certainly happier than mine, and I have the United States of America to thank for that.

From the bottom of my heart, I want to thank Judge Griffin Bell, my mentor, for his endless encouragement and invaluable assistance. His help was always there when I needed it.

I am indebted to the legal advice from my friend Quinlan J. Shea, Jr., the attorney who took on the monumental task to assist me in dealing with the CIA Publication Review Board — especially with my stubbornness and unwillingness to let the CIA censor my family's story. I thank him for his untiring efforts to protect my rights, and I cherish our friendship.

I would like to express my thanks to my friend and warm supporter Richard Matthews at the *Atlanta Journal*, who shared with me his knowledge of the art of writing.

I want to thank Chuck Perry and Suzanne Comer Bell of Longstreet Press, who made me feel ten feet tall when they accepted my manuscript for publication. It was a pleasure to work with Suzanne in many different stages of this book, and I thank her for her meticulous work in editing the final manuscript.

Credits go to Alexa Selph, my editor, in formulating and substantiating the contents of the censored manuscript.

I want to take this moment to thank my friends Dinh Thach Bich, Larry Engelmann, John Martin, Douglas Pike, John Peterson, Dale Pruna, Don Rochlen, Wick Tourison, Gary Vancena, Chuck Wilcox, and Kit Tang-Wilcox — whose words and deeds in no small ways led to the publishing of this book.

But most of all, I want to thank John, my husband, who always stands by me and whose personal contribution has made the last chapter of our family a happy one. John's love and encouragement helped make the completion of this book possible.

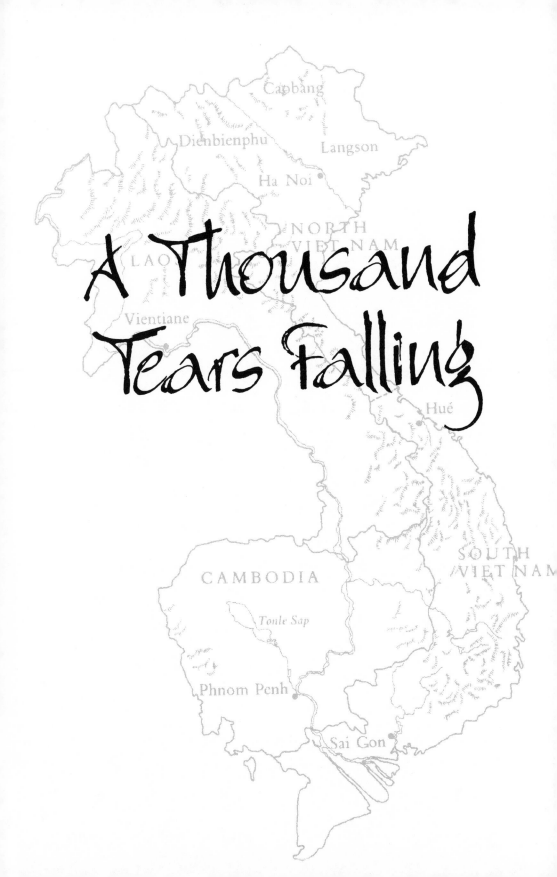

A Thousand Tears Falling

Chapter 1

May 1954

When I was a child, a great notion was imprinted on my heart about the colors on my country's flag. The broad field of bold red symbolized courage; the bright yellow star stood for the courageous race of the Vietnamese people. Other colors had meanings, too. My big sisters had said that blue is the color of hope, and when the revolutionary troupe came to our village to perform their plays, they festooned the village gate with beautiful blue banners.

And then one day it rained blue from the skies.

Airplanes from the peacekeeping force soared over our land and dropped blue leaflets throughout the Liberated Zone, the area in the Mekong Delta of South Viet Nam controlled by the Vietnamese known as Viet Minh. The Viet Minh drew a line in the rice paddies — in the countryside or deep jungle — to keep the French out. Running about in the downpour of blue paper, I caught a leaflet that was still twirling in the air. Hurrying home as fast as I could, I sat down and tried to read it.

At this time I was only halfway through my dog-eared reading primer, so many of the words printed in black ink on the leaflet were unfamiliar to me. The words "Hoa Binh" leapt out at me from the page, however, words I knew well. Hoa Binh is my baby sister's name, and it means "peace."

The word "Geneve" wasn't in my primer, but it was a household word in my family. My parents and my brother had talked about it for many months. Standing between the two earthen water barrels under the rainguard of my house, I struggled to make sense of the leaflet, but I couldn't. Finally, my mother saw me and came to help me figure out the words I didn't know.

That evening, at dinner, I pulled the paper from the pocket of my shorts and showed off my reading ability. When I finished, I asked my father what the message meant. He told us that Ha Noi and the French had reached an agreement at the Geneva Conference, an agreement that meant peace for us at last. The French will no longer be able to kill our people, he said. They lost at Dien Bien Phu, we won, and the French will soon have to sail back to France.

Dien Bien Phu — a battle zone I knew by heart, a place that gave our people hope. Many of our men had died for the red and yellow flag there, but, more important, thousands of French soldiers had died, and with them the French goal of ruling over our land. General Vo Nguyen Giap, the commander of the historic battle, became our brother, our hero, our national treasure. The families who had sons and brothers on the side of the revolution felt enormous pride at the mention of Dien Bien Phu; others who had no one in the fighting felt an emptiness in their hearts.

My mother counted on her fingers to show me that I was eight years old, and told me to remember that day forever: When I had turned eight, the French had lost the war. There were no eight candles for me to blow out to win my wishes and dreams, but wishes came true on every inch of the land when the news of the victory reached us. I had learned the meaning of the showers of blue paper that day.

Hoa Binh! Hoa Binh! Hoa Binh! The joy showed in my father's face, in his smile, and in the brisk, light steps of his stride when he took me to our makeshift classroom the next morning. All the children gathered for the flag-raising ceremony, something that had become a rather routine chore over time but something that was today a special honor. As the children sang the national anthem, my father joined in, and I caught sight of the twinkle in his eyes as he sang the words. Even though it was a warm and sunny morning, I suddenly quivered, and goosebumps ran from the top of my head to every part of my body.

In those days, even Mother Nature seemed in tune with the mood of the people. The moon was bright, the tide was high, and fish jumped in the river. The family talked about "going home" to our grandparents' village. I thought about what it would be like when Uncle Hai Hoi, a village handyman and builder who worked for my grandparents, came to take us back there: He would no doubt repeat his familiar phrase about how we "kicked the French's asses," and he would celebrate with a bottle of rice wine and smell awfully bad.

Life was going to be different from now on. The villagers where my grandparents lived, in the area that had not been liberated, would not have to talk to the French with their hats in their hands anymore. The "coolies," slave-like workers for the French, would be able to return to their farms to work with dignity. Most of all, I was happy to realize that we would never have to run to the underground shelter at the sound of an airplane. No more air raids!

I could tell that my father shared some of my feelings. I could hear it in the tone of his violin, when he played music from foreign lands that he had not played in a long time. The spirits of our brothers who had died at Dien Bien Phu were still with us, and freedom was so close we could almost touch it.

But the "peacemakers" in Ha Noi had other plans.

Hoa Binh alone, the way simple people wanted it, was not the kind of peace Ha Noi had in mind. I didn't understand it at all, even when I heard snatches of my parents' arguments. The spirit of the Dien Bien Phu victory hadn't lasted very long in my family's home. My mother and father argued late into the night about "socialism," whatever that was. They fought about it, my mother cried over it, and all the children were upset by it. Sometimes I had bad dreams because of the arguing, and I wasn't the only one disturbed. One night my brother Hai Van, who was five years old, was jolted awake by the loud voices of the unending argument. He stood up on his bed and shouted out, "*Cam noi!*" which meant, "You are not allowed to talk!"

One night my father spoke to all of us and told us he was going to have to leave for Ha Noi, to continue his work for the revolution. He gave my mother a choice: We could go with him, or go back and live with our grand-parents in Long Thanh and wait for him — for two years.

My twin sisters Kim and Cuong welcomed the idea of going back to Long Thanh. My mother didn't seem to like either of the choices. That night we all went to bed troubled. I crawled into bed with my oldest brother Khoi, who was seventeen, as I liked to do when anything kept me awake — when the moon was too bright, or when the night insects made too much noise outside the house. That night Khoi stayed awake for a long time. I could hear his angry breathing, but he wouldn't talk about what was bothering him. He just told me to close my eyes and "count the falling leaves."

The argument raged for days. Hai Van and I were "too young to under-stand," everyone said, but I listened to the discussions just the same. "Tap Ket" became the new household word — meaning "regroup." Father said the rev-olutionary forces had to gather in Ha Noi to help Ho Chi Minh, or Uncle Ho, prepare the way for a real peace, a permanent peace. The Geneva agreement, he explained, had divided Viet Nam into two parts, North and South. In two years there was to be an election to reunify the country, and so much work would be necessary to prepare for that day. Finally it was decided that my mother and the children would stay in the South, while my father and his comrades went north for the "regrouping." I couldn't understand why he wasn't going to take us with him; after all, weren't we on his side, too, even closer than the men of the revolution?

Ours was not the only family being split by the need for "Tap Ket." My mother's brother Diep, whose wife had died only recently, was going north as well. He would leave his eight children — ranging from a son about three years old to a daughter in her early twenties — with our grandparents in Long Thanh. My mother's youngest brother Thuy would also leave his new wife with them to go to Ha Noi.

Then I learned news that was even more shattering to me. At dinner one night it was decided that my brother Khoi was going with the other men. The talk between my parents and Khoi centered on how great it would be for him to attend Ha Noi University, and maybe win a chance to go on to Russia for higher study. Chances like that meant nothing to me; I only knew that I was going to lose my father — and now my big brother as well. For some reason, I had accepted the fact that my father would have to go, for any decent man must fight for his country in time of war. But why my brother? When my father had been away on his many earlier trips, everyone had said that Khoi was "the man of the family." But if Khoi left, too, then who would be the man of our family?

I was more angry than sad. I jumped up from the table and ran from the room, giving my dinner to the dog. Later that night I said to Khoi, "If you love me, don't go to Ha Noi." He tried to convince me that a man must have a good education for his family and his country, but I argued that our grandfather in Long Thanh had never gone to a university and had still become a good grandfather and a great chief of his village. Khoi countered by saying that "Granddad is a prince and I am not. He is a genius, and I am just an ordinary boy." No matter how much he talked, I could not accept it. There was no way for me to understand my brother's wishes then.

Khoi and I stayed up very late in his room that night. He even let me play with his violin, which was rare, because violin strings were among the most valuable items in our house. In those days of "antiluxury," when we were expected to share in the hardships of those who were fighting for the revolution, my father wouldn't allow us to accept gifts from our friends in the city, such as perfumed soap or fabric that was too brightly colored — or, naturally, any French products. There were just two exceptions: violin strings and quinine tablets.

As the time came closer for the men to depart and for us to move to Long Thanh, I became more and more apprehensive about going back to the "city" — that is, the area outside the Liberated Zone. I had been born in the city in Can Tho province, but when I was only six months old my parents had taken the family into the Liberated Zone, and the only thing I had left from my brief stay there was the birth certificate that the midwife had filed for me at the city hall. Ironically, even this was not going to be of any use to me when we returned to the old French-held areas. My father had instructed my mother to file a new set of birth certificates for all of us to hide our true identities from the national secret police. We could keep our given names, but the name of our father had to be left blank. If the court pressed her for the father's name, he said, my mother was to say he was "missing." The word was terribly disturbing to me, because I didn't want to think of my father as missing, but Khoi told me that to survive you must be strong and learn to live with all kinds of difficulties — yet always "remember who you are."

Soon our friend Uncle Hai Hoi arrived in a big boat to help us move. The boat, rented from someone in our grandparents' village, had a huge old sail and four poling paddles, two in front and two in back. I had no idea how long it was, but it was roomy enough for Hai Van and me to run around and play hide-and-seek in it. We liked the decoration on the front and sides — a great water dragon, dramatic in red and green paint, its tail stretching half the length of the boat.

Uncle Hai Hoi, who built nice houses for us and loved his creations, was hoping that he would take our house apart, as he had done in a previous move, to rebuild in Long Thanh. But my father disappointed him; he had already promised to leave the house standing and give it to another "comrade" and his family.

The grown-ups got busy packing and getting things ready for the trip. My mother was outside watering the eggplant rows in our garden. Pointing to the okra, which were as big as my thumb, she remarked that the new people would be able to pick them as soon as they moved in after our departure. Angrily, I blurted out that we ought to pull them up and throw them away since we wouldn't be able to eat them. My mother was disappointed at that, but at the time I didn't care. I was so upset and filled with feelings of contempt that I just wanted to hurt somebody or something. I looked at my dog as if I wanted to kick him, but he looked even sadder than I.

Uncle Hai Hoi took charge of things, telling my mother to stand aside and watch over my little sister Minh Tam, who had been born just three months before. He and my father made trip after trip to the boat, lashing the furniture onto the roof and covering it with straw mats, packing pots and pans and linens into any space they could find. Khoi took apart my mother's sewing machine so they could store it in a lower deck away from the rain; it was probably the most valuable item in our house.

Father's instructions about the birth certificates were only the beginning of the precautions he forced us to take. As we were preparing for our move, he had told us we wouldn't be able to take anything along that could be used to identify our backgrounds or link us to him. As we were going through our belongings, he took away from me the khaki backpack that Khoi had given me as a keepsake; it was North Vietnamese government issue, he said, and if I was caught in possession of such a recognizable piece of military equipment I would be questioned, and our family might be endangered. All I was left with to remember Khoi by was his old slingshot, a dried bird's nest that he had hung in his room, and a piece of old wax he had used for his violin.

One day, shortly before our departure, Father had asked Kim and Cuong to show him the "family album." It wasn't much of a photo collection, because we didn't have a camera and the only time we had our pictures taken was when visitors from the city came with their cameras. Kim and Cuong pasted the pictures in a scrapbook, and were considered the "guardians" of the collection.

When Father asked for it, the girls at first played coy. Cuong said she didn't know where it was; Kim said she hadn't seen it for a long time. They must have known what was coming. Told to find it right away, they went off and Kim brought the scrapbook to him, and he told them the bad news: We had to get rid of the pictures.

There were long faces as he went through the pages removing the pictures of our family's past. My mother was in tears. He saved a few, such as a picture of my grandfather, whom we would be living with anyway, but most had to go. One photo showed Hai Van and me posing with Uncle Le Duc Tho, one of the leaders of the revolution. Tho would one day head the delegation to the Paris Peace Talks and eventually be awarded the Nobel Peace Prize with Henry Kissinger. Tho refused to accept the award, claiming that peace had not yet come to Viet Nam. My mother took the photo and a pair of scissors and carefully cut me away from him; she then trimmed Hai Van away from the other side. She handed what was left, just the skinny body of Le Duc Tho, to my father and said, "Here, you can have your comrade."

We all laughed, but the process wasn't funny. Father came to one picture that showed him, Hai Van, and me together. I could tell from the fact that we were wearing our best new clothes that it had been taken on the first day of Tet, the Vietnamese New Year celebration. When he took that photo out of the album to be destroyed, I panicked. I decided to steal it back, and when my father looked away I slipped it under my seat. Kim and Cuong got upset when he took out pictures of them with their teachers and classmates at the boarding school, and stalked away from the table. Father calmly continued his inspections without us.

The night before we left Cang Chu Hang hamlet, my father left for a trip. He kissed my infant sister Minh Tam for the longest time. Hoa Binh walked him to the boat and stayed until the man untied the rope and pushed away from the bank; she cried. Hai Van sat on the dock with his feet in the water. The woman who owned the land where our house stood — we called her "grandmother" — came with her family to say goodbye, and she was extremely emotional. For the first time I heard her say to my father, "Forgive me for saying this, but I love you like my own son. Hurry back, please!" Father kissed me repeatedly and told me, "I'll see you in Long Thanh," but I still wasn't sure if I would ever see him again. The grandmother cried, and my mother cried, my sisters cried — but I couldn't.

Early the next morning we got on the boat to leave this dearest home, but after everyone was on board someone realized our dog, No, was missing. Mother said she wouldn't leave without him, so we tied the boat back to the dock, clambered out and went searching the fields for him. Uncle Hai Hoi kept looking at the sun, climbing higher and higher in the sky, and urging us to leave. Finally he persuaded her to come with us. We set sail, but Khoi walked along the riverbank beside us, calling out the whole time for No.

That night my mother cried so much that Uncle Hai Hoi relented. Early the next morning she and Khoi walked back toward the village while the rest of us waited in the boat. Shortly before noon they returned, with No trotting alongside them. They had found him lying by the guava tree near the play-house Khoi had built for us. He had made a crying sound when they approached, but wouldn't get up; Khoi had to pick him up and carry him a long way before he would follow them away from his home.

We kept telling No that Long Thanh would be a much better place for him — there weren't as many mosquitoes as there were in Cang Chu Hang, we insisted. He was unconvinced. For some reason, No lost his playfulness that day, and he acted like an old dog for the rest of his life.

Underway again, the boat sped along with the current and with the sails shaking in a full breeze, as if it were in a hurry to reach Long Thanh. All of us were full of chatter about what kinds of things we would like to have "when the war is over." Usually, we weren't allowed to talk of such "materi-alistic" things at home; my father would give us a disapproving look and would scold my mother for failing to teach her children properly. But in the boat, with my father away and with Uncle Hai Hoi's encouragement, we talked about new clothes, new shoes, umbrellas, perfumed soap, bras, tooth-paste, candies, and everything the capitalist society could offer. I felt guilty for enjoying my father's absence that way, but the chance to talk about such things without whispering was an unexplainable feeling of freedom — like the feeling I had when guests came and I could get away with naughty behavior because my parents were too busy with the company.

I measured the length of our journey by the meals we ate: three breakfasts, three lunches, and two dinners before reaching the outskirts of Long Thanh. We had to sleep in the boat the last night waiting for Aunt Bay, my mother's older sister, to come out and give us the signal that it was safe to go into the village.

A few days after we got there, Uncle Diep's children arrived. Yen, the oldest, had a four-year-old daughter and an eighteen-month-old son, and was hugely pregnant. One of her sisters, Thu Van, had decided to go to Ha Noi with her father to enter the university and pursue her dream of becoming a doctor. That left Yen, whose husband also went to Ha Noi, the responsibility of looking after her own children as well as her three other sisters and her youngest brother, Quoc.

Uncle Thuy's new wife arrived soon afterward, and the household was complete. There would be thirteen grandchildren and two great-grandchildren (and one more on the way) crowded into my grandparents' house. Despite it all, they seemed happy to have us. My aunt spent her days in the kitchen feeding this little army, my grandmother shuttled back and forth tending first one child and then another, and my grandfather looked forward to being a tutor to all of us when we registered for school in the village.

Grandmother hired people from the coolie hamlet to empty the fish pond, a common practice to "catch" all the mature fish. They built a dam at the mouth of the pond and then bailed furiously with scoops made of bamboo and sealed with tar. My cousins Thao and Yvonne and I sloshed around in the mud for the joy of catching the fish that were flopping about in the dwindling pond. Some of the big ones we caught were stored in earthen barrels, some were put into bamboo containers and immersed in the river to keep them alive and fresh. Later the pond would be restocked with fish and water from other ponds in the area.

We had fun, but our minds were never fully at ease, because we knew that soon our fathers would be coming to say goodbye to us for a long time.

Long Thanh village had never been "liberated" by the Viet Minh, so when my father and my uncles finally came, they disguised themselves as peasants coming home from a day working in the rice fields. We recognized them right away just the same.

My grandmother began weeping when they arrived. My grandfather, who hadn't seen them in three years, remarked sadly, "So my heroes come home to say goodbye again?"

For a while there was laughter as everyone greeted everyone else, but there were other feelings, spoken and unspoken, among all of us. I heard my grand-father asking his sons and son–in–law, "What will happen to these children?" I didn't hear their answer.

My grandmother hugged Uncle Thuy over and over. She touched Uncle Diep's gray hair, she held my father's hands, and her face was full of sorrow.

Grandmother's hearing was poor, a side effect from medicine she had taken to cure her tuberculosis, so she spoke louder than the rest of us without real-izing it. "This morning the nationalist soldiers were here," she boomed out to Uncle Thuy. "They said they want to see the senator," which is the title my father held. Uncle Thuy gestured at her to speak more softly, but she just gave him a tolerant smile. "Your father was angry. He told them to sit in the shade and wait, and if they were lucky, they would get to see the senator."

My father and my uncles were all Viet Minh, like many other men and women who were against the French domination. As revolutionaries they were slowly recruited by the Communists from Ha Noi, as Ho Chi Minh sent cadres to the South to spread Communist ideas in the hearts of these patriots. My father joined the Communists and became one of the founders of the South Vietnamese Communist Party; he was elected senator in the southern region, inside the liberated areas. By going to Ha Noi that year, he would be linking up with the National Liberation Front, an organization formed by the Ha Noi government for the Viet Cong and Southerners who joined Ho Chi Minh in the North in 1954.

Ha Noi, of course, wanted control of the whole country, but they knew the Southerners would not accept them. So the NLF became the "front" for their invasion. During the Viet Nam War, Ha Noi often mentioned that they "helped" their Southerners to rid the American imperialists.

We thought Grandmother's loud announcement was amusing, and we laughed, but my father's response reminded us that war was serious business: "Mother, don't worry. I have people to secure the road."

My grandfather was bitter that the men were going to be leaving their fam-ilies again. He believed that a country needs more than a great leader, it needs people — people with families and women and men with purpose. He didn't like the socialist system, either. Living in a socialist country, he told us, is like a child growing up in a closet. "Imagine your limitations in that kind of sys-tem," he said. "You have the sky, the air, the rivers, the freedom to roam free. One must bear a curse to put himself in such a system." My grandfather and his sons had great love for each other, but they disappointed each other with their opposing ideals.

Our world was a small circle. Up to that point the village that was under my father's control had been our cradle, just as the moon, the rivers, and the rain had been our lullabies. (In any village we came to, people gave us their land, their homes, their hospitality. It was the Communist way to help their leaders, but my mother didn't think it was right, and she would pay rent without my father's knowledge.) On that day, the family reunion marked the end of my father's protection for us. I felt lonely and uncertain, and I wondered what would happen to us after he and Khoi had gone.

A lavish meal was prepared and placed on the high table at the ancestors' altar in my grandparents' house. Grandmother lined us all up to burn incense sticks with her as the meal was offered to our deceased relatives — our great-grandparents, Uncle Diep's wife, his daughter who had died when she was eight, my cousin Liem, my uncles Sac and The. Grandmother prayed earnestly before the altar, asking the spirits of all those loved ones to protect those who were leaving and to see that they returned home safely. We children liked the religious ceremonies at my grandparents' home — for the food, the fragrance of the smoldering incense, and the unforgettable warm smell of fresh lotus blossoms my grandmother always placed near the portrait of her mother.

That night, at our last dinner together, the talk was interrupted by another reminder of the harshness of war. While we were eating, one of the men who guarded my father and my uncles came in and asked to speak to Uncle Thuy outside. They left, and my father followed a few moments later. The air around the table became stale, and the meal continued in a heavy silence.

Returning to his seat, my father explained that there was a man who wanted to cross the highway. He claimed that his mother was very ill and he wanted to be with her, but because no one knew who he was my father had asked him to wait until dawn before leaving the village.

Grandfather sipped his rice wine slowly while Father spoke, then said he didn't think my father should make such decisions involving other people. Put yourself in his place, he said. "If my daughter was ill, I would want Khoi to rush home to be with his mother," he said.

Uncle Thuy justified their position with the explanation that they weren't sure who the man was: He might be telling the truth, but then again he might be an informer for the nationalist secret police. Or he could be captured and tortured by the nationalist soldiers. (Life wasn't easy for Vietnamese on either side!) The man wouldn't be allowed to go on that night, nor would he be allowed to return to his farm.

After we cleared the table, Uncle Thuy brought the man into the house. He was a peasant, his bare feet covered with mud, his black trousers rolled up to his knees and wet up to his thighs. He was nervous and frightened, and didn't know what to do with his hands. He greeted the family without looking directly at our eyes.

The guard pulled the man closer to my father and pointed at him: "Do you know who this is?" "No, brother cadre," the peasant replied, "I do not know him." My father signaled for the guard to leave, and Uncle Diep got a chair for the man. He sat on the edge of the chair, wringing his hands, while my father explained why they could not let him go right away. The man didn't seem to be listening. "My mother is very ill," he kept saying. "I wish to be there before she goes."

My aunt took me and my cousins away from the dining area, but I went to my grandmother's bedroom and peeked through the doorway. I saw the man cover his face with his hands; he sobbed, and I winced at the sound. As I watched him humiliating himself in front of my father and my uncles, I thought for the first time that my father might be wrong.

Later that night I tried to talk to Khoi about it, but he said it was too late to talk about anything. I believe he just didn't want to talk about the man at all. The pitiful scene had touched us all.

Khoi went back to sleep easily, but the sound of the mosquitoes grew louder and kept me awake, so I went to my father and got him out of bed. He thought I needed to go to the outhouse, but I told him I just wanted to talk. We went out onto the porch so we wouldn't wake the others.

It was unfair to hold that man, I told him, and I couldn't sleep because I thought he was wrong. Father told me that life is not always fair. "Then you make it fair," I said. "You are the senator."

It wasn't just for their own protection that he and my uncles had detained the man, my father explained. If the man had gone across the highway and the canal that night, he might have been captured by the nationalist soldiers. They might have interrogated him, and if he didn't cooperate they might have killed him, he said.

I didn't know what to say. My father kissed my forehead and said, "You are my daughter. You will always care for other people before you care for yourself."

We sat there for a long time, watching as the morning light began to emerge from the darkness. We didn't talk any more about the man. Father sat on a ceramic stool, and he picked me up and sat me on his lap. He kissed my hair and held me tight. There was enough light for me to see tears on his face. We sat there until the cock crowed.

That last morning, Uncle Diep and his children and grandchildren sat close together on one side of the table at breakfast. My father held Minh Tam in his arms all morning, while Hoa Binh clung to him like a baby monkey. My mother stayed away from him but talked almost continuously to Khoi. Grandmother went around repeating herself endlessly: "Take good care of yourselves, my sons." She told them to write, and they promised they would.

Kim and Cuong were so quiet in those last few days; they didn't even fight, as they usually did. I wondered what was in their minds, and what was in my mother's mind. I wasn't even sure what I thought. I felt lost and lonely in that house full of people.

That day my father left for his two-year stay in the North. We had no way of knowing then that our family would never be together again.

Chapter 2

A revolutionary is always on the move — fighting, recruiting, teaching, sometimes hiding. The best his family can hope for is to be with him, even if it means uprooting everyone and carting the entire household for miles to new and unfamiliar places. My father had known no other kind of life since he had become a man and dedicated himself to the struggle to rid Viet Nam of its colonial masters, who had ruled the country since 1862.

He was born in 1909 as Dang Van Quang, the son of Dang Van Can, a district official in Vinh Long province. Like many others in the revolution, he changed his name after the 1954 move to the North, and was thereafter known as Dang Quang Minh.

At the age of eighteen, while in college, he joined the Liberation Movement against the French and made nationalism his life commitment. Then as a young teacher, he and his comrades roamed the countryside and the cities, recruiting young men and women to join the movement. Perhaps because he was young and new at the game, he was caught by the French in 1930. They threw him into prison for two years. After his release, he went back to his work and for the next decade was a thorn in the side of the French and their Vietnamese collaborators, hopscotching around the country, eluding their spies and soldiers while doing everything he could to make their lives miserable.

At twenty-eight, he found time to marry Tran Thi Pham, the youngest daughter of a village chief and the sister of two of his comrades. After the wedding, he brought her home to live with his parents in their own village of Ba Cang. In 1937, their first son — my oldest brother, Khoi — was born.

Life for this new family was hardly ordinary. Besides being busy with his revolutionary work, my father was a fugitive, with a handsome price on his head, so his time spent at home was limited and precious. When he could, he would sneak into the village, disguised as a peasant farmer or fisherman, for surreptitious visits to his wife and his new baby boy.

One French intelligence officer who was assigned to my father's case had developed an obsession about catching him. The officer had studied his profile until he knew him better than my father's own brother knew him — details about his family, his acquaintances, his personality, his hobbies, his passion for the Vietnamese people. One thing he knew was that my father would come home to visit his sick father, so one afternoon, at the time most people were taking their midday nap, he and a Vietnamese henchman showed up unannounced at my grandparents' home.

That is, they thought they were unannounced. In fact they had been spotted as they trudged up the village dirt road by a youngster, who ran ahead of them through the woods and sounded a warning. Father quickly dressed himself as a farmer, took his sister's country scarf and tied it around his head, then climbed a fruit tree near the house and began to pick fruit. The henchman strolled up the street, stopped beneath the tree, looked up, and asked the "farmer" about the whereabouts of "Teacher Quang." "I don't know," my father muttered back, "but ask his wife or his mother in the house."

The French officer and the Vietnamese did just that. In the house they tried to butter up my mother, telling her they were my father's admirers and had come to see his artwork (some fine pieces of woodcarving he had done while in school). The intelligence officer looked at Khoi and remarked how much he resembled his father. Asking her to tell them where her husband was, the Vietnamese aide tried to reassure her: "I am his friend. We used to teach at the same school in Vinh Long until I decided to study art. You can trust me." My mother was unmoved. "It's not easy to know whom to trust," she replied, "for dogs even eat other dogs."

The French intelligence officer patted his enemy's child on the head as they left. "Tell your papa that I'll return," he said.

After they had gone, my father came down from the tree and held his wife, who was then pregnant, and told her never to give the enemy any other answer than the one she had given: "I don't know." He hugged his son for the longest time, asked his aging parents to love and look after his family, and then vanished into the countryside once again.

For many months, my mother neither saw nor heard from him. Word came from one of his trusted comrades that he had been sent to Thailand to buy arms for the revolution, so she decided to move back to her home village to deliver her second child. She had been in poor health during this pregnancy and needed the care of her family. When the time came for the delivery, my father mysteriously appeared once again, sneaked into Can Tho hospital, and witnessed the birth of his twin daughters, Kim and Cuong. There was little time for celebration, though, because he had to leave once again soon afterward for his safety.

Two years later, in 1940, my father really "disappeared." It was hard to know if he was actually missing, since long absences were the rule, but this time there were reports that he had been arrested. My mother didn't want to believe them, but one day the French intelligence officer came to her house and arrogantly announced that he had captured his prey. My father was now imprisoned on Con Son Island, 125 miles off the coast due south of Sai Gon.

She hid her disappointment as the French officer began to offer her deals — if she would cooperate by telling him about my father's revolutionary activities, she would be allowed to visit him at the prison. She said it didn't matter anyway, because she was too sick to travel and had a family to take care of. Besides, she told him, "I am his wife and the mother of his children, but I am not his political comrade. Therefore my information contains nothing more important than my girls' diaper and feeding schedules."

For weeks there was no direct word from my father or from her brothers, who had been arrested at the same time. Other men released from the prison visited my mother and told her how brave her husband and brothers were, enduring horrifying interrogation sessions. They urged her to write my father and ask him to give in to escape the brutality of the questioning, and when she heard the details she wanted to take their advice. Still, she remembered his instructions never to say anything. As a desperation move, she went to her father and asked him what to do. "Listen to his words," he told her. "He knows what he's doing. Be patient, my child — don't write."

No letters came from my father or my uncles, only reports from other released prisoners: "They are alive," "They are still in prison," "They are sick." My mother continued her efforts to keep the family going, using her sewing skills to earn enough money for food and even enough to put aside a little for the future she still believed she and her husband would have.

August of 1945 brought the end of World War II and a revolution in the country. My father and thousands of his fellow revolutionaries regained their freedom and returned to their homes. There were many broken bones in my father's body from the cruelty he had endured during countless interrogations. There were visible scars on his back and deeper, invisible scars in his heart, but his captors had failed to break his spirit — the spirit of a man who wanted his country to be free.

— — —

August of 1945 didn't bring an end to the struggle against the French, only a new beginning. The family was back together again, but little was ordinary about its life.

In 1946 I was born, and three years later my brother Hai Van came along. My father's revolutionary activities went on, and so did the horrors of war. One of my earliest memories is of the family fleeing a burning village, being rushed into boats by my father's people, and moving to a new village where we made one of our many new starts in a new home.

I remember most vividly our house in Ong Deo, the village in Can Tho province to which we fled this time. I was five, Hai Van was two, and my mother's stomach was large with a child on the way. It was a beautiful house, with a red tile roof and pillars in front that seemed gigantic to me, and it was always full of people. My mother's two cousins lived with us, and a girl named Hien took care of Hai Van. Once in a while two prisoners whose job it was to take my father by boat on his official trips would stay with us for a day or two. (These were not hardcore criminals but civil offenders who worked for the government without pay.) And almost all the time there were some of my father's comrades, taking up nearly half the house with their meetings and often sleeping over afterward.

One of the regular guests was Le Duc Mai, younger brother of Le Duc Tho. He thought of us as his surrogate family, since his relatives were all in the North. Khoi was his best little friend and my mother was his favorite cook. Later, after the Ha Noi government took over South Viet Nam, he became the chief of security of the Department of the Interior of the Socialist Republic of Viet Nam.

We lived near the dentistry department that belonged to the Liberation government, where *bo doi* (Ho Chi Minh's soldiers), revolutionary, and other government officials came from all over the Mekong Delta for dental work. It was this clinic that eventually ruined Ong Deo as a safe place to live. The French found out about it, and the revolutionary organizations located around it, and the village became the target of endless terrifying air raids.

We had to practice emergency drills over and over, and continually changed our hidden underground shelters. My mother told her cousins to grab up the most valuable items when they fled during an air raid and stash them far from the house in case it burned. I don't remember that we had much in the way of valuables, except for the sewing machine; every time there was a bombing, my mother's cousins had to drag it out of the house with them. I was taught to stay close to my mother, while she grabbed Hai Van in her arms and hurried to shelter. For a time Khoi, Kim, and Cuong were away in a boarding school in Bac Lieu, but that town burned in another air raid and they came home to join us. We had to learn to listen for the sound of approaching aircraft even in our deepest sleep.

Despite the heavy bombings, Ong Deo seemed mostly a happy place to live, at least to my childish eyes. We lived a little distance from the village center, and it was fun to go there where people gathered in the morning to trade their goods and in the evening to meet, drink, talk, and listen to local authorities repeating anti-French slogans. Once Hien took Hai Van and me to see the "half-man, half-woman" — a pitiful, filthy creature who was kept in a cage for a time in the middle of the village, her face covered with ugly bruises and her hair long and slimy and tangled, a *bo doi* standing guard nearby with a gun on his shoulder. I was too young to understand what this person was, and I couldn't make any sense out of her screams. "I am a woman, I am not a man, let me out," she shouted, banging her fists on the cage. When people walked by she opened her shirt to expose her bra and cried, "Look at me, I am a woman!"

But he wasn't. The local revolutionary authority displayed this unfortunate man who dressed in women's clothing as an object lesson to anyone else who might be tempted to practice any form of homosexuality or sexual deviation.

In Ong Deo, my father was lucky to be working close to home most of the time, so he had free time to spend with us. He played his violin and helped Khoi perfect the pieces he would play for his first recital. With his help I learned to play the national anthem with Khoi's mandolin. Father had a small garden in the back that he loved, and he and mother spent a lot of time there almost every morning. He grew ginseng for her to use in preparing special meals for her and for the baby growing inside her.

One day he came home from a party in the village excited because a man he had met had offered to teach him how to raise silkworms. My mother shook her head at the size of the task he described, but he was like a child with a new toy and would not be dissuaded. He decided on a space on the porch, and Khoi helped him clear away the old furniture from the area and clean it up. They added a door, and soon afterward Father came home with his first two small trays of silkworms. His hobby soon turned out to be my mother's and her cousins' chore, and as the worms multiplied they had to hire people to help them. My mother would be up early in the morning to feed the worms, and Aunt Man and Aunt Chi were kept busy shredding huge amounts of mulberry leaves that seemed to disappear into the hungry worms' bellies in no time.

We were told that we had to be extremely quiet if we entered the room during the period when the worms were spinning their silk cocoons. Mother said it would take three days, and if a storm came up and lightning and thunder startled them they would stop spinning and that would mean the end of the harvest. Luckily everything went well, and my mother made a small profit from the silk that autumn. The silk mill sent my father a piece of raw silk material woven from it, so my mother made him a shirt from it. He loved the shirt, and every time he showed it off to his friends, the story of his famous silkworms went on and on.

Near Tet, my father came home from a trip with a boy who was about my older brother's age, fifteen or sixteen. Nha was tall and skinny like a stalk of temple bamboo, and his hair was cut short in the sort of shearing that made my brother burst into tears when he got his cut from a strange barber. Father introduced this shy, soft-spoken boy to my mother as their "son," and told the children that he was our brother. Later, when we were alone, Khoi told me that Nha's mother had been killed during an air raid on their village, his father was dying of tuberculosis, and he had been living with his aged grandfather. When my father met him during his travels, he adopted him with the consent of Nha's father and grandfather.

In North or South Viet Nam, adopting orphans or other people's children was a noble thing to do. It was simple, not costly or complicated like adoption is in the United States. Later, in Ha Noi, my father would adopt a little girl whose parents, also Viet Minh, were killed in a bomb raid. He said he missed his own children, and raising a needy child helped fill that void in his life.

When Nha came, I was jealous of this new rival for my father's attention. Khoi must have detected it, because he told me to share our parents' love with Nha and to love him. I made no promises, wanting to wait and see if I could like him. As it turned out, Nha was friendly and cheerful, and he pleased us younger ones with magic tricks he could do using a coin and a handkerchief. Nha became very close to my mother, and always seemed to be more helpful to her than Kim and Cuong were.

One morning my father was sitting on the front porch with all of the children, telling us how valuable a source of energy the sun can be. At times during his stay in the French prison he had been placed in solitary confinement, which turned out to be a pit dug in the wet ground, too small to move around freely in. The only contact with the outside world was a small hole, just wide enough to pass food and water through. The pit was dark and damp, and my father began to have trouble with his skin. So each morning he took off his clothes and painstakingly gave himself a "sunbath" by the narrow beams of sunlight that peeked through the feeding hole. When he was finally released from the pit, the guard looked at his sun-baked shoulders and face in surprise, then saluted him out of respect.

My sisters always wept when they heard my father's stories about his days in the French prison. Khoi was angry, but Nha and I were impressed with his courage and self-discipline.

The next day, after hearing the story about the great power of the sun, I decided to get some of it myself. Not only could the sun give us energy, he said, it could also kill tuberculosis germs. At that time I had a lot of fears, like any child, ranging from leper's blood to ghosts wailing in the farmhouses. One of them was a fear of TB germs, and I was worried that Nha might have brought some from his dying father. So I took a straw mat and spread it in the middle of the walkway between our house and the river, laid down on it, and after a while drifted off in a kind of half-sleep. In my drowsy state I thought I heard the sounds of the water buffalo herd from Mr. Tu Nho's plantation nearby. The sound grew strangely louder, too loud for a dream. I opened my eyes and, terrified, saw the herd stampeding toward me, hundreds of them pounding along the dirt road to where I lay. I heard my mother scream, and my sisters yelled out for me not to move. As I lay there, not daring to move a muscle, the herd changed course slightly and split into two columns; one by one the massive animals passed around me. When the last one had gone, everyone rushed out to the road. My mother was the first to reach me, and she sank to the ground to scoop me into her arms. Miraculously, I was untouched.

— — —

Nature wasn't the only danger we faced. Since the French had discovered the dental clinic and the other Liberation activities in Ong Deo, the revolutionary government had begun making preparations to move its headquarters to another secret location. They weren't quick enough. One day, when we were still there, the village was attacked by French planes.

At this time my father was away on an official trip, and since the prisoners had gone with him there was no man in the house except my brother. Suddenly we heard the roar of low-flying bombers, and Khoi rushed about, making sure Kim and Cuong got into the shelter. Mother carried Hai Van, and I stuck close to her as we ran from the house. As we crossed a small footbridge, a burst of machine-gun fire sprayed down from a swooping aircraft and hit the bridge. Mother and Hai Van fell right into the muddy creek, and Hai Van cried out so loudly that I thought surely he had been hit by the bullets.

Mother shouted out that both were unhurt, however, and started trying to scramble out of the creek. I tried to pull her out of the mud, but she was too heavy, especially since Hai Van wouldn't let go of her. She looked around and spotted a brass shell casing, picked it up and gave it to Hai Van to play with; while he was distracted, she managed to hand him to me, and then was able to pull herself onto the bank.

We sat there for a time, not knowing whether the planes would return or not; sometimes they returned immediately after a strike, sometimes we didn't see them again for days or weeks. Suddenly, we heard the sound of their engines as they came back for another pass at the village. Mother slipped back into the creek and took Hai Van from me; I flattened myself on the earth with my face down and my eyes shut tight. This time two planes roared over us, dropping bombs and strafing the ground. Bullets struck all around me, kicking dirt into my face. I pressed myself even more tightly to the ground and prayed hard.

When the ordeal was over, my mother and I found the rest of the family safe and unharmed. But one part of the rich man's land we lived on did receive damage: the small cemetery behind our borrowed home had been destroyed by the bombs. Old bones lay exposed on the top of this sacred earth. Mother went to the village center and found a man to rebury the shattered remains; she burned incense and prayed for God to protect the spirits of the people whose rest had been disturbed.

We left Ong Deo late one evening in a big boat, able to carry with us only part of our belongings. For many years afterward my mother still talked about the village, the green garden, the silkworms. She missed the rows of sugarcane that had brought in a little money to help feed our family. My sisters always wondered what happened to the pigs we had to leave behind.

I missed the guava tree that stood in front of our house. Khoi had built a treehouse in it for me and Hai Van, and I practically lived in it. It was there I overheard Le Duc Mai tell Khoi where babies come from; it was also there that I heard many wondrous tales about Ho Chi Minh, as Mai spent hours telling my brother about Uncle Ho's teachings.

Our next home seemed to promise few such pleasant experiences. The small hamlet of Ba Ngon, in Can Tho province, was thick with water coconut trees and its river was smaller and muddier than the one at Ong Deo. Even the mosquitoes were worse — big, fat, and louder in the night. The houses that had once stood there had been destroyed, and grass grew over the foundations. Broken, red roof tiles were scattered everywhere, and there were bomb craters all around. The tadpoles, moss, and marsh lentils that flourished in the stagnant water of the craters seemed to have been there since long before the French invaded our land. My mother looked sadly around, shook her head at this devastated ground, then resolutely started looking for a suitable spot to build our new nest.

Ba Ngon looked like a deserted place, and it would have been if not for a man and his dog who came to greet my father. He took Father and Uncle Hai Hoi and Khoi around to inspect the ground, since Uncle Hai Hoi would be the one who would build a house for us. The rest of us stayed with my mother in the boat, which was to be camouflaged with water coconut leaves to hide it from French patrol planes; that boat would be our home for several weeks until the house was ready.

Uncle Hai Hoi said Ba Ngon wasn't fit for a dog, and perhaps he was right, because we weren't even able to swim in the river. Local people warned us that it was full of *ca bong*, a type of killer fish that would attack anyone who happened to swim near their school of babies. One man told my brother about a fisherman whose net got stuck in the river bottom; leaving his son in the boat, he dove down to free the net. Suddenly the son saw blood flowing up to the surface, so he screamed for help. When the fisherman was brought up, his manhood was gone! Khoi told us that story and said that no matter how much he misses the water he would never take a swim in that river.

One day a few weeks later, at low tide, he and my father hung a net in a small section of the river around our new dock to keep the killer *ca bong* out; despite their effort, swimming in that river was never the same for us.

The desolation of this new village was brightened considerably by the birth of our new baby sister in 1952. My father was extremely excited and happy, and he named her Hoa Binh after one of the five provinces in the North that had been taken back from the French. "Hoa Binh" means peace, and Father said peace would soon come to our country. I didn't really understand what "peace" would mean to the country, but I knew it would mean my family's lives would be safer because the French would stop bombing our homes. There were nights when I woke up in terror from dreams that I had been hit with a fusillade of bullets from a machine gun pointed at me from the door of a low-flying aircraft. In my dream my stomach was full of those empty brass shells that littered the villages, but strangely there was no blood. When Father talked about peace coming soon, I hoped it would mean that I wouldn't have that dream any longer.

In wartime, tragedy is never very far away, even in what seem like happy times. Our joy over Hoa Binh's birth was interrupted by the news that my cousin Liem, oldest son of my mother's brother Sac, had been killed a few months earlier. He had been on his way from Long Thanh village to his boarding school in Bac Lieu when he was shot by a French river patrolman. He died at the home of a villager in a hamlet far from ours, and the people there buried him in a deserted piece of land. Only through his last words did they have any idea who he was, and it took months for a person from that village to find us and bring us the terrible news. Liem was just seventeen when we lost him.

Life has to go on, though, despite tragedies and despite living in places like our "goddamn hamlet," as Uncle Hai Hoi called it. After he turned the earth for a garden, he and my mother started to plant vegetables — eggplant, onions, dragon beans, and many other "nutritious" ones that Hai Van and I didn't like. Lemon grass grew like weeds. Once we had a visit from my cousin Hong Nga, who was studying nursing and was something of a nutritionist, and she told us that according to her traditional medicine teacher lemon grass would prevent tuberculosis. Did we eat a lot of lemon grass after her visit! Marinated fish with lemon grass, lemon grass chicken, lemon grass in stew, lemon grass barbecue fish. My favorite meal was finely chopped lemon grass mixed with roasted soybeans in rich coconut milk on barbecue chicken.

We lived in Ba Ngon for almost two years. Mother made friends with people who lived in other hamlets nearby and started bringing in money with her sewing. She even had four students who came to learn how to sew; they were daughters of rich landowners, who wanted to learn to sew for their families and also to prepare themselves to become good housewives when they married.

Shortly after we moved in, the revolutionary government came along. Officials set up a military school to train young soldiers; my uncle Thuy came to set up his newspaper headquarters, and many different offices were established to teach men and women "socialism." A number of houses were built for *bo doi*, and men who spoke in the northern and central accents started to come to the area. My mother told us they came from Ha Noi and Hue, which were faraway places to us.

My father promised my brother and sisters that the revolutionary organization would soon open a high school, but in the meantime he told them to study with the books he brought home for them. Khoi, who thirsted for knowledge, had no trouble disciplining himself to study on his own, but Kim and Cuong complained that they couldn't study without classmates. They studied anyway under Khoi's "supervision" — sometimes in tears, but they studied.

As miserable as we had felt when we first came to Ba Ngon, we were even more upset when my father announced that we would be moving again because the revolution needed him elsewhere, in a far-off village called Kim Qui, still within the Liberated Zone. Funereal faces filled our home, as my mother, my sisters, and Khoi whined about having to leave just when we had gotten comfortable. An enormous silence grew between my parents over the issue. I don't think if God had come down and ordered my father to stay that he would have done so; he didn't have to go to Kim Qui — he wanted to go because he was needed by his people. To my young mind it was beginning to seem that it was just too much trouble to be needed by other people.

The journey from Ba Ngon to Kim Qui was a long and tedious one. I don't remember how many days it took us to get there, but we could travel only by night, hiding during the daylight hours from French patrol boats and planes. We had no idea what to expect at yet another home. Kim Qui was a beautiful name, because it means "golden turtle," but Khoi said maybe it was so bad that someone had to give it a pretty name to "fool fools like us."

As we came closer to our destination, our boat turned out of the river into a small canal filled with marsh weeds, as if it hadn't been used by travelers in a long time. The canal was so narrow that Uncle Hai Hoi had to take off the rowing paddles and pull the tiller onto the deck. At some points my father and Khoi had to push the boat with long bamboo poles while my uncle sat in the bow and whacked a path through the thickets with his machete. On both sides of the canal tall reeds blocked our view of the horizon, and sometimes I felt as if we were lost in a different world, like the strange places in the tales my father sometimes told us.

The mosquitoes were the worst I had ever seen. Our dog No was tormented, his face covered with the fat and blood-gorged insects, until at last Khoi decided to let him stay inside the boat. When night fell, Kim and Cuong got in trouble because they became so obsessed with killing mosquitos that they abandoned their chores. Holding small candles, they went from one corner of the mosquito net to the other searching out their victims; when they touched the flame lightly to a mosquito, we could hear a little "poof!" and smell the insect burning. Of course, many times they also burned a hole in the net, so they got safety pins and patched up the openings. My mother and father got angry at them, but their strange ritual continued anyway.

The trip through this water wilderness was a miserable one. Khoi was unhappy, Kim and Cuong cried behind my father's back, my mother tried to conquer the forest with her silence, and Uncle Hai Hoi worked like a water buffalo to keep the boat moving through the marshland. Only my father seemed happy, looking forward to his work at our new home.

The confinement finally got to me. The mosquitoes were so bad that I had to sit beneath the netting inside the boat even in the middle of the day, while small charcoal stoves at the front and back puffed out smoke to keep the insects away. Frustrated, I asked Khoi if I let the mosquitoes bite me and then got deadly malaria, would our father feel sorry for me and let us move back. Khoi just shook his head and said, "We are here to stay, sweetheart." Undaunted, I thought of the poisonous snakes Uncle Hai Hoi had killed when he went ashore for firewood, and asked Khoi if Father would let us return if I were bitten by one of them. This time he got angry and told me not to ask any more questions like that.

We finally arrived at our destination at the edge of the thick forest, where a fisherman and his family came to meet us and to invite us to dinner at their house. It was quite a feast, with fish from the canal and ducks the man's wife had killed. The man's name was Thao, but Father called him Anh Tu (brother number four) and told us to call him Bac Tu (uncle number four), a polite way of referring to another person. Bac Tu wore short pants, and his black shirt was faded and frequently mended, but he wasn't poor; he had his land and had fish stocked in many ponds, and he looked healthy and happy.

At dinner his wife set two tables, one for the men and one for the women and children, as was customary in our culture. There was no actual table, just a thick black wooden slab that was also used for sleeping, sitting, and many other things. The children watched us, not really joining in the conversation except to answer my brother's questions, usually just "yes" or "no." They whispered to each other from time to time and giggled. My brother explained that they had never met anyone from outside the forest, so it was no surprise that they looked at us strangely.

A few days after our arrival, Bac Tu and my father took the family to a strip of land to inspect a lot where we might build our new house. Even a non-participant like me was discouraged by the sight: It was a wild jungle, with reeds twice as high as my father's head. Uncle Hai Hoi snorted and stalked back to the boat, not believing what he had seen. My mother tried to reassure him that we would all be fine once we cleared the land and built a home. In tears, Uncle Hai Hoi asked, "How can you be fine in this godforsaken place?" He was genuinely upset. In the past, he said, he had always been truthful to my grandparents when they asked how we lived, but this time he would have to lie because the truth would break their hearts.

Nevertheless, the project went on. Early one morning my mother took us to the site where she placed a bowl of rice and some salt on the ground and burned incense. She prayed for the god of the earth to protect us and asked the unknown spirits who lived in the land to accept our presence there. Then the work began. Helped by men from the area, my father and uncle began cutting down trees and burning off the underbrush. We were told to stay on the boat because the workmen had just killed some poisonous snakes. We didn't see any snakes, but we did see roasted turtles, and the workmen ate them with glee. I was glad my father didn't join them in that feast, because later Uncle Hai Hoi told my brother that the workmen were "savages." Uncle Hai Hoi was quite religious; he fasted twice a month, and on Buddha's birthday he bought pigeons and turtles to set free as part of his sacrifices. He told me that since turtles do no harm to people and are helpless, we shouldn't kill them, even for food.

The house was built on the highest part of the lot, the front of it facing the canal and the back facing the forest. Nearby was a big lake that had been stocked with fish; when I put my face close to the surface I could see them swimming in the cold, clear water. Bac Tu's wife brought my mother a basket of newly hatched baby ducks to raise in the lake, and Mother said that taking care of them would be Kim and Cuong's responsibility.

My father and Khoi were not homebuilders, so most of the time they stayed out of the way. Anyway, they had another project that was almost as important as building the house itself: putting up an outhouse.

We moved into the house just before the monsoon season. It rained hard for "a hundred days and a hundred nights," as we always said, and the wind howled and the thunder roared. The storms washed clay into the canal and made the water red and mucky, but that was the only time the water was warm from the heat of the earth. Khoi and I loved to swim in the rain.

Maybe Kim Qui was a "godforsaken place," but when God went elsewhere he left some of his creations behind. The land was not abundant, with nothing edible in the forest, but there were fish in the rivers, in the canal, in ponds and lakes, and even in the forest when the water was high. One day when he walked into the forest, Khoi discovered that the fish went upstream to spawn. He came and got Kim and Cuong and me and took us to the spot, where we thrashed about in the water catching the fish with our bare hands. In no time we had filled three baskets full, and they were so heavy we had to throw back part of our catch to lighten our load.

The excitement of fishing there is still warm in my heart. I used to dream of catching fish. Even Hai Van got into the act, fishing with a string Mother tied onto his finger. Sometimes I could hear him talking in his sleep, saying "I got a bite! I got a bite!"

The only food that grew in Kim Qui was bananas, but even they were skinny and meager like the land itself. Fish was our staple diet — fish for lunch, fish for dinner, dried fish, roasted fish, fish stew, barbecued fish. We got tired of it, but it was almost impossible to buy pork there. Khoi said he could hardly wait for the ducks to grow so we could eat them, but Kim and Cuong protested that they had become pets. I remember that Mother killed the ducks for a special occasion anyway — when my father came home from one of his long trips.

My sisters were unhappy at Kim Qui, because life wasn't easy there. Along with the loneliness of being far away from cities and other people, we were deprived of many necessities. We ran out of toothpaste and had to brush our teeth with salt. We treated soap like medicine, because the supply was low and there was no way to know when we might be able to buy more. In Ong Deo we had been allowed to take a bar of soap with us to the river to bathe, but in Kim Qui it was different. We had to get wet in the river, then run back to the dock and soap ourselves up, then run back and jump into the river to rinse. Mother was afraid the bar might slip out of our hands in the river and be lost forever.

The bacteria in the deep jungle ate holes in the soles of my sisters' feet. (Everybody except my mother had foot problems, as we romped about catching fish or just exploring nature. My sisters complained the most; I was too young to care.) They soaked their feet in a solution that my father brought home, but it didn't seem to help much. Father told them that when we moved from Kim Qui the bacteria would die and the problem would be solved, but that promise only got him in trouble, because their next question, in plaintive chorus, was, "When will we move away from Kim Qui?"

I guess I was just too young to know what was going on, as my sisters said, but I always took my father's side when they complained. I told them Kim Qui was God's favorite place, for I enjoyed my days and there was always something exciting happening. Maybe I was being too optimistic, but I did know that in Kim Qui we didn't have to run to the air-raid shelter as often as we did in other places, and as far as we knew no one had been killed in the raids that did take place.

Still, life in Kim Qui was usually quite lonely. My father was always busy and often went away on trips with people who came in from Ha Noi, and when he was gone we rarely had visitors, not even his friends. But near the celebration of Tet in 1952 there was exciting news that my father's nephew Cau would come to spend his vacation with us. We had never met Cau, but the fact that he was a *bo doi* made his visit even more exciting to Khoi and me.

Unlike most of our relatives from Long Thanh who came bearing presents for everyone, Cau arrived only with his backpack, which held a soldier's scanty belongings. He had a towel, a khaki shirt, a worn-out toothbrush, a rice bowl made from half a coconut shell, and a pair of chopsticks usable from both ends (in the *bo doi* the men used one end to pick up food from the serving dishes and the other end to eat with). My silent disappointment at not getting a gift quickly went away, as Cau's warm and cheery personality brightened up the house.

Cau was older than Khoi, perhaps twenty at the time. He was as tall as my father and looked like him, even more than Khoi did. Talking with my mother, he described how difficult it was to see his family because of the problems of going back and forth from the Liberated Zone. At one time he had been able to visit them in Can Tho city, but now, since conditions wouldn't allow him to leave the liberated areas, they would have to travel into the zone if they wanted to see him. He said he discouraged them from doing so, because families of *bo doi* who crossed the line took great risks; sometimes they were arrested by one side or both for interrogation, others got caught in cross fire between the military forces, and some struggled to reach the Liberated Zone only to discover that their son's unit had moved elsewhere. Despite these risks and perhaps thousands of others, I remember my family housed many friends and strangers who had made the journey in an effort to visit their loved ones who were fighting in the revolution.

Cau told my brother something that truly excited him for the first time in months — that the boarding school had been reopened and that Khoi should plan to go there whenever our father could take him. My brother was a different boy after that, doing his chores diligently and even doing things my sisters asked without argument. He sawed wood and stacked it all around the house, cut grass, and cleaned up the walkway to the outhouse, which Kim and Cuong had begged him to do for a long time.

During his vacation, Cau wanted to do some fishing, since my father had told him about our bounty. I took him to the best spot, which was the pond that Bac Tu had stocked with fish. As soon as his line hit the water, a fish snapped at the green frog bait and he had a catch. A second bite followed, then a third, and many more. What a wilderness guide I was, I thought. But Cau said that kind of fishing wasn't enough of a challenge, so we went off in a sampan and fished in the canal where there was a bit more sport to it. Cau spent all of the New Year holiday with us, then went back to his unit the next week.

One day my father came home from another long trip. I don't remember how long he was away, but I remember my sisters and I had contracted pinkeye after he left and were over it before he returned, so it must have been for two or three weeks. At dinner that night he told the family that he would take Khoi back to Bac Lieu to go to school. My brother screamed with joy and my mother looked happy, but I was sad at the thought of losing my brother for a whole year again. (It had been about a year, during our moves, that he had been out of school.) Besides, I had come to harbor the terrifying fear that they might get killed on their journey and never come home, like my cousin Liem. All through my childhood it bothered me that Liem's body was buried on some stranger's land, and the thought that the same thing might happen to my brother kept me awake many nights. I didn't talk about it, though. I used to keep negative thoughts to myself, because my brother used to tell me that if we think something is going to happen to someone we shouldn't say it, because our words have power and we might cause our fears to become real.

The idea of education wasn't very exciting to me, but to Khoi it was more important than food, more vital than quinine tablets to ward off malaria in the deep jungle. Khoi had dreams, big dreams, and he was always frustrated when circumstances kept him from going to school.

As he prepared to leave, my mother took out a piece of fabric she had saved for a long time and made him two new shirts. The night before he left, Kim gave him new handkerchiefs she had hidden away, and Cuong opened her "frog bag," a little cloth purse, and shared part of the money she was saving to buy earrings "when the war is over." I didn't have anything to give Khoi. Hoa Binh gave him many kisses and even ate her dinner "all gone" for him that night. Hai Van played the mandolin for him; of course he played the national anthem, the first song any of us learned on any instrument.

For days after Khoi went off to school, there was very little noise in the house. Mother cried quietly to herself a lot. Kim and Cuong and I became a bit closer; they even let me sleep with them when I asked, and I asked often because I was afraid of ghosts and believed they were everywhere — in the house, in the river, in the forest, and even in the outhouse!

My sisters had memorized a play they used to watch in boarding school, so we "produced" it in their room many afternoons when no one wanted to take a nap. I got to dress up like a nurse, Hai Van played a wounded *bo doi*, Kim was a military doctor, and Cuong particularly liked the part of the widow of a *bo doi* who had fallen in battle. Only Hoa Binh didn't like the play; maybe she didn't like the part when Cuong cried at her "husband's" funeral. When we had buried the soldier I always asked, "Where would his spirit go?" At that time we believed that spirits didn't go to heaven; sometimes they stayed near their loved ones, sometimes they wandered everywhere. Hien, the girl who took care of us in Ong Deo village, taught us many such beliefs and old wives' tales; I've never been sure whether my parents sent her home to her parents because they were worried about her safety or whether they didn't like her teaching us all those things.

In late autumn of 1953, my father received an order to transfer, so we prepared to move yet again. My brother came home to help and worked like a water buffalo, joking all the while that he wished he were a girl so he could find himself a husband to do all this hard work. Uncle Hai Hoi came to help again, and with help from men from the fishing village we got everything packed into a long boat and set off for our new home, Cang Chu Hang.

One of many small villages in Chuong Thien province, Cang Chu Hang was a place where the red flag was proudly raised every morning and revolutionaries struggled to hold on to their principles and a piece of their forefathers' land. The village was named for Chu Hang blockade, one of many built in an effort to keep the French patrol boats from penetrating the Liberated Zone, and just on the other side many Vietnamese chose an easier life by cooperating with the French. Each time my parents took us near the blockade, I had an enormous sense of security, a certainty that the French couldn't invade our territory. The barrier was impressive to me, with countless large wooden posts driven into the river bottom and weeds and water plants growing all around them for nearly half a kilometer of the river's length. Khoi said it should have been a great spot for fishing, but we didn't dare try because the patrol boats had fired randomly at fishermen there before.

We lived about three kilometers south of the blockade, in yet another house Uncle Hai Hoi had built for us; in fact, every room was identical to the one he had built in Kim Qui. The house stood on the edge of some land that belonged to a rich and respectable lady, who insisted we call her Ba Noi (paternal grandmother).

When he came to build the house, Uncle Hai Hoi found himself in the middle of a minor difference of opinion: My mother wanted a big front yard, but Khoi wanted the house built right on the bank of the river (my father was away again, so he didn't get to vote). Uncle Hai Hoi saw he couldn't win by taking either side, so he compromised right down the middle — he put the house in the middle of the lot, giving my mother something of a larger garden in the back and putting Khoi and the rest of us children only a few running steps to a cold swim. We practically lived in the river during the summer months.

Cang Chu Hang was a happy home for us. Since it was closer to both my parents' home villages, visits from relatives were much more frequent. The arrival of aunts and cousins and grandparents was always exciting because they brought news from home and warm family feelings, but best of all for me they brought presents!

My father was away from home alot, but only on short trips of a week or two. Each time he returned, people would come to see him. He didn't have visits from relatives, but his many guests who were involved in the revolution were equally exciting to me and my brother Hai Van. They came from all over the country, and from all walks of life, but they shared one common interest — independence for Viet Nam. There were doctors, lawyers, pharmacists, professors, college students, villagers, rich men and women, the "intellectuals" and "bourgeoisie." Some of them lived and worked in the cities under French domination, but they were as much against the French as the people in the Liberated Zone. There were many such people, but I especially remember one man whose visit seemed more important than all the rest. Before his arrival, my father seemed very anxious as he talked to my mother about plans for his short stay. For the first time I remember, my mother even wrote down on a piece of paper the menu for the dinner for this honored guest. She had suggested that my father and his distinguished comrade have dinner alone, but he insisted that the whole family be included, so for days my sisters nagged Hai Van and Hoa Binh and me about dos and don'ts at the table. My father wasn't worried about those things, but he did ask Hai Van and me not to be shy when we were asked to sing and play the mandolin for our guest.

At last the day came, and we met this man from Ha Noi. He was Le Duc Tho, the older brother of Le Duc Mai, who had been our frequent house guest in Ong Deo. When "Uncle" Le Duc Tho visited us in Cang Chu Hang, he brought with him a strange little box. We children were dying of curiosity to know what it was, because he told us that we would hear Uncle Ho's voice from the box. It was, of course, a radio, which we had never seen before. When he turned it on, all the older members of the family listened intently to Ho Chi Minh's speech; Hai Van and I didn't pay any attention to what he was saying, because we were more fascinated to know how this magic box worked. At the end, everyone clapped their hands and cheered when Uncle Ho declared his determination to bring about "peace in our entire nation from Nam Quan to the Ca Mau peninsula."

Cang Chu Hang was paradise compared to the Kim Qui forest. The green grass, the tall trees, and the fertile land were embraced by the rich river. We had many reasons to be happy, and it showed. My father began to comment that "Cang Chu Hang must agree with your mother, because she looks so radiant." Actually, as it turned out, she was radiant because she was carrying another baby.

The only disappointment for us in our new home was that our father still didn't have as much time for his family as he had hoped. He didn't go away on trips quite as often, but there were so many visitors and meetings that he was constantly busy with his work. Many nights the meetings started after dinner, and I never knew how long they lasted. I only remember my father coming in to say good night, often waking us from a sound sleep. My brother Hai Van was most alert at these times; even in a half-awake state, he never failed to tell him, "I love you, Father."

My parents had a habit of getting up early in the morning and sitting together in the dark kitchen, talking in near whispers to each other while waiting for the sound of boiling water in an aluminum kettle on the stove. It was odd that, even though they often argued about politics or the family's business at night, they never spoke harshly in this quiet morning time.

After having tea, usually my father did his exercises. *T'ai chi* and a balanced diet were musts in his daily routine; he believed that if you take care of body and mind you can prevent illness. He encouraged all of us to emulate him, but only Khoi and Kim were faithful followers of these principles.

All the children used to take long walks with my father to the rice field at dawn to watch the golden sun touch the thatched roofs of the nearby village. Khoi always volunteered to walk after the dog, carrying Hai Van on his shoulders, stirring the tall elephant grass and scaring the snakes away. The grass and leaves were still wet from the night's mist, and sometimes I stopped to drink the dew from the leaves. My sisters tried to discourage us from drinking it by telling Hai Van and me that the morning mist was actually the tears of wailing ghosts, but Khoi made up an even more convincing story. Every drop of water on the leaves, he said, was formed slowly out of the mist that settled on the land throughout the night; since it was there so long, there was every chance that a poisonous snake or insect had come along and tasted the water before we did — so if we drank it we might be poisoned. I believed him, sort of, but every now and then I would drink a little and then wait to see if I got sick, testing his story.

Hoa Binh was terrified of the grass leeches, so she refused to walk as soon as we reached the grassy area. My father loved to carry her on his shoulders, and when we heard her giggle we knew that he was nibbling on her little toes to tickle her.

In this land of plenty, there were always harvest seasons — after the rice crop, the rain would fall and then the straw mushrooms were in season. The "grandmother" on whose land we lived had many large stacks of rice straw in the fields, and she had the farm workers put one of them near our house. Khoi and I watched the process from the beginning. At first, the workers stacked the rice straw tightly in a large circle, higher than my brother's head; then it rained for many days and many nights, and soon a strong, musty odor reached our noses every time we went near the stack. Khoi and I poked through the straw, looking for mold and watching as the tiny mushrooms appeared and grew. It was an exciting time when the whole family came out to the field with baskets to share this wondrous creation.

In Cang Chu Hang, Khoi was usually busy with his studies. He had to teach himself at home with the textbooks he brought from the boarding school, since it was now too far away and the school had been destroyed in an air raid. I often begged him to come and play with me, but he brushed me away, telling me, "I can't play, I have to study." I never understood why it was so important to him, and when he told me he had to have a high school diploma in order to go to college, I only responded, "But why must you go to college?" It was natural, perhaps, that I didn't understand, because adults always said girls like me didn't need an education, because we would find a man with a good education to take care of us.

Khoi's greatest concern was that he might have to go through life as an illiterate man. He said he could live without clothes, without soap, but he absolutely had to have violin strings and a good education.

For all my father's travel and our family's frequent uprootings, I don't remember that we children had ever been alone without at least one of our parents, but one day we learned that this was going to happen — my father canceled all of his meetings because he had to take my mother to a maternity clinic. She must have felt that the baby's time had come, so she took her bath, packed her things in a small cloth bag, then wrote down a list of instructions for the older children. Khoi was not to bother the grandmother unless it was "life or death," she insisted. "Like if one of those brats drowns in the canal," he joked. Kim and Cuong didn't appreciate the humor, and they threatened not to cook for him. My mother hushed them and made them promise all kinds of things: not to fight, to take care of the younger kids, to lock the doors at night, and so on.

After all that noisy discussion, the house seemed absolutely still and deserted when the sampan carrying my parents disappeared around the turn in the river.

Hoa Binh walked into our parents' room, took out my mother's pillow, laid her head down on it, and began sniffling. I wasn't very helpful; being a sometimes mischievous sister, I said to her, "I'll tell the leper on you if you cry!" Hoa Binh threw the pillow on the floor and ran to Kim for protection. My mother didn't like for me to say that, but it worked on Hoa Binh every time.

That afternoon we ate dinner earlier than usual because we couldn't think of anything else to do. After dinner Khoi started to play hide-and-seek, but halfway through the game, even before I could find Hai Van, they all came out of their hiding places and called it off.

Later the grandmother and her granddaughter came to visit, bringing a basket of goodies like the rice cakes called *banh tet* and *banh cam*, tangerines, and half a jackfruit, the sweet tropical fruit with short spikes all over its skin. She reminded us to keep our voices down when mother returned from the clinic, and told Kim and Cuong not to cook for my mother because her daughter-in-law would prepare a "nutritious" meal for her. "Your mother needs lots of rest and the right food to produce milk," she explained. With great earnestness she also warned us that we shouldn't praise the baby, because old folks believe that if you praise a newborn child, the devil might hear and come to take it away. The high rate of sudden death among newborns made stories like that seem all too real. My father said it was an epidemic when several of our neighbors' children died, but their parents made offerings to the evil spirits to protect their future children. I believed them both.

That night, Hai Van and I slept with Khoi, while Hoa Binh slept with Kim and Cuong in our parents' bed. Hai Van asked my brother, "Will our mother die when she gives birth to our baby, Khoi?" Khoi snapped at him, "No! Don't ask me a stupid question like that again."

We all stayed awake for a long time in the dark and silence of the lonely house.

Early the next morning, we heard my father's voice calling out to us from the river, his boat still far upstream. We raced to the dock to meet him, but I couldn't bear to wait there. Tearing off my shirt, I dived into the river wearing only my shorts and swam as fast as I could toward the sampan. From the water I heard him shout happily, "Your mother gave birth to a baby girl!" From the shore, Khoi called back, "Oh, no! Another useless, mean creature coming to our house," laughing as Kim and Cuong pummeled him in mock anger.

At the house, Father told us all about the birth, answering our excited questions about our new sister and about our mother's health. Then he said he wanted to take a bath and rest for a while, because he had to leave again almost immediately to go on a three-day trip for his work.

He said he was sure he would return in time to bring Mother home from the clinic, but when Cuong asked what would happen if he couldn't make it back, he replied, "Your mother will understand." Khoi, momentarily angered, confronted him: "Why should my mother be the one who understands?" Father was a little upset by the question, but even more disappointed that Khoi had questioned the priority he had to put on his activities on behalf of the country. He sat all of us down, even little Hoa Binh, and made us listen while he scolded my big brother for his attitude.

He expected more of Khoi, he said, because Khoi was the oldest and should be setting an example for the other children who looked up to him. "I'm tired of being a good example," Khoi retorted. "I feel like an old man at seventeen. I am tired of responsibilities. I have to have my education. I must go to school before it's too late."

My father listened quietly, then responded with a solemn reminder: "You are the man of this house when I am gone, son." I listened to the exchange without fully understanding everything, but there was one thing I did know — I didn't want Khoi to be a "man," I just wanted him to be my big brother.

As it turned out, Father came home from his trip in time to go to the clinic. The grandmother let him use her covered boat so my mother and the baby would be comfortable on the return trip. He took Hoa Binh and Hai Van with him, but the rest of us remained behind to listen to more coaching from the grandmother about how to keep quiet when the baby was sleeping and our mother was recuperating from the birth. She even offered to let us play at her house during the day and eat dinner with her for at least a few days after

Mother and the baby came home. I didn't mind that at all, because the food at her house was always better than ours, although we weren't allowed to talk at the table as we did freely at home.

When my parents brought the new baby home, my father named her Minh Tam. We all just called her Baby for a long time; the grandmother, still worried about spirits, suggested we give her an ugly name to "fool the devils."

When Minh Tam was one month old, we had the grandest birthday celebration of all. (In the Vietnamese tradition, people celebrate a birthday after one month, another after one year, and then no more until they reach the age of sixty.) The grandmother and her family came with armfuls of gifts, and a few neighbors from across the river came to celebrate with us. There were many different kinds of food prepared as offerings to God, and we sat through a long ceremony conducted by the grandmother. Holding three sticks of fragrant incense, she prayed earnestly as she turned to face the four sides of the house. I don't remember much about it, except the pleasant odor of the incense — my mother seldom burned incense, but my grandmother faithfully lit the smoky sticks every night at the ancestors' altar.

I do remember watching Minh Tam during the birthday celebration. Even though the grandmother had warned us not to praise her, I couldn't help smiling every time I looked at her. I thought she was the most beautiful baby in the whole village.

Sadly, the glow of this wondrous event didn't last long. The happiness we felt at the arrival of our new sister was soon submerged beneath the conflict and sadness created when our father began to talk of going to Ha Noi — of leaving us for two years — and worse, taking Khoi with him. The thrill of having our family increased by one was dashed when we learned that it would be decreased by two.

Once more we were moving, to our grandparents' home in Long Thanh, but this time the move meant far more. Father and Khoi were going north to join the revolution.

Chapter 3

For a long time after my father and my oldest brother had left us in Long Thanh, I didn't fully understand what had taken them away from us.

I knew about the war, of course, and I knew about the hated French intruders and the need to drive them out so our people could be free. I thought I knew a little about socialism.

When I was very young, socialism was like a new breeze, fresh and somewhat fascinating — although for me it was fascinating mostly because my father was the fundamental representation of it in our lives. The international workers' songs, the dances, even the red Russian flag with the yellow hammer and sickle didn't seem foreign to me, perhaps because the Russians were not "foreigners" to my father.

"Socialism" was a household word in our family, yet I knew that other villagers and even some of my relatives were fearful of it. It seemed an ill wind to my mother's cousins when I heard them talking when my father was not around. I was confused about these differing attitudes, but it was not important to me — the fact was, my father was a socialist and I trusted him with my life, and that was all that mattered to me.

The term "communism" was not openly used, because "socialism" had a better sound to it. It softened the harsh treatment of the Communist organization already applied in Ha Noi. Up north, they killed landowners, they took money from the rich and gave it to the poor; but Communists in the South were more socialist thinkers than they were tyrannical Communists.

If I had been a little older than my nine years and more astute at the time, I might have expected the family to split along political lines. My parents viewed politics in two absolutely different ways — my mother a traditionalist, my father believing devoutly in his heart that revolution was the way to grow — yet as parents they were a good team, complementing each other in every other way. She made him the best possible revolutionary, while he made her the most devoted wife and mother anyone could hope for. He pulled our roots from one village to another hamlet, again and again, and my mother created a new home life wherever we went. While my father was planting seeds of revolution all over our land, my mother brought seeds to each new home to grow our food. The strength she gave us all helped my father feel content and happy with his family.

Unlike most other families, we talked openly about childbirth, marriage, death, war, peace, Ho Chi Minh, fidelity, betrayal, and everything else on this earth, but there were a few restrictions. Materialistic ideas or yearnings were not discussed, at least not around my father. He wanted us to learn not to depend on the outside world (i.e., the French) — "self-sufficient" was his watchword, a principle he tried hard to instill in his people, the men who worked under him, and his own family. When he took us to the Liberated Zone, he cut all material ties to the outside and we were independent and self-sufficient; we lived by the discipline that the party insisted on.

Friends of my parents who lived outside the Liberated Zone admired my family, respected my father, and praised my mother for her devotion — yet when they came to visit and saw our "model proletarian lifestyle," they sometimes could barely disguise the sympathy they felt for us, especially the children, because we did without so many of the comforts available on the "outside."

But I knew then that my father was happy with himself, his family, and the life he had chosen, so I was happy, too. My mother told us that any man with a decent attitude toward his village and his homeland would defend them if there was a need, so we should be proud that our father was one of those decent men. Even as a small child, I thought I had a pretty clear picture of the difference between decent and indecent people: the decent ones were those like my father, like Uncle Diep, Uncle Thuy, Le Duan, Truong Chinh, and Le Duc Tho who struggled and sacrificed for their country; the indecent ones were those who betrayed Viet Nam and served the French in order to live more luxurious lives, those who were willing to give up their heritage to the French in exchange for a bar of Cadum soap.

Gradually, I came to see that there were actually three kinds of people, not just two. A year after we had moved to Kim Qui, four more revolutionary families moved in. Across the canal from us was Mr. Cu and his daughter Ky Hoa; farther on the south side of the canal came the family of Mr. Thanh, who was the financial officer of Nam Bo (the southern region) for the revolutionary forces; near him were the families of Mr. Hung and Mr. Thach Son. These people were "intellectuals" who had abandoned their comfortable positions in the city and had joined the Viet Minh.

Mr. Cu was a Viet Minh, but he wasn't a Communist like my father; in fact, he and my father argued vociferously many times and criticized each other's ideology. Mr. Thanh and Mr. Hung were on the same side as my father, and in fact belonged to the same secret Communist organization. Mr. Thach Son, however, was neutral — "a cross between a horse and a man," as the others put it. I was greatly confused by all these factions, because these men all opposed the French domination, they all wanted to liberate the country, they all wanted freedom and good schools for the children in our country — yet they seemed to be divided by a great invisible barrier.

Even at seven, I came to realize that there were many different kinds of people. There were of course the ones who sold their future to the French, the ones we called Viet Gian (traitor); there were the ones who opposed the French and became followers of Ho Chi Minh; but there were also those who opposed the French but did not believe Ho Chi Minh had the answers for our country either. I had the feeling that my grandfather was in this last group, for he ran the village of Long Thanh his way, without the French, but he didn't like Ho Chi Minh's philosophy. He used to call Ho "that old goatee," and it hurt my father's feelings to hear the scorn in his voice.

As a true child of my father, I grew up with the notion that revolution and war were the normal style of life, and that good men and women were made to be revolutionaries. But since Uncle Hai Hoi came so many times to rebuild our house almost every time we moved, I began to understand that there are other kinds of virtues, other kinds of heroes.

Uncle Hai Hoi taught me that there were good people outside our world who also enjoyed life or suffered with their families, who had responsibilities as real and as important as ours in the Liberated Zone. There are many interests and beliefs in life besides being good children of Uncle Ho, he said, and he promised that I would get to experience them all when the war ended and we could all go back home.

In our house my mother worshiped our ancestors and once in a while talked to God, but Uncle Hai Hoi talked to God all the time. God was like an invisible friend of his, and he told him about the joy of building a good house for us, he told him about his problems, and he thanked him for keeping us safe in our journeys every time we moved. Uncle Hai Hoi asked if I ever talked to God; I just shook my head and smiled, because I thought it was silly. But he moved closer to me and said, "Talk to God, my child, for he listens to you." I challenged Uncle Hai Hoi by telling him that if he would let me see God's face in my dreams, then I would talk to God, but he became angry. He told me, and he told Hai Van, that we should never ask God for favors, but only show him our virtue. I thought it was easier to be one of the children of Ho Chi Minh than a child of God, but Uncle Hai Hoi said Ho was only one of God's billions of children on this earth — and that Ho had gone astray because he didn't worship God anymore. Uncle Hai Hoi left me confused, although I would appreciate his wisdom.

Meanwhile, the men and women in the Liberated Zone dedicated their lives to ridding Viet Nam of the French and bringing freedom to the Vietnamese people. Quietly and effectively, though, the people in Ha Noi — Ho Chi Minh, Le Duc Tho, and, yes, my father — planted the seeds of social-ism into the land. Just as quietly, just as effectively, the Soviet Union provid-ed the manure to make it grow.

At the same time, our family struggled to live without a father, and with-out an older brother to be "man of the house." As we embarked on our new life alone, I had no way of knowing when I would see my father again. And I would never have dreamed that when I did see him, it would be as a spy for the nation that was to become more of an enemy to him than the French had ever been.

— — —

After most of the men in our family had gone off to the revolution, life in Long Thanh settled into the kind of constant roar of activity common to any large family. There was some jealousy and fighting among the children, espe-cially among the girls. My cousin Yvonne used to tell me, "*We* are children of their (our grandparents) oldest son, therefore we are more special to them." I fought back with, "But my mother is their daughter, your mother is only a daughter-in-law." Yvonne cried at that and told our Aunt Bay about it, and I had to apologize. Still, Yvonne never mentioned that subject again.

At three years older than me, she tried to intimidate me in other ways. For instance, she used to call my mother by her first name as a kind of insult. (In Viet Nam, it is especially impolite for children to call adults by their names; they should use a term that denotes the order of their birth in their family. My mother was the eighth daughter, so her niece should call her Aunt Tam, or Aunt Number Eight.) When Yvonne made up songs with my mother's name in the lyrics, I turned the trick back on her and sang songs using her mother's and father's names in the worst manner. Of course, I got caught, and Yvonne got great glee out of seeing me confined to the house for punishment. Soon I learned that trick, too, and when she sang her song I ran to tell Aunt Bay and Yvonne would be put in "solitary." The competition never ended between my cousin and me, but no matter how often we fought, making up was almost instantaneous.

The whole family was very close, although my cousins often were a little distant toward Uncle Thuy's wife, Aunt Bich Loan. Her mother was a rich widow who lived in a hamlet outside the city of Can Tho, and from time to time she came to visit her daughter. When she did, she always came in a large and luxurious boat, and she wore gorgeous silk clothing. She didn't like it when she saw her daughter wearing the kind of cotton clothes our family had to wear. I used to think Aunt Bich Loan was beautiful no matter what she wore, so her mother shouldn't make such a big fuss over it. My grandmother seemed to have a special place in her heart for the wife of her youngest son, so Aunt Bich Loan's room was the only one in the house that had curtains — a special treat that added to my cousin's jealousy of this pretty newcomer to the family.

Grandmother hired men from the village to build some smaller houses for all the extra people who had moved in with her and my grandfather. My cousin Yen's house was first, since she was expecting and my grandmother wanted everything ready for her when the baby came. She even bought a crib for the "future spoiled brat," as Yvonne called the baby.

Our house was built between Yen's and the main house. The foundation was an old china tile that had been used in my great-grandparents' first home. This house had been burned down by the French after they failed to capture my uncles, Sac and Diep, in 1939. When my grandparents returned to their village after the war, grandfather had refused to rebuild on the old foundation; we didn't know why, because he would never talk of the old house or the fire that destroyed it. So our home would be raised on top of the thick, ruddy tiles that had lain as a bare symbol for so long.

There was a fish pond between our house and the main house, and a vegetable garden stretching all the way to Yen's house. I used to find the garden so attractive — the lavender blossoms of the eggplant, the yellow mustard flowers that attracted the bees.

We didn't have toys when we were growing up, except for our mandolin, so we played alot with what we found in nature. Once we figured out how to make a "record player" using the carpenter bees that swarmed everywhere in the spring. We would catch bees and put one underneath a piece of cheesecloth that was spread over the surface of a tin drum, so the bee was wedged between the cloth and the drum cover; then, placing a small bowl over the covered bee, we would guide it around on the tin surface. The vibration it made was amplified by the tin drum, and we pretended the sound was a kind of music. A bee could usually play for about 30 minutes, and after we let it rest it could play some more. Eventually it died, and we would give it a formal burial in a matchbox. We buried almost everything in our animal "graveyard" — from birds to crickets to geckos and field mice.

My great-grandparents had had fifteen children, but many of them died early in life, so by the time we moved to Long Thanh there were only four remaining — my grandmother, her two younger brothers, and one sister. As the oldest daughter, Grandmother kept the family house, but her youngest brother Ut had the honor of receiving the family inheritance as well as the responsibility of caring for his parents' graves and observing their memorial days.

— — —

The beginning of the school year in 1955 coincided with harvest time in the tangerine and orange orchards on my grandparents' land. Produce brokers from Soc Trang district came to Long Thanh, walked through the orchards time after time to make their estimates of the amount of fruit on the trees, then presented their bids. Some of them even stayed overnight and walked the rows of trees a second day to be certain of their calculations. That year the highest bid was 55,000 piasters, a lot of money for our family. To celebrate, Grandfather took all the children to the village center for dinner and to buy school supplies.

There were sixteen of us plus my grandfather, so the owner of the eating house had to run to his home for more chairs. The cook nodded eagerly when my grandfather told him, "Serve anything they ask for, except wine and coffee." Everybody looked at my cousin Quoc and me and laughed when he said that.

This was the first time Hai Van, Hoa Binh, and I had had root beer. I don't remember how many bottles we drank, but it was enough to make me sick. It may have been the first time my grandfather had taken so many children to the eating house, too, because when he paid the bill he said to himself, "Your grandmother should give me more money next time."

He had plenty of money left to take us across the lane to the country store, however. There he told us, "Buy all the things you need first, and buy what you want next." Hai Van and I let Kim and Cuong pick out the school supplies for us; we didn't know what we needed, because this would be the first time he and I ever attended a real school. Besides, my mind was on the list of things I had always said I wanted "when the war is over" — lemon drops, red sandals, and an umbrella.

I couldn't find the sandals anywhere in the store, and the only umbrella they had was far too big for me, so I settled for the lemon drops. I had little concept of weights and measures, so I asked for two kilos. My grandfather smiled, but told the Chinese merchant, "Weigh out two kilos of lemon drops for my granddaughter!" I was overwhelmed and embarrassed when he handed me the gigantic bag of candy. I offered to share it with my grandfather, but he told me, "An old grandfather only has one set of permanent teeth. I can't afford to lose them." He told me to share with my cousins, and they dug in eagerly, insisting all the time that they were only doing it as a favor to me.

Hai Van and Quoc bought bags of marbles. My sisters bought mirrors, combs, and colorful pins for their hair. We all enjoyed the shopping, but somehow the things we had always thought we wanted became less important now that we could have them. Maybe they were never very important at all, I thought.

My grandfather introduced us to people he knew, and of course as the former village chief he knew almost everyone. Before long, I was tired of folding my arms to greet the grownups, but I remembered that before we left home Aunt Bay and my mother had repeatedly told us to be polite. Yvonne had asked my aunt when the last time was when we were not polite, and her sister had told her, "That was the time your bottom was black and blue, sweetheart."

Grandfather took us to the Nha Viec, the town hall where he had worked as chief. The new official was a younger man who told us proudly, "Your mother and father were my classmates when your grandfather was our teacher." Later I overheard him asking my grandfather why he hadn't stopped our father from going off to Ha Noi. I couldn't hear all the answer, but I did hear Grandfather say that my mother will manage — "After all, it is the mother's job to raise the children." The new village chief looked at us with a sympathetic expression. Ironically, I felt fortunate just to be alive, to have survived the many air raids and to be able to walk among my grandfather's friends in his village.

Up until this time I had only known my grandfather slightly, from three visits he had made to see us in the Liberated Zone and from my mother's stories. She had told us he was a generous person whose loyalty to his fellow men and his family made him a most respected and beloved man in his village. When he had been chief, she said, he had spent his salary to make up taxes for people who couldn't pay, and he had lent money to poor farmers whose crops had failed.

It wasn't until I got to know him that I understood why my brother Khoi had always said, "Grandfather is a prince." His high spirits and warmth made me feel safe, and he always made us feel wanted. When I walked with him in the village for the first time I didn't know a single face, but I felt perfectly comfortable and knew absolutely that I belonged there.

Even with more than a dozen grandchildren to deal with, Grandfather was a fair referee. He was gentle and tolerant. He always told us we shouldn't think of him as a father because "fathers are loving but firm," and he could never be firm with us. I think he was so good at keeping us in line because we all respected him. Even when we had our own houses, most of us children ate breakfast with him at his house, after the farm workers had finished and gone off to the fields. We did our homework there, too, because Grandfather could help.

His pleasant demeanor sometimes failed him, though, when he read the days-old newspapers he picked up at the village office. I heard him curse the Geneva Conference, the Russians, and the people who divided our country and gave the North to the Communists and the South to "a Catholic Northerner." He made my Aunt Bay cry when he called Ho Chi Minh "the SOB who converted my sons." Grandfather never called Ho Chi Minh by his name, only "the old SOB"; it was the only swear word I ever heard him use. One day I tried it out on one of my cousins, and she went into hysterics; the next thing I knew I was grounded from swimming for two days.

What gave my grandfather the most pleasure was to teach us how to write Chinese characters, using a brush and the dark black ink from a big inkwell. We wrote them on sheets of red paper that were left over from the traditional Tet scrolls. Often the phrases we wrote were from the teachings of Confucius.

Grandfather filled our days with all the love and energy he could give us; the only time he was alone during the day was his nap time. By comparison, the nights were always lonely for us. When I came back to my own house I missed my father, and I missed Khoi. Sometimes I looked out the window and closed my eyes and wished that when I opened them my father would be there. When he used to come back from his trips he would stick his head in the window and surprise us, his broad smiling showing us his strong Dang teeth.

My Aunt Bay was one person who could make my father seem closer, because she shared his passion for politics and for the revolution. She was emotionally involved with the Liberation Movement, and supported the effort by taking on the duty of looking after my grandparents, which by tradition would have been the job of the oldest or the youngest son. She had turned down all proposals of marriage when she was at the eligible age, because with her brothers away on revolutionary work and my mother married and living with our family, Aunt Bay was the only one left to take care of her parents. Getting married would have meant leaving home, as my mother had done, because that was the tradition and Aunt Bay was a strong traditionalist and wouldn't bend or break the rules. My grandfather said Aunt Bay had "a perfect mixture to make an ideal Communist follower — a vulnerable quality that the old SOB looks for in the mass population."

Aunt Bay was admired and respected in the village, and it was never a problem for her nieces and nephews to get a ride across the river or other favors from the people there. She worked very hard, and her calloused hands were always busy. If she wasn't preparing a meal for our family, she would make our favorite cookies with a sugar flower on top. She tended the garden, picking beans or watering Grandmother's betel plants, which produced the wide green leaves that women chewed instead of smoking cigarettes like the men.

When I got to sleep over at the big house with Aunt Bay, she let me stay up late with her. She often read me some of her poems and tried to teach me how to write them. "You write poems first in your head," she said. "You write them when you work, you write them anywhere. Then, when you have time, you put them down on paper." Some of her poems made me cry. There was one about a young orphan who had survived after an air raid. A strange officer comforted her as he listened to her story of how she had lost her parents: The French burned her home and killed her parents. There were happy poems that she wrote toward the end of the war with the French, celebrating the "victory at Hai Van Pass, the triumph of Dien Bien Phu, the farewell to the French." She shared her poems with the Women's Liberation Association, where they were read aloud and learned by heart.

Aunt Bay was always full of hope and optimism about the revolutionary government in Ha Noi, though her dreams were modest — she wanted freedom for Viet Nam and for our family to have our fathers and brothers back. When I felt a need for my father, she was always there for me.

— — —

When we lived in the Liberated Zone, we were so "liberated" that it was unlawful to possess French francs; the only legal tender was Ho Chi Minh currency. When my father and Khoi had left, my mother gave all our HCM currency to them, because when we moved to the area controlled by the South Vietnamese government it would be worth less than old newspapers — at least the butcher could wrap fish in old newspapers, but one could get arrested for having HCM notes. With no money, except for her share of the sale of the orange and tangerine harvest, my mother had to look for work so she wouldn't be a burden on my grandparents.

Two dress shops in Can Tho city, about twenty kilometers, or twelve miles, away, gave her jobs sewing *ao dai*, long native dresses split from the waist down, worn with long, loose pants made from the same lightweight fabric. Once a week she would go there to deliver the clothes she had finished and to pick up fabric to make more. Each time she went into town, she would take one of the children with her, and we all waited anxiously for our turn. Elsewhere in the world, twenty kilometers may not be a very long distance, but it was a big deal for us to make the trip to Can Tho. The buses ran only when they were full at the stations in Soc Trang or Ca Mau or Bac Lieu, so when they stopped to pick up roadside passengers like us they were packed tight. The drivers always stopped for us, though, because roadside pickups were a bonus for them — they kept our fare for themselves.

I was very nervous when it was my turn to go to the city with my mother. I couldn't sleep the night before, so I got up before the sun and ate breakfast with the farm workers, who were very surprised to see me. After breakfast I sat by my grandmother and watched her cook *tam heo*, a rice gruel, for the pigs. I helped her feed firewood into the stove, and she held my hands and showed me how to stir the earthen pot without poking holes in it. When I started stirring too fast, she told me to be patient: "Give your heart to the things you do," she said. "That way you will become good at it." Later she took me to burn incense at the shrine of the Tho Than, the "god of the good earth," at the end of our property. She didn't ask for anything, but I heard her thank the god for the bounty that we had received.

I wore my best clothes to go to the city, including a new straw hat with a pink ribbon that Grandfather had bought for me. Grandmother gave me some money and said, "Buy yourself a present, anything you like — but no more rubber bands and marbles, please." I already had scads of those, because I won them in the marbles games I played at school.

The noise and bustle of my first big city overwhelmed me. I was terrified of getting separated from my mother in the crowded marketplace, so I clung tightly to the corner of her blouse as we walked along. I made one embarrassing mistake when we went to visit the home of my mother's old teacher. In the countryside, where we lived, people didn't have Western-style furniture in the living room; instead, there would be only a *bo ngua*, a thick slab of dark wood as big as a double bed, for people to sit on. The teacher's house had Western furniture, however, and when the maid asked us to sit and wait for the lady of the house to come, I sat down on what looked like a small *bo ngua*. Unfortunately, it was a coffee table, and even though my mother explained my mistake gently, I was red-faced.

My heart lifted later on when we went to a shop that had hundreds of umbrellas. I had wanted one for so long, and I thought I was in heaven when I started browsing through them and listening to the saleslady explain the different kinds. Oddly, though, the longer I looked the less interested I was in having one. When my mother asked which one I would choose, I surprised her by whispering to her, "Mom, I look so stupid with an umbrella!" My red sandals were a different story, however. We went to a shoe store and I finally got something I had been determined to have "when the war is over."

We went to other shops as well to pick up things my grandmother had put

down on a list. I asked my mother to help me buy a lighter for my grandfather; I had noticed that the wheel on his old one was so worn that his thumb
slipped off of it when he tried to ignite the wick.

Gradually I came to love the city and its variety of people and shops and
occupations. I imagined thousands of other things in the city that would keep
the wheel of life turning through eternity, people sharing their tasks as well as
enjoying the fruits of their labor. I couldn't help comparing this animated
town with the places I had lived in the Liberated Zone with my father —
where we had to tame the forests to build our houses, indeed to bear many
hardships as a revolutionary's family. I felt a little guilty when I realized I much
preferred having the freedom to participate in the marketplace, to buy and sell
whatever I wished. My brother Khoi had once told me, "Anyone can live in
the city, but only a few special people can be happy with our father's way of
life." My sisters retorted that we had been happy because we were with our
father, not because we fancied so dearly the life of a forester. In fact, they fancied a better life, as I did.

I came home feeling good about my experience in the city. The impres-
sions lingered the way the characters and music of a play will stay in your mind
after going to the theater. My cousins Thao and Yvonne, dedicated children
of the revolution, scorned my enthusiasm. "The city is a bad place for anyone
in our family," they tried to convince me. "We go there only for business. We
wouldn't go there to live."

— — —

It was early afternoon. The golden sun shone on the surface of the river. Kim
and Cuong were sitting on the bank watching Hoa Binh and Minh Tam swim,
while Hai Van and I skipped broken tiles across the water. Mother had gone
off to Can Tho to look for a place for us to live; it had been perhaps a year
since all the men had left for the North, and my mother wanted Kim and
Cuong, who were now fourteen, to have a chance to continue their schooling in the city.

Suddenly Kim stood up and pointed at the orange orchard. Her mouth was
open, but she was speechless with shock. We all followed the direction of her
finger and saw a man walking toward us. He looked tired, and his trousers
were wet to the knees. He came closer, and his image became clearer and
more real.

It was our father.

Recovering from our surprise, we took off running toward him, Hai Van
and me in the lead and Kim and Cuong coming behind, carrying the smaller
girls. My father sank to the ground, with his arms open to embrace us as we
arrived in a crush. He kissed us as if he had missed us for a thousand years.

"Where is Mother?" he asked Kim after the welcome died down a bit. Kim looked at the ground. Then, in a sentence that captured so vividly the strange division in our family, she mumbled, "I don't know. Mom told me not to tell anyone where she is."

"My daughter, I am not just anyone. You can tell me where Mother is." He looked almost angry at her response.

"No, I don't know where she is," Kim insisted.

"Kim, I came back to take Mother and all of you to Ha Noi with me. I changed my mind, I want my family with me and I have permission to bring you with me now."

"My mother wouldn't want to go to Ha Noi," Cuong interjected. "She has already made up her mind." Her face was cold and impersonal, as if she were speaking to a stranger.

"Please let your mother make her own decision," my father said. "Now let me have the address of your mother."

Kim looked panicky when Hai Van said, "Mom is staying with Aunt Sau Chuc." Mrs. Chuc was a close friend of my parents, and my father knew where she lived.

Both Cuong and Kim told my father that he would be taking a great risk if he went to Can Tho, because the Cong An (the South Vietnamese security police) had been coming around recently looking for him. He told us not to worry, because he would disguise himself with a "kit" in his bag. I felt confident then, because I remembered when my father had first gotten that kit and had made himself up with scars on his face and neck like a burn victim. Hai Van and I had laughed at the demonstration, but now it was serious. This time he said he would make himself up as a beggar. I could picture him coming to Mrs. Chuc's door, and I was sure that my mother would be fooled by his disguise and would give him money, as she often did the beggars in the marketplace. She would be shocked when she recognized him: I wondered if she would feel sorry that he had to wear beggar's garb, or would she cover her mouth to suppress laughter at his appearance?

My father took us to our house, and Kim asked if he wanted to see Grandfather before he left. He shook his head and said he had to go quickly, adding that only Aunt Bay should know about his visit. He also told us not to wander away from the house; if our mother decided to join him, she would come home immediately, and Aunt Bay would take us by sampan to a rendezvous point that only she knew about. "Will you remember my instructions?" he asked Kim. "Yes, I'll remember," she promised.

He kissed Hoa Binh goodbye, and held Minh Tam and kissed her little hands and feet. My father uttered the words, "Papa, Papa." I think he wanted to make sure Minh Tam knew who he was. He didn't want his baby to forget him. He wept as he walked out the back door and disappeared into the thick orchard.

Kim and Cuong locked the door and then pushed the table in front of it to secure it further. I wondered if they were trying to keep out my father or the Cong An, but I didn't dare ask. Hoa Binh and Minh Tam both cried, and Hai Van rocked Minh Tam in the hammock that was hung inside a mosquito net. I was confused when I discovered that my father's brief presence could create such a stormy reaction in all of us. I was torn inside, part of me praying that he would find my mother in Can Tho, the other part hoping desperately that he wouldn't. I didn't want to go to Ha Noi! But more important than that, I knew my mother didn't want to go. The people in charge in Ha Noi would not let her operate her own little sewing business. She would have to work in the government factory, and the word "factory" somehow sounded impersonal and disgraceful to my ears.

I sat on the cool wooden slab in our home, and for the first time I felt a sense of having to protect my mother. I wasn't quite sure whom I was against — the government in Ha Noi or my father. I thought back to the countless arguments I had heard between my parents as I pretended to sleep. My mother had said a hundred times that what makes people different from animals is that we have feelings and we express them, but the Communist party wouldn't allow people to speak their minds. She was for "free enterprise," he believed in "socialism." She insisted that she didn't want to exploit any person, nor would she allow another person to dictate to her.

But what about Papa, I thought. He will be lonely. We will deprive him of our laughter, our love. We will grow up apart from him, and he won't know what is going on in our lives. He had told my big sisters and Khoi that when the French put him in solitary confinement, the thing that was most painful to him — more painful than the physical punishment, more painful than his broken thumb and collarbone — was missing his wife and his children.

My heart ached and my eyes burned. I looked to Kim and Cuong for help, but both were occupied with their own thoughts. They must have been bad thoughts, because both were angry and crabby. "Go to bed!" Cuong grumped to Hai Van and me.

I went to bed without even going through the ritual of brushing my teeth and washing my face and my feet. In the absolute quiet of the night, I heard my heart beating. The mosquitoes went "zooooo . . . zooooo . . . zooooo" by my ears. I couldn't sleep. After a while I got up. I knew the squeak of the big door would wake my big sisters and they wouldn't let me go out, so I crawled out through the dog's hole low on one wall.

Once outside I realized how dark and late it was. I saw some fireflies against the trees and remembered that someone had told me they were "ghosts' eyes." I ran as fast as I could to my grandparents' house, and sneaked in through the dog hole there. I woke my aunt up when I came to her bed and crawled in with her. She welcomed me in and rubbed my back with her hand to help me go to sleep, but she drifted off while I was still awake. I put her hand back onto her chest and lay there listening to raindrops on the roof; they sounded like a thousand tears falling. I missed my mother.

In the morning, Kim came to find me and took me back to our house for breakfast. While she was helping me dress for school, I asked her if she wanted to go to Ha Noi with our father. She just shook her head and wouldn't talk about it at all.

My mother didn't come back the next day or the day after that. Truthfully, I didn't want to see her come back right away because that could well mean that she had agreed to join my father. I felt bad for thinking that way, but more than half of my heart wanted our lives to stay just the way they were.

The next few days passed and gradually I forgot all about my father's visit. As a child of nine, my mind was easily swayed to some new topic, and I began thinking about a Cambodian soldier who lived and worked at a fort along the highway that led to our school — one of many soldiers posted in Viet Nam when France ruled both Viet Nam and Cambodia. Quoc and Hai Van and I thought he must be crazy as we stopped to watch him each day. He had a bamboo basket that looked like a fish trap, but he was using it on dry ground, digging into animal holes in the earth and then putting the basket over them. Quoc asked what he was trying to catch, and he said in his Cambodian accent, "Snakes." His breath was pungent with rice wine, and his body odor was worse. We watched in fascination as he peered down into the hole and cackled, "Look here, look here, this is enough for the whole fort to eat and drink all day long!" Then he aimed a long wooden pole with a forklike spear into the hole and brought up a big snake. He broke its neck, yanked it off the spear, and went after another one the same way.

When he was finished he took a string from inside his shirt and strung his catch of eight snakes together, then started walking toward the fort. Hai Van asked to carry the snakes, so the soldier let him. "Do you kids like snakes?" he asked.

"Never tasted one yet," Quoc said.

"Come to the fort after school," he invited. "Cambodians make delicious snakes." He roared with his strange laughter.

That afternoon, Quoc and Hai Van told Yvonne and Thao that they wanted to stay at school to play. I knew they were going to the fort to try the snake.

The next day Hai Van told me that the meat was tasty, especially when it was barbecued, but he confessed that when he thought of the shiny dead reptiles on the string he had almost gotten sick. Quoc said the Cambodian soldiers had invited them to come back again for another taste treat "when they butcher somebody's dog from the village."

Not long after my father's sudden visit, my mother came home from Can Tho. My brother and I were told to "go out and play." That meant the adults in the family needed privacy for some grown-up talk. I never found out exactly what my father had said to her, or what she said to him, but after the family conference that day she told us briefly that we should make up our minds that we would be staying in the South once and for all. Our future had been decided.

Chapter 4

Though my grandfather considered himself to be a farmer, he was really only a "gentleman farmer" — he never actually worked a single day in the fields. He used to go out on walks to inspect his land, but he never went farther than the end of the tangerine orchard; there was a shaky footbridge there leading to the rice paddies, and we all knew that at his age he would never cross that bridge. That made the land beyond a perfect place for my Aunt Bay's secret vegetable garden.

The plot of green beans, eggplant, okra, tomatoes, cucumbers, and other foodstuffs had to be secret because Aunt Bay was growing them to sell to raise money to funnel to the cadres living in the bush, and Grandfather would have been furious if he had found out. She couldn't hire anyone to help tend the plants, because word of the garden might get back to him, so all of us children helped her with the weeding and picking.

We were told that what we did was very important, because the money we helped earn went to buy medicine for the wounded men and women of the resistance forces. Truthfully, I didn't share Aunt Bay's political motives. I helped her and kept her secret just because I liked her and wanted to make her happy. Still, I understood enough to know that, regardless of why I worked in that garden, I helped the Viet Cong; every time innocent people were killed by the Viet Cong, I secretly felt deeply responsible for their deaths because I had indirectly contributed to their cause.

Sometimes I asked my aunt to explain to me why the cadres sabotaged the good highways that the people needed, why they killed busloads of innocent, ordinary citizens but seldom attacked military convoys or any important officials in the "puppet government." All she said to me was, "You are too young to understand guerrilla warfare."

From time to time my mother was asked to help the movement, too. (The Viet Cong cadres approached her through Aunt Bay.) I never knew whether she did it of her own free will or was forced to, but once when she came back from Can Tho she brought back a lot of black cotton fabric, from which she sewed many sets of *ba ba*, the "black pajamas" that Westerners always called the peasants' garb.

My grandfather usually visited my mother after his afternoon nap, sitting on the divan near the sewing machine and sipping tea while they talked. The afternoon she was making the *ba ba,* he walked in and spotted them. He knew who they were for. He walked out of the house and called for Aunt Bay. When she ran to him from the main house, he confronted her with his discovery and demanded to know who had made my mother "support the evil." My mother tried to calm him, insisting that it wasn't very important because it had only cost her two weeks' salary and some of her time, but he was terribly upset. For the first time he showed his anger without first telling the children to go outside and play.

"Do you know that the people from the Front are terrorizing your sister?" he said to Aunt Bay. "Isn't it enough that she has already sacrificed her whole youth to be the wife of that Communist, and she has ended up with six children alone without a man and every night she strains her back on that sewing machine to make a living?"

My aunt looked down and didn't speak, and he continued his tirade. "I can't save those who wish to go to hell, but I will make sure that none of the SOB's make my daughter go to hell with them!" He turned to my mother. "Today you put clothes on the Communists' backs, you fill their empty stomachs. Tomorrow you refuse them and they will hang you. Revolution! I don't believe in this revolution! They are men, hungry men. There is no goodness in this revolution! It's an organized crime. They will rob and rape the South when they march down here, and we will all be their slaves and servants. I don't want to see your money and effort used in killing women and children. From now on none of you are going to leave this land without a good reason."

His word was usually final in our family, but to my Aunt Bay her meetings with the members of the National Liberation Front were "good reason" — next in importance to taking care of my grandparents. She never stopped helping the cadres, but she and my cousins had to become more discreet about their activities.

My mother continued to help now and then, too. When I was a little older, she explained to me that we couldn't refuse, that we had to support the Front even with our limited ability. If we refused, she said, indirectly it meant we denied everything my father was doing. We had to play along, to cooperate, she said. To be neutral was considered the same as being reactionary, and as wife and children of a revolutionary leader we could not be seen in that light.

The cadres who came around to ask for help were not the only people who kept politics in our lives. Like many other former Viet Minh and the sons and daughters of those who went north, our names were on the Cong An's "blacklist." From time to time the secret police came around seeking information about my father and the others. Once a man came to my grandfather's house and told him, "Just hoping we might run into one of your sons, or your son-in-law, Chief." Grandfather was more hostile toward President Diem's henchmen than they were toward my family. He retorted, "I will reward you if you bring my sons back to their children, but don't bother me here." The secret police kept coming back anyway, even though they got a cold reaction from my grandfather, who wouldn't even invite them into the house for a glass of rainwater.

One can't fight the powerful forever without being hurt, however. One day something happened that terrified us all and left me with an awful dread of being left alone.

My mother had gone to Can Tho, this time taking Thao with her. At the end of the day Thao came back alone, terribly frightened, telling us that the Cong An had arrested my mother and were holding her at their headquarters for "questioning." My grandfather swung into action immediately. It was too late for a scheduled bus, since they didn't run after dark, so he chartered a bus and headed off to Can Tho to try to get her released.

The family was in turmoil. Most of the children cried, though Hai Van just fell very silent and wouldn't talk to anyone. I was so scared I couldn't cry. That night we all went to Grandmother's house to sleep. She burned incense sticks and prayed at the altar.

Grandfather had told us that he would wait until morning to bring my mother home, because it wasn't safe to travel at night; still, every time we heard a noise we all ran out to see if it was them. As the night wore on, all the cousins and great-aunts and -uncles gathered in my grandparents' kitchen, showing their support and trying vainly to comfort us. I appreciated their concern, but all I wanted was to see my mother walk through the door. Deep in my heart I was afraid that the secret police would kill her, and I knew that that would destroy my father as well.

My brother woke up at one point and came to the kitchen. "Mom should tell the police the truth, where Daddy is, so they won't hurt her," he said.

My cousin Yen picked him up. "Sweetheart, they are not going to hurt Mom. They will only question her, and they will let her come back to us."

Hai Van argued, "If she doesn't tell them what they want to know, then they will hurt her. They can't catch Daddy, he is too far away now. They can't catch him even if she tells them exactly where he is." I didn't try to argue with my seven-year-old brother, but the grown-ups had their own ways of dealing with the situation.

We were told repeatedly that we had to tell strangers, the police, school officials, and classmates that "our father is missing in action." There were nights when I couldn't sleep for thinking about my father and Khoi so much, and I lay awake memorizing that instruction and thinking how awful the word "missing" was. What if he was really "missing"? It hurt me each time I said the word, but I knew I had to protect my father and the interests of the Front and the security of my own family. I often told myself that I must stay alive, to be there as a revolutionary's daughter to welcome my father when he came marching home in victory so that his sacrifice would be worthwhile.

The following morning, as he had promised, my grandfather brought my mother home. She walked in on his arm, looking like a wounded bird. I remember thinking, "We will take good care of her. Grandmother will say the right things, as she always does to comfort us, she will make things right. And Grandfather will protect her." But when I saw my grandfather's worried expression, I felt as if the sky had fallen on us. If this was a situation that even Grandfather couldn't defeat, then no one could help us.

He had been able to get her released, he told us, by meeting with the chief of the secret police and demanding that she be let go. He told the official of his past position in Long Thanh, and insisted that if he didn't know where his sons were, then my mother wouldn't know either. Trying the human touch, he told the chief how many children were back home depending on my mother; and just in case that didn't work, he also threatened to take the matter up with the mayor if the Cong An didn't release my mother to him.

When she was freed, my grandfather had taken her to the home of his adopted son, Uncle Dinh, where they had stayed until it was safe to travel back to Long Thanh. Still, he knew that he couldn't stop the Cong An from coming around and harassing us, and he couldn't prevent them from arresting her or any of us again.

A short time later my mother told my grandparents that she could no longer cope with the anxiety of being caught between the government on one side and the Front on the other. She wanted to move away from the Can Tho area entirely, to find someplace where no one knew us and we could be left alone. She begged them to understand her need, and not to be upset that we would be leaving them.

My grandfather was hurt and frustrated that he could not resolve this problem for her, and he had to give in. "Wherever it is safe and decent for you and the kids, I would be happy to see you go," he told her.

My mother decided to move all the way to Sai Gon, 375 kilometers (about 230 miles) away from Long Thanh — far enough, she hoped, that there would be no more secret police and no more Front cadres who knew us and wanted to use us for their conflicting purposes.

— — —

Before we could go to Sai Gon, my mother had to work even harder for a while to earn money for the move. In the meantime, she needed to ask some friends in the capital for help in finding a place to live. Kim and Cuong would manage the work and younger kids at home, so she decided to send me there to take a message to a woman she knew. Thus it happened that the first time I ever went to Sai Gon, after a lifetime of living in jungles and the country-side, I went alone.

My mother didn't have the address of the woman she wrote the letter to, but she did have the address of the home-economics school run by a mutual friend, Mrs. My Ngoc. I got off the bus in Sai Gon, the letter pinned safely inside my pocket, and took a cyclo — or pedicab, a kind of three-wheeled bicycle — to the school. Mrs. My Ngoc wasn't there, but fortunately one of the students knew my mother's friend and took me to her house.

The woman, a beautiful lady named Mrs. Thanh, came to her door and asked who I was. I waited until the student had left and then said, "My dad is Mr. Dang Van Quang." The lady hugged me as if I were her long-lost relative and poured out so many questions about my mother I couldn't answer them all. Inside the house, we sat on the couch and she read the letter I gave her. Halfway through she stopped and looked at me with a sad and sympathetic glance. "Your father is a fool, a noble fool like many other good men, including your uncle" (using the polite form of address to refer to her husband).

We ate dinner together and then she went out to see some friends, apparently to try to get some help for my mother's effort to move to Sai Gon. While she was gone I took a shower, as she had suggested, and was impressed with how sweet the soap smelled and how soft and fresh the towel was.

Suddenly I realized I was in this strange house all alone. It was so quiet I could hear the mosquitoes and the geckos on the ceiling. I looked around and saw a figure of the Virgin Mary on the wall, and beneath it a photograph of a man in his forties. I assumed the man was deceased, because religious people often put pictures of their departed loved ones beneath a picture of Buddha or Mary or Jesus. As I thought about that, I remembered a ghost story my father had once told us about a woman who lived in a mansion all alone. Her husband and son had died, and so to mourn them she kept their bodies in the mansion, and every day she would open their caskets and look at them through glass windows. As I stood there in the silent house, I imagined I could hear someone breathing. I scared myself, and so I rushed out the door and sat on the steps until Mrs. Thanh came home.

I felt a little more at ease when she arrived because she brought me a small carton of ice cream, jackfruit flavor. I wished my little brother and sisters could have been there to share it with me; I didn't want Mrs. Thanh to know, but it was the first time I had ever tasted ice cream in my life.

As we sat there that evening, Mrs. Thanh asked if I would like to become her adopted daughter, since she didn't have any children. She promised to love me like my mother loved me, but I thought that was impossible; no one could love a child as much as my mother loved me. But Mrs. Thanh added another reason: "You see, sweetheart, Mom has to support six children. I could help her by taking some of that load off her shoulders."

"I'm not a load," I insisted. "I am a big help to her. Besides, if I go to you my mother would be lonely for me."

She still talked about it, looking off dreamily as she thought of having a daughter. I wouldn't accept, though I did promise her, "When we move to Sai Gon, I will come to spend the night with you if you like. I will bring my little brother and sisters here, too."

"You do that, darling," she said, rubbing my head. "Now go to bed, I have to write your mother a letter."

The next morning Mrs. Thanh woke me up very early and took me to a coffee shop, where we had breakfast in the French style. I had a croissant and a glass of hot chocolate milk; it was a great change from all the eggs we ate at my grandmother's house. Then she took me to the bus station in Cholon for my return trip. I tried to pay for my bus ticket, but she insisted I keep the money "for candy." I tucked the money and the letter she had written my mother into my pocket and again secured them with a safety pin, remembering all I had heard about the skillful pickpockets in Sai Gon.

Mrs. Thanh told me to tell my mother she would find a place for us, and that we should just pack our clothes and hurry to the city. "Tell your mother not to worry about a thing," she said. "There are friends of your father and friends of your uncles all over Sai Gon, and they will be delighted to help your mother." She stayed with me at the station until my bus left, and I enjoyed the smell of her perfume and the warm feeling of my hands in hers. I was terribly happy that I was going to be bringing good news back to my family.

— — —

We moved to Sai Gon shortly afterward, when Mrs. Thanh helped us make arrangements to move in with Mrs. Giau, another friend who had been my mother's classmate. This was a case of a favor returned: My mother had taken care of Mrs. Giau's son, a *bo doi* with a stomach ulcer, when we lived in the forest of Kim Qui.

Mrs. Giau owned a dress shop in one of the expensive shopping areas on Le Thanh Ton Street, so my mother was able to get a job sewing for her; we were also lucky enough to rent a room on the second floor of her three-story townhouse on Le Cong Kieu Street. My older sisters and Hai Van started school right away, but I would have to wait. My mother said she needed me to take care of my two little sisters while she worked in the dressmaking shop on the first floor.

Our living space was small and the ceiling was low, so the hot summer days seemed almost unbearable inside, hotter than it had been in Can Tho. My sisters and I spent a lot of time outside. I took them for walks on Cong Ly, the tree-lined boulevard near our house, and Hoa Binh had a great time watching all the cars roaring by. We walked to the Cathay movie theater to look at the posters for the features "now showing" and the "coming attractions." We could never afford to actually go in to see a movie, but we enjoyed standing around in the cool lobby where a powerful air conditioner was working away.

My mother worked long and hard, always the first to get up so she could fix breakfast for all of us. She ate hurriedly and then went downstairs to begin work; when we went to bed at night she was still at her sewing machine, toiling away. Yet she seemed happy — here in Sai Gon there were no secret police and no members of the Front coming to our house to bother us.

Mrs. Giau's first husband had been a close friend of my parents and sympathetic to the revolution. They were divorced, however, and she married quite a different kind of man, a very rich merchant. Their two children went to a French private school in Sai Gon. Every morning a green school bus with two attendants came to the front door to pick them up. I watched from my upstairs window as the children sometimes argued with their nanny, complaining that they didn't want to go to school; when that happened I always thought, "I will take their place and go to school for them." They had no idea what it meant not to be able to attend school, to learn the things one might need just for survival.

Their father had a big red convertible, and he often came home in the late afternoon to take his daughters for a ride. I heard their laughter and saw that the younger girl got to sit in her father's lap when he drove. Seeing them having fun in a car wasn't the hard part for me, though — it was hearing them shout gleefully, "Papa!" when their father came home. I realized I hadn't been able to say that for a long time, and I became afraid that someday I might forget how. When I was alone, I tried to utter the word "Papa," but it stuck in my throat.

At night, while everyone else slept, I often lay awake thinking about my father and Khoi and all the villages we had lived in together, and trying to imagine what Ha Noi must be like. Mostly, though, I thought about my father's promise when he left that "Daddy will be back in two years." All the men who left had told their loved ones that; Uncle Thuy had told my grandmother that he'd be back in two years to have her grandson, and he promised his new wife Bich Loan that they would have their own home in two years.

I always trusted my father when he made a promise, because he was so careful not to promise something he thought he might not be able to keep. I remembered once when I had asked him to bring me back a magpie from one of his trips. His answer was quite carefully phrased: "I promise I will buy you a magpie if I see the man who sells birds, but I won't promise to buy you a magpie, because I might not see him at all, then I won't be able to keep my promise to you." At the time I was hurt, because I thought he just wasn't going to try very hard to bring me my present, but later I understood the importance he was placing on keeping one's word.

At that hot house on Le Cong Kieu Street, however, I finally stopped believing that my father would keep his last promise, this most important one, to come back to us within two years. It had become clearer to me that it would not be so easy for my father's side to win the victory they sought. The refugees from the North, together with Diem, seemed very strong and very united in fighting Ha Noi. My father and Ho Chi Minh would have no chance to defeat them as quickly as they had predicted.

On weekends Mrs. Giau's children came up to play with me and my brother and sisters, and sometimes the older girl, about ten, would bait me about my father. "Where is he? Did he leave you and your mom?"

I snapped at her, "No!"

Then she would say, "I'll bet you don't have a father. I'll bet you are an illegitimate child!"

I wanted to punch her, and then I wanted to tell her that her own stepbrother was in the same place my father was, but I knew I couldn't. "Leave my house!" I demanded. She reminded me that this was her house, but I insisted: "My mother rented it, therefore it is mine." I threw them out and closed the door, calling them SOB's on the way out for good measure. I was still angry, though, so I went downstairs and told their mother everything (except the SOB part). She promised it wouldn't happen again, and that night her husband came to see us with his two daughters and the older one apologized for what she had said.

We spent six long months in that hot, tiny apartment in Mrs. Giau's house. My mother never complained, but I knew she was exhausted. She lost weight and she looked quite strained; I hadn't heard her laugh since we left my grand-parents' house. Only when she spoke of my father and Khoi was there a trace of a smile in her eyes. She often talked about what would happen "when your dad and your brother come home." I don't know if she really believed they would be back after two years or if she was just trying to keep our spirits up, but she always expressed only good thoughts about them.

Mother had been saving as much money as possible since we first arrived in Sai Gon, and as soon as she had enough to pay for a place of our own we moved from Mrs. Giau's. She found a house in a place called Xom Dao, a Catholic community. My Aunt Bich Loan came to live with us so she could learn to sew, since my mother was thinking ahead to opening sewing classes for half a dozen young girls when we could get a bigger house.

The term "Dao" literally meant "religious," but it was used to refer only to Catholics, since they huddled together in their own communities with a sense of pride of being "children of Jesus Christ," not to mention having the clout of sharing the religion of President Diem. The first few days we seemed like strangers from outer space when the Catholics asked us, "Do you have a religion?" We children knew what they meant, and said we didn't, but my mother told us it would be better to reply that "we worship our traditional religion."

The nearest public school was far, far away, and the only private school within walking distance was run by the Huyen Sy Catholic Church. The school accepted underprivileged children with no charge, so my mother took Hai Van and me there to register for classes. The mother superior who was principal had a beautiful face, pure and delicate as if she had never been out in the wind and sun a day in her life. She was quite serious, however, about her religion. When my mother told her we "worship our traditional religion," she asked why we wanted to register in a Catholic school. My mother was hon-est: "Because we live in Xom Dao and there is no other school nearby."

"Will you let your children become Catholic?" the mother superior asked.

"They are free to practice any religion as long as they honestly believe in it, Mother."

The principal put her reading glasses back on and filled in blanks on the applications, both mine and my brother's. I don't know what my mother was asked to agree to on that form, but she signed it.

For most children, going to school for the first time is a traumatic experi-ence, but I had been deprived of it for so long I was looking forward to it eagerly. I loved school, if not always for learning then for socializing. It was a place where I could just be a kid for five or six hours a day. I didn't think of my father or my brother while I played with the other children, beating them at marbles and jacks and telling them stories of my life in the countryside. But the Catholic school also became a survival test of sorts, too, because I learned for the first time the pressures that people can put on others when they believe they are acting on behalf of God.

On the first day in my third-grade classroom, the stern-faced nun who was the teacher asked me again if I had a religion. I told her I didn't, and she demanded, "Why not?" She didn't wait for a reply, however, but strode briskly to the last row of chairs and tables. I stood, not knowing what to do. "Come down here," she demanded. "I don't have all day. You will sit here with the rest of the non-Catholics!"

At that moment I thought about the village school I had attended several years before, where all the children were considered equal — Communists or not, boys or girls, children of farm workers, town officials, even the Cambodian guards. Nobody had talked of segregation then, but I was now firmly immersed in it.

As the nun walked away a girl sitting next to me whispered a warning: "You'd better learn how to say Hail Mary and Our Father or she will kill you!"

"I'm not a Catholic. What is Hail Mary and Our Father anyway?" I asked.

"Prayers," she said, and she told me the nun would give me a book and order me to memorize them.

"What will she do to me if I don't remember them by heart?"

"No recess," she shrugged.

The class began — with a reciting of the Hail Mary. The Catholic children said it smoothly and heartily, while those on my side of the room read along in their books. The nun made a face as she looked at us.

I was told to stay after class during the first recess to study the Bible. I wanted to find Hai Van to see how he liked his class, so I lied to the teacher that I had to go to the bathroom. She refused to let me go, forcing me to stay and go over the Hail Mary time and again to learn the correct intonation. After a while I really did have to go to the bathroom, and she finally allowed me to leave. Then I discovered that I didn't know where it was! I thought that if I couldn't find the girls' room in time, I would have to quit this school.

I spent my second recess with the nun in the classroom, too, going over the Hail Mary and Our Father. To me these were less like prayers and more like dogma; with each sentence I uttered, I felt somewhat ashamed, as if I were betraying my ancestors by worshipping some strange religion. But no matter how I felt, I knew it wasn't important to anyone; the important thing was to stay in school, and that meant memorizing the prayers.

My brother was stronger than I about such things. Being forced to learn the

Catholic rituals didn't bother him. It was a free school, he said, so they wanted something in return, and that was a chance to try converting us to their religion. "They can't beg me to be a Catholic," I told my family, "what makes them think they can humiliate me into it?" Hai Van said someone had told him that "they killed kings and dictators who refused to become Catholic in the old days, so you'd better watch out!" I knew he was joking, but it bothered me all the same.

On the third day I was told to stand and recite the Hail Mary to the class. I thought I did it all right, but the nun was not satisfied; she ordered me to write it twenty-five times and submit it to her at the end of the day. Even that wasn't as bad as when I had to recite the Our Father. I stumbled on the words, and the nun pinched my ears and called me "dunce." It was like a nightmare. The Catholic children roared with laughter, and I wished I could disappear. In fact, I gathered up my things and started to leave the room, but the nun just said without even looking at me, "If you walk out that door, don't you come back." I thought of my mother and how she would react, and so I stayed.

All the way home at the end of that day I cursed that nun and wished that she would go to hell — the Buddhist hell that one reaches only after going through nine purgatories!

Hai Van was far more intelligent than I, and far more forgiving. He tolerated mistakes and stupidity in other people, bending like strong bamboo in the face of unfortunate pressures. "If it makes the nun happy to think she can convert you, let her believe it," he told me. "What is going on inside you is a different matter." He memorized his prayers like a Catholic kid, and his teacher rewarded him with a brand new Bible. He had limits, though — when the nun asked him to go to Mass on Sunday, he made the excuse that he had to babysit his sisters and couldn't attend.

Adults liked Hai Van, because most of the time he met their expectations. He hardly ever argued with grown-ups; he simply proved to them that he was right by his actions. He brightened my mother's spirits with his countless "achievement awards," while I was bringing home endless "poor conduct" notes. I always admired my brother, but I didn't envy him or feel a need to try to copy him. I thought of him as the gifted child of the family, and I was content with myself and my abilities.

Actually, I liked the story of Jesus. I could relate to him when I heard that he was a poor boy who had devoted his youth to helping his carpenter father, and that he had worshipped God. I had a notion about God, that he was good, but still when they talked about loving God and loving Jesus I couldn't feel what they felt even if I tried.

One day Hai Van and I walked into the church next to the school yard just to see what it was like. Above the altar there was a gigantic cross, with a figure of Jesus nailed to it. I was moved by the realistic bloodstains on his hands and feet, and by the crown of thorns on his head. His eyes were lifelike, but so sad, and they seemed to be looking at me no matter where I stood. I felt a real sympathy for him, and a strange idea that I owed him something, but I didn't know what it was. The feeling was genuine, and it came from my heart, not from a book.

Suddenly a nun came up from behind us and whispered sternly, "Children, you shouldn't dress this way in church!" She walked us outside and told us that we shouldn't come into the church wearing our khaki shorts. I must wear an *ao dai*, she said; all the Catholic children wore either *ao dai* or proper Western clothes.

It was the last time we went to that church. I was too small to have an *ao dai*. Hai Van and I looked at the building from outside after that, and talked about having a house someday with stained-glass windows, but after a while I forgot about Jesus since I couldn't go into the church to see him. The feeling I had had that day beneath the giant cross never came back to me when the nun tried to teach us religion out of a book.

By midterm, my teacher asked me if I wanted to become a Catholic. I certainly didn't, but I was afraid to tell her that, so I said I would have to ask my mother. My mother said it wouldn't displease her if one or all of us became "religious," because there is only one God and most religions teach the same good principles, but if I didn't want to become Catholic then I didn't have to. I asked her to tell the nun for me, because I was afraid she might mistreat me if I declined. My mother just replied, "You don't allow people to mistreat you."

"She will kick me out of school, then," I worried.

"Then let her kick you out," my mother said matter-of-factly. I felt great relief then, because my mother was willing to support me in whatever I decided, and especially because she promised she wouldn't be mad if I got kicked out of school. I thought getting kicked out of that school would be the best thing that could happen to me.

Still, when the teacher asked me for my answer the next day I was tongue-tied. I had never been afraid of anyone the way I was afraid of that nun. I shuffled my feet and looked at the floor, until her patience ran out: "What did your mother say?" she shouted. Perhaps strong fear can sometimes be converted into strong confidence, because her rough voice seemed to give me the nerve to respond. I looked her in the eye and said, "Maybe later, Sister, when I understand Catholicism and believe in it."

She accepted that, and promised to teach me all about her religion. I told her she would be the first to know when I was ready. After that I spent recess like the other kids, playing outside, because I was studying at home with my brother.

The more I learned about Catholicism, the more I knew I couldn't follow it, at least not then. The religion required that its followers worship only the Christian God, and no other. But in my grandparents' home there was our ancestors' altar; there was the God of the Good Earth that blessed our land; there was the godmother that my grandmother worshiped. If I became a Catholic I would have to abandon all of them, and that was too much of a sacrifice for me to make.

I felt a great burden all during my year at the Huyen Sy school, especially because we were being given an education without having to pay any tuition, but I couldn't pay the price they wanted from me. Sometimes I thought it would be so simple just to tell the nun, "My father is a Communist, and I am an atheist." Then she would scream and leave me alone forever.

The summer in our house in Xom Dao was almost unbearable with the heat baking in through the galvanized roof and hanging in the rooms even throughout the night. Suddenly, to my surprise, my mother announced that we were going to pack up and move back to Can Tho. Kim and Cuong were going to remain in Sai Gon with an old "comrade" of my father's who ran a home economics boarding school for girls, but the rest of us were leaving.

It wasn't until years later that I found out why we left in such a hurry. Aunt Bich Loan, who was living with us, was young and very pretty; a man who lived in the neighborhood came to like her and believed he was in love with her. He was married and his two children went to the Catholic school with me, but he told my aunt he wanted her to be his concubine, or mistress. That would have been abhorrent to our family, even if Aunt Bich Loan had not been married to my Uncle Thuy, and she of course refused. But when she told him she was married to my mother's brother, the man somehow figured out our situation — that the men in our family were members of the NLF. He threatened to tell the authorities if my mother wouldn't help him talk my aunt into becoming his concubine. She said she could only think of protecting her sister-in-law, so we gave up everything we had gained in Sai Gon and moved away. We thought we had escaped the Cong An and the Front cadres by coming to the capital, but our "secret" had caught up with us anyway.

Chapter 5

*M*y mother found a house for us, about three kilometers from Can Tho market, between the Can Tho stadium and Tham Tuong bridge. This was a busy, populated area, and she said it would be good for any business, including the sewing shop she was going to open. She and other members of the family installed cabinets and glass windows to convert the front of the house into a shop, and before they were even finished she had already recruited six students for sewing classes.

Even though my sisters Kim and Cuong still lived in Sai Gon, the size of our household grew; in addition to Aunt Bich Loan, my cousins Hoang Mai, Yvonne, Thao, Thuan, and Quoc came to live with us, the girls planning to learn sewing and help in the shop.

My mother worked hard, as usual, but the house was alive with all our relatives and the students and the customers coming and going, and our days were relatively happy.

It was here that my mother bought the first expensive luxury item we had ever had: a radio. It wasn't for entertainment, however; she never even turned it on during the day. At night, though, very late at night, she and Aunt Bich Loan and my two older cousins would huddle close to the set and listen for hours — to the programs broadcast from Ha Noi.

Ha Noi had begun a program called "Relay a Message," in which men and women who had gone to Ha Noi would send messages to their families left behind in the South. Countless times, members of the resistance forces told my mother that they had heard my father speaking on this program and encouraging us to listen for further word. They had heard Khoi, too, they said; in fact, they told us, one time he had played his violin on the radio for Hai Van and me.

The chance to hear from one of the eight members of our family who had gone to the other side was irresistible. It was also terribly dangerous. Listening to Ha Noi broadcasts was illegal under the Diem regime. The government tried to jam the signal from the North, and Cong An patrols roamed about the towns and villages trying to catch people listening to their radios. When my mother and the others listened, one person would always stand by a small window looking out for the Cong An patrol jeep, worrying about what would happen to them if they got caught.

One night we were asleep. Suddenly an angry hammering on the front and back doors woke us, and the Cong An came storming into the house. I don't remember how many there were, but they confiscated the radio and handed my mother a notice commanding her and Aunt Bich Loan to appear at the Special Police station the next morning. (The Special Police force was created to catch Viet Cong and any activity concerning them.) After a restless and nerve-wracking night, they dressed and went to find out their fate. We didn't know if we would ever see them again. Luckily, they were only fined, but they were given a stern warning never to listen to the Ha Noi broadcasts again.

Two days later everybody chipped in enough money to buy another radio.

Throughout the nightly vigil, the effort was a constant disappointment. Many times my mother would tire of listening and hearing nothing from her loved ones, turn off the set and go off to bed in frustration. "What a waste of time," she would say. "This is my last time. I am not going to be a slave to that radio again." The following night would find her snuggled up once again in my aunt's room, her head bowed close to the set, trying in vain to hear her husband's voice.

The frustration was even greater because time after time the people in the bush insisted that they had heard my father, telling us he was doing well and that he missed his wife and children. My mother complained once that she must have terrible luck because everyone heard his messages except her. To that, my grandfather retorted, "The insiders give you hope — and at the same time they get you to listen to their propaganda."

It would be twenty years before we would discover how wise my grandfather had been. When we finally met with my father, my mother asked him why we had not heard any of his messages on the program. He told us he had not even been in Ha Noi at that time. From 1954 to 1960, he said, he had been working in NLF-controlled areas in the South; it was not until 1961, when he was elected as a member of the Central Committee at the second congress of the NLF, that he had moved to the northern capital. The people who had assured us that they heard his voice had lied. The purpose of the program was, basically, to get people to listen to the propaganda that surrounded the few real messages.

For years we had received no letters or word of any kind from my father; we were easy prey for that kind of deceit. All during that time, my grandfather kept reassuring me, telling me to "keep good thoughts about your father." To me, "good thoughts" simply meant "he's alive." But when other people whose relatives were in the resistance said they had heard from their fathers and I hadn't, it was hard to keep those "good thoughts." Revolution and politics can be beyond the understanding of a child, but the child is not beyond the reach of the pain they can create.

— — —

Our lives in the house near the stadium were like a dream, but a short one from which we were abruptly awakened. My mother's business was going great, and financially we were in better shape than we had ever been. She hired a nanny to take care of Hoa Binh and Minh Tam, allowing Hai Van and me to be more like normal children with fewer responsibilities, nicer clothes, and even new school satchels in the middle of the school year.

Along with this success, however, came many female cadres who knew my cousins Thao, Yvonne, and Hong Nga (Yen's younger sister), who had been their comrades in the countryside. They began to show up at our house and use the living area behind the shop for clandestine meetings, exchanging information with the city cadres. Sometimes they even stayed overnight, behaving as if they were just friends of Thao and Yvonne coming to enjoy "girl talk." They never caused us any inconvenience — they usually came when most of us were in bed, and at other times refused to eat dinner with us even when my mother invited them — but they kept the political pressure on the entire family.

I began to see that our house had two different parts. The front was an ordinary tailor shop where my mother's customers included government workers and wives of high-ranking officers in the city and even Cong An. The back was a place where the resistance built yet another of its nests.

I wondered if my mother really had any choice. Like the villagers and wives of other Communists, once the Viet Cong wanted your house or anything else you had, there was no way under the sun to refuse. "It is your country, your land, your revolution," the cadres would insist, and if you refused to participate you were a "reactionary" — and wives and children of revolutionaries simply were not allowed to be that.

When the Viet Cong claimed that some hamlet or village was "behind the movement," I understood clearly what that hamlet or village had to go through. Some nights I lay awake and cried in anger, or cried in fear. The people in those places had to live by the Communist rules at night — attending meetings, learning the Communist doctrines in group sessions, parroting the anti-Diem slogans — while during the day they tried to have ordinary lives, keeping in harmony with the land and enjoying the advantages the freedom of the South offered them. People were forced to cast away their honesty, their pride, and their virtue. I realized that I was no different from any of them: I attended public school, I sang the South Vietnamese national anthem, I quivered when I saluted the South Vietnamese flag, and yet my family hid Viet Cong cadres in our house.

My mother sometimes resisted the Viet Cong's demands for assistance. Once they came to ask her to sew hundreds of NLF flags, working at night while the shop was closed; she did it once, but the second time she refused, giving them money instead and telling them it was too dangerous to have those flags in our house. She often told them that so many of the members of our family were already involved in the resistance that she should not be asked to do so much. It worked most of the time, but as she put it, "It is like leprosy, you can control it but you can't cure it."

While the Viet Cong were pressing us from one side, the Cong An were beginning to become more suspicious of my family. My mother didn't tell me directly at the time, but I overheard her telling my grandfather's adopted son, Uncle Dinh, that the Cong An had asked her to come to their headquarters. There they demanded to know whether she had gone "to the bush" to visit my father, and insisted that she identify each and every person who came to our house. The first part of their demand was serious; our next-door neighbor had gone into the bush for a rendezvous with her husband, had been spotted by a government double agent, and was at that moment in jail.

A few weeks after I overheard that conversation, a group of Cong An in plainclothes suddenly appeared in the door of our shop. It was Saturday, and everyone was busy helping a lady who had come to have a wedding dress made. The government agents shouldered their way roughly into the shop and ordered the place cleared so they could interview each of us in private, and the lady had to take her fabric and leave.

During their questioning of my mother, the Cong An asked if she had seen my father recently. She glanced over at us and said, "I will not lie in front of my children, so you had better believe me. No, I have not seen my husband in the last two years." I don't know whether they believed her or not, but they kept pressing her to take sides, to prove her innocence by reporting anyone she knew who had gone into the bush. My mother told them it was not her duty to do such a thing. They finally departed, but left behind the clear impression that they would be back and that my mother had better cooperate.

They did come back, repeatedly. Their visits were so disruptive and so threatening that business in the shop began to fall off and fewer girls registered for the sewing classes. People just didn't want to be there when the Cong An were throwing their weight around. The pressure became so great that Aunt Bich Loan had to leave and go live with a cousin in Sai Gon. Hoang Mai went back to Long Thanh.

Eventually, there was just no way we could continue. Caught once again between the Communists at the back door and the Cong An at the front, we had to close the shop and give up our house in Can Tho.

My mother sold the house and everything in the shop except her sewing machine; wherever we went, she knew that would be our only source of support. Everyone in the family tried to persuade her to move back to Long Thanh to live with my grandparents, but she couldn't agree. It is perfectly all right for parents to provide for their children's needs when they are young, she told us, but she was no longer young and "you don't run home every time you have a problem." My mother wanted most of all for us to continue our schooling, and that would have been impossible in Long Thanh because the school there went only as far as third grade. That would have been all right with me — I had loved third grade and would have been happy to stay in it the rest of my life — but my mother was determined to see us grow up with a good education.

By now, in 1956, conditions in Viet Nam were the worst since 1954; the Diem government got tougher on the Viet Cong, and the resistance increased its efforts in response. We all expected major battles to flare up in every village that was a Viet Cong stronghold — like Long Thanh. And with things getting hotter, the one thing we didn't expect was that my father would come marching home anytime soon; he had already missed his promised two-year deadline, and there was little hope of an end to the fighting. As my mother used to say, "To believe in that 'two years' is like believing in a fortune-teller."

I was sad to leave the house near Can Tho stadium, where we had enjoyed such rare financial success and so many happy times, but once again politics decided our family's course for us. We were going to Sai Gon again, hoping this time we could find some way to be left alone and to live our lives in peace.

— — —

The five of us — my mother, me, Hai Van, Hoa Binh, and Minh Tam — crawled out of the motorized pedicab we had packed ourselves into and stared up at the imposing villa before us, at 38 Chi Lang. Near the big iron gate was a sign that read, "Beware of mean dog," and a picture of an ugly beast that made our old dog No look like a prince. The sign was no bluff; when my mother rang the bell, there was an explosion of barking from inside the villa's wall, and about a dozen fierce canines rushed to the gate and snapped and snarled at us. We had arrived at the home of my mother's former teacher, Mrs. Huynh Ngoc Nhuan, where we would stay for several months.

My mother explained to her that she could have gone to Ha Noi, but had declined. She said she was afraid that in Ha Noi all of us children might have to be "turned over to the party."

"I am glad that you can see that far ahead, child. Can you imagine your own flesh and blood, one belonging to the party, one to Moscow, one to Ho Chi Minh, and one to the army?" She shook her head at the thought.

They talked for a long time about people they had known in the past, including my mother's classmates when she had been a student of Mrs. Nhuan's in the Nhu Van home economics school in Can Tho. When she asked why we were in Sai Gon, my mother told her how we had been caught in the cross fire of pressures from the Cong An and the resistance. Before she could say that she had come to ask for advice about finding a place to stay, Mrs. Nhuan had issued a flat invitation for all of us to live with her at the villa. My mother tried to caution her: "I am not what I used to be when I was in your boarding house. I have four children besides myself." But Mrs. Nhuan brushed off her concerns. "I know, my child, I know. But the kids will be good for me, too. They will make this place more lively, wait and see!"

With that she took us to see our new home, soon urging us children to call her and her husband "Grandma" and "Grandpa." We walked through a breezeway covered with red China tiles, with big pillars on both sides supporting the pantile roof. Green vines hung down everywhere, laden with beautiful, lavender bell-shaped flowers. Hoa Binh stopped and touched one of the blossoms, and Mrs. Nhuan picked some and gave them to her and to Minh Tam.

Just past a huge, restaurant-sized kitchen, we came to our living quarters, which consisted of a large living room and a big bedroom, all furnished. Next door there was a bathroom, and Mrs. Nhuan told us we could cook in the main kitchen and eat at the dining table there. I was excited, because for the first time in our lives were were going to be able to use a refrigerator.

Back in the main house a little later, Mrs. Nhuan told us we were not the only guests she had from time to time. "I stopped giving money for the cadres to buy guns and bullets to kill innocent people, but this way I can still help the revolution and feel good about it. I house your husband's friends and comrades. I house the 'fugitives.' The Viet Minh come and go from this place without Diem knowing."

I noticed that she still referred to the cadres as "Viet Minh," perhaps because of her long history of supporting the Viet Minh against the French. Oddly, she called herself a "Cong San," or Communist, because to the French one had always either been for them or against them, and if you were against them they called you a Communist.

— — —

The villa that was our new home in Sai Gon had many rooms on the second floor. One of them was occupied by a young nephew of Mrs. Nhuan's named Amin. He was too sick to go off to Ha Noi, so he had to stay behind and let his aunt take care of him. For security reasons, he couldn't visit a doctor, so instead a doctor who was sympathetic to the revolution came to him. Usually he ate dinner with his aunt and uncle in the big dining room, but when Mr. and Mrs. Nhuan had dinner guests, Amin stayed hidden in his room and ate a meal brought up to him by the butler, Mr. Oanh.

In another room upstairs lived Mr. Ho Thu, who was a French-educated pharmacist who had joined the Viet Minh to use his Western knowledge to help end the French occupation. He wasn't sick, but had been assigned by the movement officials to stay in Sai Gon and be active there. He had served as secretary-general of the NLF Central Committee, but was also secretary-general of the Democratic Party of South Viet Nam. That connection made him quite useful to the resistance, but his principal function was to administer the various NLF medical facilities.

Mr. Ho Thu had been in and out of French prisons like most of the other Vietnamese nationalists, and he was still on the blacklist of Diem's secret police. As a result, he never left his room to go to any other part of the house, having his meals brought to him there and ringing the bell for Mr. Oanh whenever he wanted anything. He did go outside the villa, however, through a secret tunnel that started in the basement and emerged at the back of the property. From that tunnel he went out to many clandestine meetings with the cadres.

One quiet afternoon when everyone in the villa was taking a nap (except my mother, who never stopped working at her sewing machine), four Jeeploads of police came roaring up to the gate, jumped out, and began ring-ing the bell. Mr. Oanh was off that day, so my mother went to see who was there, and I ran along behind her. The police told my mother they had a war-rant to search the place and ordered her to open the gate immediately. She pretended not to understand what a search warrant was, and told them she would have to go and inform "the masters of the home."

We hurried into the house, and as soon as we were out of sight of the police my mother told me to run upstairs quickly to let Uncle Ho Thu know that they were at the gate. We had always been told not to go near his room, so when I stood at his door I had a strange feeling, as if this was one of those mystery stories in which a madman with a hairy body and a wild face had been locked away by his family. Hesitating only a moment, I pressed my ear against the door and called out to him. When he asked "Who is it?" I told him, "The police are going to search the house, sir."

"Good girl," he replied. "Your mother knows what to do. I will leave right now."

I went back downstairs, intending to look for my mother, when suddenly a herd of those ugly, mean dogs went running past me to the gate, where they raised an unholy howl at the police. For the first time, I thought those awful animals may have been worth having around after all.

My mother had just come from Mrs. Nhuan's room, and she went back into the house as Mrs. Nhuan took my hand and said, "Come with me, child." We walked slowly to the gate, where she scolded the dogs and to my surprise spoke extremely politely to the head of the police team. "Captain, may I be of help to you today, sir?"

The captain held up a piece of paper and told her it was a warrant to search the house. Mrs. Nhuan strained to look at it through the gate, then asked him to pass it to her under the gate so she could see it more closely. She pretended to try to read it, then searched in her pockets for her "reading glasses" — which I knew she never used. "Would you gentlemen excuse me please, I can't read without my glasses."

She took my hand again and we started back to the house. The police captain said to her, "Please, Madam, put the dogs away and hurry back."

"Of course, captain," Mrs. Nhuan replied, and so we wasted more time in a vain attempt to round up the dogs and lock them away. Eventually we got into the house, and Mrs. Nhuan dropped her pretense and ran upstairs to see if Mr. Ho Thu had gone yet. He had, so she told me to drag one of the dogs into his room and put a dog dish on the floor and a rag on the bed to make it look like the dog lived there. Uncle Ho Thu had already stripped the linen from the bed, so the room looked bare enough to house an old dog. I smiled to myself at the prospect of a policeman coming into this room and finding the dog I put there; she was the meanest one of all, especially since she had become the protective mother of five new puppies.

The search team was finally admitted, and the captain ordered his men to "carefully search every square of the tile, and every room in the house." About this time Mr. Nhuan came wandering downstairs, still in his pajamas from his nap, and looked around at all the activity going on. He was quite calm, and I knew they had both been through this sort of thing many times before. He looked at the police captain. "With your protection, *mon capitaine*, we feel safe in this violent society. Isn't it true, Grandma?"

After their futile search, the officers asked to see the registration of the household, then did a head count of everyone there until they were satisfied that everything was proper. Amin was there, but he was not on the blacklist, so his presence created no problem. Finally they left, and the traumatic incident was over.

That afternoon, we were all called to a meeting with Grandfather and Grandmother Nhuan. They instructed us that from that day on, the iron gate must be locked day and night, and that we kids must remember to lock it even if we went out only for a moment for a walk or to buy a treat from the man with the ice-cream cart. We were told never to open the gate for strangers, and always to let the dogs out if the police showed up.

A few days later Uncle Ho Thu came back. Grandma Nhuan must have gained confidence in me because of the way I behaved when the police were there, because now I was allowed to take tea and newspapers to his room. On my first visit there he asked me to stay for a chat, and he told me that he knew my father. "You should be proud of your Papa," he said. Another time he asked me to buy some white shoe polish and a hundred grams of sesame candy for him at the general store. The shoe polish was for him, but the candy was a present for me and my brother and sisters.

I grew to like Uncle Ho Thu more and more each day. He was only a year younger than my father, and one night I caught myself wishing he were my father. I lay in bed and fantasized that my father was upstairs in that very house. I got up and went to the kitchen to make a cup of tea and took it to Uncle Ho Thu's room. The sleepy look in his eyes reminded me how late it was to be drinking tea, but he took the cup and asked me in. I sat on the edge of the bed, since the only chair was full of dirty laundry.

"It is lonely here," he said. "I am glad you came, and thank you for the tea."

"You don't have to drink it if it will keep you up all night," I told him.

"Your father used to drink very strong tea to stay awake," he said with a smile. "It won't be long before he is with you and your mother again. Be brave and try to keep good thoughts."

I left him to take the empty tea cup back to the kitchen. As I started down the hall, he stuck his head out the door and whispered, "Tell your brother to come up to play checkers with me tomorrow after school!"

We found comfort in each other, this young "fatherless" girl and the old revolutionary, but because I was told not to disturb him too much I had to restrain myself from visiting his room too often. Still, for some reason, knowing he was up there in the room gave me an odd feeling of comfort. I missed him when he was away on his clandestine missions, and when he came back it was like a holiday in my heart.

— — —

Hai Van, Hoa Binh, and I entered a Baptist elementary school, and our days there couldn't have been more different from our last experience with religious teachers. The principal was always called "Minister" — I never knew his name — and he was a lot of fun for us kids. We all loved him, and he somehow managed to remember the name of every student in the school, more than two hundred kids.

In the hours he spent with our class he made us understand that each of us is one of God's special creations, and that our differences make the world go 'round. "If we were all alike, we would bore each other to death," he said, and the class laughed. He was a peaceful person, and he taught the big kids to look after the smaller ones, not only on the playground but on the way to and from school as well. There were always older boys stationed along the main street to help us cross safely in the heavy traffic; on rainy days, the minister himself watched his children coming and going, sharing big umbrellas as they walked.

This fine man taught us to respect our elders, to respect other people's property, and to honor the Southern flag. He was a powerful moral leader for all of us; the most dreaded punishment at the school was to be sent to the minister's office and have to face his disappointment over one's transgressions, then to have to listen to his long lectures on how to behave.

I followed and accepted the minister's instructions that we should honor the flag of South Viet Nam, but I had a rather striking conflict in my mind in that regard. Along the way between our home at Grandmother Nhuan's and the school, there was a large villa protected by a long brick wall with barbed wire on top. Above the villa flew the North Vietnamese flag! This was the headquarters of the North Vietnamese delegation to the International Control Commission, the body that had been set up to monitor the requirements of the Geneva peace treaty. The villa's property was about fifty meters long, and its entrance was guarded by two soldiers — one South Vietnamese, one North Vietnamese.

The first time I saw the red flag, I thought I was dreaming. Then the national anthem of the North came trumpeting from loudspeakers mounted outside the villa, the anthem I had sung with my family since I could remember. I stopped to salute the flag, but the South Vietnamese guard chased my brother and Hoa Binh and me away. Each morning after that I tried to be outside the compound at 7:45 when the flag was raised (carefully out of sight of the South Vietnamese guard). I took my hat off and stood still while other children streamed past me on their way to school. They often reminded me that we didn't have to salute the Communist flag, thinking I simply didn't know because I was from the small town of Can Tho.

I used to peer through the windows of the main house of the villa, thinking that this place was some kind of link to my father. I could only see vague figures inside, but I recognized the khaki uniforms and caps with little red decorations, the kind my father's comrades had worn. Sometimes I had the urge to go up to the North Vietnamese guard and tell him I wanted to talk to someone inside. I knew if I told him who my father was, I would surely be admitted, but on the other hand I also knew that if the South Vietnamese guard heard me I might as likely be dragged off by the nationalist secret police.

I never worked up the courage to try, but I continued to linger around the villa, thinking that it represented something concrete that was connected to my father. It was a way to know that the world in which my father was struggling was real, not something so distant that it was beyond the reach of my everyday existence. Somehow, the people in that villa, even though I never spoke to them, brought the North closer to me.

— — —

The focus of our family in those days was on spending money sparingly and wisely, so we could have our own home someday soon and Kim and Cuong could come to live with us. My older sisters liked to show off their family to their friends, but they weren't proud of the fact that we had to live under someone else's roof. My mother told them she understood, but that we must all be patient and wait until she could give us all a better life.

Many nights, when everyone else had gone to bed, she sat beneath a flickering light and sewed clothes for the rich friends of the Nhuans. Sometimes I woke up and could hear her quietly singing her favorite tune, "The Returning Day." Her voice would choke on the lyrics, and I knew she was crying.

I don't know how much my mother had saved toward our new house and our new life, but the amount wasn't enough to cope with the tragedy that befell the family next.

One Sunday afternoon Minh Tam woke up from her nap with a high fever. Mom picked her up, and she gasped, "Oh God!" We all rushed over to them, and I saw that Minh Tam's face had changed. When she cried, her expression was all twisted — the right side of her face was paralyzed!

Doctors at the children's hospital in Cho Ray told my mother that Minh Tam had polio. I had never heard the word, but she knew what it was. The prognosis was bad: The doctors said there would be a permanent effect on Minh Tam's face, and only time would tell if there was brain damage. It was the saddest day of our lives.

My mother wouldn't give up, however. She took Tam to other doctors for a second opinion, then for a third, and a fourth. She tried Chinese "natural" medicine; she took Tam to countless acupuncture sessions. Nothing seemed to do any good. She wanted to take her to some so-called healers, but my grandfather discouraged her from doing so.

Tam's illness became an obsession for my mother. She abandoned her sewing business and concentrated on searching for a cure. Each day I came home from school and found her in distress, her face filled with sadness, her eyes rimmed with dark circles. She lost the confidence and toughness that had always characterized her voice and her gestures, and she looked smaller and older than I had ever seen her. That change worried me terribly; it was silly, but I kept worrying about how fast she seemed to be aging because I still had vivid memories of how young and vigorous my father was.

For six long and terrible months, my family lived with fear and desperation and very little hope. I don't remember that it ever occurred to me to pray or ask somebody "up there" to find a cure for my sister, but I do remember hoping that someday one of us in the family could send Minh Tam to America, to its best hospitals, to find an answer for her.

Finally my mother ran out of doctors to visit, and about the same time she ran out of money. All her savings were exhausted, and we were back to square one on our finances — worse, in fact, because now one of us was suffering from a terrible illness. Everywhere we turned, the problem stared at us; every word we spoke seemed to echo with sorrow and sadness.

When summer came and the My Ngoc school broke for vacation, Kim and Cuong came to stay with us. Their presence was something of a relief for me, because they took over many of the chores I had shouldered and also kept Mother company, giving me a chance to escape at least for short moments from the depressing atmosphere in our home.

One afternoon I overheard my mother talking to Kim and Cuong. "Your first word was 'father,' but Minh Tam might never know your father at all," she said. She was clearly at the end of her rope. "I am so tired, tired of running, tired of living like a nomad. We will move back to Can Tho. I will change our identity if I have to in order to protect your father and his work, but we should return to our birthplace. I must go home. I can't do this all alone." She broke down and cried.

I was so occupied with our own problems and truly eager to get back to Can Tho that leaving Grandmother and Grandfather Nhuan's home wasn't hard for me. Through the years, though, I thought many times of their wonderful generosity. They had taken us into their home and helped to teach me the real meaning of kindness. By their actions they demonstrated the sense of unity and loyalty "within our own kind."

Grandfather Nhuan died in 1972 after a long and painful battle with cancer. Grandmother Nhuan remained in the villa with her son Uncle Chau and her daughter-in-law, Phi Nga, the daughter of a Viet Minh, Cao Minh Chiem. It wouldn't be until many years later, in Paris of all places, that I would learn of the terrible fate that was to befall this wonderful lady and her family and their beautiful home at the hands of the revolution they had worked so hard to support.

Chapter 6

We had planned to spend only the summer months in Long Thanh with my grandparents before finding a home in Can Tho, but our stay stretched on into fall. My mother hardly made enough money to provide the necessities for us during that time, so Aunt Bay and my grandparents took care of most of our needs so she could continue her efforts to help Minh Tam.

At Can Tho hospital, the doctors experimented with a new therapy to restore the normal functions in the muscles of Tam's face, but even after months of trying, there was still no improvement. Finally they told my mother there was nothing more to try. She stopped taking Minh Tam to the hospital, but she kept hoping that new research would turn up something someday that would provide the answer.

When harvest time came in the orchards at Long Thanh that year, 1956, my grandmother decided to give my mother an extra share so she could find a house in Can Tho and start a new sewing business. Mom and Hai Van went into town to look for a house, and they found one at a busy location in Ca Dai township on Vo Tanh Street. Unfortunately, it cost more than my mother had, but her adopted brother Uncle Dinh gave her a loan for the difference, and she had her new place.

Once again there was a massive effort to turn the front part of a home into a shop. My Uncle Met helped with the renovation, Uncle Khai built a glass display cabinet, and Uncle Dinh bought a female mannequin to show off my mother's dressmaking skills.

When it came time to paint the house I wanted it to be red, after the color of the flag I had saluted since I was old enough to walk. My mother said we could have a red door or a red chair, but not a red house. Aunt Bich Loan suggested pink, Hoang Mai wanted light green; Yen said to paint it blue, the color of hope, and so that was what we settled on.

When I had been much smaller, I had welcomed the chance to take on responsibility; the first time my mother had let me babysit for Hoa Binh and Minh Tam, I had been as pleased as ever. Just two or three years before, if she had named a shop after me, for example, I would have been proud and would have made sure all the kids in my class came to see the sign for themselves. But now I had turned twelve and I was afraid that childhood was passing me by. I wanted to be helpful to my mother and my family, but I wanted a chance to enjoy the carefree times of childhood as well. It seemed to me that since the day my sisters, who were seven years older than I, had moved to the boarding-house in Sai Gon, I had taken their place and had aged five years myself.

On the day of the shop's grand opening, my grandparents and all the other members of the family came from Long Thanh to celebrate with us. Only Kim and Cuong were missing, because they couldn't afford to come all the way from Sai Gon and my mother didn't want them to miss school anyway.

Business was booming from the very next day. Four students enrolled for sewing classes, and customers poured in to have clothes made. There was plenty of work for my mother; too much, in fact, I thought. A few weeks later when my grandmother came for a visit, she confided in me that "your mother looks so pale, and she has lost weight." There was nothing I could do except to agree and to try to take on as much of the workload as I could. I kept the books, took inventory, shopped for supplies, and even delivered clothes to customers' homes. Delivery wasn't required, but I thought it would be good for business. Sometimes I had to walk three or four kilometers on those errands, however, so my mother finally decided to buy a bicycle for me. That bicycle helped our business grow even more, because it made delivery easy at a time when most other dressmakers didn't even offer the service.

Only two weeks before the opening of the school year, my mother suddenly remembered that this time we would have to submit our birth certificates to the authorities at Can Tho elementary school. It would be too risky to submit certificates with my father's name on them, because the watchful eyes in Can Tho would recognize it and know who he was. Our identity had always been important to us, and we put off changing our birth certificates as long as we could. We never wanted to take our father's name out of our lives, but this time we had to, to be able to go to public school.

My mother discussed the problem with a judge who was an old friend of my Uncle Diep's. He advised us to file for a new set of birth certificates for all of us, papers with new names and with a father listed as missing — and thus in legal terms "unknown." Getting new birth certificates wasn't an unusual thing to do; during the war many people had been too concerned with survival to go to the trouble of recording the births of children, so it was not uncommon, years later, for someone to come to court to file for certificates for a whole family of kids at once.

The night before we were to go to court, I lay awake and wondered how I would feel when it appeared in black and white that I didn't have a father, that my mother was the sole parent of our family. I talked to Hai Van, who comforted me with the assurance that "it is only a piece of paper to fool the fools out there."

The whole matter took less than ten minutes. My mother stood before a judge and swore to the "truth" about her "missing husband," and the children of Dang Van Quang became children without a father. To complete the illusion, Hai Van and I got new names. I became Tran Ngoc Yung, since Tran My Yung didn't have a very pleasing sound in Vietnamese. Hai Van became Tran Van Van; he had been named after the Viet Minh victory of Hai Van pass, and in those times that sounded too much like a Communist name. Only Hoa Binh and Minh Tam had the luck to keep their given names.

The only good thing that came out of the whole process, to my way of thinking, was that my cousins Thao and Thuan became my legally adopted sisters. They had their real birth certificates, too, but their father's name on them made them no more useful than ours, so it was better for us all to have a new family name and "no fathers."

Since the day my father left, I had always known that we had little chance of ever becoming rich, but we had something more valuable than money. We knew who we were and were proud of the circumstances that had put us in our situation. For days after that brief appearance in court, though, I felt as if I had lost something very precious, very personal, and very powerful — my identity. I heard myself repeating Hai Van's statement about the "piece of paper," but I knew that without that piece of paper I couldn't go to public school or any other school, and that when the time came I couldn't get a job to help support my family. That miserable piece of paper that said I was a bastard child was important — important to the Diem regime, to the society we lived in, and worst of all to me, because it tore me to pieces and I couldn't tell anyone or complain to anyone about the lie I was forced to live.

— — —

Ever since my mother had gotten our new birth certificates and legally adopted my cousins Thao and Thuan, I looked forward to having them live with us permanently. I particularly hoped that Thao, who was four years older than I, would be able to help around the house and to relieve me of some of my numberless chores. I never actually said that, of course, because I knew it would sound selfish and my mother would have been disappointed to think her daughter was so lazy.

I waited for Thao and Thuan to assume new duties, but it seemed their jobs were only going to be to make their own beds, do their homework, and take care of themselves. Thuan didn't like to do the dishes or wash clothes, because she said it would ruin her "pretty hands." I told her one day that if she didn't like to do the chores that the rest of us did, she ought to stop eating and go naked. She cried, but she didn't tell my mother; Mom found out anyway, and I had to apologize to her.

My mother always told us to treat Thao and Thuan with "extra sensitivity" because they were orphans — their father, my Uncle Sac, had died when they were young and their mother had left them with our grandparents, not for another man but for Communism. I often told my mother, half-seriously, that "I am half an orphan too." She shushed me: "Just count your blessings and have some kindness for your cousins."

Thao was strong, determined, and as stubborn as a water buffalo. She was ambitious and worked hard for my grandmother, and she was the youngest member of our family who had joined the resistance forces.

Thuan was weaker, lazy, and somewhat timid. She was always passive and ready to cry over any argument we had. I must admit that I didn't give her much of a chance to crawl into her shell and stay safe; I wanted her to fight back, to argue with me, but it never happened. She would always just clam up after a fight, and sometimes her "silent treatment" would go on for days and bother me a lot. My Aunt Bay also felt sorry for her and told Hai Van and me to be extra nice to Thuan because "she needs sisterly love."

My brother Hai Van — or Van Van — went to the boys' elementary school, which was only about five hundred meters from our house. Thao, Thuan, Hoa Binh, and I had to walk about three times as far to the girls' school. On my first day in class, when the teacher called the name of Tran Ngoc Yung, I didn't recognize it as my new name and I failed to respond. The whole class laughed when the teacher called on me for the third time.

We all had to write our names in small labels and glue them to the front of our notebooks and books; when I looked at my new name on the labels, I thought it looked so strange. My grandfather had reminded me earlier, though, that "Tran is my name, and Tran is your mother's name, so it shouldn't be strange to you." I thought a lot about what he said and suddenly I felt fortunate: It could have been other names, worse names, the name of a stepfather or stepmother!

At Can Tho elementary children rarely saw the principal except when they were in trouble; when their teacher couldn't put up with them anymore, they were sent to "purgatory" to see the fat-bellied Madame Principal, who would greet them in her stern fashion. I was never sent to "purgatory," but as the class leader I was sent to report to the principal from time to time on our class social activities. On one occasion when I went to the office, the principal wasn't there, but someone else was sitting at her desk.

I realized that I had seen this woman somewhere before — but not at the school. I thought for a moment, and then it came to me that I had seen her one weekend at Long Thanh. She had been visiting her brother Mr. Dan, who lived across the canal from my grandparents. Her younger brother, Mr. Phat, was a Viet Minh who had been our neighbor in Ong Deo when I was five years old; Mrs. Phat used to take me home to keep her company while he was away on assignments. Mrs. Phat later died, and when Mr. Phat had been ordered to go to Ha Noi, he had left his son Chau in the care of this lady, who turned up now as the vice principal at my school.

As I walked into the office, I greeted her by saying "Hello, Mrs. Ba," instead of calling her by her title. She was startled. "Who are you?" she demanded. "How do you know me?"

Placing my class report on her desk, I said, "I met you once when you visited my grandparents in Long Thanh."

Mrs. Ba got up quickly as if she had just heard a frightening noise. Her face wore a troubled expression. She walked close to me and in a very soft tone of voice asked, "Come here, child, who is your father?"

Since I knew she was "one of us," I answered without hesitation: "Senator Dang Van Quang."

Her face turned cold and stiff. "I would rather not explain to you why, but this is our last conversation in public. We don't know each other, we never met at your grandfather's. Do you understand?" She strode briskly back to her desk, her eyes never meeting mine.

I was confused, humiliated, and embarrassed; no one had ever denied me in such a way. I wanted to run away and hide, but my feet were stuck to the floor. I choked a bit as I said to her, "I don't understand that, but I will remember it." And I did remember it. For the entire two years I spent at Can Tho elementary school, despite countless trips to the principal's office as class leader, I managed to avoid the vice principal entirely.

I never talked about that painful incident to my mother or my grandparents, because I thought it might hurt them more than it did me, but I did tell my Aunt Bay about it. I knew she was quick to forgive people and could always accept them whether they were right or wrong. She told me that people reacted as Mrs. Ba had only to protect themselves and their families from the secret police, and that I shouldn't hold it against her.

I told my aunt that I suspected that when my father came home in victory Mrs. Ba would be one of the first to come to ask if I remembered her. "You don't have to say that," Aunt Bay said. "You earn your respect. When you lower yourself to her level then you two are even, but it won't serve you any good."

"It would make me feel good, though," I retorted.

"She must feel bad that she had to tell you what she did, believe me," my aunt insisted.

"You are not asking me to feel sorry for her, I hope. If someone punches me one, he will get four from me."

I remember the tears on my aunt's face that day. She told me she had grown up in a circle of love and caring, from her parents and her brothers and sister, from other relatives and the villagers where she lived. She had never been hurt by them, she said, so she had never had to build up a protective shell. My childhood was not like that, she said, so she knew it was harder for me. "Don't let it take away your goodness," she urged. "Be yourself, be tolerant. You will be rewarded."

I was still too young to see it her way. "You taught me to be good, to be kind," I said. "How can I accept those who are no good and unkind?"

I recognized that I had many of the qualities of my father, even to my high cheekbones, my deepset eyes, and my overbite. Our personalities were similar, too. He was a fighter, having fought the French, capitalism, and the "American imperialists," who had supported President Diem when he rejected the Geneva Agreement in 1954. I was a fighter in my own way, not a noble one, perhaps, but a fair one like my grandfather had taught me to be. I also realized that our family was not unique; there were thousands more wives, sons, and daughters of the Vietnamese Communists struggling to survive in the South under the "adversary's" power. I knew I wasn't alone, but I never thought it meant I had to be timid because my father was a Communist. In Can Tho or anywhere else on this earth, why shouldn't I be able to walk tall?

That day I cried with my aunt, and she held me in her arms. The wind gently caressed my hair as it had stirred the stalks of rice in the nearby field.

I would have traded everything just to be in the village with my grandparents — forget school and education. But my grandmother told us that a child must grow, just like the green field out there had to reach its harvest time. I used to think it was a rude law that nature had set out for us, the law that we must all grow and change and learn to live on our own. But growing is learning, experiencing pain along with the pleasure. I had learned to be my father's child, to be apart from him and to accept loneliness. I learned not to feel sorry for myself, but to help my mother as she struggled to keep our family together and well.

I had learned that life is like the earth, with seasons that change and rivers that ebb and flow. A child must grow and become a man or a woman. No matter what happened, though, I wanted Long Thanh always to be my cradle, a place to come home to. For that reason, more and more I began to see the Viet Cong cadres who prowled the land as great threats to me and my chance for a happy life.

— — —

Each time I came home to Long Thanh on weekend visits, I found the cadres thicker on our land. They glided silently up to the edge of our property, and if they got a safe signal from one of their own, sometimes from my cousins, then they came onto the land to meet with "city cadres" to pass on information and receive reports of activities of the "city task forces." Those activities included propaganda, recruiting agents, intelligence work, sabotage, and even assassinating South Vietnamese officials. The task I heard mentioned most often was infiltrating cadres into all levels of the South's organizations and forces.

My cousins and Aunt Bay supported the NLF regardless of the duty they were assigned. They hid the cadres and protected them from Army of the Republic of Viet Nam (ARVN) soldiers from the South. Even the youngest member of our family knew this and understood implicitly, without any formal promise, that we were to act accordingly. Even if we had to lie to the soldiers, we were told, "It is all right to lie to our enemy in order to protect our interests."

I had no qualms about that. On one Sunday afternoon I even went out of my way to lie to a patrol soldier who crossed the canal over to our house and asked if I had seen any Viet Cong since morning. Usually we didn't talk to the soldiers at all, but I thought I was having fun as I chatted gaily with him, pretending to be friendly, just so I could insist that he was the first stranger I had seen that weekend. The soldier asked to have a drink of rain water from the barrel my grandmother always kept full, and I handed him the coconut-shell dipper from which his enemy had drunk only an hour before.

Suddenly I felt sad, and was not proud of my skill at lying at all. I looked at the young soldier, who might have been eighteen, and thought that he could have been shot because of me. I thought that if he lived to have a wife he might make her a widow early if he continued to trust kids like me. I offered him a ride on the sampan back across the canal and he accepted. Asking him to wait a moment, I ran back into the kitchen and took one of the rice cakes my grandmother had made and gave it to him. I didn't share our food out of compassion but out of guilt.

Not until this soldier had moved on with his compatriots did I find out that we had been watched the entire time by my cousin Yvonne and several Viet Cong cadres from the rice warehouse. They asked me what we had talked about, and I told them repeatedly the exact words we had exchanged and about the rain water and the rice cake. I lied in part, however, by telling them the soldier had asked for the rice cake because he was hungry. I also didn't tell them how I had felt when I had to lie to the soldier, because, knowing them, they would have considered those feelings degrading. One of the cadres rubbed my head and said, "Very good, my little friend." I felt a rush of hot blood to my face, and I stared down at the ground and tried to escape from them.

Everyone in our family was involved in the clandestine business except my grandfather and my mother. Thao and Yvonne told me not to tell Mother, because "she has other things on her mind, other duties to fulfill." They told me not to let Grandfather know everything that went on, either, because if he knew "he would be furious, and that is not good for his health." I agreed that protecting my grandfather was a good enough reason for keeping him in the dark.

There was too much activity to hide completely, however, and gradually the attention of the ARVN patrols was more fully aroused. They patrolled our area more often, and the soldiers became hostile toward us. They not only tried to pry information out of us, they stole our property as well; they took chickens without asking, they chased ducks into the pond, and finally they shot the ducks. My grandmother was in tears as the feathers flew into the air. She offered to have her nephew catch the ducks for the soldiers, but they preferred to shoot them.

The fact came home to all of us that we were no longer "innocent citizens" in the eyes of the South Vietnamese authorities. Our land was no longer our simple home, but a "Viet Cong nest." By law the soldiers had every right to intrude upon our property; by law we were undesirable citizens under the Diem regime. We didn't like it, but we were told by the cadres to "persevere." My cousin Thao urged us, "Bite your tongue until you can bite them back."

Each time the trip home from Can Tho became more unpleasant and more risky. One time Hai Van, Hoa Binh, and I got off the Lambretta, a small carriage that was pulled by a motorcycle-type engine instead of a horse, and were about to walk toward the new bridge that Uncle Dinh had built when a group of soldiers approached us. Two of them pointed their guns at us, and the others tried to scare us by loading their rifles. The sound of the bullets clicking into their chambers certainly had the intended effect on the three of us. Hoa Binh clung to me and whimpered softly.

I looked into the dark barrel of the gun that was pointed at me and thought somehow that it seemed to fit with the man who was holding it — dark, cold, and impersonal, yet powerful. I was limp with fear, but I had a minute to think. I looked up at the soldier's face with a broken smile and said to him, "We are going to visit our grandparents, would you like to come with us?" He shook his head, with no expression on his face, and said, "Drop your basket, kid. Let me see what you have in it."

I emptied the shopping basket; the French bread I had bought for my grandfather rolled onto the ground with the barbecue ribs and rice cakes for my grandmother and the newspapers for Aunt Bay. Another soldier who had been pointing a gun at my brother like a robot finally moved, examining our possessions gingerly. He tore up the newspapers and tossed them into the air, and he put the tip of his gun on the barbecue ribs to inspect them. Hai Van was about to stop him from stepping on the rice cakes with his boot, but I pulled my brother back just in time as the soldier swung his gun away from the ribs and back in Hai Van's direction.

The first soldier then ordered us to leave. I took my brother's and sister's hands and left everything behind, including the basket. As I walked the soldiers were laughing behind us. I thought our lives were in the hands of heaven at that moment, until I could no longer hear their voices. Then I knew we were safe. We started to run, but Hoa Binh was too scared, so Hai Van and I had to take turns carrying her until we reached the boundary of our land.

There was a shrine at the edge of our property, the sacred place where my grandmother worshipped her "god of the good earth." When we passed it I took my hat off and thanked God without realizing I had done it.

— — —

In 1959, when I was thirteen, I was in the last year of elementary school, and all my attention was focused on studying. In Viet Nam in those days, every student who wanted to go on to public high school had to take an entrance examination, and because a high school education was terribly important, the drive to study hard and pass the exam was strong in all of us students.

This year, however, brought a momentous distraction for me and our family: We heard from my father for the first time in five years.

A man came to see my mother one day, and beginning his conversation he used a curious phrase: "Hai loi." She was startled to hear it, because it was the secret password that she and my father had agreed to use if they ever had to send a message to each other. "Hai loi" was my brother Khoi's nickname when he was little: *Hai* means the first son in a family, and *loi* was Khoi's most private fault at childbirth — an unusually large belly button (which eventually became normal as he grew older).

The message brought by the man with the secret code word was at once thrilling and troubling. My father wanted to see all of us in Phnom Penh, Cambodia, the man said. He gave her instructions on how to get to the rendezvous point, and told us we had to hurry because my father was going to be leaving soon and we might miss his boat.

We all wanted to see Father, of course, but the cost of doing so would be devastating. Traveling from Can Tho to Phnom Penh in wartime was not only dangerous, it was costly; Mother said if we went to see Father, it would wipe out all our savings and put us back where we had started after the family separated — broke. I hated the thought of returning to those days of hardship, but the more we talked about the possibility of seeing my father only a bus ride away, the more we realized that everything else was far less important. We began to work on the secret plan for a reunion.

It was not to be a complete reunion, however. After Mother went home to consult with my aunt and grandparents, they came to the conclusion that some of us would have to stay behind — including me. My mother said she needed me to look after the shop while she was away so we wouldn't lose all our customers. Hai Van had to stay because the message instructed my mother to go to an address in Phnom Penh and wait with the family there for further word, and she didn't want to impose on that family with too many children.

An even more important reason was suggested by Aunt Bay: If we all left town with my mother, it would arouse the attention of the secret police. During that time many wives and children of NLF members tried to visit their menfolk in the jungle, and the police were eager to follow them and make arrests. I knew of a woman whose brother-in-law was a police officer in Can Tho, and her husband was in the resistance stationed in the Ca Mau region. Once she sneaked away to visit her husband for about a month, and not too long after she returned we noticed she was pregnant. Soon afterward the police showed up to ask how she had gotten in such a condition if her husband wasn't home. To protect her husband's location, she had to lie to the police by telling them she was having an affair with a married man. Then, cleverly, she asked them not to reveal that secret in order to protect her ten-year-old daughter. They fell for her double ruse, and I often wondered what the police officers had thought about their duties and obligations to these not-so-innocent citizens.

These were complex times, forcing people to say and do things that did damage to all of us, to our principles and our moral codes. There were quiet moments when I walked along the riverbank at a Buddhist temple near our home, thinking about these psychic costs of war. If the Vietnamese people survived all our tragedies, I thought, we would not only have to bury our dead and mourn our lost loved ones, we would also have to bury a part of the wonderful Vietnamese character within ourselves, our honesty, pride, and courage. Along with that I wondered what would happen to the smiles on young maidens' faces that had inspired poets for centuries, and how we could ever again live our lives according to the teachings of Confucius. For the time being, all that was a dream; we lived according to the rules of war and the terrible demands of a divided nation.

My mother asked a friend on the west side of the city to look in on Hai Van and me from time to time while she and Hoa Binh and Minh Tam were away. Then she told everyone at the shop that she was going to Sai Gon to visit Grandmother Nhuan because she was ill, and slipped out of the city. Everything happened so suddenly that I didn't even think of sending a small present to my father until it was too late. For days I was kicking myself, but Hai Van said it probably didn't matter; remembering our days in the Liberated Zone, when "materialistic" things were frowned upon, he said, "Maybe he isn't allowed to have anything that was made in the city anyway."

Once Hai Van and I had gotten over our disappointment at having to stay behind — I desperately wanted to go but didn't want to endanger our family — we resolved to make the best of it and have fun while we were on our own. We were going to stay up late, stay out with our friends longer, and break all the rules without our mother knowing about it. It was funny, though — as it turned out, we both behaved ourselves unusually well. I took an extra interest in cleaning the shop, and I even took my mother's sewing machine apart and cleaned and oiled it. Then I almost panicked, because I couldn't put it back together; fortunately, my little brother figured it out and everything went smoothly. Our behavior was noticeably untypical; one of the girls who worked in the shop kept saying, "Your mom should take more trips, because when she is not home you and your brother are such angels!"

After three weeks my mother came back home. She was crestfallen; she had never seen my father. On her second day in Phnom Penh, the wife of the family she stayed with had taken her to an unknown location quite a distance away, a place by a big river. By prearrangement the woman went to an unattended dock and picked out a sampan laden with fresh fruits grown in the area. They left the shore and sailed up and down the river, pretending to be selling the fresh produce, searching the faces of people in other boats looking for my father. For days, my mother said, they had gone out early in the morning and stayed on the river until nightfall, but they never spotted a familiar face.

Eighteen years later, when my mother and father finally met again in London, she asked him about that time. His eyes filled with sorrow and he looked down at his hand — the hand the French had broken in the prison at

Con Dao — and said: "I never left the South until that year, so before I went to Ha Noi I wanted to make one more attempt to persuade you and the children to join me. I wanted you to bring them all to Cambodia so we could all go to Ha Noi together. But we missed the rendezvous date because our plan had been revealed to the enemy by some of their agents."

After the failure of the meeting in Phnom Penh, my mother threw herself back into the business of supporting her family. There were six of us, almost useless to her in a financial sense; all we did was eat and sleep and go to school. She struggled to pay off loans and the other debts she had incurred when she bought the shop, yet she never gave up hope of finding a cure for my sister Minh Tam, spending a lot of money to take her to doctors near and far. My grandfather once told us that "there will not be any way on this Earth that you can repay your mother, but you can make her happy and you can make her proud."

My adopted sister Thao didn't like sewing — she didn't have the patience or the skill to make a simple buttonhole. On weekends Mother let Thao go home to Long Thanh to look after my grandparents; Thao loved working on the farm, and she was good at it. Thao had a secret, however. Every Friday afternoon she would come home from school and gather a few things and then head off to Long Thanh, telling us she would return early Monday, just in time for school. But at Long Thanh, she told my grandparents that she had to return to Can Tho on Sunday to study for her high school exam, and of course they believed her as she waved goodbye to them each Sunday morning.

While neither my mother nor my grandparents got to see Thao on Sundays, the NLF organization saw a lot of her. Thao was being trained by them to work secretly in school and in the town, to tell them who was doing what. As Hai Van put it, "Every Sunday Thao's brain is being washed with Russian soap." We children knew where she was going, but Thao told us not to say anything to the grownups: "You will only make them sad, but you can't stop me from being away on Sundays," she said. And so we kept the secret for Thao.

Unlike most of us who worked very hard to get into public high school, Thao made certain that she didn't pass the exam; she wanted to get into private school so she could keep a low profile and work for the Viet Cong. Public school was actually more prestigious in Viet Nam; for private school all you had to have was money. Grandmother, who was always big on education for her family, paid Thao's tuition. Her trainers suggested she take English because "it is useful to know your enemy." Sometimes Thao looked ahead to a Communist conquest and told me that if she knew how to speak English, she could be of use as an interpreter during interrogations of the "American imperialists." I couldn't share her viewpoint; as a survivor, I thought only of using English as a means to get a good job.

Thao spoke with contempt and hatred for the Americans and for President Diem and his family. Every Monday I got a new list of crimes committed by the "American imperialists" in our country. Her language was even new to us, slogans full of Communist terminology formulated by an organization that was expert at hating the Americans and the Diem regime.

Thao repeatedly tried to get me to go with her on those Sundays to meet the cadres; she wanted to introduce my father's daughter to them. Each time I told her the same thing: "Even a Catholic priest failed to bring me to his church for just one Sunday; what makes you think I would refuse heaven and choose hell?" She always smiled with confidence, and tried again the next week.

Finally, she managed to get me involved without my knowing exactly what was happening. One Saturday I was at Long Thanh with her, and she asked me to go back to Can Tho with her. I refused, because I had just arrived that morning, but she said it was important and that my help would never be forgotten, adding that "if Dad knows you helped in this task he will be proud of you."

I gave in and went with her, still not knowing what she wanted me to do. We boarded a bus and started toward Can Tho, but after a short time we got off and waited a while for another one. A few kilometers later we got off again, waited a while, and then got on a Lambretta and headed for Can Tho. "What a waste of time," I said to Thao. "If we had stayed on the first bus we could have been home by now." She gave me an elbow in the ribs to keep me quiet.

I could tell that Thao was awfully nervous, especially when we approached the Tham Tuong bridge about one kilometer south of the Can Tho city limits. All the traffic had stopped in a long line in front of us; it was either a fatal accident or the police were searching all the vehicles coming into the city. Thao told me to get out when the driver shut off the engine and see what was going on in front of us; I did, and found a checkpoint manned by military and civilian police and a lot of men in plainclothes. Climbing back onto the Lambretta, I told Thao what I had seen. Immediately she handed me her school satchel and said, "Hold it for me. I'll be right back." Then she walked into the rice fields and disappeared behind the bamboo hedges. An old woman sitting next to us smiled at me and remarked, "I guess she had to go pretty badly."

I waited as the traffic crept forward, not knowing what Thao was up to. Then suddenly I saw her coming back toward the Lambretta, but from the opposite side of the highway. As she came closer, I couldn't believe my eyes — she looked completely different. She was barefooted, and the clothes she had on were not those she was wearing when we left my grandparents' home that afternoon. Instead she was wearing her work clothes, and not only that her long hair which had hung to her waist was gone! She had chopped it off roughly in the field, and now it was all uneven and shabby looking. The whole costume made her look like a poor Chinese farm girl.

When Thao got back on the Lambretta, she ignored me completely. Walking up to the driver, she paid him the fare for a ride into Can Tho, even though we had already bought tickets earlier. She found a seat next to a young man, who moved a bit away from her to avoid getting his clothes dirty from Thao's wet, muddy trousers. Our eyes met once but there was no gesture or expression of recognition from either of us. I couldn't help watching her in her peasant image, because her imitation was complete — from time to time she snapped her knuckles and even scratched her head as if she had lice. "Oh, Thao," I thought, "if Mother caught you in that getup you would be hung." Finally it was our turn to be searched by the joint police forces. Every passenger voluntarily handed over their bags and ID cards, but when he came to me I was worried because I didn't know what was in Thao's school satchel. When he opened it, it contained only school books, several colored pencils, a ruler, and a thick Vietnamese-English dictionary. I breathed a silent sigh of relief when he handed the satchel back to me without saying anything.

The MP was carrying three photographs, black and white pictures about three by five inches in size. He handed them to the driver and asked if he had seen any of the three women in the pictures. As the driver looked at them one by one, I glanced over his shoulder and saw one of them: It was my cousin Yvonne's student ID card picture! I was shocked, and sat back in my seat in silence as the police finished their search and we finally moved on into Can Tho.

After we got off the Lambretta, I didn't know what to say to Thao. We crossed the wide street at the corner of Hoa Binh and Ngo Quyen Boulevard, and Thao said to me, "You handled yourself well back there. I prayed that you wouldn't talk when I came back from the field."

I pulled myself together and looked her in the eye. "I wonder who answered your prayer," I said to my Communist sister. She only smiled at my comment.

"I saw Yvonne in one of those pictures, Thao."

"She is already here in town, don't worry."

"Are they looking for you, too?" I asked.

"I don't know, but I won't make it easy for them," she responded with a determined look.

"What about your hair? Grandfather will be angry at you. He doesn't like us to cut our hair!"

Thao shrugged. "I won't go home until my hair grows back. It's simple."

She asked for her satchel back, and when I gave it to her she said, "I want you to know what you have done today was very important, and you did it well."

"What did I do besides being scared and not wetting my pants?" I pouted.

"It is not a joke, sweetheart. You have carried one half of a plan from the Front to our cadres in the 'city task force,'" she told me. The first half had been delivered to the city cadres two weeks before, and the other half had been hidden between the hard covers of the Vietnamese-English dictionary in Thao's satchel. It had been in my possession the whole time the Lambretta was being searched, and the policeman had actually held it in his hands.

I had mixed feelings when I learned what had happened. I was a little angry that my own adopted sister, who was actually a blood relative, had put me at such risk, yet I knew that if it hadn't been me it would have been her carrying the satchel. I admired Thao's courage, and secretly I wanted to be as brave as her, but I knew that I would use that great quality for some other cause — perhaps for my family, but never for the Viet Cong.

That night, after dinner, Mother calmly trimmed Thao's chopped-off hair and the family felt sorry for her; she had told everyone that she had been stirring the rice gruel for the pigs out on the open brick stove in my grandparents' back yard when her hair suddenly caught fire, and she had done a terrible job trying to trim it. Everyone believed her, but I thought that one day her lies would catch up with her. That night, before going to bed, I whispered to her: "When you go down to purgatory, they will stretch your tongue at each gate, and by the time you get to the ninth purgatory your tongue will be one meter long, Sis." She took it as a joke and just smiled. "I know," she said quietly.

Day by day Thao became more active, more deeply involved in her secret work for the Front. Like a nun who had dedicated her life to God's work, she devoted all her time to worshipping the Communist ideology. She spent hours at the American library, trying to get to know her "enemy" by reading all the books she could find about America and its people.

I had a friend who worked at the library, a man named Hung, and because of that Thao asked me one day to do her a favor. She wanted me to find out from Hung when his American library director would visit the office, and to learn his rank and full name. Thao was convinced that the director wasn't any ordinary librarian, but a CIA officer. I refused Thao's request, telling her I didn't believe in using people I considered my friends.

Angrily, Thao flared up at me: "He is not worthy to be your friend. He is an American lackey." I lost my patience, too, and shot back: "If you were not my sister, I would turn you in!" I snapped my fingers in her face. "Just like that!"

"You won't do that," she insisted confidently. "You belong to the same organization that your father and my father lead. We are the children of the revolution, and we are obligated to carry out certain duties."

"Like blowing up buses and killing pregnant women and old folks?" I interrupted.

That ended that conversation, and we didn't talk any more about my spying on the library director for the "cause." But that wasn't the end of the matter for Thao's friends, apparently. Two days later, someone tossed a grenade into the library's front yard, killing the South Vietnamese guard who was posted there. God knows that "mercenary" had probably been drafted into the army, and had been nobody's agent, but just a servant to his country.

Chapter 7

As the numbers of American personnel increased in our small town, Western-style homes and hotels once occupied by the French were being remodeled to suit the Americans who were moving into them. These buildings were privately owned, and the owners were renting them out after inspection by the South Vietnamese security forces. I knew a man who was working on one of these remodeling projects, a man named Mr. Tu. Ironically, he was a former Viet Minh, but after the Geneva agreement he had left the Liberated Zone and the new Communist revolution to come back to Can Tho, where his wife had a fish stall in the city market. He got a job as a carpenter for a lumber company that had contracted to renovate a downtown building that was going to house American personnel — and he lasted two days. On his second day at work a plastics bomb went off at the front lobby where he was working, and Mr. Tu was killed. The work went on, though, and the Americans eventually occupied the building, living behind heavy security, while they continued their mission in South Viet Nam.

I didn't know what to think about this war. Of course I wanted my father and Khoi to come home, but I never thought about whether they should have a victory or not — the outcome didn't mean much to me, except that if the fighting ended they could return to our family.

The cadres insisted that Americans were our enemy, but I also saw that the Americans did many things to make life easier for the Vietnamese people. During the daytime, American engineers built roads and highways throughout the South; they had military uses, of course, but they also made it possible for people to travel from town to town to do business or to see other members of their family. (I noted that they built the roads in the daytime, because that was the only time the Americans and the South Vietnamese could move more or less freely. At night the countryside belonged to the Viet Cong, and by dawn they would have blown up most of the fine new highways. The next day the Americans would just come back and build them again.)

In the rural areas, where most children had never had the opportunity to go beyond the fourth grade, schools were being built with American money, and teachers were being paid through a special program funded by the U.S. government. The Viet Cong believed the money came from CIA funds, but it seems unlikely the CIA was involved very closely in the program: One of the teachers accepted for the "rural school program" was my cousin Yen, whose husband was Captain Nguyen Hoang Phat, a member of the famous 307th Battalion of the North Vietnamese army.

Many things bore the "handshake" label from CARE, a nonprofit organization which matched funds with the U.S. government to provide aid to our needy communities. The American "trademark" was everywhere in Can Tho, at the Ninh Kieu park by the waterfront which the Americans built for us, in books in our library, on the tables and chairs in our classrooms, even on the office equipment in the principal's office. At Can Tho general hospital, modern equipment filled the operating rooms where American doctors worked alongside the French-trained Vietnamese doctors. Fertilizer shipped from the United States was being tried out by farmers everywhere, even on our own farm, and new agricultural technology was replacing the water buffalo.

I didn't know what to expect from the Americans in Viet Nam. What did they want? What would they do to us? To the Vietnamese? To my heritage? Many of my closest relatives, and others who identified themselves as "your father's comrades," told me the Americans were there to conquer our country as the French had done, and that as a patriot I must seek ways to destroy them. I was a stubborn kid, though, and I didn't believe anything until I saw it, so I resisted propaganda from both Right and Left. I didn't know what they intended, but I remember one hope I had at the time: If they ever teach my people anything Western, please don't teach us the French way — their legacy was a bureaucratic complexity that had gotten into every aspect of Vietnamese society. I hoped the Americans would leave behind something more pleasant, as the French left the baguette. I expected no more from these powerful people.

The Vietnamese I knew were independent and proud of their heritage, certain that the Vietnamese people were superior to any others. The Communists played on these emotions, using nationalism to rally people to their side. At one "political education" session in Xeo Mon hamlet, when I was in the fifth grade, the Front cadre told us that "the American imperialists will Americanize the Vietnamese. They will add Viet Nam as one of their states. They will exploit our natural resources, our oil, our fertile lands. The Mekong Delta will go first into the hands of American capitalists." Often this kind of appeal worked, because very few Vietnamese would have been willing to discard the thousands of years of their civilization to become French or American. To most Vietnamese I knew, that would have meant degrading oneself.

That summer of 1959, I spent most of my free time at the American library, trying to learn about the United States of America so I might figure out what they wanted in Viet Nam. Of course, there was one small problem: I didn't know a word of English. There were some books about the United States written in Vietnamese, but I had to ask my friend Mr. Hung to order them for me from Sai Gon. In the meantime I plowed through the English books as well as I could, learning some things from the pictures in the books and using Mr. Hung's English-Vietnamese dictionary. I asked to borrow the dictionary so often that eventually as soon as Mr. Hung saw me coming toward his desk, he just said, "It's in my office, sweetheart."

Struggling through the books, I compared maps and learned that the state of California alone is bigger than my whole country. I remember thinking, if the Russians really help North Viet Nam invade South Viet Nam, Cambodia, and Laos and put all that territory together, the state of Texas would still be larger and richer.

Questions about the things the cadres had said about America ran through my head constantly as I read the books. Some of them had told us the Americans want the rice in the Mekong Delta — but I learned that they grow far more rice in California, Texas, and Louisiana. Do they want our land? They already have land that stretches all the way to Alaska. I thought the Americans would have to be stupid to want our people, because by now they surely knew that we would make rotten slaves.

I read about President Abraham Lincoln, and hoped so hard that he had left a lasting tradition to his people. I felt so lonely when I quoted to myself one of his sayings I had learned by heart: "Stand with anybody that stands right. Stand with him while he is right and part with him when he goes wrong." But in this confused war, who was right and who was wrong?

I had had a wonderful time with my father, up until the day he left for Ha Noi. I believed in him, I trusted him, I was proud to be his daughter. I had been especially proud that he had given up his personal life to work with the Viet Minh, for the cause he believed in and the people of Viet Nam believed in. But the Viet Minh era was now only a past glory, and the reality on the revolutionary side now was the NLF. The only other choice was the Diem regime.

I couldn't take either side, because I didn't think there was really a side I could believe in. I didn't like what the Viet Cong did to my own people, but I rejected the regime in the South as well, with President Diem letting his brother and his sister-in-law terrorize the people. There was enough propaganda from both sides to confuse anyone, not to mention a teenager. Both the NLF and the Diem government did their best to win the hearts and minds of the Southerners with their fabrications and lies.

Sadly, the Viet Cong won over those who were least fortunate and most forgotten by Diem's government — the poor and the discontented. Poverty-stricken people are ready for any kind of promise, but they especially liked the promise that they would become "equal" if the Communists won. I lived in a mixed neighborhood, ranging from a millionaire in an imposing French-style villa to destitute people living in homes with thatched roofs. People whispered about politics all the time, but most of them had the same attitude: "*Chanh phu nao cung vay*" (whatever government it is, it's still government). But the very poorest ones waited to be "liberated" and looked forward to being "equal" under socialism. And the political dissidents waited for the harmonious relationship between government and the people that the Viet Cong promised they would enjoy in the socialist system.

I had friends who had fled North Viet Nam after the Geneva agreement in 1954, and they told me about the suffocating life under the Communist system. I was happy they had found a refuge in my homeland, just as people fleeing North Korea found a haven of freedom in South Korea, or people fleeing Eastern Europe found it in the West. The knowledge that thousands of people were constantly struggling to escape from the "equality" of the socialist way of life gave me courage all through my youth to be impartial and to resist the pressures from the Front cadres to "follow in your father's footsteps" and to "keep your family tradition" — something they could say because all my uncles and cousins were dedicated Communists.

— — —

There was a brick house with a red pantile roof on our street, not too far from where we lived, that reminded me of a house in Ong Deo where we had once lived with my father. I asked my mother if my memory was accurate, so she went with me to look at it. While we gazed at the house, I reminisced about our old home, remembering that it had four wooden pillars in the front and reminding Mother that she used to hang a hammock between them. We went on and on about the old days in Ong Deo, enjoying the chance to recall a happy period when our family was still together. We seldom had private moments like that at home, because two of my mother's students lived with us and the house was so small we couldn't share intimate feelings, not to mention secrets about our father's activities. Her students didn't know about my father; they believed my parents were separated for ordinary reasons, as so many unfortunate families had been divided.

That day when my mother and I talked about Ong Deo and our life with my father, I hid my tears and discovered yet another warm feeling inside me — the feeling that comes when one knows that her parents truly love each other. My mother looked radiant as she talked about the old days and what "your father" had done or said.

The brick house was for sale, we learned, and I couldn't sleep that night for thinking about the idea of living in it. I knew it would be too much for our strained budget, but the thought of living in a better house was tempting. Besides, I thought, "maybe it will be a good omen to live under a red pantile roof like the one in Ong Deo. Maybe Dad and Khoi will come back to join us."

To my surprise, my mother decided to buy the house — not because she believed in my "omen" theory but because she wanted a better place to raise her children. We had no difficulty in selling the old house and the shop, and after that Mother gave the students two weeks to go home to visit their families while she got the new house ready. She wanted to build a section on the front of the house to use as her new shop, so she went to the city hall to apply for a permit. There a civil servant let it be known that if she wished to obtain a permit, there would have to be some private payment to him as well as the fee to city hall. She left uncommitted, not wanting to pay a bribe, but she knew she needed the permit in her hands if she was going to find a builder to do the work.

Hai Van had heard her report, of course, and that evening he surprised us with some news. From a friend of his, an older man who was a policeman, he had learned that most people don't bother with getting a permit in advance because they run into the same obstacle my mother had; they just go ahead and build, then when they get caught they pay the fine. The money comes out about the same, and you avoid all the trouble with the corrupt bureaucrats. So my mother found a builder and started the work. When it was half-finished, two police officers showed up one day and charged her with building without a permit. She paid the fine, and the whole matter was over in ten minutes. I remember that I didn't feel proud that my country's government worked that way, but that's the way it was.

I went over the family books one night and realized that we had overspent the shop money on the construction, and that the first payment on the new loan was coming up. We didn't have enough to meet that payment, so a week before the payment was due I went home to my grandmother's house and asked her to give me the gold earrings and necklace that she had been keeping for me since she had bought them for me at harvest time some years before. My mother thought everything that came from my grandparents had great sentimental value, but to me the jewelry was our last resource — and so we sold them to make the first payment on time.

On one short trip to Long Thanh, I told my grandfather I thought life wasn't fair to my family. He asked me to tell him about my friends and their families that I was comparing with ours. I told him that my friend Tuyet's family lived very comfortably, and the only problem they had was that her father had another wife and other children. Hanh's father was rich, I said, and even though her mother gambles all week long they still have a lot of money.

As I rambled on about my "lucky friends," he interrupted me. "You are the luckiest one, my child. Your father doesn't have a second family, and your mother is not a gambler." I hugged him and said, "Being poor is not an honor, either, Grandfather."

He kissed my hair and rubbed his whiskers on my face, then looked at me intently and said with a serious tone: "You are not poor. The poor are those who don't have clean clothes on their backs, food in their stomachs and a roof over their heads. You are allowed to dream, but don't expect your mother to make your dreams come true. You will have a better chance than your mother had. Be patient, my child."

— — —

When I heard my name over the loudspeaker in the school yard, I couldn't think of anything except running home to tell my mother the good news. I had passed the exam for public high school! It was not only an honor, but more important, it meant my mother wouldn't have to pay tuition for me for seven long years.

Racing through the streets, I suddenly had a silly thought: "What if there is another Tran Ngoc Yung, who was born May 24, 1946? I will kill her!" Then I picked myself up and ran another half-kilometer to our house.

My mother was at the sewing machine in the shop as usual. I rushed up behind her and unplugged the cord, and the machine ground to a halt. She looked me sternly, and then I took the question from her eyes: "I passed!" The happy smile on her face was worth all those nights and days I had shut myself in the kitchen to study for the exam.

The girls in the shop were excited, too. They volunteered to make my white *ao dai,* which was the required dress for the girls in public high school. I wasn't too eager to start wearing what I thought was big girls' clothes; I still slept in my khaki gym shorts.

When I got back to Phan Thanh Gian school a little while later, I elbowed my way through the crowd of anxious parents and older brothers and sisters standing in front of the bulletin board where the examination winners were posted. I already knew I had passed, but I just had to see it in print. And there it was: "Tran Ngoc Yung, born 24/5/1946, Long Thanh, Can Tho. Mother, Tran Thi Pham. Father, Unknown." My sister Thuan was on the list, of course; she had studied so long and hard I knew she could have passed with her eyes half-closed.

Later I walked in the school yard, and it felt strange to know that I was tracing the footsteps of my father and my uncles who had gone to the same school. My Uncle Diep had taught at Phan Thanh Gian high school when it was known as Bassac, and Thuan's father had been an art teacher there before they all left to join the revolution.

Thuan and I sat by the flower garden in the school yard, and we could see our house through the brick wall across the street. Hai Van and I had climbed over that wall many times to play badminton in the school yard, and Thuan reminded me that I wouldn't be doing any wall climbing in my new *ao dai*. She was always very feminine and romantic, and was looking forward to high school and new clothes, makeup, high heels, and boys. I wasn't thinking about my *ao dai*; I wanted to join the track team and to head the student sports committee and be an assistant coach in the sport. I did have one fashion-trend ambition, though, and it was about to come true: I had made a deal with my mother that if I passed the exam, I could get a permanent, and I got it the very next day.

Of course, not everyone thought it looked good. A few days later Grandfather arrived for his annual preschool visit when he took all the kids out to buy school supplies and then treated us to a meal at his favorite eating house in Can Tho. I had thought about tying a scarf around my head, because I knew he wouldn't like my permanent, but in the end I decided to face him. I came into the room with a happy greeting: "Granddad, I passed the exam!" His smile faded and his face fell when he turned to look at me. He didn't express any anger, but turned to my mother and asked, "Who's that?"

I broke out in tears and jumped into his lap. "It will grow out in no time at all," I whimpered. I tried to put my arms around him, but he kept brushing them back, so I picked up his arms and put them around me.

Finally he said to me, sadly, "Is it worth it?"

"No," I replied.

He didn't let me off easy even later, when we went shopping. At the Tuy Hue Lau eating house, before we sat down, he said, "I don't sit next to any curly-hair now." I took the chair next to him anyway and told him, "But curly-hair wants to sit next to you, Granddad." Everyone around the table laughed except my grandfather. I reached inside his pocket and got his tobacco pouch, rolled him a cigarette, and laid it between his fingers as my brother and sisters and cousins looked on and giggled.

— — —

My last year in elementary school had been like hard labor in a prison camp, at least by a child's standards. I had spent hour after hour studying for the high school exam, desperate that I wouldn't pass. "If I flunk," I often swore to myself, "I will bury my head in the mud." Now that it was all over, I could relax, because in the Vietnamese school system then, the first couple of years in high school were a time for fun and adventure.

I had many friends, but my closest one was Hiep, who was the class leader. She was as old as my sisters Kim and Cuong (because of the turmoil in the country, many kids had been unable to go to school for long periods, and so the sixty-two girls in my class ranged in age from twelve to nineteen), but she had the patience to put up with her little friend. Hiep used to call me "my tail," because whenever people saw her at school they usually saw me trailing right behind.

Hiep and I had one very important thing in common: Her mother and father were members of the NLF, operating inside Cambodia with the Khmer Rouge. Until 1959 she had been raised in the jungles of Cambodia while her father, a Viet Minh, was fighting the French alongside the Khmer Issarak. Then her mother took her to Phnom Penh, where she attended French schools for four years and earned a high school diploma. Her Vietnamese language ability was still limited, however, so she had to start several grades behind when she came to Can Tho. When I first heard her talk I said, "You speak like a Cambodian."

She swore in French, saying "Merde!" then asked, "How do you know? Are you Cambodian yourself?" Then she told me her life story, and a powerful bond formed between us.

Hiep's mother had died from malaria not long before then, when Hiep was seventeen. At that time the war in Cambodia was intensifying, and she was taken out of her boarding school and sent to live with a family of Vietnamese Communists operating under cover in Phnom Penh. After her mother's death, Hiep said, she began to see the work of the Communists more clearly, and to see how it affected her family and others; she secretly rejected the Communist way at that time, although she couldn't do anything about it.

Then one day the family she was living with told her that her father had made arrangements for her to go to Ha Noi. She could not bear the idea of going into the heart of the system she had come to hate, and so she fled the family's house, finding sanctuary in a Buddhist temple in Phnom Penh. After the monks' hospitality wore out, she moved in with a Cambodian woman who was elderly and blind, taking care of her in exchange for food and shelter. Meanwhile, she sought help from a classmate, a half-French, half-Cambodian girl named Monique whose father worked at the French consulate. Monique's father helped Hiep make contact with her aunt, who lived in Can Tho with her dentist husband. Then, using a forged birth certificate that identified her as her aunt's daughter, she bluffed and bribed her way across the border at Tay Ninh. She didn't have the proper passport or visa, she said, but "Monique's father told me that money was far more acceptable at the border than travel documents."

I was afraid to think about how a girl in her situation might have come up with enough money to bribe the border guards, but she spoke of it first: "Aren't you going to ask where I got the money?" She went on to explain. "I had a good-luck charm made of pure gold, given to me by my mother and father. I had that necklace blessed by a Cambodian Buddhist monk; you see, in Cambodia we believe the high monks have that much power. Anyway, I had to sell the necklace to Monique's mother, but so far my luck is still with me."

Luck, and talent, and a lot of guts, I thought. Hiep did well at school, often skipping classes while I had to struggle along to understand math, chemistry, and French. While she was studying about Viet Nam and learning how to be a Vietnamese, she still thought in French and had the temperament of a Cambodian. Once when she had trouble answering a teacher's question in Vietnamese, he got tired of waiting and told her to sit down. Hiep let loose a long sentence of French and Cambodian all mixed together, and when she sat down I whispered to her, "What did you say to him?"

"I told him, Goddamn it, I am going crazy being French, Cambodian, and a new Vietnamese all at the same time."

Hiep and I usually did our homework together, either at her aunt's house or in my kitchen. One day I started telling her about my father, but before I got very far she said, "I suspected it since I first knew you, kid." I asked if someone had told her and she replied, "Remember I am five years older than you. What you are going through as a Communist's daughter is an experience that I have already graduated from. A kid like you doesn't match the description in your birth certificate."

I thought it was a privilege to share Hiep's most private life story, although for any teenage girl it can be tough keeping a secret. But having a trusted friend was a great feeling for me, and so we kept each other's confidence throughout our relationship. Now and then, joking when the two of us were alone, she would call me "Communist's daughter." Of course, she was one, too, and like me she didn't know where her father was. She had written to him twice a year while he was operating in Cambodia, but after he had gone to North Viet Nam she lost contact with him, although sometimes she got word from his friends that he was in good health. Hiep didn't like politics. Sometimes I would try to discuss our country's situation, speculating about a day when we might not have to worry about either the North Vietnamese government or the Diem regime, but she wouldn't hear any of it: "Let the politicians fool each other on that subject," she snapped. Hiep's world then was simply learning almost from scratch about being a Vietnamese, which included learning about Vietnamese boys.

Because Hiep was older and had other interests, I spent more of my time outside school with friends my own age. Le Thi Bach Tuyet and Nguyen Thi Mai were my two favorites. Tuyet and I were both born in the South, and we found Mai refreshing because she was a refugee from Ha Noi. She never minded when we called her "Bac Ky," which was a not-very-nice way to say "Northerner."

Mai and her family were among the million Northerners who fled Ha Noi in 1954 when the French lost and the Communists took over. They had to leave everything when they came south, bringing only enough money to last about six months. Mai's father had died a few years before, so there was only Mai, her mother, her oldest sister, Thai Lan, two teenage brothers, and a younger sister. Thai Lan, a teacher, was the provider for the family. After their exodus she had taught for a few years in a refugee community school in Sai Gon. Then, just that year, she had been accepted as a teacher in a regular school in O Mon district, about twenty kilometers from Can Tho, and her family had moved to Can Tho to live with her.

My first meeting with Mai didn't seem to promise a deep friendship. On my first day at Phan Thanh Gian, someone had told me that she had seen "a Bac Ky in 7C" that she thought was me. I laughed: "There can't be another me in this world." But indeed, when I went to 7C at recess, there was a girl who looked almost exactly like me — about my age, my size, even a head full of curly hair. I watched her for a while, then signaled for her to come outside. At first I found her rather haughty, and I was irritated by her manner and especially her Northern accent.

"How long have you been here?" I asked.

"Five years."

I doubted that, because I was sure I would have known my "twin" if she had lived in Can Tho for five years. "Where did you go to school last year?" I asked, and she told me the name of an elementary school somewhere in Sai Gon, almost as if she was trying to test my knowledge of geography. I almost gave up on her then and there, but her resemblance to me was so magnetic, and her curious look and the smile at the corners of her mouth were intriguing, so I told her, "Come to see me at the next recess." She responded, "Maybe we can get together after school, too, if you like."

After that rocky start we gradually became like one another's shadow, spending hours together. Mai and her family lived in a rented house at the edge of a field; it was in poor condition, but they couldn't afford anything better on her sister's teaching salary. Our friendship helped both of us escape from unhappy situations at home — she from her gloomy house, I from the pressures of a house with more than half a dozen people. Together we were like two happy, self-centered children with "a rich daddy and a good-looking mommy." We laughed at everything and at everybody, especially anyone who was fat and phony like our principal and her daughter. We both liked music, and she would sing along while I played the mandolin. She had a great voice, but I was the only one who could enjoy it because she was too shy even to sing along in classroom functions.

Mai knew the South only through her years in the refugee community in Sai Gon, and she merely lived on the land rather than cherishing it as I did. She talked about Ha Noi often, and had great pride in being a Northerner, just as I was proud to be from the South. Mai made it clear that she considered herself an outsider in Can Tho, and was living there only temporarily "until the Communists are destroyed and we can go back to Ha Noi."

One night I told Hai Van how I felt guilty about the Communists, but he said that if we took personally everything the Communists did we might as well die with shame. He noted that our father had never tried to teach us about Communism, but had only demonstrated his love and his feeling for our country. "We don't have to be a Viet Minh or a Communist to be a patriot," Hai Van said. We were still too young to take sides, he insisted, so all we could do was wait until we were able to act on our own beliefs.

Hai Van seldom mentioned our father and Khoi, and he didn't like to go back to Long Thanh as much as I did since we had been asked a few times on visits there to attend "hoc Tap" (Communist study) classes at a nearby hamlet. He dreamed of his future, thinking about being a pilot, traveling the world, meeting foreign women; he didn't express his feelings very often, but kept them inside and under control.

I have always thought I was fortunate to know my father more than Hai Van and Hoa Binh and Minh Tam, but I also suffered more because he wasn't with me when I needed him. His memory nourished my life, but his absence often ruined my spirits. With Hai Van, Father was a vague image; a shadow can appear only when there is light, and for Hai Van only my mother could shine that light. Sometimes Hai Van said, "I feel more like a Tran than a Dang," and I could see how sad my mother was.

Chapter 8

In 1960 my grandfather passed away. The loss of a loved one is hard for any family, but in our case it was a terrible blow. We had all depended on Granddad for so long, as the only man still with us, and somehow we had imagined he would live forever. Even at eighty-five, he was still in good shape and never sick, and we must have all thought that natural laws didn't apply to him. Friends and relatives came from many cities to mourn with us. His body was laid in the middle of the great room of his house in Long Thanh, his favorite room where he used to sit and look out at the canal.

Perhaps the members of my family had forgotten how to help each other; we tended to drift apart and dwell in our own sorrow over Granddad's death. My mother cried, my grandmother looked a hundred years older, and everyone else sat around sobbing, but I couldn't shed a tear. I learned a lesson from that sad day in my life — that I could only please the people I love while they are living, that I shouldn't wait. When they are gone we can only miss them and regret what we didn't do for them. "Love the living and have fine memories of the ones who are no longer with us," I promised myself as I looked down at my grandfather for the last time.

After the funeral, Kim and Cuong left for Sai Gon and we returned to Can Tho. The house was strangely quiet for a long time. Mother worked late into the night, and I could hear her crying often, but she wouldn't talk about Granddad. I found ways to hide my own sorrow. We were supposed to wear a badge of mourning for the required period of three years, but I had to take mine off, because people would always ask whom I was mourning and it was just too painful for me to say, "My grandfather passed away."

Many things changed in our family after that. My mother had never been a temple-goer, but she began going after Granddad's death. Her hair began to turn gray, and for some reason she became much more protective of her children. Even a year later she still spoke of Granddad as if he were still living back at home in Long Thanh. Grandmother's health declined, and Aunt Bay began to take control of the family land there — which meant making it available to the NLF for their use.

Grandmother had always tolerated the Front activities, because to her the Front was her sons and grandchildren. She knew my grandfather's feelings against the Viet Cong, but she had never spoken against them because to her a loyal and faithful mother had only one duty: to support her children in whatever they did. Now that Grandfather was gone, my cousins and the Viet Cong had one less obstacle on their way to "liberation." With Aunt Bay's urging, the home in Long Thanh became a common meeting ground for them, as well as a connection to the city to further their destructive aims. They finally had room and the freedom to practice "socialism" right in our back yard. Sometimes I saw them in my grandfather's favorite room.

My grandmother had tuberculosis and had to make regular visits to the doctor in Can Tho, so one Friday my aunt asked me to come to Long Thanh to take Grandmother to town for her checkup on Saturday. That evening, we were roasting jackfruit nuts on an open fire in the back yard when a young cadre came in from the field. I was introduced to him by another cadre who had arrived earlier, and the two of them invited me to a "film show" in a nearby hamlet. I knew it was more than an invitation, something like a "command performance," and said to the young man, "Only if you can guarantee that there are no leeches on our way to the hamlet." I knew he couldn't guarantee that, because we would have to walk in water up to our thighs at some places after we left the boundaries of our land.

I had to go along anyway, so I changed into peasant clothes instead of the nice things I had worn from the city. That seemed to please Aunt Bay, because it seemed I was showing more willingness to listen to the Front's pleadings; my attitude had become more passive since my grandfather's death, and I didn't quite have the "reach for the jugular vein" attitude that I had once displayed. Before I left the house with the two cadres, she called me to her room and reminded me, "Behave yourself. Remember, you are your father's daughter and people will watch you."

We walked a long way in a difficult passage through the night. The two cadres moved silently and steadily, as if the darkness was their world; the only sound I could hear was my own heavy breathing, and I thought to myself, "I would make a rotten Viet Cong." As we made our way through the woods, I thought about my father and my uncles and their resistance careers that stretched back to boyhood. They had walked miles of this country and they knew it well; they knew its wants and needs, too, but I couldn't accept that the Communists' way was the answer to those wants and needs. I must have thought out loud, because one of the cadres asked what I had said. I said, "My legs are tired," and they laughed and assured me we'd be there soon.

The "film show" turned out to be a propaganda film sent down from Ha Noi, made by "comrades from Cuba." I don't remember the title, because the beginning was scratchy and had a lot of upside-down numbers, but the film stressed the friendship between Ha Noi and the Communist countries around the world, especially the Third World countries, all hand in hand on the road to socialism. The film showed a friendly chat between Ho and Chairman Mao, the visit of Russian officials to Ha Noi, the hugs and kisses and handshakes and smiles all aimed at putting more confidence into the guts of the Viet Cong guerrillas. Thousands of factory workers in Yugoslavia welcomed Ho Chi Minh in his 1957 visit, and peasants in Mongolia, North Korea, East Berlin, Bulgaria, Cuba, and many other Communist countries cheered him in their lands. Surely all that recognition must have proved his popularity and justified his cause — at least that was what the filmmakers intended.

After the show a young cadre introduced me to an older man, "Brother Than," who I believe was a high-ranking cadre. He asked what I thought of the film, and I decided to discard my aunt's advice. "My uncle Diep used to draw cartoons about Chinese airplanes when he was an editor of the Liberation newspapers," I said. "I wish I could express myself about the quality of Cuba's film industry in cartoons."

The young cadre was amused by my comment, but "Brother Than" was irritated. "I'm not sure I understood you, sister," he grumbled, staring intently at my face.

"I said the Cubans don't make good enough films to suit an occasion like this."

"It is the intention behind the report that counts," he insisted.

I argued his point. "The Catholics, the Buddhists, the Muslims put their gods in monumental places, in cathedrals and the most impressive temples and mosques around the world. I believe that 'Uncle Ho' deserves more than this modest kind of film. After all, the Liberation only has one 'Uncle Ho' and he is your god, isn't he?"

"Sister, this is wartime . . . ," he began, but I interrupted him.

"My father would not agree with you, but I understand this is the best you can do."

The bait was tossed out, the trap was set, and he fell into it. "Do you have anything better in mind?" he asked.

I pretended to look cautiously around, and leaned toward him and lowered my voice: "Let's make the Americans pay for our propaganda operation."

That was the end of the "lesson" for me, and shortly the same two cadres escorted me back to my grandparents' home. I invited them in for snacks, but for security reasons they declined and left me at the property line. Normally, I would never have been there alone that late in the night; our family's cemetery was there, and a short distance away were others, and I was scared to death of the spirits I believed were lurking all about. I ran as quickly as I could from the spooky place and, without thinking, burst into the house, interrupting another meeting and frightening the participants more than the ghosts had frightened me. Like machines, everyone — my aunt, my four cousins, members of the "coolie community," and two young women I didn't know — leapt off the table and into a ready position. When they recognized me they calmed down and laughed about it, but I was embarrassed.

Long Thanh had been my cradle, but now it was a nest for growing the "socialist future." The Viet Cong came and went, cutting through the bamboo hedges and using the house and land as they wanted. Nothing was sacred anymore, except perhaps the shrine of Tho Than, the God of the Good Earth, by the corner of the property. My grandmother still went there faithfully every evening, burning incense sticks and praying to her shepherd.

The Viet Cong stepped up their efforts and became better organized. The road to Long Thanh was unsafe, and land mines had killed countless travelers on the road from Ca Mau to Can Tho, but we still went home to visit Grandmother as often as we could. "You bring life into this land when you are here," she told us. She was very interested in politics and always asked us about things in the city, such as whether Madame Nhu, President Diem's influential sister-in-law, was behind the recent string of arson incidents. (Hundreds of homes all around Sai Gon had caught fire under mysterious circumstances, so the government had ordered homeowners to replace their wooden or thatched roofs with sheets of galvanized metal. Madame Nhu just happened to own a factory that produced galvanized metal, so the rumor spread throughout the country that she had paid henchmen to set the fires intentionally to win "customers" for her business.) I knew Grandmother wanted it proven that Madame Nhu was the real culprit, but I had to tell her that "nobody knows."

Grandmother always asked me, "Have you heard from your father?" I shook my head every time. She earnestly believed that her sons and grandchildren would come marching home in victory one day and that she would come to the village center with the rest of the people to cheer their triumph. "Be patient, my child," she often told me. "Your father will be here before too long." Whenever she said that I only held her big hands in mine and squeezed them with love.

In my search for understanding I wanted to know my family better, so I had traced my roots on my father's side. I kept in touch with his sisters and other relatives, and went to his native village even though his parents had died long before I was born. His stepbrother told me about the rise and fall of the Dang clan. I learned of my great-grandfather, who had been an officer from the Court of Hue, the ancient capital of Viet Nam, and of the endless love stories among my ancestors. There were heroes and cowards, leaders and followers, lovers and thieves in the Dang family. No wonder my grandfather Tran had sometimes said, "I never thought I would marry off my daughter to a Dang." But above all the other things I learned about my father's family was the love that extended throughout all its members.

I cherished what I had learned about that side of my heritage, and felt myself growing more like my father. I started to think about others, not just myself. Viet Nam and her people were constantly in my mind. I heard the cries for peace and freedom, and I witnessed the powerful urges that made men become ruthless Viet Cong. I could sympathize with their desire to destroy the Diem regime, which was no savior of Viet Nam. At the same time, however, I felt a need and desire to do the same thing to the Viet Cong who were killing my innocent countrymen.

So the question of "When will your father be home?" became painful and confusing to me, and I wished people would stop being "concerned." I loved my father as a man and as a sensitive human being, and I admired him as a leader; through him I learned to love something else, perhaps as much as I loved him: Viet Nam. I had had a fine childhood with my father, the first man I ever loved, and I hoped to find a man to marry someday who was like him — but I knew that if the Ha Noi government invaded the South, I would never have a chance at that good life, nor would the millions of others who would suffer under Communism.

I would have preferred that they just give up on me and leave me alone — kick me out of their "hoc Tap" sessions, denounce me, call me a black sheep, forget me. But they persevered, always trying new approaches to recruit me to the glorious cause.

When we came home for my grandfather's memorial day, a year after his death, Thao and Yvonne asked me to help them bring firewood from the woodshed to the kitchen. When we were alone outside, Thao asked if I had noticed the political leaflets that had been secretly left in our classroom one recent morning. I knew that they had been responsible for the leaflets, and as I told Thao about the students' reactions her face grew brighter and her eyes got bigger. "Did you hear that?" she asked Yvonne.

"You surely know what kind of information we look for from a test like that, don't you?" Yvonne asked me. The leaflets asked such things as whether students were satisfied with their education, whether they wanted more rights, whether they would join a student union.

Thao broke in eagerly: "Yung, join the Front! People need you, the country needs you. It is your chance to prove your love for Viet Nam!"

"Of course you know we are not begging you," Yvonne said. "It is a matter for you and your conscience."

"The land mines on the highways already blew up my conscience, Yvonne," I replied. I saw Thao kick Yvonne slightly as a signal for her to keep quiet.

"You would make an excellent recruiter," Thao said. "You have the potential, and a perfect location, your high school." She was sincerely trying to sell me a place under the red flag, but as always I turned the pitch into a joke. "I didn't study my tail off to get into Phan Thanh Gian just for a recruitment job, you know," I told her.

Yvonne's patience wore out, and she picked up the wood and started back to the house. "It is your choice," she grumbled.

I thought maybe they were through with me for a while, but that night after the memorial service for my grandfather they resumed the drumbeat once again. Calling me out to the rice warehouse, they asked me if I would do them a favor — to distribute more leaflets like the ones we had found in our classrooms. I refused immediately, but they were prepared for that. "The leaflets will be in your best friend's desk this weekend. Please don't let her seize them."

God, I thought, *which* best friend? I was so angry that if we hadn't just come from the memorial service I might have forgotten they were my cousins. I stifled my fury, pulled myself together, and said as calmly as I could, "I will make sure that my friend won't see the leaflets before I do. Now, whose desk is it?"

"Hiep's," Thao said with a satisfied smile.

I was the first one at the school gate that following Monday, and the school guard let me in when I told him I was on classroom-cleaning duty. I raced up the stairs and flung open the top of Hiep's desk. There were the leaflets, a stack of blue papers about three centimeters thick. I stuffed them into my school satchel and went back downstairs and out the gate. I was nervous carrying the leaflets, because just across the street from our school was the Cong An headquarters; from time to time, when its huge green gate swung open, we could see prisoners squatting uncomfortably on the floor inside in their awful situation.

I hurried past with the "time bomb" in my satchel and went to a public outhouse in the worst section of a community near the school. I had never used that facility, but I walked right in, placed the stack of leaflets on the floor, and hoped that people would use it as toilet paper. I almost laughed out loud as I left, thinking, "At least I have done something good for the poor this time."

Later Thao thanked me for carrying out my "task." I refused to tell her my method of "distributing" the leaflets, because I didn't want to lie to her. As it happened, my little rebellion didn't amount to much, because the Viet Cong had many more undercover distributors; the principal later reported that leaflets had been found in all three of the classes at the school.

When I had passed the exam for public high school, my family treated the event like big news — perhaps because they didn't have much faith in me, or perhaps because it was obvious I was struggling so hard in studying for it that no one thought they should get their hopes up too much. I was continually weighed down with a heavy mind: I missed my father and Khoi, I worried about the outcome of their return to the South, and my anti-Communist sentiment was growing. When the time came for Hai Van to sit for the exam, however, it was almost like a routine day. He breezed through the two days of testing, the two days most of the kids called "purgatory," and then went off to Long Thanh to go fishing, confident that he had gotten nearly all the answers right. I envied that brilliant, carefree little kid!

I didn't envy him his turn as the potential recruit for the Viet Cong, however, a turn that wasn't long in coming. About four months after he entered the boys' school at Phan Thanh Gian, my cousin Thao started paying a lot of attention to him, always wanting to "talk" to him. I warned her to stay away from him or "I'll tell Mom on you, and everything else you've ever done, including the time you cut your hair!"

Hai Van didn't like it when I watched him like a mother hen, of course. "I can take care of myself," he insisted. Actually, I thought he probably could, but I worried sometimes what loyalty might make him do. I was afraid he might secretly join the Front, even though he didn't really share its beliefs, simply because he was the son of one of its leaders and felt it was his obligation.

— — —

For years I ran everywhere I went, and it paid off when I began taking part seriously in sports at school. I made the track team, and one day in the summer of 1963 I learned that I had been chosen along with two other girls to represent the school in a big track meet in My Tho with other schools from all over the Mekong Delta.

Track meets call to mind such things as high hurdles, but the biggest hurdle

I had to cross was getting my mother to let me make a four-day trip nearly one hundred kilometers from home. It would be quite a change from my normal routine, since I still lived under a 9:15 curfew that she and the mothers of my friends had set for us. On top of that, two of my classmates had just turned up pregnant, and few of the mothers were in a mood to be lenient with their daughters. Luckily, my coach was able to convince her that I would be safe and well cared for, so she relented and let me go.

The meet started on a happy note for me — I won the first race of 1,500 meters — but the joy didn't last long. While I was waiting for the second race I took my tennis shoes off to walk around in the deep, green grass; I stepped on a piece of broken glass and suffered a deep cut on the back of my heel, and my athletic career was over for that day and forever.

The team didn't have any money to take me to a doctor, so the coach sent me to a friend's home in My Tho to have the cut tended and to rest while my teammates finished the four days of the meet. As usual, I was to end up embroiled in politics once again.

The coach's friends were an elderly couple, the Thanhs, a retired high school history teacher and his wife. The lady washed my heel with a solution of mercurochrome, and I felt the burning all the way up to the top of my head. If it had been my mother treating me, I would have screamed bloody murder, but when the kindly stranger asked me "are you hurt?" I gritted my teeth and said "no."

The man and his wife were devout Buddhists, and their home was filled with a religious aura. As we were eating a light lunch of fruits, they told me that they didn't eat meat anymore but would ask the maid to buy whatever I wanted for dinner. I assured them that I would eat the same things they did.

Mrs. Thanh told me they were going to visit the great Tan Hiep Buddhist temple not far away, and invited me to come along. Since I was going to be stuck for the entire four days of the track meet, I decided I might as well make the visit as interesting as possible, so I accepted. Mr. Thanh chartered a Lambretta for the three of us and their maid, Chi Sau, and off we went with sacks full of rice, yams, beans, coconuts, and other food for the temple.

Tan Hiep temple was well known, and thousands of people usually visited it on Buddhist holidays, but things had changed somewhat because the area where it stood had recently fallen under Viet Cong control. Chi Sau told me that "the Viet Cong don't like strangers to come to the temple anymore, but my masters paid a tax so they are friendly to us now." Mrs. Thanh didn't seem to like the maid's statement. "If we could exchange money for peace, we should be grateful for that, my child," she said.

During the trip Mr. Thanh whispered to his wife and me that "the news from Sai Gon is not good for Buddhists. In Hue our people are not allowed to fly the Buddhist flag on Buddha's birthday, and the government has killed several people who tried to raise the flags." He bombarded me with slogans and arguments against President Diem, but I didn't buy them all. I knew that Diem, for all his faults, was both intelligent and religious; he honored the Vatican flag, and I was sure he would allow others to pay respect to their religious colors. I thought about the discussions I had had with my cousins about "psychological warfare," and I suddenly had the almost certain feeling that the Communists had orchestrated the whole incident but the Buddhists were too religious and too emotional to see it. I knew the Communists were perfectly capable of manipulating crowds, temples, and thousands of other innocent and unsuspecting people in this country.

I suggested my theory to Mr. Thanh, quietly so only he could hear, but he shook his head without even a moment's consideration. Perhaps he wanted to believe the rumors about Diem's role; in this way he could have a visible figure to blame for the wrongdoing to his fellow Buddhists. I knew better than to argue with an old teacher, so I didn't say anymore. Still, I thought it was unlikely that President Diem would have been responsible. There were more Buddhists than Catholics in Viet Nam, and if Diem wanted to win over the hearts of the citizens it would have been illogical for him to deny them the right to practice their religion. That was only the opinion of a seventeen-year-old girl, though, so I didn't try to press it on my elder Mr. Thanh.

When we arrived at the temple, I wouldn't have recognized it from Chi Sau's earlier description of a place "full of animation." The front court looked deserted and the temple flowers were wilting and unkempt. The young monk who came out to greet us seemed unchanged by events, however. I couldn't tell his exact age; he looked so pure, without a trace of the dusty world on his face. He held his hands together calmly in front of him as we were introduced, and his deep, black eyes against his pale complexion made me think of stories of the mandarins and young scholars of the olden days.

"Have you noticed the stillness out here?" he asked me.

"Yes, I have," I replied, "but the stillness can also make the sound of mortars seem louder." Somehow I felt that this monk should not forget the war going on in other parts of Viet Nam, where lives were being lost and the land torn apart.

He asked where I was from, and I told him Can Tho. "My village is also in the cross fire now," I said. Then, for some reason, I asked if he had heard about the militant monks and their violent protests in Sai Gon against the Diem regime.

"I haven't heard any news from the outside," the monk said.

"The police found guns and materials belonging to the Viet Cong at Xa Loi pagoda in Sai Gon. How would you feel if it happened to Tan Hiep?"

He spread his arms in a sweeping gesture and looked around us: "The temple is always open to everyone."

I wondered if Buddha had said the Viet Cong were welcome, too, but I resisted the temptation to ask him. Instead I said, "The venerable monk who burned himself to death must not be a genuine monk. Monks are not violent people, they are compassionate."

"Allow me, Miss," he responded. "Venerable Thich Quang Duc was indeed a great monk. To tell you the truth, I have heard about that incident. It is sad that we must lose the venerable to get our message across." His cool and unconcerned tone proved to me that he was merely following the party line.

"President Diem is a devout Catholic, and Catholics don't believe in suicide," I retorted. "Suicide may not move him at all. Madame Nhu has already laughed at the 'barbecue.'"

"The free world will see our problem more clearly."

"To hell with the free world! Forgive me, Monk, for my language. The world doesn't control our lives, the future of this country is in the hands of the Vietnamese people. The French, the Americans, the Russians shouldn't have any impact on our future or on our actions. You can't burn yourself to death to tell the world your story."

He smiled and walked closer to the water-lily pond, and I followed. Dark clouds moved in and covered the sun, and the hot, heavy air became a little easier to breathe. "Are you still in school?" he asked.

"Yes. Next year I'll take an exam for the baccalaureate, and then I'll try to either join the army or maybe work for the army."

The monk had not looked at me directly as we talked until then. He stopped and turned toward me, and for the first time there was a lively expression on his face.

"Are you serious?" He understood that I meant the South Vietnamese army.

"I am serious."

"Why?"

"When you love someone or something, you have the need to express that love, to show it. It may sound old-fashioned and funny to you, but I honestly love this country." I could feel my throat tightening, and my voice broke a bit.

The monk was silent for a moment, and then he said, "I'll not fight for the Americans."

"Who asks you to fight for the Americans anyway? This land is ours, half of the 'S' shape is ours. It isn't important to me why the Americans are in Viet Nam; it's only important to me that they are here. Let's believe that they are here with a very noble mission. We need them to defeat the Communists in Ha Noi."

The monk shook his head. "They will take Viet Nam. They will dominate us like the French once did."

"You think the Vietnamese will let them even if they try?" I shot back.

"We may not have the power to resist," he said sadly.

"Our people have been warriors for thousands of years and professional soldiers for life; we will not be dominated again! At least the Americans will give us the freedom to fight them. The Ha Noi Communists will never give us that opportunity."

"You seem to be so sure about that, Miss."

In those days, in talking to a Viet Cong sympathizer, one would normally speak of *we* the Vietnamese people. It was safer to double-talk to get one's message across; besides, we *were* Vietnamese and had suffered great losses in the war. In my conversation with the monk, while I meant the anti-Communist nationalists when I referred to the Vietnamese people, he used the same language but believed all were pro-Communist.

I was a bit embarrassed that I had gone so far and gotten so excited. "I should take this rare opportunity to ask you about Buddhism rather than talking about war and violent death."

"It is interesting to know how people think and feel," he assured me. "I find you rather refreshing, different from most of the female students who used to come around here."

As we walked toward the temple, the monk said to me, "You are very intelligent." I laughed and tilted my head back. "My grandfather used to say that intelligence is what your parents gave you, but wisdom is what your fellow men will give to you. My bag of wisdom is still empty yet."

Later, when everyone else was taking a nap, I couldn't sleep so I wandered back out to the garden. I loved the smell of the air after a big rain in Viet Nam; it was as familiar to me as the aura of my mother or the aroma of Granddad's tobacco, all of them saying to me, "You are home." The cool, gentle breeze caressed my face, but inside a storm was still raging. As I sat on the edge of the lily pond, I became frustrated with how difficult it was in this critical time for my country to get the facts straight in order to know what to think. The phrase "I heard" was on everyone's lips, but you rarely heard anyone say "I know." When no one had any information but rumors and gossip in the marketplace, a simple Viet Cong bandit in the city jail could become as big as a North Vietnamese commander in people's minds. Hearsay was like an uncontrollable disease among the mass of the population.

President Diem was the first leader of a democratic government after two thousand years of feudalism, yet the "intellectuals" demanded an overnight change to a total, Western–style democracy — while in their living rooms they entertained Communist cadres with French cognac and American cheese, all served by an underpaid maid. Yet these people had gotten much of their message overseas and had persuaded many naive Americans to push their government for "total democracy" for Viet Nam. I should have been the one screaming for more freedom for my country and less secret police snooping in our lives; but I realized that under the present circumstances more freedom would just mean more freedom for Ha Noi's agents to operate in the South so they could eventually deny us any freedom at all.

I came gradually to accept that my father, my uncle, my brother Khoi, my cousins, and so many other Southern patriots were firmly in the claws of the Northern Communists, and there was nothing I could do about it. They had made their beds, and I had to let them lie in those beds.

As for South Viet Nam — the land that nourished my life and the life of my family — I just wished the war could end and life could be normal, but wishing wasn't enough for Viet Nam. I wanted to be twenty-five, old enough to wrestle with the real-life horrors of the world. I was in what writers call the "spring" of life, supposedly the brightest time of a girl's life. I should have been sensing the awakening of a woman's body and the emotions that come with it, but the war made that impossible. I felt myself hating the Communists for what they were doing to my country and to me, and because I knew hatred was a most unhealthy feeling, I became terribly unhappy.

For the first time, though, I felt myself missing someone back in Can Tho, someone who had become special to me. I couldn't sleep on my last night at Mr. and Mrs. Thanh's home, because I knew I would soon be returning home and could see him once again.

Chapter 9

Running up the stairway that led to Phong's house, I suddenly stopped halfway. Phong was standing by the threshold watching me.

"Where are your medals, kid?" he called out as I climbed the rest of the way. I turned around and lifted my foot to show him the white bandage wrapped around my heel. That was my only "award" from my expedition to the track meet. (As a typical Vietnamese, I was too modest to show off my medal for the first race.)

Phong was not exactly a boyfriend. Twelve years older than I, he was sometimes like a best friend, sometimes like a big brother. I never asked if he had a sweetheart; I didn't know what I'd think if he said yes!

Phong was perhaps an unlikely person to be the object of my first "crush" — he was a lieutenant in the military police under the Diem government. He never asked about my father, though; as far as I knew, he assumed that my father had died like so many others during our country's long years of war.

That afternoon I had lunch with Phong, and he asked me about My Tho, where the track meet was held. I told him all I knew about it was the bus station, the school, the stadium, and one particularly nasty piece of broken glass. We all laughed at my unfortunate track "achievement." I also told Phong about my conversation with the monk I had met; he just shook his head and said, "I only hope that someday you will be missing one Viet Cong monk."

We chattered on about many things, but Phong could sense that I had something serious on my mind. "Something is troubling you, lady, what is it?" he asked me.

"I don't know. I feel as if I am wasting my time in school. I want to do something, something useful. I want to be productive. I'm just not happy with myself." As a sixth-year student by this time, I had one more year to go in high school to earn my baccalaureate.

"Look," he said in his best brotherly tone, "this is the world of a seventeen-year-old. Enjoy it! Slow down and smell the flowers along your path. If you are in a hurry, you'll miss it. You'll be twenty-five in no time, but you will never be seventeen again."

"Promise that you'll be honest with me?"

"I promise."

"You may think I am out of my mind, but I feel I can fill in my brother's place, and some nights I feel that I should fill in my father's place, too."

"You are not out of your mind," Phong assured me. "Since my father passed away I became the man of the family. It is an honor to me, but I had to pay a big price for it." He stopped abruptly, as if he had said more than he intended. Then he continued, "You can do that, but it takes someone bigger than a seventeen-year-old."

Something was troubling Phong, too, I suddenly realized. It became my turn to question his mood, but when I asked he just shook his head and poured another cup of tea. I pressed harder, and finally, reluctantly, he spoke.

"This whole town was lonely while you were gone. I also discovered something about you."

A cold terror stabbed my heart: Had he found out about the Communists in my family? I interrupted him. "If it's bad, then don't tell me."

"Remember the night you and Mai walked in the rain?" he asked. He gestured toward the front of the room. "I was standing by that window and I heard your laughter. I saw you take off your raincoat and let the rain pour on your face, and you two laughed again. It made me happy to hear you laugh, and I discovered how much I care for you — more than I ever cared for anyone. It is more than love from a man to a woman. I wanted to tell you I love you when you first got here this morning, but it wasn't enough."

"Try it," I said in a joking tone, grinning at him.

"Can you be serious for a while? I have an obligation to see that our friendship stays healthy and lasts. And I want you to have more friends besides me."

This was an important discussion, I realized. I sat on a big chair and stared out the window, while Phong pulled up a chair and sat in front of me.

"You have a father, whom I happen to admire and respect," he said, to my amazement. "You may have to withhold the truth about your family, about your father, to strangers. But don't ever let it fool you. You have a father, a great man for a father."

I had started to cry. Wiping my tears, I asked how he knew about my father.

"I work for army intelligence. It isn't important how I know about your family, but it is important that you know who you are."

"When did you find out about it, before we met or after?"

"After."

"I want to know how!" I demanded.

"It is not important anymore."

"It is to me, Phong."

He relented. "The chief of staff called me in one day and handed me a file. Your whole family tree was in it. He warned me about you, although he said he was informed that so far you hadn't shown that you have any connection with their networks."

"Did he tell you to spy on me?"

"Yung, he was just doing his job."

"Why is it that my world seems so complicated all the time?" I wailed.

"Let's forget about the whole thing, huh? I'll always be your friend, always be here when you need me, but I want you to take advantage of today, the best time in your life. Enjoy it, live it, and let tomorrow come in its own pace. Someday I'll tell you how I lost my golden years."

"I am numb," I told him. "Why didn't you tell me when you learned about my father?"

"I didn't want to give you the wrong impression."

"Wrong impression!" I threw back at him. I was devastated, and for a moment I thought I would swear never to see him again. But how could I make a stranger out of this man, the closest male friend I had at the time? We had laughed together, he had helped me with my math and volunteered to be my audience when I rehearsed speeches I prepared for our school plays. No stranger could know me the way he did, or care about me the way he did.

Phong told me that if the Cong An ever called me or anyone in my family into their headquarters for an interview, "Don't talk to them. Let me handle it."

"I can take care of myself," I boasted. I got up from the table and picked up my things to leave.

"Are you angry at me for knowing about your family?" he asked.

"I am angry, but at myself for walking through the real world blindfolded," I replied. I wanted to say more, perhaps to hurt him, but I left the house. The steps at his front entrance somehow seemed much longer, and I wanted to run.

That afternoon I let my feelings rule my life. I broke off the beautiful friendship we had shared for eighteen months. I knew I would miss him. My classmates would miss the chance to use his membership card to play tennis at the mayor's court, but my loss would be far more serious to me. He came to my home twice after that, looking for me, but the relationship was never the same to me.

Phong was killed one month after our talk, on October 15, 1963, the victim of a Viet Cong land mine that blew up under his Jeep while he was on an inspection tour near Tra Noc Airport.

I didn't go to his funeral. His brother knew me and perhaps knew that my father was a Communist. His boss knew me, and I was sure that whoever had told him about me would also be at the service. So I endured my sorrow alone, telling him goodbye in my own private words.

Sadness wasn't the only thing I felt after Phong's death. Because of the awful suddenness of the way he was killed, I began to feel a penetrating fear; I saw Viet Cong in every living thing, every shadow. One day in O Mon village near Can Tho I saw a little girl about eight or nine, Hoa Binh's age. She had something in her top pocket that triggered the thought in my mind: "It is a hand grenade!" I grabbed her hand and searched her pocket without even thinking, and when I found nothing I meekly apologized and ran back to a friend's house where I was visiting. It was horrible to realize that I had come to fear even little children. But I knew it could have been some "innocent" woman or child who had planted the land mine that took Phong away from this earth, someone like me who had decided she must "follow in her father's footsteps."

The war's casualties had just been statistics to me up until then, but they had begun to touch me more than ever before. I lost much of my feeling of comfort and security when they buried my friend Phong. What I had left was an enormous empty space.

Fighting and tragedy continued to spread throughout my country. Then, in the midst of my loneliness, an incident occurred that stirred up everyone's life — the coup d'état that took place in Sai Gon in November 1963. "The president is dead," the cry rang out in the streets, as the whole town ran about in chaos to inform one another.

— — —

During the first two weeks of November, after the deaths of President Diem and his brother Nhu, my country suddenly became like a jungle. The animals were those who had betrayed the president at his death, and even afterward.

Those who were still loyal to him had to mourn him in silence. I saw a charcoal peddler in tears when he asked an elderly woman, "Have you heard the news? They said the president took his own life while he was surrounded by the traitors. That was a lie! He was a good Catholic, and good Catholics don't do that!" The charcoal peddler wore a silver cross around his neck. I felt sad for him.

Many others were far from sad at the Ngo brothers' deaths, however. The man who came to our home every Friday to sell bread was an old Viet Minh who used to serve my father as a crew member when he traveled by boat throughout the country. On the morning after the coup, he showed up unexpectedly at our door. "Sister Nam," he said to my mother, "Diem and his brother were killed!" He came closer and lowered his voice to a whisper: "Maybe brother Quang will be home soon. The event seems to be in our favor." His face was positively beaming with delight. My mother responded quietly, "I hope their father will be here soon, too, Mr. Ba, but how can I be happy at someone's death?"

At my school the principal ordered every class to take down President Diem's portrait, and I volunteered to climb the ladder to take down the one in our room. When I lifted it from its nail I recalled the times when it had been my turn to clean the picture. Often I had gazed into Diem's eyes and chewed him out: "You shouldn't let Madame Nhu run the palace and your brother run the country!" Others had done more than criticize; three times we had all been asked to chip in money to buy new glass for the portrait, because someone had stoned his image while no one was looking. My homeroom teacher Miss Huong asked to have the portrait for herself, so I wrapped it in newspapers for her. Outside, in the school yard, students from the boys' school were burning all their pictures, smashing the glass, and tossing even the frames into the bonfire.

The NLF had been quick to claim "credit" for the Ngos' deaths, as I heard when I was taken to a rally in the countryside. At the rally I noticed everyone's faces showed hope and encouragement and joy at the deaths; I was ashamed even to be there. The fall of the Ngos was the occasion for the NLF to pursue new schemes to round up the peasants and try to swing more of them to their cause.

I was deeply hurt when a spokesman got up on stage at the rally and told the crowd, "The U.S. imperialists backed the military coup d'état! The CIA engineered the murder of the Ngo brothers!" Later, on our way back to Long Thanh, I asked one of the high-level cadres to explain something to me. "At first we claimed the victory at their death, but tonight the cadre said the 'U.S. imperialists' murdered them. Who was really responsible for it?"

"We are, the NLF," he answered.

"You are not telling me that the CIA cooperated with us to overthrow them?"

"You see," he told me, "Diem and his brother were very stubborn. They only wanted to take the U.S. dollars and spend it in their own ways. The Americans are not that stupid, so they had no choice but to get rid of the Ngos and find another puppet who will be more obedient."

I was brought up by two very loyal people, loyal to each other and to their beliefs. I knew some of the Viet Minh had left the movement after the Geneva agreement, but I had never known of such betrayal as this cadre was describing. Why must the Americans murder their allies, I wondered. I asked the question a hundred times on the way back from the rally, but could not resolve it. I had not yet taken the Americans into my confidence or given them a gram of trust, but I thought what the Viet Cong was saying was hard to believe. I thought I should remain objective, and give the Americans a chance to demonstrate their real intentions.

In the midst of all the turmoil, I felt even more alone than before. On weekends I went to Long Thanh to see my grandmother and Aunt Bay, and there I visited my grandfather's gravesite. I wished I could communicate with him, because I was sure he would know the truth about who had killed the Ngos.

Just a few weeks after the Ngo assassinations, we received another shock, this time over the radio. I heard over North Vietnamese Radio that President Kennedy had been assassinated. I felt a sudden sadness and emptiness. If someone could kill President Kennedy, there was no safe place in the world. I had counted on him to get rid of Communism, not only in my country, but everywhere else. I thought of his children, his little girl and the little boy who sometimes would play under his desk. I thought about the fact that they, like me, would grow up without their father.

Sometimes I feared that one day I would prove to be an embarrassment to my father because I hadn't followed his footsteps as so many other youngsters I knew had done. Yet other days I said to myself, "If he had really wanted me to be a Communist, he would have told me so." He had never insisted, and in fact had not even pressured my mother to raise us in any particular way. My grandfather had once told me not to be concerned: "The Catholics believe that when a man becomes a priest, he saves his whole family. Well, the same goes for the Communists. You have already sacrificed your father to Ho Chi Minh, so you don't have anything to worry about." My aunt had cried when he said that, but my brother and I were greatly relieved.

The problem in Viet Nam was that, for all their obsession with rumors of war and politics, most people were political illiterates and terribly susceptible to clever propaganda from dedicated men. In this war for minds, the Viet Cong were far better equipped than the South Vietnamese government; they were talented, hard-core cadres, they were cunning and experienced, and on top of that they went into war with true hatred. After that meeting in the hamlet with my distant uncle, I grew more discouraged about the situation. My country was being manipulated by people far away, some in Ha Noi, some in Sai Gon, perhaps even some in Washington, and there was little that ordinary Vietnamese people could do. Again, I felt that we had been cheated — cheated by foreigners at the Geneva Conference who divided Viet Nam without consulting a single Vietnamese farmer or fisherman, the people who were the backbone of our country.

— — —

In the spring of 1964, my last year in high school, my grandmother passed away and was buried in the family cemetery in Long Thanh, next to my grandfather. Her name did not go on the stone marker, however, because my Aunt Bay had no money to spend on stonecutter's services. The money Grandma had saved for her funeral expenses was spent instead on the "struggle movement."

After Grandma died and Aunt Bay began to devote more and more of her energy and resources to the NLF activities, I didn't enjoy going back home as often as I had in the past.

I told my mother I wanted to go to work to earn money to help pay utility bills or part of the food costs, and she cried, "But you are only eighteen!" I wouldn't listen to any arguments, though, and so I began my effort to find someone who would hire me.

In my mind, stores would be a last resort, because the pay was too low to make it worthwhile. So I started with the post office.

"How old are you?" asked the manager, peering at me through thick glasses.

"Eighteen," I said, "but in the lunar calendar I'm already nineteen."

He smiled. "Where did you work before, young lady?"

When I told him I had just finished school, he handed back my application and said, "We don't have anybody to train new workers at this time. We need somebody with experience."

As I left the post office I was fuming. "I could go back in there and beat him up for experience," I muttered to myself. That was characteristic; my brother had always told me I ought to study judo, because every time I got angry with someone I threatened to beat him up.

Next I visited three theaters in Can Tho and applied for a job selling tickets. The owners were willing to hire me, but told me the job required a deposit of 2,000 piasters, apparently as a bond to make sure the cashiers didn't run off with the theater's money. The only thing I had that I might have been able to sell to raise the deposit was my bicycle, and it had only cost 1,500 piasters when I bought it four years earlier; besides, if I sold it then I wouldn't have any way to get to a job, or to deliver clothes for my mother.

My initial eagerness faded, my confidence seeping out of me like air from a punctured tire. I decided that I would wait awhile and let the matter cook itself like my grandmother's stew: "The longer it cooks the better it tastes, and for God's sake don't stir it," she always said. There was plenty for me to do at home, anyway. There is a season for everything, they say, but not for mothers' work; that goes on 365 days a year, as regularly as the sun rises and sets. I could keep myself busy almost all the time doing housecleaning, feeding my little sister, and making a dozen deliveries a day for the sewing shop.

Then, one day, the "stew" showed signs of being ready: I earned a completely unexpected 200 piasters for something I did as a favor to a neighbor, who happened to be a reporter for a newspaper in Sai Gon. Mr. Quan, the reporter, was a quirky kind of man, an unfriendly person who rarely talked to anyone in the neighborhood and who hated kids because "they're too noisy." He lived with his common-law wife, a friendly and outgoing person who ran off to her family about once a month and always said there was "no future with him" even though they had been together for fourteen years. The reason she said there was no future, even though he made good money, was that his money went up in smoke: He was an opium addict.

One evening the Viet Cong blew up the gasoline storage depot near Cai Rang bridge about seven kilometers from our house. I went to Mr. Quan's house to tell him, because I knew he would want to cover it, but his mother said he wasn't there. He had gone off looking for his wife, who had run away again, she said. We later found out he ended up at one of the "smoking houses" and slept there. I still thought the sabotage at the gasoline dump would be a good story, so I decided on the spur of the moment to hop on my bicycle and cover it myself.

The heat from the blazing gasoline kept onlookers from getting very close to the scene, and police were stopping everyone except local residents even from going into the general area. I told them I lived there and had to get home because my parents would be worried, so they let me through the barrier.

I joined a crowd of people standing about a thousand meters from the fire and watched people fleeing the flames. One man strode angrily across the bridge, his arms loaded with possessions from his house, cursing the Viet Cong, the firemen, and even his little girl, who scurried to keep up with him. "If my house burns down, I'll kill three generations of any Viet Cong I can get my hands on," he raged.

Moments later a convoy of military trucks roared up, and the crowd divided to let them through. Whistles blew, MPs and other officials lined up, and then soldiers piled out of the trucks and began pushing people to the edge of the bridge. I was afraid that if I didn't hold onto the railing I would be pushed into the river below. The authorities told everyone to leave the bridge, but since it was the only spot high enough to see the fire from that distance most people stayed put. Then one of the soldiers fired a shot into the air and everybody started running. I had to leave, too, and since the south bank of the river was closer to the fire I went that way, still determined to get my story.

I could feel the heat and hear the crackling noises of the spreading fire, but I couldn't see much because of the thick rows of coconut trees and the houses along Rach Ban bridge. As I stumbled along in the near-darkness, I bumped the front wheel of my bicycle against an elderly woman who was sitting on the ground. I put down my bike and went to help her; she didn't seem hurt, and she began talking to me in a calm and strangely uninvolved tone of voice. "I saw that rocket with my own eyes, it went over my house, just right on top of my head. Yooooooo, it went, and it missed the tank. The one that hit was the third rocket." I asked if her house was safe, and she said, "Beats me, how do I know?" Looking around at the nearby houses, I asked if she wanted to walk to one of them to rest until it was safe to go back home, but she said, "My damn son evacuated me and dropped me here. He went back to get my pigs and the chickens. I am paralyzed, I can't walk, girl!"

"Can you hold onto my neck? I'll carry you, Grandma."

She laughed, and said, "You are too tiny to carry me. If you drop me, I'll be dead."

I was small, but I knew I could do it because I moved heavy furniture at home all the time. So I put my right arm under her legs and my left arm under her neck and picked her up and started walking. A few people looked at us, but they were too busy watching the fire to help. I found a house where the people knew the lady and they took her in, and I went back to my bicycle. It was getting late, and I had to get home because my curfew had been set at 9:15 ever since my classmates turned up pregnant. (That had been a long time ago, and the babies in question were already walking, but my mother had kept the curfew in effect. She wasn't amused when I said, "My friends have already had their babies, can we stay out later now?")

On my way home I was disappointed that I hadn't been able to get close to the fire or to get any good solid news to give to Mr. Quan. My mind kept going back to the brave old lady on the ground: Why didn't she cry? Why was she so calm? Then it came to me — I would tell Mr. Quan about how the Viet Cong couldn't even break a helpless, paralyzed old woman. And I would tell him about the man who cursed and threatened to kill "three generations of Viet Cong." I tore two leaves of paper from my school tablet and wrote down what I had seen and heard, and the next day I took it to Mr. Quan's house and gave it to his mother.

That evening his wife came over and said, "He wants to see you." Because he was such a grumpy man, I wasn't keen on talking to him, but I went anyway. At his home he offered me a chair and read out loud what I had written. "Why didn't you write the conclusion of the incident?" he asked me.

"The joint police kept everyone out, they even fired shots to keep people from standing on the bridge. I couldn't stay to the end."

Mr. Quan smiled, the first time I had ever seen him do so. "Reporters must be aggressive and brave," he told me.

I was at least brave enough to tease Mr. Quan. I added, "And always be available when it happens, too. Your mother told me you were out on a different kind of mission last night."

He thanked me for the information I had brought and said he would check further with his police sources, and we said goodbye. That night his wife came back to my house with 200 piasters he had sent to me. I had never expected 200 piasters; it wasn't a great amount of money, perhaps enough for two bus rides to and from my grandparents' farm, but the idea of getting paid for that kind of work opened a new door for me. I went to bed with the money under my pillow and my head full of thoughts about a new career: I dreamed of reporting, writing, the editor accepting my stories, my family sitting around in front of a radio listening to a report I had written for the station in the capital.

— — —

When I woke up the next morning I was filled with excitement about my dream and my new idea for a career. I told Thuan about it, but she just smiled, and all day long she went around singing a popular tune that made clear what she thought of my prospects: "*Em oi neu mong khong thanh thi sao?*" (My darling, what will happen to you if your dream never comes true?)

And there was plenty of reason to be dubious. How could a young girl, just out of high school, with no work experience or special training, get a job as a writer? I was never one to let simple impossibility stand in my way, however, so I vowed to make it happen somehow.

I had always wanted to join the ARVN, but as a female my mother would never let me. Besides, my aunt and cousins might disown me from the family. But working and writing for the army as a civilian would be a bit less "rebellious." It was a job I needed with good pay, a great outlet for me to speak out against the NLF. My family in the bush would not find out easily, I figured, because I would only write news for the army radio; no writers' names were mentioned on the "Voice of the ARVN" radio program.

Luck was on my side already. In a boardinghouse just two doors down from our home there lived an army lieutenant who had been trying for some time to get me to go out with him. He wasn't having much success, because each time he came calling my mother greeted him politely and respectfully, then made certain she never left him alone with me or any of her students.

My mother was determined that none of the girls in her care would be caught dating soldiers.

The lieutenant, whose name was Nguyen Ba Phuoc, was interesting to me, however, because of where he worked — at a newly established military office called G-5, a propaganda and communications section under the command of the Fourth Corps of the South Vietnamese Army, known as IV Corps. One of the many programs G-5 was responsible for was a radio station in Soc Trang, a little south of Can Tho, that broadcast news of a military nature to the troops and to anyone else who was listening. To my eager young mind, the recent creation of this radio station seemed to have been done solely for my benefit, to give me an opportunity to get a job and begin fulfilling my dream.

Lieutenant Phuoc had been looking for a house to rent for his boss, the chief of G-5, Captain Nguyen Dat Thinh. This man was the author of many novels and a theater critic in private life, Lieutenant Phuoc told me; before being transferred to Can Tho as part of his military service he had been editor of an army journal and had worked in psychological warfare headquarters in Sai Gon. I was impressed by the captain's credentials, although I had to admit that I hadn't read any of his books. To high school students in this city in the extreme South, the famous authors were the ones from the prewar era and the poets of the ancient past. One went to bed with a pillow over the head to block out the mortar sounds and dreamed of the world of the endless love stories of the classic writers Khai Hung and Nhat Linh.

Still, I realized that Captain Thinh could represent the door to my chosen future, and that Lieutenant Phuoc could be the key. So one day when he came calling on me I told him I wanted to get a job at G-5 and asked him for an introduction to his boss. "We are going to have a party to christen our new offices," he began, but I shushed him and walked him out to the front yard, away from the house. "Don't let my mother hear that," I said conspiratorially. He laughed and invited me to come with him to the party.

The day of the gala event I met Lieutenant Phuoc at the tennis club and we walked back to Le Loi army base where the IV Corps headquarters was located. He warned me to prepare myself to be disappointed, because all the captain's staff writers in Sai Gon were army officers and enlisted men, not civilians, not women, and certainly not inexperienced young girls. "If he says he doesn't hire civilian news writers," he suggested, "maybe you can come back through the regular channels and apply for a typist job."

I stopped in the middle of Hoa Binh Boulevard and laughed out loud. "I don't know how to type!" I admitted.

"It's a thousand times easier than learning how to write," he said. "You can take typing courses."

That was hardly my style. "I can do harder work than that, so why should I take courses to do an easier job?"

I was the only fresh face at the G-5 party. The other girls and women displayed the most fashionable makeup and clothes — they were friends, lovers, and concubines of the men in attendance, men from the base commander's office and friends of Captain Thinh who had come from Sai Gon to help him celebrate his new office and his new position as head of one of the most important sections in IV Corps. As usual, wives were not included in these parties. I had told Lieutenant Phuoc I only wanted to be introduced to the captain that day; I was waiting for a more appropriate moment to bring up the subject of a job.

I wanted to come back the very next day, but I was afraid of seeming too naive and eager; I didn't want to wait too long, either, because he might have forgotten who I was. So I calculated that two days would be the best, and on that second day I showed up at the base. Captain Thinh had to come to the sentry gate to sign me in because the only identification I had was my expired student ID from the last year at Phan Thanh Gian. I apologized profusely for having put him to the trouble, but he told me not to worry, adding with humor that he hadn't had anyone visit him with a student ID in a long time.

The G-5 office looked quite different from the way it did on the day of the party. Everyone was in combat fatigues and was hard at work. I felt a little odd among all these military people, because even though our country's survival depended on its soldiers they were not in general highly regarded — my mother was not the only one who warned her daughter to "stay away from the soldiers."

The men in the main office worked away under a rusty, squeaky ceiling fan that looked like a survivor from the French era, but Captain Thinh's private office at the end of the room had an air conditioner. He seemed a little embarrassed at the special treatment, and insisted that the air conditioner was necessary because his office was also used as a recording studio. Besides, he said, he shared the office with an American correspondent who spent most of the time in the field and came back every now and then to file reports to MACV (Military Assistance Command Viet Nam) in Sai Gon.

Before we entered his office Captain Thinh peered through a glass window, then opened the door. "OK," he said, "the boss says we can come in." The "boss" turned out to be a second lieutenant, as frail as shrine bamboo, and the captain introduced him to me as "Lieutenant Nam, the poet and soul of the 'Voice of the Armed Forces of the Republic of Viet Nam.'" We shook hands and Lieutenant Nam left us alone in the office.

As we sat down, Captain Thinh drew a King Edward cigar from his desk drawer and lit it with a Zippo lighter. I thought how this was my first real encounter with the American style of things, and I looked around. Everything about the room was un-Vietnamese, I thought. I realized that the gray chair I was sitting on must be a product from the United States, and so must the gray steel desk that matched it, the captain's swivel chair, the carpet, and even the in-and-out box on his desk.

Captain Thinh must have read my mind. "It makes you feel like you are in a different world, doesn't it?"

"It's certainly different from my school desk," I said.

"Everything is American except me," he said. "Now, what can I do for you, little lady?"

I knew it was customary to address military personnel by their rank, but I couldn't hear myself doing that, so I decided to call him mister.

"Mr. Thinh, I want to work for the radio program if you have an opening for a news writer," I blurted out.

"Why do you want a job instead of going to school?" He meant go on to college, since I had finished high school.

"Right now I need a job more than an education. I want to help my mother." I told him about the post office's demand for experience and the theaters' requirement of a 2,000-piaster deposit, and he nodded in understanding. "It's a Catch-22, huh?" I must have looked puzzled, because he added, "That's the name of an American novel." Then he told me flatly, "I'm sorry, but we don't hire civilians for that job."

"Lieutenant Phuoc told me the same thing, but that is somebody's rule in Sai Gon. This is IV Corps — your office and your rules, Mr. Thinh."

"Tell me," he asked, "are all the women in Can Tho as persuasive as you?"

"If the Viet Cong let G-5 live long enough in Can Tho, you'll know."

"I want to believe that our future is not in the hands of the Viet Cong, little lady."

"I want to believe that, too, Mr. Thinh."

He asked me how old I was, and I suddenly grew a year older on the spur of the moment: "I'm nineteen."

"Can I believe that nineteen is a correct number?" he asked with a doubtful smile on his face.

That wasn't important, I insisted. What was important was getting the right kind of job. "I can't picture myself selling fish at the morning market or shaving snow cones for kids at elementary school," I said.

Captain Thinh laughed. "I can't picture you doing that either." Then he shook his head slowly. "No, but I can picture you going to school."

"Mr. Thinh, I never had to tell a total stranger that my family is poor, that my family needs my help now, but I am telling you. Of course I would rather be in school. I love school! But I must work to help my mother now." I broke into tears and fled from the office without even saying goodbye.

I knew my writing career had ended before it had even begun. But much to my astonishment Lieutenant Phuoc came around to the house that evening and told me that Captain Thinh wanted me to have dinner with the two of them that night.

I shook my head. "I made a fool of myself this morning in his office."

"I don't think so," Lieutenant Phuoc replied. "I think you made a good impression on him. Why don't you see him tonight."

At the restaurant, Captain Thinh had brought his own bottle of Three Stars cognac and ordered soda water and ice, while I asked for Limonaide, a lemon soda bottled in Can Tho. He didn't even wait for the drinks to be served before breaking the good news: I was going to be hired. I was so excited about the chance to work that I forgot completely about salary — we had never discussed it. Again it seemed that Captain Thinh could read my mind, because he brought up the subject. He was going to try to get me on a special projects payroll, where my salary could be 3,000 piasters a month. That was twice what the girls in the typing pool made, he said. If he couldn't get me the special rating, however, he wanted me to promise him that I would go back to school. I agreed that 1,500 piasters wouldn't be enough to make it worthwhile to quit school, so I made the promise.

When I returned home, I told my mother with great glee that I was "99.9 percent sure" that Captain Thinh would manage to put me on the special payroll. That night, however, I lay on my bed next to Hoa Binh, tossing and turning with anxiety about my decision to go to work. The money would be wonderful, but I worried a little that one day I would regret not having stayed in school. More than that, I had another worry — a fear, really. What would happen if Captain Thinh had the army do a background investigation on me and found out about my connections with the NLF?

Finally, I decided that the only way to eliminate the uncertainty and the fear of discovery was to eliminate the risk of being found out: I resolved to tell Captain Thinh about my background myself, rather than let army intelligence throw a cold, harsh report on his desk as they had done to my late friend Phong.

Captain Thinh came to the cafe at the tennis club the next day as I had asked. I had arrived about twenty minutes early and had coached myself over and over on how to tell him about myself. I rehearsed the "right words" that would convince him that I had not been sent to him by the Viet Cong or my father's people, and I thought sure I could do it. When he came, however, I was speechless. He sat and sipped his beer while I fidgeted in my seat, breaking toothpicks and saying nothing. Then suddenly I forgot everything I had planned and blurted out the simple truth.

"I thought I should tell you that my father is in North Viet Nam, as is my whole family except my mother, my sisters, my brother, and myself, but we have nothing to do with the Communists or the Front, and I thought you should know before you hire me, Mr. Thinh!"

He puffed on a cigar and looked at me for a moment. Then, calmly and quietly, he said, "We have one thing in common from the start. I have two younger brothers who are officers in the North Vietnamese army." Thinh was one of 800,000 North Vietnamese who went south in 1954. His two brothers remained in the North.

He extended his hand, and I felt as if he had thrown me a life preserver. As I breathed a sigh of relief, Captain Thinh told me he would talk to army intelligence when the time came. "We don't show them the scars on our backs," he said, letting me know he would be discreet and choose an appropriate time.

He told me I could start work anytime, and since it was Thursday I decided to wait until Monday so I could spend one last long weekend of summer vacation with my friends before becoming a working woman. He asked me what I would do that weekend, and I told him I had already planned it in my head: "My friends and I will race across the Bassac River." He remarked that swimming in the river was an odd pursuit for a girl who had just a few days ago sworn that she was nineteen years old. "My mother doesn't like it, either," I said, "but I grew up in the Mekong Delta and the river is my cradle. There is nothing unfeminine about swimming in the river at all."

The captain turned a bit more serious and asked me how I felt about my father's role with the NLF.

"I am confused," I admitted. "When I witness the wrongdoing by the Viet Cong, I believe that my father would not approve of them, but then again my father is the most loyal person I have ever known."

"Do you think of him often?"

"As often as my heart beats."

"Have you heard from him since he left?"

"Only by relayed messages, and I doubt very much if the messages really come from him."

"Can I ask you a personal question?" Captain Thinh said, looking at me intently. I nodded. "Do you still love him?"

I couldn't speak my answer, but tears began to run down my face. We sat in silence, I don't know how long, before I pulled myself together and said, honestly and a bit formally, "I hope I won't be too big of a burden to you, Mr. Thinh."

"Look, little lady, it seems to me that you have enough to worry about for your age," he reassured me. "Let me worry about the intelligence people."

I felt a great release of pressure from the man I would work under in the ARVN, but it still left a family full of outspoken people with mixed alliances. My aunt, mother, and cousins would always believe that I worked as a clerk for the program, which is what I told them. Only Hai Van knew exactly what I did. He was proud of me when he occasionally listened to the radio.

Chapter 10

One of the girls at my mother's shop made me a new *ao dai* to wear to my new job. It was the first printed *ao dai* I had ever owned — my school uniforms were all white and I had had one sky-blue *ao dai* for holidays.

The news team at G-5 consisted of the editor-in-chief, Captain Thinh; the editor, Lieutenant Nguyen Nam; three civilian typists; and an announcer, a gorgeous twenty-two-year-old woman who turned heads every time she walked from the gate to our office.

I was assigned to work as a reporter with Lieutenant Nam, and we shared a wide desk, facing each other. The first week all I did was read the army journals he gave me, paying special attention to the articles he had marked with a red X. These were commentaries written by army commanders and the director of psychological warfare; it was Lieutenant Nam's way of letting me get used to the style and content of army technical propaganda writing. The material was awfully dry, but I digested it all.

I called Lieutenant Nam "mister," too, even though he didn't like it much. We didn't get along wonderfully at first. He was the son of a mandarin from the North and had come south with more than 800,000 other refugees after the Communists took control in his home area. I never knew much about what had happened in his past, but he didn't seem to like women — or at least he treated them very rudely. By contrast, he would sometimes show me poems he wrote in which he expressed beautiful thoughts about women.

Nam chain-smoked Camels while I inhaled the fumes. After about a week he asked me if the smoke bothered me and I said, "Just don't change your brand and then I'll be fine." From that day on he was a little nicer to me, and he gradually began talking to me about the techniques and rules for writing the news. I wasn't allowed to write anything for actual use, but I began to practice by taking rough field reports and trying to turn them into finished articles. Lieutenant Nam read the first few attempts, crumpled them up, and tossed them into a wastebasket across the room.

One day after he had finished his final touches on the radio program, he asked me to read over it from the opening to the end of his commentary. When I finished, he told me to hand it to Miss Thao, the beautiful announcer. From that day on it became a routine, and gradually I began to learn how the reports should sound. I kept writing my practice versions, and I began to notice that Lieutenant Nam was not tossing them into the wastebasket any more. He spent time on them, correcting them with his red ballpoint pen and filing them away in a folder. About a week later, after I'd been there about three months, he turned his work over to the technicians, picked up the folder, and asked me to go to the cafeteria to have a cup of coffee with him. I knew the time had come for the "verdict" on my tryout as a writer.

His criticism was sharp, professional, and legitimate. My biggest problem, he said, was that I didn't take sides strongly enough. "If you are not prejudiced, then try to become prejudiced when you tell millions of people out there about our brave men at war. Even if you don't hate the Viet Cong, you must still lead people to that trail and show them their savage enemies. Be more convincing, and don't forget that your listeners are mostly soldiers. Make them feel needed, important. In this way you can bridge the gap between the army and the people."

He went on. "You can write, all you have to remember is that you are not a news reporter, you are a propaganda cadre. The field reporters furnish you with statistics, and they become your tools. You use them to boost the troops' morale, to discourage the enemies and make them disillusioned. You can do wonders with your imagination. Your pen is another weapon to fight this war."

"You mean to win this war, Mr. Nam!"

"You've got it!" He turned a bit contemplative. "Sometimes I get used to this old war like a favorite old shirt or a living companion — she is so bad but I can't do without her." He shook his head. "I don't know what I'll do when the war is over."

"Publish your poems, write novels," I suggested. "Live a good life!"

"My poems are personal, and I write better when I am depressed. Besides, what is a good life?"

"A good life is life without flares in the sky at night, no rockets, no more bombs, no more assassins, no more land mines. I lost my best friend and I still don't know exactly how he died or what happened when the mine exploded."

"This war will never end!" Lieutenant Nam spat out the words.

"You owe it to the South to give her hope and optimism," I told him. "You left the North because you hoped the South would be a better place. And it is better, because the Communists are not here yet." I realized that it was a good thing Nam never put his true feelings into his work, which was supposed to be inspiring and optimistic. Once, much later, I asked him about the two different Mr. Nams I saw, and he said, "In your early days here I told you that propaganda doesn't come from the heart, it is the work of the mind."

As I sat outside the recording room and listened to Miss Thao reading the words I had written, I felt a tremendous sense of pride and security that I could have such a job and be able to do it well. My first payday came two months after the day I started working — there had been a delay because of the problem of getting me onto the special-projects payroll — but somehow by that time the salary didn't seem as important as the work itself. Even though I had originally sought a job because my family needed the money, now I really enjoyed what I was doing.

I brought home 6,000 piasters on that first payday and spread it on the table in front of my mother. "It's all yours, Mom," I beamed. She put the money away in the sewing machine drawer and thanked me, but she didn't seem as happy as I had expected. She still felt guilty that her daughter passed up college to help out, despite my efforts to convince her that I loved my job and had no regrets about my decision.

— — —

An urgent message arrived at G-5 around midday from the military hospital in Can Tho. Casualties from nearby fighting had been heavy, and they were running low on supplies of blood. Dr. Hieu, the medical director, had sent a teletype appeal to all the military bases for donors, stressing the critical need. I decided to volunteer, so I took the afternoon off and rushed to the hospital.

An enormous crowd had gathered around the gate of the hospital — not a sudden crush of blood donors, but the usual mass of relatives of the men who had been wounded in the military operations. Huge throngs of women, children, and old folks were sitting on the ground or resting against the wall or the trees outside the hospital, waiting for visiting hours. Most of these people had not seen their soldier-relatives for months, and now that the men had been wounded the hospital became a place for reunions, though often tragic ones.

When I said I had come to give blood, a guard directed me to a room inside where four other people were lined up to make their donations. A nurse drew blood from their arms while I waited my turn and looked around uncomfortably. Just being in the hospital made me feel ill; I decided that if I ever got sick I wouldn't go there because I would never get well.

The first nurse took the bottles of blood from the first four people and hurried out of the room. A second nurse entered, smiled at me, and asked if I knew my blood type. I had never been sick or injured, so I had never had a chance to find out. I shook my head. "Nobody knows his blood type!" she complained.

"I know my blood is one-half Mongolian, one-half Chinese, and 100 percent Vietnamese," I told her. "Does that help?"

"In that case, sit down," she ordered, and she stuck me with the needle and took a sample to test the type.

It turned out to be O positive, and the nurse said there was a soldier who was waiting for just that type. As she began draining my blood into a bottle, she heaved a deep sigh and said, "It has been nothing but chaos in this place. I didn't get to sleep at all last night." Innocently, I asked why not. "Why not?" she snapped. "We are short of everything, from doctors to blood to hospital beds." She finished and left without even taking the rubber band off my arm, hurrying down the corridor with my blood in a stainless steel box.

That evening I came back to the hospital. I had become curious to know what had happened to the soldier who had received my blood, so I went to the blood-donor room and found the same nurse still there. She told me the room number of the soldier, and I went off to find his ward. When I entered the room, I saw a blood-stained sheet covering the soldier's body from head to toe. I was too late to meet the man who had my blood.

A woman sat sobbing at the corner of the bed, her hands covering her face and her shoulders shaking. I wanted to leave, but I felt sorry for her because she was all alone. I put my hand on her shoulder and she looked up.

"Are you his friend?" she asked, wiping her tears with the corner of her *ao dai*.

"I just came to see how he was doing."

She sobbed again. "How do you know my son?"

"I didn't know him. This afternoon the nurse told me he would receive my blood."

The mother got up and walked to the top of the bed; she lifted the sheet and caressed the hair of her dead son. I didn't have the courage to look at him. I just said, "I want to share your sorrow."

"If my husband were here they would have tried harder to save my son," she wailed. "He had just turned twenty. Oh, God, why my son, my only son?" I didn't have an answer for her.

The mother told me that her husband was still at the front near Chuong Thien. He was heading the operation in which their son had been killed.

Two men dressed in hospital green came in then with a stretcher, and they lifted the young soldier's body onto it and took it out of the ward. The mother followed them, one hand held out to help support the stretcher. Her crying nearly tore me to pieces.

I stood there for a moment and touched the cold metal frame of the empty bed. A nurse came in and changed the sheets, and while she worked silently I heard a strange moan from a nearby bed, one I hadn't even noticed until then. There was a man in a cast from his head to his waist; a green sheet covered the lower half of his body. I moved closer to his bed, and noticed there were holes in the cast for his eyes, mouth, and nose. "How are you feeling?" I asked the faceless figure.

"Is he gone? The young kid?" he asked.

"Yes."

"Fuck the Viet Cong SOB's, fuck my destiny," he groaned in a muffled voice. He swung one free arm and pounded violently on the steel bed.

"You will get well," I said to him, not knowing anything else to say.

"Are you blind?" he roared back. "My legs are blown off, my neck is in a cast — how can I get well?" His voice was a horrible mixture of bitterness and raw pain.

There was nothing I could say, and in my embarrassment I took a few steps backward and hurried out of the ward. A few meters down the hall there was a small chapel, its door open. I walked in, although I didn't know what to say to God, either. "A young man died, and another man's world has been shattered," I whispered. "Perhaps you are as helpless as I am, God. My grandfather once told me that you love your children but you don't interfere. If that's true, then what can you do, God?"

— — —

My worries shrank to nothingness on the day the news arrived that shattered our family: Our cousin Yvonne had been caught and arrested by the intelligence forces of South Viet Nam.

Her sisters knew that she was being questioned at a local Cong An jail, but they were instructed by the Front not to try to visit her. We could only sit by helplessly as she went to court on countless charges of "criminal acts," since we were forbidden as well from attending the trial. Alone before her prosecutors, Yvonne was sentenced to five years in prison.

Five years! For all our differences in our beliefs, my heart went out to her when I tried to imagine her sitting for five years in a dark, dank prison. I tried to conceive how long the sentence was in terms I could understand: The whole time I had spent in elementary school was five years, my stay in high school was five years, it was 1,825 days, 43,800 hours, more than 2 1/2 million minutes. My God! I could not imagine what a person could do for all those days, hours, minutes in a cell. And what might they continue to do to her in her imprisonment? I hoped the interrogation had ended by now for my Viet Cong cousin.

One day a man came to our shop and hand-delivered a letter to my mother. We all recognized Yvonne's handwriting and gathered around to read what she had written: "To my family. As you read this letter I may well be on my way to Con Son Island. Don't worry about me. Don't visit me. I will not accept any presents. Take good care of yourselves." Ironically, as a revolutionary, Yvonne's father, who was opposed to the French, was sent to Con Son prison in 1940 for five years.

I knew that Yvonne was thinking of our safety when she told us not to visit her, but I couldn't bear to let her go off to Con Son Island without a single word of goodbye from her family. The blood in our veins was the same, for she was my uncle's daughter, and I resolved to go to the Can Tho main prison, where she was being held before final transfer to Con Son. I didn't tell my mother, but went off on my own with a package containing a few things I thought she might need: two hand towels, a bottle of aspirin (to help with colds, because she would be sleeping on a bare concrete floor), a few spools of thread and some needles to mend her clothes, and two bottles of eyedrops for the itching she got from an allergy.

It was easy to get permission from the prison officials for the visit, but it wasn't easy to see Yvonne. The guard came back to the waiting room and told me, "She said she doesn't know you, she doesn't have any relatives." I thought there had been a mistake, and begged him to go back and tell her I was her cousin. He was kind enough to make another trip into the cellblock, but again he brought back only her refusal to see anyone. My effort to reach out to her was unsuccessful.

No one in the family saw her again until she completed her sentence five years later. When she was released, the prison officials said she had been a "model" prisoner with a record of excellent behavior. They didn't realize that she had spent the time making connections with other political prisoners in Con Son, and together they had worked to recruit common criminals to join the "struggle movement" once they got out. Like her father, when Yvonne stepped out into the free air, she was stronger, more mature, and even more dedicated to her cause. She walked home to her sister Yen's house on Ngo Quyen Boulevard in Can Tho, then walked straight back into the underground to resume her work.

Yvonne's imprisonment had even deeper effects on me. My heart was no longer in the work of writing propaganda for the radio program, and apparently it showed. Lieutenant Nam looked at my scripts and complained, "Are you in love or out of love? Your writing is going downhill!" For a time I simply gave up trying to write editorials; luckily Lieutenant Nam didn't mind, because there was nothing he liked better and he was happy to take up the slack.

A short time later, Captain Thinh was promoted to major. Before we had finished celebrating the good news, however, we were all shocked to hear that he was being transferred back to Sai Gon. We shouldn't have been surprised, but because he was such a good boss we hated to lose him. As Lieutenant Nam said, "There is no other boss like Captain Thinh, and you just have to take what the army gives you."

I hadn't bargained for what the army gave us next, however. The new bureau chief, Captain Nguyen Van Chanh, was more a poet than a bureau chief or even a soldier, for that matter. I didn't get to know him well, however, because he seemed to avoid me as much as possible. He seldom talked to me except for the minimum conversation necessary for our work, and I had no idea why.

Captain Thinh — now Major Thinh — happened to come back to Can Tho on a temporary assignment, and I asked him if he knew why his replacement was so cold toward me. He did. He told me he had had to tell Captain Chanh about my background, and even though he had assured him I was a genuine nationalist, Chanh was unconvinced. He saw me as a threat, and that was why he wouldn't have anything to do with me. In fact, if it weren't for Major Thinh's authority, he wouldn't have allowed me to stay on at G-5 at all.

If Chanh had been the only person concerned about my background, I wouldn't have had too much to worry about, except for an unfortunate tension in the office. But there were others with doubts — people who could make trouble far worse than unhappy relationships with coworkers. One morning I came to work and found a message on my desk: I was to report to G-2 (intelligence) "at once."

G-2 was just across the base driveway from my office, so I hurried there and was greeted by a second lieutenant named Chuong. He asked me to be seated, and then went back to reading a thick file on his desk while I waited for at least twenty minutes, drawing on all my mother's teaching of patience to calm my fears about what this summons could mean. I had no way of knowing that I was about to endure one of the most terrifying episodes of my young life.

When the lieutenant finally looked up at me, his face was cold and impersonal.

"Tell me, miss, who is Senator Dang Van Quang?"

"Mr. Dang Van Quang is my father, Lieutenant."

"Are you sure?"

"I don't understand your question."

"Your birth certificate reads 'Father: Unknown,'" he said.

"Mr. Dang Van Quang is my father," I repeated.

"Dang Van Khoi, what is he to you?"

"He is my oldest brother."

Lieutenant Chuong handed me a sheet of paper and a pencil. "I want you to write down their mailing addresses," he ordered. I ignored the paper and pencil and just shook my head. "I don't have their mailing addresses, Lieutenant."

He stiffened in his chair and shouted at me: "You are lying to me!"

"Lieutenant, that is a rather harsh accusation."

"Answer my question, and put it in writing," he said angrily, slamming the paper and pencil down in front of me.

My mind flashed back for a moment to a similar scene I had once witnessed, when a security man who worked for my father had interrogated a farm worker who was suspected of being an informant for the French. I was only five and Hai Van was two, and we were both being fed breakfast by our nanny. She said to us, "Hurry up and eat and we will go see the *viet gian* (traitor)!" We gobbled our food and she took us to watch as the farm worker was questioned by my father's men.

There is a saying: "There will be a time when the fish eats the ant, and there will be a time when the ant eats the fish." Well, I thought, perhaps my father was a fish, and now, because I was his daughter, it was my turn to be eaten by the "ant" who sat before me in a lieutenant's uniform. I decided to get control of myself and "cooperate" with my interrogator.

"I don't have my father's or my brother's address," I told him. "I wish I did."

"Did they tell you to lie to government officials?" he asked.

"Who are 'they'?"

"The Viet Cong, the Red imperialists' lackeys."

I bit my lip to suppress a smile at hearing him use the same terminology about the Russians that was used not twenty kilometers away by the Viet Cong when they referred to the Americans.

"Answer me!" he shouted when I hesitated.

"I am not being dictated to by anyone. As a matter of fact, I defy the people you have just mentioned."

"Lie! Don't you lie to me! When was the last time you heard from your father and brother?"

I counted on my fingers, the bad habit of a lifelong poor student of mathematics: 1955, 1956, 1957. . . . "It was nine years ago, Lieutenant."

"How many letters have you received from them?"

"None."

"Are you sure?"

"I am sure."

"Doesn't your father love you or your mother since he joined the Communist party?" he asked, trying a different tack in hopes of shaking my story.

He shook me all right. I was furious, my face reddening. I wanted to call him a son of a bitch, but I knew better than to say it — he would probably throw me into a dark box somewhere and I would never see my mother again either. I gripped the sides of my chair and replied as calmly as I could, "I like to believe that he wrote to us but the letters got rained on and they never got here."

"Do you love your father?"

I smiled, and for the first time looked the officer in the eye. "Yes. I love my father very much."

"Even though he never wrote to you and your mother for nine years? Other people who have family members in Ha Noi have been getting letters from their loved ones, you know."

"They are luckier than I," I said quietly.

Lieutenant Chuong went for the jugular vein. "From what I read here, your father is only fifty-five years old, young enough, powerful enough, and perhaps popular enough to have many women in line waiting for him. You know what I mean, don't you, Miss?"

"You are insulting my family!" I almost screamed.

"Please answer my question. Do you think there are other women in your father's life?"

"What do you want to hear from me?" I demanded.

"You are his darling daughter. You must be his follower, too, aren't you?"

"I am proud of my father, but I am not his follower."

"That makes you a disobedient daughter."

"I've been told the same thing by people who have tried to force me to 'follow in your father's footsteps.'"

"And why don't you follow in his footsteps?"

"I can give him an arm, a leg, or any part of my body, but I'll never give my soul to the Communists, even to please my father."

"You are a very good liar. Tell me who ordered you to get this job." He walked around the desk, closer to where I sat, and the cologne he reeked of bothered me almost more than his arrogant attitude. "I don't take orders, Lieutenant. I've never been trained to take orders."

Lieutenant Chuong stepped back to his desk, picked up a stack of photographs, and threw them in front of me. "Look at them. Tell me who they are!"

There were pictures of me riding on buses and Lambrettas on my way to and from Long Thanh. There was a photo of me with a boy I used to date, whose brother was a high-ranking army officer. I recognized the guava orchard where he and I went with six other kids on the last day of our school year in 1963. I told the officer this, telling him the names of my classmates in the pictures, but that wasn't what he wanted. He was far more interested in knowing the names of the other people on the buses and Lambrettas. I had no idea who they were — as far as I knew, they were just innocent passengers like me — but he didn't believe me. His people had spotted me with those same passengers at every stop and on every change from one vehicle to another; therefore there must be some connection, he insisted.

Abruptly, Lieutenant Chuong cut off the "interview" and told me to go back to work. I returned to my office and spent a nervous day and then a sleepless night at home. Somehow, I just knew that I hadn't seen the last of him.

Sure enough, the very next morning I was summoned to the G-2 office again. Lieutenant Chuong got out his stack of photographs and started to pump me for information about the passengers once more.

This went on for three more hours, then suddenly he got up from the desk and pronounced the meeting over. "We shall meet again," he said menacingly, "I don't know when." As horrible as it was, I almost wished the questioning would continue so we could get it over with. In the next few days I couldn't eat or sleep, and I didn't even like being alone because I was gripped with a feeling of helplessness over this interrogation. A horrifying thought came to my mind: What if Lieutenant Chuong's awful questions were just the beginning? What if they had far worse in store for me? Would they hang me upside down and pour water in my nose? Would they shoot me in the leg and watch me bleed? Or worse yet, put me in a room with snakes! I had heard from a classmate that such techniques were actually used — her father was a Cong An, and interrogating prisoners was his job.

It was a terrible burden, but I couldn't ask my mother to share it. She had enough to worry about already, with five students to teach, a tableful of clothes to be made each week, the house payment, utilities, and other bills. On top of that, Dr. Ngoc had told her she had developed an ulcer — no wonder, with all that weighing on her — and she was feeling ill more and more often. The last thing she needed was to learn that an intelligence officer was battering hell out of her daughter's mind.

I turned to my diary as something of a release, and wrote this in its pages: "This land belongs to me and those who love her, as the sun belongs to the earth and the rice fields belong to the calloused hands of the farmers. The fact that I belong here shall not be denied."

A few days later I was again seated in front of Lieutenant Chuong's desk. The officer was tense, more formal than before, and somewhat more abrupt. Curiously, he spoke to me in the Northern dialect, whereas he had used the Southern style of speech in the first two sessions. "Did you talk to your mother about our meetings here yet?" he began.

"No, there is no need for that," I replied.

He seemed to be searching his mind for a moment. "All of the men in your family joined the Communists. There are only women and children in your family now, is that correct?"

"There will be a man in my family when my little brother grows up, Lieutenant." For some reason I felt cocky when I answered.

"What makes you so sure of that?" He wrinkled his face in an expression of disrespect for me.

"Because I know who we are. Only you try to doubt us. Perhaps the Communists wish that every child born to a Communist father would turn out like he was stamped from a mold, but they will be disappointed in my case."

"Where is your little brother?" he asked.

"He lives with my sisters in Sai Gon."

And, to my surprise, that was all for the third session. I returned to my office, to the stares of my coworkers. They knew I had been to G-2, and so most of them were afraid to speak to me.

One day Lieutenant Phuoc, the oldest friend I had in G-5, took me to the cafeteria for a cup of coffee. We talked about my problem with the intelligence officer, and he bravely offered to help in any way he could. "No," I said quickly. "You helped me get this job, and you taught me how to get along with soldiers and how to follow the chain of command. You are not going to stick your neck out for me this time, Phuoc."

He offered me one piece of advice about dealing with Lieutenant Chuong: "Don't put your hand in the tiger's mouth." I didn't tell him, but I thought that was a bit funny. I didn't see Lieutenant Chuong as being like a tiger at all, but more like a boil on my rear.

Still, the office he represented and the authority he had over me were a genuine threat, and I couldn't find any peace of mind while I was at his mercy. One night I couldn't sleep, and when I got up and walked through the house I found my mother still up, working at her sewing table. My resolve to protect her from my problem dissolved in a weak moment, and I told her about the interrogations.

I was surprised at her reaction, because I guess I had forgotten how strong and how logical she was. She didn't panic, or seem frightened or worried at all. After listening to my long story she just said, "Talk to people who want to believe you, don't talk to people who have already accused you. Find out the name of his boss. Not his immediate boss, but the highest boss, the director of army intelligence in Can Tho. He might be in a position to listen to you."

"What do you mean?" I asked her.

"A lieutenant wants to advance to a captain, but a director who is already comfortable with his position doesn't have to lie or catch Viet Cong to prove his talent. Go to him. If you don't, I will."

I was buoyed by my mother's courage, and the first thing the next morning I found out what I needed to know from Lieutenant Phuoc: The director of the office of army security in Can Tho was Captain Tran Duy Binh. I knew nothing else about him, except that he was a devout Catholic, a family man, and a refugee from Ha Noi, but I made plans to visit him as soon as possible.

The receptionist at the director's office, a man in civilian clothes, asked me to write down my name and my reason for wanting to see Captain Binh. I signed myself in as "Tran Ngoc Yung, daughter of Mr. Dang Van Quang," and handed back the logbook, saying, "My purpose is a classified matter. I can't write it down." The man said nothing, but took the paper into the office behind him. A moment later he came out and said, "The captain asks you to come in, Miss."

Captain Binh was about thirty-three, with his dark hair neatly combed and his army fatigues sharply creased, unlike most other men's uniforms. There was an aroma of expensive foreign-made cologne and imported tobacco in his office. He held his pipe in one hand and extended the other to me as I entered. His eyes looked at me with a powerful gaze, but he had a friendly smile. After the pleasantries were over, I told him why I had come.

"I believe you are aware of the investigation being conducted on me," I said.

"I haven't received the report yet," he replied.

"It is more than a simple background investigation, Captain. The way G-2 is conducting this investigation has forced me to come to see you today."

"I was informed by Lieutenant Chuong that you would be asked to answer a few questions concerning your father," he said.

"He is not interested in my father. He is interested in accusing me of being a spy! I don't think he is doing his job correctly, sir."

Captain Binh seemed disturbed. Perhaps my candor was a surprise to someone who is surrounded by his men but never has much contact with outsiders. I pressed on with my complaint.

"Captain, this is my home, my birthplace. I belong here, and I expect this government to honor my rights. You owe it to yourself and to my family to find out the truth about us in a better way, not from accusations and harassment by people like Lieutenant Chuong."

"Is Tran Thi To Loan related to you?" Captain Binh asked.

He was speaking of Yvonne. "She is my cousin."

"I met her here after her arrest. She is a courageous young woman."

"She was sent to Con Son prison."

"If she would cooperate, her sentence would be lighter and she might not have to go to Con Son at all," he said. "But she never breathed a word throughout her interrogation."

"It is not easy for me to convince you which side I am on, with the history of my family and the present activities that my cousins are involved in, but I ask you to help me with this problem."

Captain Binh listened carefully, his hands folded on the marble top of his desk. He was calm, while I was a bundle of nerves sitting in front of this mighty authority — the man who had put my cousin in prison for five years.

He looked at me. "Do you like the job at G-5?"

"Yes, I do."

"Do you have any reservations about it since your cousin got arrested?"

"My heart went out to her, but knowing Yvonne, going to prison was just another obstacle to overcome in reaching her goal. But she's To Loan and I'm me!"

He smiled and ended our discussion. "I'll talk to Lieutenant Chuong about this little problem," he promised.

I thanked him again as he walked me to the front of his office, and as I left the gate of the headquarters complex I thought I could fly! I rushed home and told my mother about the talk, and about Captain Binh; he had changed my idea of intelligence officers, because I had thought all of them were monsters with awesome fangs.

The next morning when I came to work, Lieutenant Nam handed me a message: "Report to Lieutenant Chuong's office at once," it said, a telephone message in Captain Chanh's handwriting. Emboldened by my certainty that Captain Binh had rescued me, I folded the message into a paper airplane and sailed it into a trash can across the room. Lieutenant Nam told me to hurry to G-2, saying that he would take over my report for me, but I sat down at my desk and started writing. He was astonished. "The son of God wants you in his office right now!" he urged.

"The daughter of God must work now," I said. "He can wait." Lieutenant Nam shook his head in bewilderment and went back to his work.

Everyone expected all hell to break loose, but nothing happened. No one came to get me, no one called to complain, and I was never interrogated by Lieutenant Chuong again. In fact, when I saw him in the cafeteria a few days later he got up and left as soon as he noticed me. Phuoc and I looked at each other, and I told him, "It's too early to drink, or I'd buy you a beer to celebrate my victory!"

Chapter 11

It was two o'clock in the morning, and it seemed I had been running through the pitch-dark streets forever looking for a pedicab that could take my mother to the hospital. It was another ulcer attack, but this one was far more serious than the others. The pain in her stomach was excruciating, and the alkaline drugs the doctor had prescribed for her seemed to have no effect.

At the hospital I wasn't allowed to go into the treatment room with her; I stood outside the door and listened to her moaning in distress. I felt so help-less, and for the first time I was really upset that my father wasn't there when she needed him. He would have known what to do; I remembered when I was five years old I had sliced a cut so deep in my finger that the fat had showed through, but I didn't even cry because he had dressed the cut and sealed it with a kiss. "It will make the scar less visible," he had assured me.

I paced the hallway or sat on the floor for the longest time, in a state of near panic. Finally they wheeled her out of the room on a long rolling bed. I could only see her hand, and it was pale and motionless; I grabbed hold of it and called out, "Mom, talk to me!" She could manage only a weak, tortured groan. The attendants rolled her into another room, where two nurses work-ing like machines lifted her quickly from the cart and swung her onto a bed. Before leaving us alone, one of them showed me a switch on the wall and instructed me, "Push that button if your mother is in great pain." I thought about the terrible agony she was already feeling and prayed to God that I would never have to push that button.

I sat on the edge of the bed and could see how tired she looked. She moved her head slightly and muttered something I couldn't quite hear. "Mom, how do you feel?" I asked.

"I am afraid . . ." she moaned.

At that moment I felt as if my last supporting pillar had been knocked from beneath me. My mother had always made me feel strong and safe and had told me not to be afraid of anything. Now she lay in a hospital bed, pained by her illness and fearful of her fate.

"Send a telegram to Hai Van and your sisters, they should know," she whispered to me. Kim and Cuong had gotten an apartment in Sai Gon, working at a bank for an undercover Viet Cong (one comrade taking care of another comrade's children). My mother sent Hai Van to live with them because the Viet Cong continued to press him to join the militia in a VC-controlled area.

"Mom, you have to get well. I'll get advance pay, we'll have money for the best care for you."

Her eyes still closed, she searched blindly for my other hand. "Look after the shop," she told me.

"Don't worry about the shop. I'll take care of the business and the other kids."

Suddenly she went rigid and grimaced at another stab of pain. I pushed the button frantically, and after a few minutes the nurse came in and checked my mother's pulse. She told me not to worry, that everything would be all right and the doctor would see her in the morning. The clock on the wall pointed to 6:15 A.M.

After a while she mercifully fell asleep, and I sat on the bed near her feet and thought about what my grandfather had said to my brother and me when he grew very old: "You take good care of your mother for me." We promised him we would, but now I talked to his spirit and told him, "Granddad, right now only God can help her." My father had given all of us children the same assignment, and Khoi had told Kim and Cuong that as the oldest they had a special responsibility to "take care of Mother for me until I get home."

Toward daylight, she seemed to be resting more or less comfortably, so I decided to go to the administration office to fill out the papers for her admission. Before I left, I put my hand near her nose just to be sure I could feel her breath, warm on the back of my hand.

I had not lived long, nor done many important and grownup things, but I had already learned that in a country like mine, a country at war, power was the key to opening many doors. I remembered that one of my mother's old roommates at the Nhu Van home economics school had grown up to become head nurse at the Can Tho hospital. When you are sick, I knew, having a friend who is head nurse can be more valuable than having a friend who is president of the country. I went directly to her office and introduced myself and told her about my mother; from that moment on I didn't have to worry about anything else at the hospital except my mother's health. The head nurse, Mrs. Tam Quan, took care of the paperwork and arranged for the best doctor to treat her and saw to every detail.

Then I left for the telegraph office, and as usual a telegram meant bad news. I have sent three telegrams to my sisters in my whole life: one said, "Granddad died. Come home"; the second was "Grandmother is dying. Come home quick"; and the last read, "Mom is seriously ill. We need you here." For my sisters in those days, no news was truly good news.

Kim, Cuong, and Hai Van arrived home on the following afternoon. I was so grateful for their presence; I had thought I would go crazy being there by myself, terrified at the prospect of losing Mom. Hoa Binh had been asking me over and over to take her and Minh Tam to the hospital to visit Mom, but I refused because I didn't want them to see her sick; that just made both of them suspect that she was already dead. If there is a law saying big sisters must be strong and supportive, I broke it a thousand times in those two days, because each time the little girls cried, I cried, too. Each time they asked "Is Mom going to die?" I almost lost my breath.

Kim and Cuong's return put things almost in order again. Hoa Binh left me alone and followed after Kim, who had always been her idol. Cuong was very good with Tam and was able to keep her mind off Mother's being sick. I went back to the hospital and rented a cot so I could sleep next to her. The doctor kept her on the critical list, and more tests were being done.

On the fourth night in the hospital, my mother was sleeping better than any other night. I was sound asleep next to her when she reached over and woke me up.

"The Virgin Mary told me that I'll get well," she said to me with a peaceful smile on her face. "She put her hand on my stomach, and I felt the pain go away." As she talked, she looked up on the wall where there was a portrait of Mary I hadn't noticed before.

"I hope your dream is real, Mom," I said sleepily.

"It wasn't a dream; it was real."

I left her very early that morning, ran down the spiral staircase of the hospital, and took a pedicab to get home quickly to report her improvement to the family. I especially wanted to tell Kim and Cuong what Mom had said. They had long been believers in the Virgin Mary, and I knew as soon as I told them they would say "Hail Mary!" which they did.

The doctor who was taking care of my mother told us her recovery was a "miracle," and was really puzzled by the good results of her tests. We took her home two days after that. Before we left the room, she tried to reach up to touch the portrait of Mary high on the wall, and said to it, "Thank you, thank you, Mother." Kim and Cuong, looking on with awestruck faces, made the sign of the cross in unison.

— — —

My older sisters and Hai Van stayed for about a week after Mother's recovery, and for the first time they began to understand how hard she was having to struggle to raise the rest of us, to run her shop, to meet the mortgage payments, and to handle all the other bills. Kim and Cuong thought the rest of the family should move to Sai Gon with them, where we could all pool our money and live together with less stress and strain, and we talked about it for a long time.

My own mind was divided on the question. I knew that we would have financial advantages if the family moved, but I also knew that I had come to think of Can Tho as the place I belonged. I had become good at my work, and I had finally gotten out from under the watchful eyes of both Left and Right; I was making it, I felt. Still, even though I had grown enough feathers to fly free from the nest, my mother was bound there by the needs of my younger sisters and the demands of making ends meet. We didn't come to any resolution before Kim and Cuong and Hai Van returned to Sai Gon, but Mother promised to give the idea serious thought.

I also had to admit a more personal element in my reluctance to leave Can Tho. There was a boy, a very special boy. I wasn't in love with him, exactly, but we had cared for each other, and recently our relationship had been torn by hurt feelings, resentment, and perhaps guilt — and I just didn't want to leave it that way.

Nguyen Viet Thanh had come to Can Tho from the Sai Gon area, looking for a place of refuge from Communist assaults on his village and a chance to study for his baccalaureate. He and his sister lived with his cousin Giao, and I had met him through her. At twenty, he was just two years older than I, but I was hugely impressed by his knowledge of the world, his sophistication and polish. My mother liked him, perhaps more than I did; he was my only male friend who could come to the house anytime and always be welcomed by her.

The more I knew him, the more I realized how complex he was — sensitive, somewhat insecure, usually keeping his feelings to himself. He was also the only friend I had who wouldn't settle for my short answers to questions about where my father was. "My parents don't live together," I told him first, but then he asked me, "Do you see your father often?" and I had to tell him that I didn't see him at all. His own parents had died "a long, long time ago," he told me, and he continued to be curious about my father. Neither of us could have known that the answer to his innocent questions would finally shatter our friendship.

152 · Yung Krall

The break came on what had started as a wonderful day. We had gone fishing with a group of friends and Thanh was sitting on a small dock watching me reel in several fish, one after another. "You must have been taught by a fisherman," he said, pointing to my generous catch. I laughed and told him that my father was a fisherman in Ca Mau. Thanh shook his head as if he didn't believe me, and then for some reason — I guess because we had become such close friends — I told him the truth: "My dad went to Ha Noi in 1954."

Thanh looked startled, then suddenly hopped to his feet and strode off down the dirt road alone. My other friends looked at me, puzzled. Giao asked, joking, "Did you say no to him?" It was clear to me that I had said something more serious than "no," and I rushed after him to find out what had upset him.

He stopped and waited for me, and when I reached him there were tears behind his glasses. We walked along the river bank, away from the others, and I told him I wanted to apologize if I had said or done anything wrong. I quickly learned it would not be that easy.

With great difficulty, Thanh told me the terrible story of his family, an incident that happened about two years before they came to Can Tho. His father had been chief of a small district northeast of Sai Gon, where the Viet Cong operated freely during the night and undercover cadres exerted a lot of control during the day. One day Thanh and his older brother were in the city, and while they were away their father and mother were found dead, victims of a Viet Cong execution. With the bodies the murderers had left a note, pinned to the father's chest by a knife: "Traitors to the Vietnamese people must die." Both had been shot and stabbed while Thanh's ten-year-old sister was forced to watch; when I met her, about a year after the trauma, I thought she was just shy, but Thanh said she had gone insane for a while after the murders and was still very withdrawn.

I went to pieces myself when I heard the tragic story. Somehow I felt responsible, partly guilty for the loss of his parents and the breakup of the family that had followed. "What can I say or do to show you how sorry I am?" I pleaded.

"Just go away, because I don't want to be reminded," he told me.

After work one day I went to his uncle's house and asked the housekeeper to tell him I was there. From outside I heard him say, "Tell her I am studying."

When she returned I didn't wait for her to speak: "It's urgent," I insisted. "Tell Thanh I must see him."

She took me by the hand and led me to his room, then left me by the door. Thanh looked up; without a trace of emotion on his face he said, "I thought you understood when I said I don't want to be reminded."

Even though I felt a responsibility for what happened to his parents, I thought it was unfair for him to tell me that I reminded him of the people who had murdered them. I sat down in a chair quickly without being asked, because I was afraid he might walk me directly out of the room and slam the door behind me.

"Thanh, if I could wipe out a whole battalion of Viet Cong to prove to you that I am not one of them, I would," I began. "Going away, never seeing you again will only make things worse for both of us. I am not the people who killed your parents! You can't find me guilty because of my birthright."

"But you feel guilty, don't you?"

"Yes, I do."

"Then you understand my resentment is legitimate. I am sorry, but I can't help it, Yung."

"You can if you want to," I begged.

"But I am not sure if I want to," he said coldly.

"There are thousands of children of men like my father in this part of the country," I argued. "If you let yourself hate me now, what about another girl who might show up in your life and you find out she is another Communist's daughter?"

"I'll treat her the same way I treat you."

"It might be harder for you," I said. I thought we were just friends, and that the next girl might be a true sweetheart.

"Damn it, what do you think I feel about you?" he said, holding his head with his hands.

I found myself outside the house, walking along the Cai Khe River, turning over confused thoughts in my mind. I asked what Thanh really meant to me, and I wasn't at all sure of the answer. I felt a rush of anger at my father, who had put me in this position, and then I felt angry at myself for blaming him. I realized that democracy was the path I had chosen for myself, by myself. It would have been much simpler if I had just joined the NLF, drawn a circle around its members, and excluded everyone else from friendship. Just pick a cadre, be blessed by the high-ranking members, and together we could go out and kill and kill and kill, carrying out our "Liberation tasks."

After Kim, Cuong, and Hai Van returned to Sai Gon, I went to Thanh's house to make one more attempt to talk to him and patch things up. I didn't see him, but his cousin told me he had volunteered for the army and would be leaving for the officers' training center near Thu Duc as soon as he got his baccalaureate.

Two weeks after that, however, Thanh was picked up by an army recruiter and arrested as a draft-dodger. It was all a mistake; he was supposed to be exempt from the draft because his father had died in the line of duty and his older brother was already in the army reserve, but on the day he was arrested he wasn't carrying proper identification to prove his rights. Of course, he wanted to go into the army, but if he were drafted before he got his degree he would go in as an enlisted man, missing the chance to go to school to become an officer.

At last there was something I could do for Thanh that might demonstrate my concern for him. I thought of my old "savior," Major Thinh. It took me three days to find him and contact him in Sai Gon, and when I finally heard his voice on the telephone I was too panicky to measure my words. I blurted out, "I need another favor from you, Major!" On the other end of the line he laughed and replied in English, "Anything you say, Miss."

I poured out my story about Thanh's predicament, anxious to make sure Major Thinh realized how urgent the matter was — no one had any idea how quickly Thanh might be pressed into the service. My old boss calmed me down and assured me that once again he would help. If I would give him Thanh's full name and his parents' names, he said, he would call a friend at the province chief's office and have him personally take Thanh out of detention. I was flustered and embarrassed to have to admit that I didn't know his parents' names, but Major Thinh was used to my youthful intensity and "dizziness," so he said he would take care of the details.

Elated, I rushed to tell Thanh's uncle the good news. This sweet man was greatly relieved, but then he looked at me and asked, "How much should I pay your friend for his generous help?"

At first I was hurt and a little insulted, but then I realized that we lived in a society where bribery had been a way of life since the French first set foot on our land. I knew that Major Thinh didn't expect any money for helping me, but at the same time I knew that I was in his debt again. When I explained that we didn't have to pay anyone, Thanh's uncle didn't seem to believe me.

Sure enough, Thanh was released from the detention center right away, and a few days after he came home I was invited to his uncle's home for a lavish dinner. I didn't enjoy the evening at all; as the uncle heaped thanks on me in a formal speech, my face turned red and I was terribly embarrassed.

Only Thanh was sensible enough not to say anything to me about his release. But when he walked me home after the dinner, he asked me one question: "Do you believe that an officer could kill more Viet Cong than an ordinary soldier?"

"In many ways, yes," I replied.

"Then it will be my pleasure to kill them for you," he said.

Gradually I came to accept that I would not be able to break through Thanh's wall of bitterness. With that prospect gone, I finally decided that moving to Sai Gon would probably be the best thing for the family, even though I wasn't eager to leave Can Tho. I told my mother she should make the decision (she didn't know about my little drama with Thanh); when she asked what I thought, I replied, only half-joking, "I am not going to influence you in this matter. If we move there and we are not happy, I'll not be blamed."

Just before we left, my old classmates threw a party for me and gave me a present wrapped in bright red paper. They all knew red was my favorite color; I had bound my textbooks in red paper, painted my ruler red, used a red fountain pen and worn a red shirt almost every day, and as a joke they had called me "Viet Cong" because of the color. As a rule in our culture, one doesn't open presents in front of the giver, so I took this gift home with me after the party and opened it in my room. When I unwrapped the paper I found a can of earth from the school garden, the garden we used to take turns caring for all through my school years. I treasured that tin can full of dirt, and when we moved to Sai Gon it went with me; at my sisters' apartment, I mixed it with other soil and used it to plant a bamboo tree, vowing it would stay with me for as long as I lived in my country. I had no inkling then that that would not be many years longer.

— — —

The first few weeks in Sai Gon were a whirlwind for the whole family, as we tried to get settled into a new home and my mother hurried about to find schools for the younger children. I spent all of my time looking for a job, something that would allow me to pull my weight as a new grownup and help the whole family.

I glued my nose to the want ads in the papers every morning, not knowing until later that the runny nose and sneezing I suffered the whole time was caused by an allergy to ink. I didn't have time to think about that, because I wasn't having much success at finding someone to hire me. I answered ads at legitimate businesses where people were quick to let me know I didn't have the qualifications for secretarial jobs, and at slightly less savory places where I was told I didn't quite have the "look" to be a hostess in their night club. Thank God I didn't have the right look, I suppose, because my mother would have been so ashamed if she had found out I had gotten that kind of job.

Finally I ran across an ad that seemed like a miracle — a job tailor-made for me and my dreams of writing. "Wanted: Young, single woman who is interested in journalism. Will train." I may have set a new speed record, injured heel and all, in getting to a taxi to rush to the address in the ad.

The location, much to my surprise, turned out to be a hotel on Tu Do Street. Before I could even go inside I was met by a glamorous woman wearing a high-fashion dress and speaking in a very polite way: "You read the ad in the papers?" When I nodded, she led me past the swimming pool and up to a room on an upper floor, where an American man about thirty greeted us. The woman left, and I went into the room.

I had never seen an American quite like this one — his blond, full hair was much longer than the military haircuts most of them wore, and he had the face of a movie actor who might play the part of a playboy or a con man. With him in the room was a Vietnamese man in his late thirties who did the talking in Vietnamese for both of them. As the door closed behind me, I became very worried about the situation, and I tried hard to keep my voice from trembling when I spoke. I told the Vietnamese man I'd like to know more about the job in the newspaper ad.

"It has been filled," he said matter-of-factly, "but we have another job opening and my friend here will be more than happy to discuss it with you if you are interested in it. He pays well if both parties agree on the terms."

"Can you tell me what the job is?" I asked.

He signaled to the American, whom he called Bob. The blond man went to his bed, opened a briefcase and spread out an incredible assortment of photographs, all of them young Vietnamese girls, all of them beautiful, and all of them without a single thread of clothing on — posed in terrible ways to reveal all their "female secrets" to anyone who saw the pictures.

I was shocked and humiliated, angry at having been lured there under false pretenses and ashamed to be under the same roof with a Vietnamese man who would help a foreigner make young Vietnamese girls expose themselves for a profit. Fortunately, my mother had instilled in me one of her good qualities, the capacity to keep my cool under pressure, so I restrained myself from saying what I thought.

"I am not qualified for this job," I said as calmly as possible.

The Vietnamese man put his hand up in protest: "Bob will determine that for you, but you look great to me."

"I am a minor," I said, thinking that might stop them.

"We are looking for innocent faces. Minors are what we want for the pictures," he replied.

Should I just vomit right into his face before I get out of here? I wondered. I was repulsed by the men, but scared as well. I knew the two of them could easily overpower me if they wanted. I could kick until they tied me up, I could scream until they put a piece of rag in my mouth, and my family would never hear from me again. I had to come up with some convincing way to get them to let me go. A thought suddenly occurred to me, and I said with an eager look on my face and what I hoped was a friendly tone in my voice, "I know two perfect girls for him to take pictures of. If I bring them here would I get a commission from you?"

He turned to interpret for the American, and I hoped that this foreigner knew so little about the Vietnamese and how our minds work that he might not suspect my offer. The American said something in response, and the other man turned back to me.

"OK, Bob said he will give you 500 piasters when you bring your friends over."

I felt so cheap just listening to him and having to carry out the ruse. "When can I come?" I asked.

"Any time," he replied, and both of them seemed so eager to see my "two friends" that they let me go quickly and I fled the hotel as fast as I could.

I knew my mother would have been crushed if she had known about that frightening "job interview," so I never told her. I became much more cautious about other ads in the paper, now that I had learned firsthand about the darker side of life in the big city.

After two weeks of unsuccessful job hunting, Kim heard about a position as cashier and receptionist that had opened at the Dong Nam A Printing Company. The job required basic mathematics skills, some typing, and French and English language ability. I could read and write French, but English was out of the question. "English is easy," Hai Van told me, brushing aside my concerns. "Just tell them you speak English, then hurry up and study it."

I put on my best *ao dai* and headed for the interview with the manager of the firm. An ancient man with Northern features and an official manner asked me three questions that he read from a card in his hand: Did I speak French? Did I speak English? Did I know how to handle money? I answered yes to all three, and then he added two more questions. "Are you a gambler?" he asked. "Can you be trusted with money?" I said yes to the latter, but then I felt bad about lying to a man who wanted to know if I could be trusted, so I confessed that in fact I didn't really speak any English.

The old gentleman gave me a look that reminded me of the way my Chinese teacher stared at us when the class cheated on a Chinese lesson, both disapproving and disappointed. For some reason, though, he forgave my lie and told me to report for work the next day. He gave me a list of the firm's regulations and added, "We like our receptionist to dress simply. The boss is a very conservative man, so *ao dai* is most suitable when you work here."

He started to get up from his chair but I pointed out, "Sir, we didn't discuss my salary." He didn't answer right away, but took his thick glasses off and polished them, then peered at them closely to see how clean they were, then polished them again. Finally he put them back on and told me, "Two thousand piasters is your base pay. We will pay you double for overtime, and at the New Year you'll receive a bonus. Payday is twice a month."

I left the office and decided to walk home and search for a shortcut, because with that pay I wouldn't be able to afford to take a cyclo except on rainy days. What a step down, I muttered to myself. In Can Tho, where I wanted to be, I made 3,000 piasters doing work that was fascinating, and I could walk to work in five minutes. Now I was in the big city, afraid of muggers and pickpockets and the unknown, doing boring work as a receptionist for a thousand piasters less, and I had to walk half an hour to the job. I hoped it was all worth it, as long as my mother didn't have to worry about money. I decided to go home with a cheerful, happy face despite my disgruntled mood.

The first morning on the job, the general manager Mr. Thu took me around to meet the other office workers, two men in their late forties, Mr. Cac the accountant and Mr. Khuong the business manager. The four of us sat in a large area behind the counter, each of us at our own desk. Behind glass doors to the right of the entrance was the office of the president, Mr. Hy. I spent most of my first day learning how to write business transactions, receipts, work orders from customers, and so forth.

I soon learned the pecking order in the small office. Mr. Thu often shouted at Mr. Cac and Mr. Khuong, exerting his authority, but it was clear that he feared the real boss, Mr. Hy. Even though I hadn't met the company president yet, Mr. Thu gave me careful instructions on how to act when I did: "When you are called to appear in front of the boss, remember not to turn your back on him. Take a few steps backward before you turn around." This ritual, an old custom that servants practiced, was to show respect to a high and mighty person.

By the second payday I was doing all right, I thought. I hadn't been shouted at yet by Mr. Thu, which was a good thing — with my temper I probably would have stalked out and never come back. In a quiet moment Mr. Thu asked me to sit and chat with him, and asked me about my family. When I told him I came from Can Tho, his eyes opened wide and he asked if I knew his son — a literature teacher at Phan Thanh Gian high school. Of course I did, I told him (I didn't say it, but any male teacher was the object of lots of attention from the girls for a while, unless he proved to be a terrible teacher). I could tell by the way he spoke of his son that he was very proud of him.

I was asked to help prepare the payroll because the bookkeeper was sick and hadn't come in that day. It was a simple job, I thought, just reading the names of employees and the salary in the next column, counting the money and stuffing it into envelopes. I did it rather fast, and Mr. Thu seemed upset. "Slow down, kid, you don't want to make a mistake! You have to recount the money three times." So I repeated the count once more and finished stuffing the envelopes. Mr. Thu checked the payroll sheets, and then with a serious look on his face he asked, "Any money left?"

"No, sir."

"Good work. Now you bring the payroll sheets to the boss to get his signature. Remember what I told you — don't turn your back on him."

I took a deep breath and walked into Mr. Hy's office. The boss was standing behind his big desk, holding a cup of tea in one hand and reading a newspaper with the other. He was thin and very tall, with the pale, polished, ivory complexion of a Vietnamese aristocrat. "You are the new cashier, aren't you," he said, putting down the paper and the teacup.

"Yes, sir."

"I hope you like working here, Miss."

"Thank you, sir."

I gave him the payroll sheets and he signed them and handed them back. I thought about what Mr. Thu had told me, but then I remembered everything I had ever been taught about individual dignity and fairness, and I walked out of the office the way I felt I should — straight and forward, not backing out and kowtowing. Mr. Thu had been spying to see how I did, and he was livid. "You didn't listen to me!" he seethed.

"I am not used to that," I said simply.

He shook his head and stomped off to his desk, mumbling to himself, "Young people don't know how to behave anymore."

I wondered about all this protocol, about who had invented all these rules. In the olden days, when it all started, had the servant wanted to lower himself in front of the master or had the master required it? I doubted very much that Mr. Hy wanted his workers to bow before him and not turn their backs, but Mr. Thu seemed to think it was critically important. The custom was as old as China, but it was new to me and I didn't intend to make myself bend. I hoped my job wasn't going to depend on following Mr. Thu's frightened example.

Apparently it didn't, because after three months I got a raise of two hundred piasters a month. That was a mixed blessing, because the extra money was certainly helpful, but it was getting harder to work under Mr. Thu. He submitted himself to the boss, and in turn he expected the workers to yield to him.

I didn't mind the idea of bringing hot tea to Mr. Hy, because Mr. Cac did that. But each time I was about to enter the boss's office, the old manager would rush over and inspect it, checking the temperature of the cup and the cleanliness of the serving tray. "Oh, God," I thought to myself each time Mr. Thu fussed that way.

Over a period of time, however, I began to find myself imitating him, thinking of Mr. Hy as someone superior, a kind of "master." I discovered one day that I was behaving the same way Mr. Thu did, timid and humbled before Mr. Hy — and that was the day I decided to quit. Although I felt guilty, irresponsible, and selfish, because I knew that 2,200 piasters was very useful to my family at that time, I couldn't allow myself to become like Mr. Thu. I gave two weeks' notice, and when Mr. Thu asked my reasons for leaving "such a good job," I told him I was going to move back to Can Tho. The idea, I realized, had always been in the back of my mind, and when I walked out of the office I felt that some kind of bondage was about to be broken.

— — —

Despite the loss of the salary, my family was quite supportive of my decision to leave the printing company. They told me to "rest your soul" for a while before plunging back into the job-hunting jungle. I slept in late for two days, and then on the third morning I went to see my old friend Major Thinh for yet another favor — advice about a job.

There were plenty of jobs at the psychological warfare headquarters where he worked, he told me, but the pay was poor and it was a long way from my house. Thinh suggested I should try to get a job working for the Americans, perhaps at MACV, because salaries there were about twice what Vietnamese civil servants were paid. I felt some resistance to the suggestion, because I was born into a family that put nationalism on a pedestal and taught that Americans — in fact, all outsiders — were imperialists and ultimately our enemies. I could never bring myself to hate Americans, as I was told, any more than I could love "Uncle Ho," but I wasn't comfortable with the idea of working for them either, at this point in time.

One day not long afterward I had gone to Nguyen Hue flower market to buy marigolds for my grandmother's memorial day. Just as I was about to leave the flower stall, a friend of Major Thinh's, a man named Yen, came up to me to say hello. Yen was a civilian, and it wasn't until much later that I found out he worked for the Americans in the Phoenix program, a CIA operation whose primary objective was to neutralize the Viet Cong. There was an American with him, whom he introduced as "my friend Mr. Bender." I spoke only a little English and didn't try to pretend, so I just said *Chao ong*, which means hello. Suddenly Yen looked at his watch and said, "My God, I'm late for my rendezvous." He excused himself and ran off down the street.

I was angry to be placed in such a situation with this American stranger. It seemed that hundreds of eyes were on us, so I just said "Chao ong" again, hoping Mr. Bender would know that it also means goodbye, and started walking away. The American followed me, however, and to my surprise began speaking to me in perfect Vietnamese. It wasn't his language skill that caught my ear, however, but what he said: "I would like to talk with you about your big brother Khoi."

When I heard my brother's name I felt as if I had just found something that had been missing for a long time, a brightness like the sun's rays when they peek through the forest after a shower. I smiled at the American for the first time and forgot my uneasiness. When he asked me to walk to his office to chat, I went along; I would have walked a hundred miles with anyone as long as he could tell me anything about my brother in Ha Noi.

The place Mr. Bender called his office was really just an apartment on the second floor of a rowhouse on Tu Do Street. The living room was large and attractive, but it had a suspiciously clean and tidy look. I couldn't see any traces of real human life there, and I realized that it must be used only for meetings like the one we were about to have. I looked at Mr. Bender closely. I was terribly interested in hearing what he had to say, because it was only the promise of information about Khoi that had led me to this apartment. Yet it was clear to me that he was a white man, a representative of the "American imperialists." I thought he looked like Cary Grant (we knew all the American stars from the movies) except for his hair, which was so blond it was almost white. His eyes were large and seemed incredibly blue. He went to the refrigerator to get us a drink, and as he put ice into two glasses he remarked, "It is terribly hot out there today."

"Viet Nam was not made for Americans," I replied. "You'll never feel comfortable in my country."

"You certainly have a way of making me feel unwelcome," he said, smiling.

I remarked on his language ability and said, "You must have been to many schools to learn about my country."

"Not enough, Miss," he said. "Not enough to really understand the complexity, the beauty, and the troubles of Viet Nam and the Vietnamese people."

I caught myself thinking like a Front cadre, because I almost told him, "If you get out of Viet Nam, my country will be free of trouble." I experienced a strange, contradictory set of emotions for a moment: One part of me was repulsed by this stranger in my homeland, but another part was drawn to a person who apparently knew something about my brother. I sat quietly while he brought Coca-Colas to the living room and sat down across from me in a rattan chair.

"You seem to be preoccupied by something important," he remarked, sipping his Coke.

"I'd like to know how much more you know about my brother," I told him.

"Let me ask you this, when was the last time you heard from him or your father?"

"Who wants to know?"

"You certainly make it difficult for me to help you, Miss."

"If you want to help me, just tell me about my brother. Beyond that I don't have any reason to be in the same room with you, sir." I moved on the sofa as if to get up.

"I thought Vietnamese people are supposed to be very patient," Mr. Bender said. "Must you go?"

"What do you want from me? I don't think you have any information about my brother, but you tried to make me believe that you do!" I rose and started toward the door.

"Would you like to see your brother again?" he called after me in a soft, calm voice.

A sharp pain tugged at me inside my chest. I swallowed hard and looked at the American. "What do I have to do in exchange for that?"

"How well do you remember your big brother, Miss?" He gestured for me to sit back down, and I did so, moving automatically.

"I remember everything about him," I said.

"What does he want most in his life?"

"To have a good education."

"Is he a materialistic person? Does he like to have good clothes, good food, a nice house?"

"My family hardly ever talked about those things."

"Did he tell you about his dreams?"

"He wants to see Viet Nam prosper, and he wishes that our parents could be together forever."

"What about dreams for himself? Did he give you any indication that he wanted to be rich?"

At this point I realized that Mr. Bender didn't know anything about my brother; on the contrary, he was a CIA agent trying to get information out of me. I remembered what my father had said when he left home and warned us never to talk about him or anyone in the family who had gone north. People will try to bribe us, to buy our loyalty, he said, but we must stand fast. It was happening to me now, I saw, and I was angry.

"Mr. Bender, in my country people make mousetraps, but you will never hear of people making tiger traps, because it is impossible to trap a tiger!" I was serious, but the American was unfazed. He smiled broadly and commented,

"So this is a typical daughter of a Viet Cong."

"Viet Cong is a poor choice of words when you speak of my father," I told him. "He is a Communist!" I reached down to the floor and picked up my marigolds and headed for the door once again. This time he stopped me with a promise: If I would write to Khoi, he could see that the letter would reach him.

God! Like a starving African child in front of a bowl of milk, how could I resist? I had no doubts that he could in fact accomplish what he said.

There was one condition, the American told me — the letter had to be a secret between him and me, and I couldn't tell anyone about my involvement with him. I refused to go along, telling him that many people on his side would know about our meeting but I would be alone on my side, and I didn't think that would be safe. I told him I would at least have to tell my brother Hai Van so that if anything happened to me he could tell my family and the whole world about it. Mr. Bender argued, "For your brother's own good, the fewer people who know about it the safer it will be for him. We must protect his life."

I replied, "You must protect your interests, and I will protect my brother."

Finally he compromised and said I could tell Hai Van, but he didn't want to see him "yet." I told him I would show Hai Van this apartment, but he said we would meet at a different place the next time. It didn't really matter, though, because I had already decided to have my brother watch me whenever I went out to meet this sly American.

Then Mr. Bender made a mistake — he mentioned money to me. He said he had heard I was looking for a job, and he suggested I should work for him. When I asked him to describe the job, he said, "At first, all you have to do is work on the letter to your brother Khoi, and I will see what we can do next."

My pride rose up in me and my head started to hurt. I remembered once, years before, when Hai Van asked my little cousin Quoc if he wanted to trade marbles for rubber bands. Quoc agreed, and Hai Van gave him five thousand rubber bands for one hundred marbles. Two days later Quoc had second thoughts and wanted his marbles back, but Hai Van said the transaction was final. Quoc asked Grandfather to be his negotiator, but he too said that the deal couldn't be undone. "You should always question the trader who offers a trade," Granddad said. "Most of the time he wants what you have, and he is not giving you anything that will cost him a lot."

I realized that this American who was offering me a deal must have some big plan behind it, one in which he would gain a lot more than I would. I lashed out at him again:

"The prostitutes sell their bodies for U.S. dollars, but children of people like my father will not sell our souls for your dirty dollars, Mr. Bender!"

He raised his hands in front of him in a denying gesture and insisted, "I'm not asking you to sell your soul."

"I hope you stay in my country long enough to learn the definition of Vietnamese integrity and loyalty," I said. "You can't buy allegiance."

This man seemed to be carved out of rock. He showed no emotion after what I said, but he didn't seem to give up his intentions, either. He walked closer to me, his arms folded in front of his chest, and said quietly, "There is an old saying — I believe it is in Vietnamese, too — that 'if you scratch my back, I'll scratch yours.'"

"Mr. Bender," I replied, pausing a moment to still my anger, "my back is perfectly fine. I don't need you. *Chao ong*."

As I relive that moment, I see a sassy, immature, cocky little girl who may have been in over her head with her brash comments. Yet, I ask myself what I would do if I had to do it over again, and I honestly don't know, but I hope I will never have to repeat it in this lifetime or the next.

I left Mr. Bender's tidy and unlived-in apartment and walked home. When I got there, the marigolds were wilted. Hai Van took them from me and put them in a vase with cold water and two aspirins, and by the time Kim and Cuong came home and my mother brought the food for Grandmother's altar, the flowers were fresh and bright once again.

From time to time after that, when my brother needed extra money for his judo lessons or for tickets to see "the best movie of the year" and I couldn't give it to him, I thought of Mr. Bender and his promises, but in reality those promises were no different from my mother's frequent sighing comment, "If I only had a magic lamp . . ."

Chapter 12

Sai Gon Cathedral was a place of refuge to me, a non-Catholic, a non-Christian, perhaps a nonbeliever in anything except the harsh realities that challenged me and my country every day. Despite my lack of firm religious conviction, I found a comfort in that great house where I could tell somebody my most secret desires and worries.

I used to argue with God about the terrible things he allowed to happen to Viet Nam. Sometimes I asked him a favor, such as "Protect my dad, and protect Khoi for my mother's sake." I never asked him to end the war, however, or to bring my father home, because my grandfather always told me, "God doesn't mingle with politics; he is too good for that." It was at Sai Gon Cathedral that I finally concluded I would never be able to hate the "white men" as so many people urged; I just didn't have that kind of feeling, that kind of obsession, inside my heart.

One Friday afternoon I found myself in the church again. The Catholics were there to say confession, but I was there seeking strength to make an important decision that I knew would upset my whole family. I wanted to go back to Can Tho, back to G-5. I had told my mother I would find a room in a boardinghouse and would be all right, but she worried about my being alone. "Mom, Can Tho is my home. I can't be safer anywhere else than I could be in Can Tho," I argued. Kim and Cuong opposed the move because they said I would fail them if I left the family.

But I knew I wasn't ready for Sai Gon. I needed more time, more experience in work. More important, I needed a job with much better pay, and G-5 was where I could get it; Captain Chanh had told me before we left for Sai Gon that if I ever came back, the job would be mine again.

I came home from the cathedral and told my sisters, "I've been to the church, talking to God, and he said, 'Go where your heart is.' I'm going back to Can Tho. I'm tired of being unemployed in the big city." Everyone finally gave up fighting me, and my mother went off to the market to buy ingredients to make *cha gio,* the delicious Vietnamese spring rolls, for my "last supper." There was still no joy in our parting, and everybody — even Hai Van's dog — cried the morning I left for Can Tho.

At G-5, Captain Chanh welcomed me back and told me to report for work the next morning. Then I faced the problem of finding a place to live. My mother had told me to stay with my cousin Hong Nga, who I knew for a fact was a Front cadre posing as a midwife. I had nothing against cousin cadres except that it would be hard to explain my living arrangements to the South Vietnamese army if the truth ever came out.

I thought about my years in Can Tho, combing my memory for ideas, and remembered a boardinghouse that stood across the street from a house we lived in when I was in the third grade. I headed there immediately, knocked at the door, and asked the lady who ran the home if she had space for me. She hesitated. "My guests are all officers," she said. "All of them are men." Don't worry, I said, I'll just be sure to lock my room. She went off to consult her husband in the garage, and from the living room I heard him tell her to let me stay. I had a new home in Can Tho!

Mrs. Nam was about sixty-two, thin and tall, with black-rimmed reading glasses. She walked with leisurely steps as if the world stood still for her. Her hair was the color of salt and pepper, but her laughter was like a young girl's. She chewed betel leaves and spat the red juice into a brass spittoon. Her husband was a little shorter than she was, about sixty-five, but his body looked strong. His shoulders were straight, and he walked with a purpose. He chain-smoked cigarettes all day, even though they made him cough and the smoke made him squint his eyes.

The family occupied the main house, which was built in Western style; the guests stayed in an addition, built above a small garden at the rear. Mrs. Nam took me to the back of the main house to show me the kitchen, the shower, and the place where I could wash clothes on Saturday. The kitchen was huge, and I imagined it would be busy every day as she prepared food for fourteen boarders, plus herself and her husband, their daughter and son-in-law and their two children, and a maid.

My room was the first one at the top of the staircase, a little space about three by four meters. There was a window, where I could look out onto the garden, a tiny bed, a shaky desk and a high, skinny dresser. I used the two bottom drawers for my clothes because I wasn't tall enough to see into the top one. I started unpacking, but by then I was worn out from the trip, my visit to G-5, and "househunting." I lay down just to rest my eyes, and the next thing I knew the maid was waking me up for dinner.

Being on my own was a new experience for me, and it should have been an exciting one. My adopted sister Thuan and I used to complain again and again to my mother about our 9:15 curfew, always wanting to stay out another fifteen minutes or so. Now, here I was in my own hometown, it was Friday after work, and the only big plan I had was to walk back to the boardinghouse and have dinner — and nothing after that.

I didn't have as many friends in Can Tho as I used to. My school friend Tuyet had gone to Sai Gon to live with her sister a few months before, and Thuan had recently gotten married. That was a big event in our family, although not in the happy way marriages usually are. Thuan's choice for a husband was the son of a rich merchant in Can Tho, a family whose anti-Communist feelings were well known. She had to get married at the city hall with only a few friends present, because neither Aunt Bay nor her sister Thao would give their consent for a marriage to a man who opposed their cause.

I felt very sad for Thuan because she had become estranged from her family after her wedding. Thao had always wanted to follow in her father's footsteps, and she achieved her goal through her Liberation activities. I wanted sometimes to be a warrior in the traditional fashion, at other times to be a famous writer like Françoise Sagan. All Thuan ever wanted was to be a wife and mother with a lot of kids. She used to volunteer to help my mother sew buttons and iron wedding dresses for customers, so she could feel the "luxury of a wedding." She had dreamed of a big, beautiful wedding and had wanted my mother to make her the softest red *ao dai* and the most luxurious white satin pants — but her dreams were ruined because of politics.

I thought about poor Thuan as I lay on the bed in my little room on this Friday, waiting for dinnertime. A house lizard made its "regret" sound on the ceiling, so I got rubber bands from my purse and "shot" him down to the floor. I hated the house lizards, because they made that awful sound and they left their little "pellets" on my bed.

I imagined my family back in Sai Gon on Friday night. Kim Chau theater, near our apartment, would be bustling with moviegoers, and my mother and Minh Tam would stand on the balcony and watch them below. Kim and Cuong would probably be out with their boyfriends. I didn't know what Hoa Binh would be doing, because she was too unpredictable, but I was absolutely certain that Hai Van would be working out with his barbells and doing his pushups, working hard to become the new man of the family.

In the next few days at G-5, I worked hard to reestablish my routine and concentrated on getting better at the "art of propaganda." Lieutenant Nam trusted me with everyday reports while he tended to a new project connected to the "open arms" program, which was designed to encourage Viet Cong to defect to the South.

For a long time I had entertained the notion of becoming a field photographer. I didn't know anything about taking pictures, but the idea of being a first-hand witness to the incredible events taking place in my country intrigued me. I started studying the pictures that Sergeant Mai Hoa brought back from his trips to the front lines. It was a sobering experience; even Sergeant Mai Hoa himself sat still and silent in his darkroom as he stared at the photos he had taken. One series of pictures was taken in a burning village: The scene was chaos, as soldiers carried children in one arm and secured their weapons with their free hand, and people ran about with their faces smeared by black smoke and tears. I could almost hear the crackling sound of the fire as I pored over the pictures.

Hoa preserved images of life in hell, and of the forgotten dead — pictures of decomposed bodies, of faces full of fear, of panicked gestures in desperate moments. His work, combined with the information off the teletype and the reports from our correspondents, made me feel closer every day to the war zones. Knowing what was happening there made me realize how much we owed the soldiers who were fighting, keeping places like Can Tho safe and quiet. If for any reason the NLF and the North should win, then I knew my whole nation would endure the kind of hell I saw in those photos and reports. But the Vietnamese people were strong, courageous, and patient, and I believed we would somehow survive this threat from the Communists.

Such thoughts often kept me awake at night, gnawing away at my hope that someday my family would be reunited with Father and Khoi. Still, I felt a great deal of honor when I reported how our men fought the battles, and a great debt to those who were wounded or killed in the effort. Living away from my family wasn't easy, but I was glad I had had the courage to leave Sai Gon. For the first time I had a chance to make my own decisions and to remove myself from the pressures to meet someone else's definition of "loyalty" to my father. In Can Tho I found myself totally uncommitted to the NLF, and was able to think about my father more freely, separating him from the politics. I knew I loved him, but I no longer felt confused or guilty when I condemned the Viet Cong's criminal acts in my radio reports.

Sergeant Mai Hoa must have heard about my background, because one day while I was looking at his photos, still wet from the developing fluids, he asked me what my father was like. "Not as bloody as you would expect a Communist to be," I said, laughing. His question prompted me to think about it more. My father was sensitive and romantic, faithful to my mother, loyal to

Ho Chi Minh. He never told his children what to do, but offered us an example to follow. He charmed many people and promoted the ideals of socialism. His stepbrother once told me, when I visited him in a rest home near Can Tho shortly before his death from cancer, that people in our family are strong, full of convictions, and quite different from one another. He loved his "Viet Minh brother," he said, but he refused to accept him after he embraced Communism. Still, he reminded me, "No matter what you believe in, love your father first; only through love can you find the understanding for the differences."

One Saturday, five months after I had moved into Mrs. Nam's boardinghouse, I walked out into the back yard and found her lying unconscious on the ground. She had had a stroke! Mr. Nam was visiting a friend, and the maid was doing errands, so we were alone. I felt very stupid because I didn't know what had happened. I screamed for help, but then I realized no one was there, so I calmed down and tried to think about what to do. Finally I picked her up and carried her to the garage, where I called a pedicab to take her to the hospital. To this day I don't know how I managed to carry her the 60 meters to the garage — I only weighed about 90 pounds then and Mrs. Nam must have been about 110.

The stroke left her paralyzed on her left side and unable to speak, so the family decided to close the boardinghouse. They asked me to stay, however, saying that they owed it to me because I had saved Mrs. Nam's life. In fact, Mr. Nam said he wanted me to be part of the family, and not pay room and board. I was grateful, and went to my room to brush my hair before going to bed. As I counted my hundred strokes, I looked into the mirror and saw my mother's image there — and then got up and went to tell Mr. Nam that I couldn't accept his generous offer. My mother wouldn't consider it right, I knew; she had a terrible aversion to handouts, which were among her greatest objections to socialism.

For a time I stayed on, coming by Mrs. Nam's room each afternoon after work to see how she was. She lay in her bed helpless most of the time, and I thought about how close we had come to losing this precious human being. Gradually her condition made me more aware of a couple of similar incidents in my life. For one, when Mrs. Nam had fallen ill, none of her family was there to help her; even sadder, when my father's stepbrother was put into the rest home, none of his five children ever came to visit him until he was dead. I began to have vague thoughts about my mother, back in Sai Gon, always at risk of an ulcer attack. The more I saw Mrs. Nam lying there in her bed, the more I felt I wanted to return to Sai Gon so I could be near my mother if she needed me.

Finally, I made my decision. I gave thirty days' notice at G-5, and told the Nams about my plan. I didn't write my family, though, because I was looking forward to seeing their faces when they opened the door and found me standing on the doorsteps.

— — —

There was one thing I had to do before going off to Sai Gon. During the whole six months I had been back in Can Tho, I had not gone to visit my grandparents' gravesites. Aunt Bay's total devotion to the Front cause and the cadres' obvious eagerness to recruit me had made me uncomfortable there, so I preferred to stay away. But I thought I ought to pay respects to my grandparents one more time, because I didn't know when I would return; this time I was ready to leave Can Tho for real.

The bus lurched to a squealing stop at the usual place in front of the footbridge leading to the village center, and I looked toward the little town I had known so well. When I was young, my cousins and I had played a game in which they blindfolded me as soon as we got off the bus and then walked me through the village center. I could always tell them exactly where we were, because I knew every turn, every sound, even every smell of Long Thanh. When they took me into my Uncle Sau Em's general store, I knew it was his store and not one of the other three in town because I could smell the brown sugar and dried fish near the entrance; the other stores all kept their fish against the wall farther in the back.

I went to my uncle's store this day to get some sugar as a present for Aunt Bay, and several customers recognized me and asked about my mother. Uncle Sau Em waited until a moment when the store was empty and whispered to me: "Have you heard from him?" I had to say no.

I left the store and started off to Aunt Bay's house, but almost immediately I noticed something was wrong. The village post — a small army to guard the village — was removed, there was not a single soldier in evidence in the village center, and the big footbridge that connected the Cambodian guard's home base with the marketplace was now only a quivering piece of dried wood. When I walked on it, I could see my shadow on the muddy surface of the river and I felt so close to falling into it.

In front of me, the green alongside the road disappeared and I saw only bare trees standing against the dry, scorched grass in the background. A sharp pain struck my chest and spread over my whole body. "Oh, no!" I cried. "It can't happen here, not in my village!"

The war had finally touched the place I called home.

I began to run past the countless skeletons of leafless, lifeless trees that had once been bright and heavy with fresh oranges. Their bareness made them look like victims of starvation in their last moments. Tears ran down my face as I looked at the dead leaves that littered the ground. It was defoliation — the latest advance in antiguerrilla warfare. I called out, "Grandma!" She had dedicated her life to caring for every shoot of the trees and every inch of the precious soil, and I felt the agony she would have suffered if she had seen it.

A villager stood watering a small plot of betel plants near the riverbank; it was the only green spot left in his garden. I didn't know him, but as I drew near he put down his pail and greeted me: "You must be the chief's granddaughter." He hadn't seen my aunt in a long time, he said, because it was no longer safe to travel to our land outside the village. I asked him about the horror I saw about me, and he told me that when the first leaves fell, his heart had fallen with them, but when all of the trees were denuded, he just gave up. He tried to encourage me, though. "Everybody has lost something in this war. At least these were trees and not humans." After the war they will become green again, he insisted. "Heaven will not let us down. One must go on." I felt a deep sense of respect for the old man, and I wanted to shake his hand, but it wasn't proper so I made a traditional gesture of respect to say goodbye — I kept my face toward him as I backed away several steps, the same gesture I had never wanted to make for Mr. Hy, the president of the printing company in Sai Gon.

I ran the last kilometer to our family land, the bare trees seeming to run in the opposite direction beside me. I tried not to look at them at all. As I reached the boundary of our property, I saw that the shrine was still standing. I wondered if Aunt Bay ever came at sunset to burn incense to the Tho Than — the Buddhist god of the family land — as my grandmother had done every day of her life, but I still harbored enough of my childhood fears of spirits that I didn't have the nerve to look inside for evidence of recent visits.

I found my aunt, living all alone in the big house that had once housed all her nieces and nephews. She assured me that during the day she was quite busy with chores, and only felt a little lonely at night. She still supported the Front with her time, with money from selling her crops, with the use of our land for access to the road. I remember thinking that I couldn't really blame the Americans for defoliating our land, or the South Vietnamese air force for dropping the bomb that had left a hole the size of a rice warehouse right in the front yard of the house. Aunt Bay and many of the others in the area were part of the "movement," and they would have to accept the consequences.

That night my aunt built an open fire in the back yard to cook rice gruel for the pigs, and I roasted sweet potatoes in the hot flames. As we worked, she talked to me once again about "patriotism" and about "following in my father's footsteps." I had to admire her selfless devotion to her movement, the strength of her patriotism as she saw it, but I wanted to tell her that I believed the "movement" was no longer a revolution but a conspiracy to take over the South. If she had been a Christian I might have told her how some people exploit churchgoers in God's name, but I knew that her religion was nationalism and her gospel was the NLF's version of events. She would never understand or accept anything that challenged her "faith" in the course she had chosen, the course she knew would lead to the salvation of her country.

We talked a bit about the terrible defoliation of the countryside. Aunt Bay said the Americans had offered to compensate villagers whose land had been harmed by the chemicals, but she had decided to drop the matter. Some of the people in the Front organization had urged her to file a claim. "Make the Americans pay," they told her, the money will come in handy. She still wouldn't do it, she said, because she would feel indecent to accept the Americans' money. Others had not been so reticent, she said. A villager, the mother of Nguyen Hoang Phat, had collected two million piasters for damage to her much smaller plot of land. The Americans who doled out the money had no idea that Nguyen Hoang Phat, who had married my cousin Yen, was then a colonel in the North Vietnamese army.

My aunt knew that I had gone to work for the South Vietnamese army; the Viet Cong had informed her. I was being watched by them, which I always assumed, but life had to go on. My VC cousins were being watched by the ARVN, and I was being watched by their people! It was sad, but it made me stronger.

Aunt Bay had been devastated when she learned about my work, despite my protestations that I needed the money for my family. She was momentarily heartened when I told her I had quit G-5, thinking maybe now I would be ready to join her cause, but I quickly squelched that idea. I was going to Sai Gon, I told her, far from my father's friends and comrades, far from the people who kept trying to make me do something I could not do. I tried to make her understand that I love my father more than anyone else on this earth, but I could not share his cause. The Front had turned down the wrong path under Ha Noi's leadership, I told her: "We are fighting for Ha Noi, and Ha Noi is fighting for Moscow." At that she stopped the conversation, and we spoke of politics no more.

Between the muffled "thumps" of mortar fire in the distance, I enjoyed the plaintive chirping and buzzing of the insects in the night. I walked along with Aunt Bay to the rice warehouse to reset the mousetraps, a ritual that had to be done faithfully every night, just like brushing your teeth. I carried the torch made from coconut leaves and she carried bananas to use as bait. She used two bananas to set ten traps, and as we walked back to the house I ate the last banana. I also enjoyed the fun of dipping the torch into the pond to extinguish it in a hissing, steaming "whoosh."

That night, the moon was just a sliver in the sky and I could see millions of stars. For some reason I remembered the appearance of a comet in 1957, which my mother's uncle had told us could be an omen of the future. He said we should watch for other comets and notice which way the tail pointed. If it pointed toward the South, as this one did, then the South would face disaster and the North would win; if it pointed toward Ha Noi, then the South would be victorious. Ever since then, on clear nights, everyone had looked to the heavens for a comet, and most of the family had wished for one that pointed south so all the men could win the war and come home. I asked Aunt Bay if she remembered her uncle's story about the comet, and she smiled. Of course she remembered, she said; not only that, her uncle had learned that Ha Noi was going to win the war, because in 1961 he had seen another comet and the tail definitely was aimed at the South, like a dagger pointed at Sai Gon's heart.

The crackling sound of the wood burning in the kitchen woke me early the next morning. It was still dark outside, but the glow from the kitchen fire brightened half the house. I decided to get up and talk with my aunt while she fixed breakfast for the farm workers.

"What is happening to our family, Aunt Bay?" I asked. "There were so many of us in this house once, and all of a sudden we buried our most precious loved ones."

"Our ancestors don't live forever, sweetheart," she said, "but the memories of them should always live in our lives."

Shortly after breakfast she had to leave me for a while to talk to a cadre who had just come in from the rice field. I walked off alone to the orange orchard, where the barren branches haunted my thoughts. Every one of those trees had been nurtured by my grandmother and by Aunt Bay; they had helped the workers with the planting, and had tended every new shoot, every new leaf. Their growth was a joy to my grandmother, because she was a farmer in her heart, while my grandfather had been more of a "gentleman farmer."

I went to the family cemetery and sat down on the dry grass between my grandparents' graves. If only Grandfather had still been alive, I thought, Uncle Ho's "children" wouldn't have been able to take over our land and the South Vietnamese air force wouldn't have destroyed the orchard to expose their hiding places. I wished my grandfather could hear me from the grave when I spoke to him: "You were right, Granddad, the SOBs cooperate with the Russians and they trespass all over our land."

Each time I had come home, the evidence of this destructive war became more obvious. Once before, Aunt Bay had been crying her heart out because

Yvonne had gone to prison. Then her cousin's husband was wounded when a Viet Cong rocket missed an ARVN post and hit his home. His two teenagers had died under the rubble, and two younger children were wounded; one of the little girls lost her leg at the age of two. His wife, my aunt's cousin Chi, had been at a neighbor's house and had escaped injury, but she never recovered from the terrible fate that had struck her children. The NLF called the tragedy an "unfortunate incident."

Around this time, I learned that the war had struck even closer to my family. Yvonne had been on a reconnaissance mission in her enemy's territory and had been shot in the abdomen. I never found out exactly when it happened, but Aunt Bay told me that Viet Cong paramedics operated on her under an oil lamp in a farmer's thatched hut by a river bank. They saved her life, but she lost one kidney. Naturally, the Front said the American imperialists were to blame.

That visit, in April 1965, was the last time I ever saw my Aunt Bay, and the last time I ever set foot on my family's land.

Chapter 13

I can't describe the surprise and delight my mother felt when I suddenly showed up on the doorstep with my suitcase and two baskets filled with fruits and other "goodies" I had brought from Can Tho. She was overjoyed when I told her I had finally come to the conclusion that "living away from home wasn't as great as I thought it would be."

Kim and Cuong were happy to see me, too, and they had what they thought was a great suggestion for me. They had quit their jobs at the bank and had gone to work as sales clerks at the U.S. Army Exchange because the Americans paid salaries that were three times what they could earn from Vietnamese companies. Both of them encouraged me to come to work for the U.S. Army as well.

The money sounded great, but despite my animosity toward the NLF and Ha Noi, I was very uncomfortable with the idea of working for the Americans in my country. A Viet Cong woman who knew our family well back when my father was a senator once told me, "You girls have made a revolution against your father." At that time we had only refused to accompany him on his chosen path; I couldn't imagine what she would have thought of us if she knew we had gone to work for the country my father considered Viet Nam's greatest enemy.

I think my mother sensed the trouble within me, and she gently suggested that I not hurry into anything. "You just came from one job, why don't you rest for a while before you find another one?" I appreciated her concern, but she must have forgotten that I have never known how to relax by resting — I relax by keeping busy.

Eventually, pushed by Kim and Cuong, I decided at least to put in my application for a job with the American forces. There were a few obstacles to overcome, however. For one thing, Vietnamese who worked for the United States had to undergo various clearances and background checks by the Vietnamese intelligence agencies. Kim and Cuong had gotten through that by showing birth certificates that listed their parents as "deceased." In my country's traditions, the dead are given more respect than the living, especially if those living are listed as "missing in action."

The other hurdle, an even bigger one, was that anyone who worked for the Americans had to be able to speak English. There was no way to bluff my way through this time, as I had at the printing company. Kim suggested I take an English course, which would cost about 1,500 piasters and take about three to four months. "I don't have 1,500 piasters," I whined, "or three or four months, either!" But she and Cuong offered to give me the money and assured me that the time would pass swiftly.

At the time Kim was dating an English teacher, a Mr. Vu Hoang, and I asked him if he could teach me at an accelerated pace. I wanted to take twice as many classes per week as was usual, so I could learn to speak English in half the time. Since I was Kim's little sister, he agreed to come to the house to teach me every day after his regular classes. I learned fairly quickly, although later I was to discover that what Mr. Hoang taught me was not American speech but British-style English. Much later, people would sometimes laugh at me when I said "water closet" instead of "toilet" or "bathroom," and when I said my family lived in a "flat" instead of an "apartment."

After I finished my classes with Mr. Hoang, he suggested I enroll in a night school to improve even more, so I began taking classes three nights a week for two and a half hours each time. I didn't want to wait any longer to go to work and begin pulling my weight in the family, though, so Kim took me to an employment agency in an American compound in Cholon to apply for a job.

At the office Kim helped me fill out what seemed like hundreds of pieces of paper, which we then turned in to a Vietnamese clerk. Then we had to go to another part of the office and wait and wait until another clerk could take my fingerprints for background checks. I kept telling Kim how sorry I was that she had to wait with me, but she was calm and cool and patient. When it was all over, the employment people told me I would hear from them after the investigation was completed, but I didn't feel things were very promising. I wasn't impressed with the clerk who had taken my application, a seemingly incompetent worker who chewed gum and filed her long red fingernails in front of the people sweating over their applications. "I have a feeling that fatso will use my applications to pad her chair," I told Kim. She just laughed and said, "You're not so crazy about working for the Americans anyway, so why worry what happens to your applications."

I was only half-joking when I said, "Because I spent all day on those damn applications, and they'd better do me some good."

My sisters weren't bothered by things like waiting for applications or slovenly clerks, but I couldn't stand it. I don't know where my impatience came from — it wasn't heredity, because I was born to the two most patient people on this earth. A few days after I applied at the compound in Cholon, as I stood on the balcony of our apartment watching the people going to the movie at the Kim Chau theater, an old black Citroen drove by. It reminded me of Captain Binh, the director of army intelligence at IV Corps, who had owned a similar car. But thinking of Major Binh reminded me of something else — that he had once given me the address of his brother, who was an intelligence officer in Sai Gon, and told me to look him up if I ever needed help. I got dressed and told my mother I was going to see Major Binh's brother to seek help in getting my clearance. If by chance they actually did their homework, I said, they might find out who my father really is, so I needed to do anything I could to smooth the process.

My taxi arrived at the intelligence compound on Tran Hung Dao Boulevard, an old villa built during the French occupation. Barbed wire stretched along the building outside its brick wall. A guard came up and motioned the taxi to move away from the building; during those days the Viet Cong often mounted suicide missions, driving cars or trucks or taxis into target facilities or getting close enough to lob a grenade over the wall.

After some difficulty I persuaded the guard to call Captain Binh's brother, Lieutenant Tran Duy Hinh, and was given permission to come in. In the waiting room the orange vinyl chair was covered with a thin layer of dust, so I stood waiting for Lieutenant Hinh. He arrived quickly, a dark-complexioned man in civilian clothes; as soon as I saw his smile I recognized him as Captain Binh's brother. After a brief introduction, he took me back to his office and asked what he could do for me.

I told him about my situation, and pleaded with him to ask his brother to clarify the matter and decide whether or not to help me. "Fair enough," he said. "I'll call my brother, then I'll take care of it for you." He gave me a pad of paper and a pencil to write down all the information he would need to locate my job applications, then wished me good luck.

Like a miracle, within three weeks I received a notice that my clearance had come in. A week later I got an appointment for a job interview. I had the clearance, all right, but actually getting a job wasn't going to be as easy as we thought. When I showed up for the interview at the Rex Bachelor Officers' Quarters (BOQ), the office manager, a Mr. Hiep, said nothing was available at that time. I was puzzled, since I had been sent by the regional office in

Cholon, so I went there and asked a person what was going on. He lowered his voice and leaned toward me. "You know, in this day and age, money can buy everything," he said, "even a job when they tell you they don't have one."

I was disappointed and angry, but not surprised; once again I realized that my countrymen had been good learners from the days of the French occupation. "How much does this guy want from me?" I asked.

"It's usually your first month's salary," he said matter-of-factly.

"You must be kidding!" I gasped.

The man put his forefinger to his lips, in a shushing gesture, and said nothing more about it.

I went back to see Mr. Hiep the same day and told him how badly I needed a job. Then I added, "When I get rich, I won't forget you, Mr. Hiep." He smelled money, and suddenly "recalled" that there was a job opening after all if I wanted it. The salary began at 5,500 piasters a month — of course I wanted it.

I started the next day, in the accounting office in the back of the terrace on the top floor of the Rex BOQ. As it happened, I didn't really need any English for the job, because my boss and his assistants were Vietnamese, and all we did was work with numbers, preparing payrolls and doing the bookkeeping for the officers' club, a large living facility for American officers and civilians. The work was tiresome, and looking at those thousands of numbers wore me out; I can't blame the job, though, because I had always been terrified of math. Mr. Hoang, the boss, was patient with me. "Once you make friends with these figures, you'll enjoy them," he assured me. I appreciated his kindness, but frankly I thought anybody who enjoyed playing around with numbers must be some kind of nut.

On my first payday, two weeks after I started, two of my coworkers, Ngoc and Le, asked me to go shopping with them. I wanted to join them, but I declined their invitation — my promise to Mr. Hiep had to be resolved first. I knew that paying bribes was a common practice, but I just hated the idea of doing it. I had very few enemies in my life; one was Communism, one was bureaucracy, and the third was corruption. Still, I had promised to remember him when I got "rich." My half-month's salary, 2,750 piasters, didn't make me rich by most standards, but even my teachers in Can Tho hadn't made that much, so I knew I had to do something to keep from breaking my word.

I decided to buy Mr. Hiep a present. I spent half my pay on a clock, asked the saleswoman to gift-wrap it for me, and bought a small card with a European scene on it, in which I wrote, "Dear Mr. Hiep: Please accept this as a token of my appreciation. I do enjoy the job that you have given me." I didn't sign my name to it.

I walked back to Rex, but the guard wouldn't let me through the gate because the clock was ticking inside the package! He told me to unwrap it if I wanted to go inside, but I decided to wait for Mr. Hiep to leave at the end of the day. Shortly he came out, and I handed him the package and left. I felt free of any obligation or entanglement then, although I suspected Mr. Hiep would feel he had been shortchanged by this "little farmer from the Delta."

— — —

Like a woman, Sai Gon had many moods. Early in the morning the city seemed passive, quiet, as young people walked to school and workers headed to their jobs with heavy, sleepy eyes. Gradually the noises grew and the city became exciting, busy, lively, and eager. There never was a day when I didn't see the streets filled with shoppers. Some had a lot of money, some had very little, but they window-shopped, they examined the merchandise, they haggled over prices, and they bought all the needs and luxuries they could manage.

Bar girls and prostitutes squinted their sleepy eyes as they stumbled into coffee shops for their first wake-up cups about 10:00 or 11:00 A.M. Like many other Vietnamese, instead of drinking their coffee at home they preferred to sip it slowly over conversation with friends. Many of these women didn't even bother to comb their hair before coming to the cafes, because from there they would go directly to beauty shops to get themselves ready for that evening's "work."

In the midday rest period, the streets of Sai Gon were almost deserted. One time I walked virtually alone on Cong Ly Street at noon and thought, "What a perfect time to have a coup d'état!" Even the guards at the various military installations took catnaps at this hour, not to mention the president, the air marshal, and all the other important men. I remember thinking, only the Viet Cong are active all day and all night.

I loved Sai Gon in the late afternoon, after the working day was finished. It seemed as if everyone in the city was milling about in the streets. The noise, the smoke, the diesel fumes, the traffic, the excited smiles of people looking forward to a night out or an early return to the warmth of home let me forget, for a while, the war that raged outside the city.

Sai Gon bore the image of a country alive and capable of prospering. The stores had plenty of merchandise for people to buy, and I said to myself, "At least we don't have to queue up for hours to buy a loaf of bread in the Communist fashion."

There were beggars in Sai Gon, too, of course. Some truly had no way to make a living, others seemed to be professionals. Every day when I went to work I saw a pregnant woman with a little girl about two years old. This woman had two eyes, two legs, two arms — a perfectly healthy human being, and yet she stood on a street corner and begged money from people passing by. I never gave her any money because I thought she ought to be working. Then, suddenly, I didn't see her at her usual spot for several days in a row. About two weeks later she turned up again, with the little girl hanging onto her leg and a cardboard box on the ground beside her. I walked closer, and discovered that the box contained her newly born baby! Perhaps she thought the baby would make people more sympathetic and generous; it worked on me, because I gave her two hundred piasters, many times more than she would ever get from one donor at one time.

A few weeks later I saw the woman again, but the baby was nowhere in sight. When I asked where the infant was, she broke out in tears: "God doesn't love us, he let her die from pneumonia!"

I walked away without a word of condolence. I could not bring myself to feel sorry for a woman who had obviously failed to take care of the baby she had been blessed with. God had nothing to do with the death of that baby, I thought; she had exposed it to sun, wind, and germs of every conceivable kind while she used it as a device to get more "contributions."

— — —

For a long time, ever since my older sisters and I had been old enough to date boys, my mother had let us know in various ways that when the time came for us to be married, she would not be a domineering, possessive parent. The decision of a husband would be left up to each of us, and she trusted that we would not make a lifelong mistake.

That resolution must have weighed heavy on her during this time in Sai Gon, because Cuong had started dating an American serviceman, and they had become serious. They had met at MACV, where Cuong worked and where he was in a signal battalion. Sure enough, after about six months of a steady relationship, Cuong announced that she and her boyfriend, Wray Allan Hall, had decided to get married.

Mother's only question to her was, "Do you two love each other?" Actually, I could tell that they were crazy about each other, and I'm sure my mother knew it, too. But she was very confused about the prospect of Cuong's marrying an American because she knew what my father would have thought about it. She agonized over it, but in the end did nothing to interfere, just as she had always promised. It was Cuong's life, Cuong's happiness, and Cuong's future, she knew, and she admitted that neither she nor our father could guarantee any of those things for her.

My mother wasn't the only one confused and upset by the upcoming wedding — I was vigorously opposed to it. I respected Cuong, and looked up to her as my older sister, but I couldn't understand how she could marry an American knowing our parents' feelings. Time and time again my mother tried to make me see that her opinions, and my father's, weren't the central issue: "The most important thing is your sister's happiness."

I refused to see it that way, and began to feel that the whole family was "against me." The preparations for the wedding were torment for me. When everyone went out to buy fabric to make new clothes for Cuong's big day, I grumped that I didn't need any new clothes, so they went without me.

— — —

After about four months of training and working at the Rex military hotel, I was transferred to the Brinks BOQ. There, my boss was a young navy lieutenant j.g. from New Hampshire, Richard Satter. Lieutenant Satter had been to foreign language school to learn Vietnamese, and he was determined to speak it to the sixty or so employees under his supervision at Brinks. I bet my coworkers that "this guy must have nightmares in Vietnamese." Unfortunately, not everyone could understand him; for one thing, he didn't know the distinctions between the northern and southern dialects spoken by the various workers. One day I told him he needed an instructor to help him with his language, and I found myself stuck with my own suggestion — I became his teacher.

Lieutenant Satter was a demanding student, always wanting to know the origin of every slang term or colloquial expression, and never satisfied to end our tutoring sessions after the appointed sixty minutes. Gradually, I got to know him as more than a boss and a student — we became friends. He talked about skiing in New Hampshire, and I could picture him going down a snow-covered hill on the toboggan he described to me. When he talked about his home, I could share his yearning to be back in one's own town. Even though I sometimes felt envy when I compared his pleasant and relatively easy childhood with my own, I came to see him — and thus other Americans — less as a threat and more like someone I could befriend. He never knew it, but he helped me realize that people everywhere have similar joys and sorrows — and he opened the door for someone very important to walk into my life shortly afterward.

Late in 1966, the navy turned over all of the officers' and enlisted men's clubs to the army; I remember our navy chief warning all of us that "the army will ruin this wonderful Brinks BOQ with their army style." We had no idea what "army style" was, but we would soon see.

Changes came, but they weren't so bad considering that there was a war going on less than fifty kilometers away. The dining room didn't have fresh flowers anymore, the waitresses complained that their uniforms were too old, and the officers griped about the food and poor choice of movies, but otherwise it was just a typical military BOQ. None of it affected me, but about that time I asked for a transfer to the Splendid BOQ — not because of the changes, but because Splendid was within walking distance of my house.

There were a lot of high-ranking officers from all the services living in Splendid, but my new boss, Warrant Officer Lugent, warned all the women working for him to watch out for the lower-ranking ones, the young officers. He had a genuine, fatherly concern for us, and didn't want us to get involved with someone and then be hurt "when the soldier goes home."

For the most part, I took his advice and just watched all the goings-on while I took care of my new duty of selling tickets for meals and drinks. I began to notice one navy pilot who didn't live at Splendid but came there with his buddies to drink; the navy always seemed to be trying to prove to the air force officers there that they could outdrink the other services.

One day this officer came over to buy more drink tickets from me. I kidded him about how much he and his friends were putting away. "If you eat your dinner first, you could get your tickets after," I joked.

His blue eyes stared into mine for a moment, and then he said quietly, "I don't like to eat alone."

I was lost in those eyes for a moment. Recovering, I said, "Ask your drinking partners in the bar to join you."

"They're a bunch of ugly guys," he said. "But if you go to lunch with me tomorrow, I'll get my dinner from you right now." He waited impatiently for my answer.

"I can't," I told him.

"Why not?"

"I'm not allowed to go out with an American." About that time, Mr. Lugent came over to the cashier's station and waited to speak to me. The navy pilot wasn't ready to give up. "Whose rule?" he demanded.

"His golden rule," I said, pointing to my boss. The lieutenant boldly turned to Mr. Lugent, who hadn't the vaguest idea what was going on, and asked, "Can she go to lunch with me tomorrow? I promise to have her back before . . ." He glanced at the work schedule pinned to the wall behind the cashier's post.

Mr. Lugent smiled, but I could see the disapproving look in his eyes. He didn't want to get involved, however, so he just said, "You'll have to ask her, Lieutenant Krall."

The lieutenant turned back to me and vowed, "I won't eat until you go out with me. Now, can I have my tickets, please?"

"OK," I said, "just so you don't starve to death I'll go to lunch with you."

And the next day I went to lunch with "the guy in the baggy pants," as my friend Hanh called him. He was trying to get his weight down to 165 pounds in order to fly a special aircraft, and his khaki uniforms were now too big for him.

He may have been trying to impress me, because he took me to the Circle Sportif, an exclusive French country club. I already knew that he didn't have to do that; if he had asked me to join him for a sandwich in the park, I would have gone out with him again and again.

By the autumn of 1967, I was completely in love. My mind, my heart, every minute of my free time were reserved for the dashing Lieutenant John Krall. I hadn't thought much about the future. More important, I hadn't told John much about my family. I realized that our relationship was coming to the point at which we could have no more secrets. That shook me, because when there were no more secrets — when John knew about my father — there might no longer be any relationship.

That night, the moment of truth came for both of us.

John took me to a cozy French restaurant on Dinh Tien Hoang Street, a lovely place called La Cigale, and we had a wonderful dinner and happy, laughing conversation about everything and nothing. While we were waiting for dessert, though, John happened to turn to the subject I had been hoping — foolishly, of course — would never arise: "You've never talked about your father," he said, his deep blue eyes looking into mine.

My heart went cold. What could I say? I had lied to John only once, and that over a trivial, silly thing. He had asked me to mend a small cigarette burn in his new coat, and I had my mother do it because I knew if he saw my handiwork he might never be able to wear the jacket again. When I gave it back to him he thanked me, and I took credit for my mother's fine job. Now, on this subject, I knew I could not lie; but I didn't know if I could tell the truth.

I didn't answer right away, but excused myself and rushed to the tiny ladies' room. Closed inside, I stared at myself in the mirror, searching for an answer. I remembered that someone in my family had once told me I have a "death wish," because I refused to compromise by telling people my father was dead, as Kim and Cuong did easily. Now I laughed and thought, maybe I do have a death wish, because I have to tell this man the truth even if it destroys our relationship — even if it kills me.

Back at the table my resolve momentarily weakened. I knew that when I told John about my father he might never want to see me again; I had been hurt that way before, even by Vietnamese friends. But he sat patiently, waiting for my answer, suspecting nothing, so I took a long drink of wine and then said in a rush: "My father is in North Viet Nam. He is a member of the

Vietnamese Communist Party. After tonight you can stop seeing me if you want, and I'll understand."

Without even a blink, John smiled at me. "Why would I want to do a dumb thing like that?" he said. He kissed his forefinger and placed it on my lips, the gesture that had become a habit with us because he couldn't really kiss me at my office.

A feeling of relief rushed through me like a warm breeze chasing away rain clouds. I spent the rest of the evening telling John everything about my father, and about my family's situation. He listened carefully without raising any questions, and from time to time I felt twinges of worry. Could he really accept this strange and difficult situation? I was terribly afraid of losing this man. He was one of the few really intelligent people I knew, and I felt happy and comfortable with him. I could laugh with him, I could be serious with him, and I discovered that he brought out the best in me. I cared for him, I respected him, and yet he gave me all the room I needed to express myself. He made me know that I was important to him, too.

We were the last two customers at La Cigale that night, and the French couple who owned the restaurant was about to say goodnight to us and close when my American pilot lifted his wineglass to me to end the conversation about my father in a most unexpected way: "I am not going to marry him," John said, "but I want very much to marry his daughter. Please say yes!"

That night, and many nights thereafter, I woke up in the darkness and asked myself, "Is it a dream?" No, I assured myself, it wasn't a dream — but even if it was, my dreams often come true anyway.

My mother insisted that, despite the anxiety I felt, this decision was one only I could make, no matter how much I wished someone would "interfere" and make it for me. "Grandfather allowed me to make my own decision when I married your father," she said. She did offer one piece of advice: "Marry him for love, don't marry him for money; that's all I want you to listen to from me."

I laughed and told her, "I don't think he has any money, Mom." In fact, the way he handled the money he did have made me wonder if we would have enough to eat after our honeymoon — which he had suggested would be a thirty-day trip across the whole United States after his tour in Viet Nam was over.

Chapter 14

$\mathcal{E}$veryone was looking forward to Tet, the Vietnamese New Year, in 1968 because President Thieu had decided that people would be allowed to enjoy all the old traditions again, including the fireworks that were such an exciting part of the celebration. Hai Van had spent most of his allowance on firecrackers, and to our surprise my mother had even asked him to buy a string of them for her. The red fragments of the burst firecrackers that used to litter the streets after every Tet were signs of good luck, prosperity, and new beginnings, and we all were thrilled to see them return.

Mother was the only one whose spirit was a little reluctant this year, because Cuong was living in California with Wray and their daughter Christina, and Kim had gone there to live with them. To brighten up the house a bit, Hai Van invited some of his friends, and I invited my fiancé and my girlfriend Hanh to come to a party at our house on New Year's Eve. All through the evening we celebrated and listened to the firecrackers going off around the city. As a gesture of encouragement, the government had lifted the curfew in Sai Gon, so the holiday seemed almost like the ones we had enjoyed in the old days before the war had engulfed so much of our country.

We wound up the party at our house about 11:00 P.M., because Hai Van's friends had to spend the last hour of New Year's Eve with their families and Hanh had promised her father she would be home before midnight, too. John and I took Hanh home in his Jeep, laughing and talking. I think I was much too loud, but I had had a little too much of my brother's "potion" that he had mixed for us to drink.

When we got to Hanh's neighborhood, a big crowd had gathered in the middle of the street. At first we thought it was just New Year's merrymakers, but then we were startled by a sight we could never have anticipated. A bunch of children had surrounded about forty North Vietnamese soldiers and were chatting with them. The soldiers wore pith helmets and had their AK-47s at the ready position while they talked to the youngsters. Hanh jumped from the Jeep and disappeared behind the crowd, while I rubbed my eyes in disbelief and turned to John.

"Do you see what I see?" I asked in amazement.

"Damn, I think we see the same thing, sweetheart," he said, wheeling the Jeep around and speeding away from the scene.

John raced back to my house, took me up to the door, wished me a "Happy Tet," and told me to stay put. Inside, all the guests had gone home except Hai Van's friend Ali; my mother wouldn't let him leave because he had drunk a bit too much and was in no shape to ride his motorcycle, even though the mosque where he lived was only a few blocks away. He slept on the couch that night.

I went into the kitchen, trying hard to keep my balance and not to appear drunk in front of my mother. Hai Van was there, "deintoxicating" himself with her special recipe of mung beans cooked in brown sugar. "This sounds crazy," I told them, "but John and I saw North Vietnamese soldiers standing in the middle of the street near Hanh's house." My mother looked at me with a disapproving frown, then handed me a bowl of the cooked mung beans. "Mom, I'm not drunk, I don't need this. I really saw North Vietnamese soldiers in North Vietnamese uniforms!" Hai Van laughed and said, "You are seeing things." "You can ask John tomorrow," I retorted. "He saw them too. I think he was as confused as I was."

My mother left the kitchen and the "nonsense talk," as she called it. Suddenly Hai Van raised his hand and closed his eyes. "Oh, heaven and earth!" he shouted. "I remember now! Thao came here last month and warned us that 'something big' was going to happen during Tet. She told us not to go anyplace, not even to go back to Can Tho for Tet. 'Stay home, have enough food in the house just in case,' she said, remember?" When he said it, I did remember, but we never took Thao or any of the other Viet Cong seriously. We always just assumed they were making threats or engaging in wishful thinking when they said things like that.

A thundering roar broke the still night air as a rocket hit somewhere in the city. The sound of gunfire began to shatter the silence all around. As if we had been trained to react to this kind of "disorder" all our lives, we all hit the floor and lay as flat as we could. Hoa Binh held her pillow under her chest.

"Now do you believe that I saw the North Vietnamese soldiers?" I called to Hai Van. "I sure do," he chuckled.

"What bothered me was that they looked at John and me but said nothing to us," I said. "Why didn't they shoot John?"

"That's an interesting question," he said, "but I think we'll find out that the Viet Cong obeyed their orders and instructions. Your navy pilot may owe his life to the Liberation's discipline. Wait until this whole thing is over. You'll smile because it might be the case, Sis."

My mother shushed us, telling everyone to be quiet so she could listen to the gunfire and try to determine how close it was.

By dawn the rockets were landing farther and farther apart, and we began to hear army vehicles speeding up and down the streets and ambulances and fire trucks with wailing sirens threading their way through the devastation all over the city. A military Jeep went up our street, warning everyone by loudspeaker that a twenty-four-hour curfew had been imposed because of the emergency. At first light we went onto the balcony and looked down; all the streets were deserted, as far as we could see.

Hai Van had left his four-band radio at the mosque the last time he visited Ali, so we had no way of finding out what was going on outside our apartment. Ali decided that curfew or not, he had to get home. We warned him that he might be picked up by the police or the soldiers for violating the curfew, but he assured us he could manage. After asking for an aspirin for his hangover, he slipped out of the apartment and sped away on his motorcycle.

Below us in the apartment building was a great stirring. About three-fourths of the people who lived in our building were rich Chinese merchants. The war had not touched them in many ways; Vietnamese politics wasn't their concern, and they even managed to keep their sons out of the military by bribing army officials or sending them to live with relatives in Hong Kong or Taiwan to escape the draft. Now, however, things were different — the rockets and guns were right here in Sai Gon, almost at their thresholds, threatening them and their stacks of money. Several of the people from the first floor came up the stairs and asked my brother, "What is going on out there, young man?" Some of them speculated it was a coup, because the Communists had long spread the slogan "Overthrow the Thieu-Ky puppet government." Hai Van told them he believed the Communists had come into the heart of the city.

We went to the apartment of our neighbors, Mr. and Mrs. Trong, to listen to their radio. Everyone was in a state of utter confusion, and even the radio station went dead and then came back on the air many times. Mr. Trong asked if anyone had noticed that we hadn't heard a word from the president, and I piped up, "Maybe they killed Thieu!" My mother wasn't fond of Nguyen Van Thieu, either — the unpopular successor to Diem, he was more of a dictator than a president — but she shot me a stern look and I shut up. To myself, I said, "I hope Mr. Ky will lead the country. If Thieu dies I'll celebrate the occasion even if I have to drink on top of this hangover."

Finally, a few minutes before 7:00 A.M., Vice President Nguyen Cao Ky broadcast a message to the people, and for the first time we learned that it wasn't a coup, but a concentrated attack by the Communists. We went back to our room to talk about what had happened. "What are we going to do?" I asked my mother. "Just stay calm," she said. We still hadn't heard the voice of President Thieu, but strangely that made my brother and me feel more confident, not less. If Ky was in charge, with his military background, he might be free to make decisions to save the country, we thought; he wasn't a politician like Thieu, and Sai Gon was too precious to be left in the hands of politicians.

The sounds of mortars and gunfire continued to rumble in scattered parts of the city as my mother gathered a few valuables, put them in a velvet sack, and tied it with a knot. She took a picture of Christina that we had gotten from Cuong only a few days earlier and put it in a folder along with photos of my grandparents and my late uncle and the snapshot of Mom, Kim, Cuong, and Khoi — the one she had sent to my father when he was in the French prison from 1940 to 1945.

Hai Van was the first one who thought about food and water. He went to the water tank in the kitchen to check the supply, knowing we would have to make sure it was full in case the electricity went off and it couldn't be pumped up to the second floor where we lived. He ran downstairs to find the "water man," but the pump room was chained shut and no one was there; the strict curfew had paralyzed the entire city and the man hadn't been able to get to our building. Hai Van came back up and got my mother's saw, cut through the chain and turned on the pump, then went through the building advising everyone to store all the water they could.

If the Communists had picked any time other than Tet to attack Sai Gon and the other cities, people would have been in a real panic because they wouldn't have had enough food in the house to last through a long curfew period. In Viet Nam, housewives usually shopped every morning and every afternoon for the food they would need each day; frozen food was almost unknown. At Tet, however, people laid in huge supplies of food to last all seven days of the celebration; it was considered bad luck to spend money on essentials during the holiday, although spending on movies and theaters and even gambling with friends was a tradition.

Our family was no exception to the pattern. In preparation for Tet we had two dozen watermelons, the traditional fruit for the holiday, three different kinds of stew that my mother and our longtime housekeeper Van had made up in advance, four chickens still alive in their cages, and live fish in a holding barrel. We had enough food for more than a week without the need to do any more shopping.

We sat in the kitchen and talked about the Tet tradition. Hai Van teased my mother: "The Viet Cong have ruined our Tet — does that mean they will ruin every day in our lives for the whole year of the monkey?" She smiled wryly at him. "They have ruined every day of our lives for the past fourteen years, I don't know if the omen still works for the Communists."

— — —

Suddenly I remembered that I was supposed to go to work at 1:30 P.M. When Kim had left her job as a head cashier at the Splendid Officers' Club to go off to California to live, I had applied for the position and gotten it. Five girls worked with me at different shifts, morning, afternoon, and evening, and I had no idea how many of them, if any, would show up. Regardless, because I was head cashier, I knew it was important for me to be there. In the four years I had worked for the Americans I had learned how demanding they could be. Once, when the Brinks BOQ had been blown up by a Viet Cong suicide squad, there was utter chaos from the ground floor to the seventh floor where the officers' dining room was — yet some of the American civilians who ate there got angry at my boss because the sausage wasn't cooked right. They complained that the service was too slow, the elevators took too long, the dining room was too hot — while below them crews were still clearing out the rubble where some of their own countrymen had been killed or wounded the afternoon before.

At that moment I was really upset that my mother had never let us have a telephone, arguing that we would just use it to talk endlessly to our young friends. Maybe so, but in this crisis I badly needed to reach my boss, Warrant Officer Lugent, at the officers' club. A Chinese man who lived across the street had a phone, so I went to the balcony and shouted across to him and asked if I could use it. When he said I could, I went to get dressed and got ready to sneak across the deserted street. As I put my clothes on, I thought to myself, "If the Viet Cong shoot me it will be so sad. I just hope my Viet Cong cousins in Can Tho don't say, 'She died for the Liberation movement' at my funeral. I'm doing this for my job, and I work for the U.S. Army."

I survived the trip across the street and back. On the phone, Mr. Lugent said that not one of his 150 employees had showed up for work! He didn't sound angry, although I could tell he had his hands full trying to prepare food for all the officers who stayed at Splendid. I told him if he would send MPs to pick me up, I'd come in. Hoa Binh was also a part-time cashier there, and she said if I was going she'd go too.

When my mother saw the Jeep pull up outside the Kim Chau theater next to our apartment and the MPs with machine guns at their sides, she looked terribly worried, but we went anyway. The MPs told us to sit as low as possible behind them, so we couldn't see anything as the covered Jeep darted through the city. In about ten minutes we arrived at Splendid, which was protected by sandbags piled high in front of the building and soldiers with rifles in their hands, helmets on their heads, and grenades on their belts.

Hoa Binh took care of the cash register at the counter, and I headed into the kitchen to help there, but Mr. Lugent said what he needed most was a bartender. I didn't know anything about mixing drinks, but I went with him, and when he opened the bar the officers cheered and streamed in, filling all the barstools and the tables in an instant. I was panicked, because there were so many people who wanted drinks and only me to serve them.

Fortunately, the officers were patient and cooperative. When they ordered a drink I didn't know how to make, they would tell me how to mix it. When it got too busy, I just handed them the bottles and a glass of ice and let them mix their own, hoping they would be honest enough to pay for what they drank. A marine captain who had been drinking beer called me over and said, "Miss, I want a brandy Alexander, and my friend here wants a Mai Tai." Everybody booed him, but I knew it was only a joke. "You are doing fine," he assured me. I tended the bar for the rest of the afternoon, while Mr. Lugent and four enlisted men managed to do the job of more than fifty workers to serve dinner to some three hundred people.

I hadn't minded serving the officers, but the next day when the civilians came to eat and drink at Splendid, my heartaches began. American civilians in Viet Nam — embassy staffers and contractors for various firms — must have thought the country and the war were created just for them. When they came into the bar they complained endlessly: "Miss, this table is dirty!" "Sir, I know that." "Miss, this drink is too weak!" I poured him a double to shut him up. I remember telling an officer that those civilians were lucky that God made America for them, because they would never survive anywhere else. A war was raging just a few blocks away, yet they griped about everything and not one lent a hand even to clean his own table.

I had very little patience with people who took life for granted. That day a woman who worked for RMK, an engineering company, said she wanted me to chill her wineglass for her, so I did; a few minutes later, though, she asked me to chill four wineglasses for her and her male friends. I blew my top. "We might chill your glasses in peacetime, but not when the Communists are running loose right outside the door!" She reported me to Mr. Lugent, but he just told her that I was in charge of the bar for the time being.

We went home in the MPs' Jeep after the dining room and bar closed, but after the second day Hoa Binh and I both decided that riding around in that Jeep might be an invitation to suicide. So we packed our clothes in an overnight bag and stayed at Splendid for several days, coming home every now and then to check on the family.

When we went home the third time, we rode in an open Jeep. The streets were indescribable: dead people were everywhere, trees were knocked down, the body of a man hung on a branch of a tamarind tree on Cong Ly Street. Gunfire was so close I could hear the whistle of bullets through the air. My parents used to tell us stories of hell and purgatory, and I imagined that Sai Gon in those days was worse than hell and all twelve levels of purgatory. An enormous amount of water flooded the street near Ham Nghi and Cong Ly boulevards; the Viet Cong must have been trying to achieve their goal of paralyzing the city. A twelve-story building that had been under construction had collapsed under a rocket attack; I had a chilling image of our two-story apartment building, but I didn't say anything to my sister.

At the department of vehicles, there used to be a beggar with a horrible-looking cast on his leg and his six-year-old daughter, who sometimes had a bandage around her head; when we drove past the spot where they used to sleep, I saw both of their bodies scattered in pieces along the brick wall.

We reached our building and told the MPs to come back to pick us up at 4:00 P.M. As we ran up the stairs, my mother was already a few steps down waiting for us. Hai Van had been gone since the curfew was lifted at 9:00 A.M., and I knew she was lonely and worried about all three of us. Her face lit up as she took the overnight bag from Hoa Binh and said, "I am so afraid for you two." Hoa Binh and I both told her we wanted to eat "something Vietnamese." The previous night, about eleven o'clock, I had had a craving for the stew we usually ate to celebrate Tet — a pork stew made with fresh coconut juice, black pepper, fish sauce, and hard-boiled eggs — but of course there wasn't anything like that at Splendid. Instead I had eaten chili con carne and a biscuit, and I had to get up and drink many glasses of water during the night.

After a shower I was ready to go back to work, but we were all worried about Hai Van. He had told my mother he had to see what was happening in the city and wouldn't be gone long, but now it was getting late and there was no sign of him. I saw my mother burning incense sticks and knew she must be praying for his safety.

He still hadn't returned when Hoa Binh and I had to leave for work. In fact, he didn't show up until the next day when we had come back for a short visit with Mom. He was tired and dirty. It turned out he had joined up with a bunch of volunteers helping the Red Cross with the emergency, trying to relocate families who had been bombed out and helping pull bodies from underneath the debris. My mother began scolding him for not returning home, but he just sat quietly, not saying anything. Suddenly he jumped from his chair and ran to the bathroom and locked the door. I sat on the floor outside the bathroom and waited for him to come out, and I could hear him being sick inside. My mother thought he had come down with the flu or had caught some terrible illness while handling dead bodies, and she was going to give him aspirin. But he turned her away, quivering, and told us, "I'll never be able to forget yesterday. People didn't die from bullets, they were executed by the Viet Cong! They were stabbed, shot in the face, in the chest. Oh, God, let me join the air force!"

The curfew hours were shortened, and people began to move about more in the city, even though gunfire was still being exchanged between the Viet Cong and ARVN troops. The streets still weren't really safe, but Hoa Binh and I decided that we ought to go back to spending nights at home. Our mother was the one most happy at that decision, because she was afraid that Splendid, a "U.S. imperialist installation," was one of the Viet Cong's targets.

I had thought that my father would be ashamed even to look at my dead body if I had been killed together with the "U.S. imperialists." Thank God Splendid was protected and safe throughout those terrible days of Tet.

— — —

In the months that followed, Hai Van spent a lot of time with friends, and a lot more by himself, thinking about his future. There were times, he said, when a person couldn't let his family's well-meaning interference get in the way of his decisions. "The turning point in each of our lives will not only make a big difference to us, but will have a lasting effect on our parents' relationship with us, too." He wrestled with that responsibility for a long time, and one day he came to me and said, "There are times in my life when I have to live up to my parents' expectations, but there is only one chance to be a man, and this is it." He told me he had decided to sign up for the air force.

Had he thought of our father, who might be among the targets of his bombs, I asked. "When I get my wings I'll bomb every single Viet Cong that crawls on the ground, and every military installation there is in Ha Noi," he said with grim determination. "I just pray to God that I miss Dad and Khoi."

Hai Van carried out his plan as soon as he graduated from high school that spring after Tet, signing up to join the air force. But, just as happened to me so many times, he discovered that being in the middle means you can get hurt by both sides. He was still in boot camp when word came down that he had been rejected for pilot training because he was the "son of the PRG [Provisional Revolutionary Government] ambassador to the Soviet Union." Hai Van was shattered by the news, and my attempts to comfort him by telling how army intelligence had denied me once didn't help much. "Perhaps you do know to a certain degree," he said, "but you are not a man — how can you understand my disappointment?"

My mother didn't say it, but she was actually glad when the air force told Hai Van to go back and continue his education or do whatever he wanted in civilian life. She was quietly proud, though, that he had not been among the thousands of boys in our country who had bought or cheated their way out of military service.

Hai Van wasn't going to take his rejection sitting down, though, anymore than I had accepted mine. He began to pound on every door he could find, to plead with every official he could think of to get the air force to change its mind. Uncle Hai Dinh, a former Viet Minh, had a son who was a colonel in the air force, so Hai Van went to see him. The colonel, Nguyen Hong Tuyen, promised to help his eager young relative. Weeks later, word came back and it was still "no." Hai Van's case was firmly in the hands of military intelligence, and the air force wouldn't budge on its own.

Naturally, mention of military intelligence reminded us of Captain Binh, who was about to hear another sad story from this family of a Communist's offspring. Binh was now Colonel Binh, and when Hai Van went to see him in Can Tho he listened patiently for a while, then helped us out once again. Thanks to a written "guarantee" of Hai Van's trustworthiness signed by Colonel Binh, my brother finally reached his goal of joining his country's air force.

— — —

With my brother committed to service in the air force, and with the horror of Tet still ringing in my mind day and night, it was hard for me even to think about leaving my family and going off to America. But on March 20, 1968, John's tour of duty in Viet Nam would end, and he would have to leave. I couldn't work out my worries that quickly, so I told my fiancé that he should go ahead and I would follow a short time later. We could get married in California.

I knew I had to go, despite my worries about my mother and my little sisters. I knew John was the right man for me, and if I let him slip through my fingers heaven might never give me a second chance. If a farmer misses planting time he can try again the next year, but chances for happiness between two people don't come along that regularly. I knew I wanted to be Mrs. John James Krall for the rest of my life, and in the end that meant more than anything else.

I told my mother in May that I had decided definitely to marry John, and her reaction was to urge me to get started immediately on the paperwork that would be necessary for me to leave the country. This wasn't a simple process of getting a passport, an exit visa, and an entry visa; in the bureaucratic maze of the Vietnamese government, it meant going through an incredible tangle of processes — and, yes, the usual quota of bribes.

The bribes started early. At the Interior Department, an official told me that I might not be able to go at all, because the Thieu government restricted Vietnamese citizens from traveling abroad. A few days later, however, this same man showed up at our apartment, having gotten the address from my application, and said that "someone" he knew could help me get the necessary permission papers. When I asked him how that could be accomplished, he was quite brazen about it: "Ten thousand piasters will get you permission." The money was twice what I made in a month at Splendid, but it was my hatred for corruption that made me slam the door in his face in a most unladylike fashion.

I went to police headquarters to find out if there was any way around the Interior Department, but they were no help. The Interior Department was the only way unless I was "the president's mother or his mistress," a police officer told me with a grin. Humbled, I went back to the Interior Department, but the man wouldn't see me; I guess I couldn't blame him. Fortunately, one might say, the supply of bribe takers wasn't limited. A girlfriend of my mother's knew an army colonel who had helped her obtain a student visa for her daughter to visit Paris once, so I asked her to contact him on my behalf.

The answer was yes, and the price was still ten thousand piasters — but only for the permission papers. The passport would still be up to me. The colonel had the nerve to demand payment in advance, but my mother's friend pressured him to get the papers first, assuring him he would get his money. Two weeks later I got word to go to the colonel's house. He didn't come to the living room to face me, but sent his wife. She handed me the papers and waited reluctantly while I examined them. When I was satisfied they were in order, I handed her the fistful of five-hundred-piaster notes that I had struggled so long to save.

I never spent money as foolishly as I did on this army colonel, and my brother teased me about it: "For love, people will do anything." He was right! I even studied Catholicism and was baptized at Sai Gon Cathedral by Father Paul Thong; John's ancestors on both sides were Catholic and he had said once he wished we could get married in the Catholic church. John's great-grandfather had been a king in a small part of Yugoslavia, and was beheaded because he refused to become a Catholic; the rest of his family converted in short order. I had some reservations about taking on this religion, too — not because I feared for my head, but because my mother had once said that our family might be divided by religion just as it had been rent by politics. "After all, there is but one God and he has been good to us," she said. But by this time Kim and Cuong had become Catholic, so it was too late to worry about that.

At the passport office, the plainclothes policeman in charge of giving out and accepting applications told me it would probably take six to eight months to get my passport. Once again, I decided not to wait for the bureaucracy. I went to visit a friend who was a police investigator at the Second Precinct. In a gentle way my friend, An, told me that in this city "success comes when one has either money or power or sometimes both." I didn't have much money left, but An offered to go with me to the passport office to find out what kind of pressures might work. Sure enough, when a fellow policeman showed up, shook hands with that same clerk, and introduced me as his cousin, the six-month delay shrank to almost nothing — only three weeks!

(I was and am still so grateful to An, who was always a kind and generous man. As I write this book, he is in prison in Viet Nam for the "crime" of serving as a policeman in the Thieu regime. He has been there since 1976. His wife and five children were sent off to a "new economic zone," and I never heard anything of them again.)

Still, even with the help of kind friends, dealing with the people in the bureaucracy could be frustrating. When I got a notice that my passport was ready, I rushed to the office, where an ancient civil-service worker took my letter and told me to wait while he went into a back office. An agonizing fifteen minutes later he returned and said, "They seem to have misplaced your passport, Miss." Fat chance, I thought! There were so few people being allowed to get passports that it would be impossible to misplace one that was actually issued. I told the man I would wait until he found it, but he just shook his head and nonchalantly went back to reading a newspaper.

I was infuriated! I reached across the counter and took the newspaper from in front of his face. "Sir, you are here to serve me. You can read your papers when I leave. Now please try to locate my passport." He yanked the newspaper back, his face flushed, and growled through his teeth: "I told you they can't find your passport!" Fine, I said, let me see "them." He changed his tactic, lowering his voice and suggesting I come back the next day and try again. "I don't have any free time the next day," I said. "I work, and I'm serious about my job."

The man seemed humiliated. "Just who do you think you are?" he demanded.

"You serve the people of this country, and I'm the people," I told him coldly. "I demand service, that's all I want. Give me my passport and then you don't have to worry about who I am." Sure enough, he pulled open a drawer and took out my passport, which had been there all along, and threw it on the desk-top. "Take it and get out of here!" he screamed, then stomped off into the back while I checked to make sure the passport was truly mine. I thought for a while about reporting the man, but in the end decided not to. For one thing, I didn't want to waste the time; for another, I was pretty lucky to have gotten a gen-uine passport without having to pay out a single *dong,* or dollar, in bribes.

I wasn't optimistic when I went to the tax office for the next step, which was to allow the government to make sure I wasn't leaving the country owing them money. This government building must have contained nearly every piece of paper in South Viet Nam, huge stacks of yellowed sheets covered with thick layers of dust. By some miraculous coincidence, the person who handled matters like mine turned out to be my father's niece, and she whisked me through the forms that asked questions such as whether I owned a busi-ness, a savings account, a house elsewhere in the country, or a private retreat. I laughed at that last one and said, "Sure, Vung Tau."

I must say I had no trouble getting my entry visa to the United States. All I had to do was pay a fee that amounted to about three dollars and respond to a few questions — which I answered almost completely honestly. When the consular official, Miss Tuttle, asked me my reason for visiting the United States, I told her I was going to visit my sisters, who lived in California. "Will you seek a job while you are visiting your sisters?" she asked.

"Why would I want to do a thing like that? I have a good job here, I'm not going to America with that intention."

Miss Tuttle asked if I met a young man while visiting America and he asked me to stay, would I stay? I smiled, thinking that I had already been asked: "I'd better not," I replied.

It took two interviews with Miss Tuttle to convince her I wasn't going to America to seek new opportunities and stay there permanently. In a way, that was the truth, because in my heart I still couldn't really believe that I was going to marry John and stay in his country.

As the time came for my departure, I seemed to lose touch with reality. I can't remember going from my house, where I said goodbye to my family on June 20, 1968, to Tan Son Nhut Airport, and then on to America. All I can remember is sitting by the window on the airplane, in a blue and white seat, the blue and white Pan Am logo printed on a cocktail napkin on the tray in front of me. I also remember falling asleep when it was dark outside, then being terrified when I woke to bright sunlight and realized that my mother and my family were on the other side of the world.

When I was young, there were very few things I was afraid of or unable to comprehend. Once when I was twelve I had killed a boa constrictor that had swallowed some of my aunt's chickens. I beat the thing with a paddle, and when it died one of the chickens was in its stomach and the other was still only halfway in its mouth. The only thing I had ever really been unable to stand was being alone, and now I was traveling a terribly long distance to be almost completely alone from everything I had known and loved all my life.

I looked over my shoulder, trying to gaze thousands of miles back across the Pacific, and said goodbye to my family, to my people, and to the country that had given me birth and life. I had no idea what lay ahead for a stubborn, impatient "farmer from the Mekong Delta" in the nation that most of my relatives considered their most hated enemy.

Chapter 15

The beginning of my new life in America was as much a blur as the end of my life in Viet Nam. I don't remember much of anything about the first days in Monterey, and very little about my own wedding on August 3, 1968. I know that Kim took me to Carmel to buy my wedding dress, but I can't remember bringing it home.

I didn't send out any invitations to the ceremony, because I knew no one in the United States. John invited his friends, of course, and Kim and Cuong invited people they had gotten to know since coming to Monterey, most of them Vietnamese instructors at the Monterey Presidio in California.

All my life I had dreamed of my wedding day, with my father standing there proudly to bless the marriage and give me away, and my mother crying over "losing her daughter." I wasn't able to share any of this most important day with them, however. The two people who meant the most to me in the world were far away, and likely to remain so for a long time.

Before we left on our honeymoon and then for our new home in Johnsville, Pennsylvania, where John was a test pilot at the naval air station, both my sisters took me aside and reminded me again how lucky I was to have married such a fine person. They didn't need to tell me; I had known that before I left Viet Nam, and John was the only reason on earth I would have left my homeland.

I don't remember a lot about those early days as a newly married couple. Once we settled down in the small community of Johnsville, I met some fine people and began to socialize and participate in Navy Officers' Wives Club functions. I wrote home three or four times a week, and in every letter I told my mother how happy I was because I didn't want her to worry. It was a lie, though. The fact is, I wasn't doing very well at all. I had dreams and nightmares of home almost every night: I dreamed of Viet Nam, of Sai Gon, I heard Vietnamese music, I dreamed of Viet Cong trying to break up my marriage. I dreamed of food my mother made and woke up thinking I smelled it, only to find myself in the middle of a cold winter in northern Pennsylvania. For almost a year the dreams kept coming. I fought them hard, and I fought them alone; I didn't want John to know how weak I was.

One night when John was away on a trip to Bermuda for the navy, I woke up from yet another dream of being in Sai Gon, window-shopping along Le Loi Street with its bookstores, restaurants, theaters, and stores. Lying there in the dark, I thought about how much I had let myself down in the last year, catering to my weakness. If it got much worse, I realized, I wouldn't be able to hide it from John. In fact, I might go out of my mind. I didn't think I was strong enough to cast away whatever it was that was making me refuse to accept reality, yet I had to find a way. I knew that my sense of humor, my boldness, my seeming ability to face anything were the things that had attracted John to me, and now those bright characteristics were in eclipse. Since I set foot in America, I had been behaving like a lost soul. Somehow, thinking of John and all he meant to me, I drew on all my courage and determined to snap out of my depression, to become once again the person he had fallen in love with. And from that day on, I never had any more of those terrible dreams.

In late 1969, John got orders to report to the Naval Post-Graduate School in Monterey where he was to study for a master's degree, and I finally had a chance to see that beautiful place, the home of my sisters and the site of my wedding, in a healthier, more positive light. It was like being there for the first time.

— — —

The fall of 1970 brought truly thrilling news: Hai Van was coming to America! The South Vietnamese air force was sending him to the American air force base at Lackland, Texas, for helicopter training.

It was the best year in Hai Van's life. He received one "outstanding" rating after another throughout his training, and enjoyed seeing the United States during his furloughs. It was a wonderful year for me, too: I was going to become a mother.

Hai Van and I called each other to share our good news. He told me about girls he had met at parties, I told him about feeling the baby kicking inside my swelling belly. He told me how anxious he was to go back to Viet Nam and to put his helicopter training to use to help our country, I told him what names we were thinking about for the newest member of the family.

From Lackland, Hai Van's class was sent to Hunter Army Airfield near Savannah, Georgia, for more training. I was so proud when my brother became one of the outstanding students in his flying class. General Robert McKinnon at Fort Walters wrote my mother to congratulate her for having such a fine son, and she was filled with pride.

On December 9, 1970, our son was born at Fort Ord hospital outside Monterey. We named him Lance David, after John's friend who had been the best swimmer on his high school swimming team, and Dr. David Goldstein, who had been best man at our wedding.

That Christmas Hai Van flew to Washington, D.C., to spend the holidays with our sister Kim, who had gotten a job teaching Vietnamese at the State Department. I wanted to see him, but with the new baby I couldn't make it to Washington. It was a real disappointment, because I knew his class would be completing training at Hunter and returning to Viet Nam in another month or so and it might be a long time before we could be together again.

Disappointment turned to agony two weeks later. On January 11, 1971, Kim called from her home in Arlington, Virginia, and said that Hai Van had been in an accident — the helicopter he was piloting had gone down in a rare Georgia snowstorm near Hunter Army Airfield. We couldn't talk to each other, we didn't want to think about anything but our brother and to pray that he would survive the crash and be all right.

A few hours later Kim called again. The air force had informed her that Hai Van was dead.

It can't be, I screamed inside my head. *Not him, not a twenty-one-year-old young man who hadn't even had a chance to fight for his country yet!* My mind raced, thinking about the chances that they might have made a mistake. I offered a deal to God: *Let my brother live, and I'll give up my arms, my legs, anything. I've had a full life, a husband, a new son, I've loved and been loved, let me die for my brother.* I went to the chapel where I had gotten married and talked to God. I went to the Catholic church in Monterey and asked the priest there for help. All he could say was, "God wants your brother to be his servant." It wasn't enough. I had made such an effort to become close to God, and now when I needed something from this great being, I felt betrayed. I didn't set foot in the church again for nearly a year, when John thought it was time for our son to be baptized.

I wanted so much to be with my family, to share our great loss and to support my mother; I knew that the pain I felt was nothing to compare with the suffering she was feeling. But I couldn't return to Viet Nam because of my visa situation — I could go back, but there was every chance that I wouldn't be able to leave again. My sister Cuong was in Bangkok at the time with her husband, who was stationed at the U.S. military headquarters there, so she went to Sai Gon to be with our mother. Kim went to Savannah, where the air force had a memorial service for Hai Van. The world seemed to stand still while my mother waited and waited to receive my brother's body; it took more than a week to get him home for the last time.

I was shattered by the loss of my brother, and I felt helpless and all alone. How can one be "strong" and "take it well" when a little brother dies? I am still bitter about his death, still angry, and I miss him immensely. Most of all I share the sorrow I know his soul must feel that he didn't have the chance he wanted so badly to fight to rid his country of the Communist evil. Even in death the Viet Cong used him, telling my father that the CIA had killed Hai Van because of who his father was. My blood boils when I think of how my father believed that lie for so long, up until the day he died.

It hurts me that my own father saw things through the eyes of the Communist ideology and didn't realize that his son was as great as he was. My brother may not have had much luck, but he was nobody's victim.

— — —

It was not until five years after coming to the United States, in 1973, that I decided to chance a return visit to Viet Nam. I still worried about getting into problems over visas with the bureaucracy there, but I longed to see my mother and my sisters once again. The power of a family's love can overcome fear of any government, it seems.

It didn't take me long to realize, as everyone who ever tries to "come home again" learns, that things had changed. A taxi driver overcharged me, the streets were filthy, there was garbage and burning trash everywhere; Sai Gon could certainly no longer be called the "Pearl of the Orient." Makeshift shelters lined the streets and sidewalks where refugees from the wartorn countryside tried to survive; I'm sure such places must have existed when I lived in Sai Gon, but the scene was especially shocking to a person coming from a peaceful, prosperous land. My world was shattered by the vision of orphans begging in the streets, former soldiers crawling along on little wheeled boards, even healthy men in uniforms pleading for money.

My spirits were revived when I got to my mother's house. Lance, now three years old, had come with me, and everyone was thrilled to see him for the first time. The maid rocked him to sleep, his aunts catered to his every wish, and almost everyone would run to him whenever he made the slightest sound.

Dinners were like big feasts every day. My mother made all my favorite foods. After our meal we would stay up very late, talking a little about life in America but mostly about conditions — the terrible conditions — at home.

During the first weekend, Hoa Binh came home from her job and the whole family packed a picnic basket and went off to the National Cemetery about ten miles outside Sai Gon to visit Hai Van's gravesite. I took along a large periwinkle plant, because my brother had always liked wildflowers; I planted the flowers at his feet. It was an unexplainable feeling to sit by Hai Van's grave. Part of me refused to admit that my own brother lay underneath that marble slab, but another part accepted it and was glad to know that he was among other men and women who had given their lives so our country could live in peace. I couldn't touch him or see him, but I felt he was there, that he would always be with us. In a way I felt Hai Van had it better than our cousin Quoc. Quoc died in a Viet Cong–controlled area at nineteen years old, two years before Hai Van was killed. He had been buried in a mass grave.

After a few days spent with my family, I decided I wanted to do something, however small, about some of the problems I saw everywhere around me. My grandfather used to tell me how lucky I was, and I never quite understood how he could see my life that way. But when Lance came into our lives I realized that I was indeed a "lucky one." I wanted to share what I could with people who were less fortunate. I started visiting some of the orphanages in Sai Gon to see if I could help the desperate, lonely children whom the war had made homeless. At some of the orphanages, the nuns told me they needed money to upgrade their "model institutions"; at others, the directors said they were too busy and asked me to come back when they had time to talk to me. None of them allowed me to see even a single orphan — they only wanted to talk about money, aid, and support. I told them all that my intention was to go back to the United States to raise funds to help the children, not to help institutions; I had no intention of giving money to anyone except directly to the children by fulfilling their immediate needs.

Finally, I went to the U.S. Agency for International Development (AID) and met a staff member, Bobbie Noflet. I told her I didn't believe in giving money to churches or social organizations to buy coffee or typewriters for any office worker. She smiled and said, "I think I understand."

The next day Miss Noflet and her Vietnamese secretary, Miss Hanh, took me to Go Vap, a little town just outside the Sai Gon city limits, where we visited a small, isolated orphanage called Minh Tri. Funded by the Catholic church, Minh Tri was run by two nuns and two other women, aided by a young lady who had grown up there as an orphan herself. Miss Noflet warned me that the institution was rather poor and had little contact with the government's social department. The nuns didn't seek help from AID, but women at the German embassy lent the children toys and made visits and sometimes donated milk and medicine.

I was introduced to Sister Ho Thi Trong, the head of the orphanage, who showed me around. More than 350 children, ranging from newborns to twelve-year-olds, were living in cramped, pitiful conditions at the institution. There were no more than a dozen beds, so all the older children had to sleep on the floor. At lunchtime, the children stood in line with bowls and spoons in their hands. When they reached the head of the line, they would get rice from one lady and a ladle of soup from another. There were bits of fish in the soup, but it looked as if the green flies had tasted their share before the children had a chance. One little boy with an open cut on his head swatted repeatedly at the flies that swarmed over his wound as he shuffled passively up the line. Amerasian children were plentiful at Minh Tri; two little blondes, hand in hand, covered their mouths and giggled when they saw Miss Noflet and me watching them.

I left Minh Tri that afternoon with a knot in my stomach, but the smile on the face of Sister Trong and the look of hope in her eyes stayed on my mind. I had told her I would go back to Hawaii, where we had recently moved, and do everything I could to raise funds for the children in her care.

Back in Hawaii, John and I raised some money from the officers and wives of his squadron. About six months later John was reassigned to duty in the Indian Ocean, so Lance and I returned to Sai Gon and we used the money to have a playground installed at Minh Tri orphanage for the first time — a swing set, monkey bars, and a slide. With the money left over, Sister Trong bought rice and a few other things for the classrooms.

When I returned to Hawaii again I called on Lois Taylor of the *Honolulu Star Bulletin,* who wrote an article about Minh Tri. The response was overwhelming; donations poured in, from as little as a single dollar bill to more than a hundred. A sweet woman who was living on her modest Social Security check wrote in, saying, "I want to share something I have with the children," and enclosed a check. A wealthy man who preferred not to give his name to the press called me to come to his office to pick up his check; I almost screamed for joy when I saw it was made out for five hundred dollars.

It was several more months before I got a chance to return to Sai Gon, this time when John was sent to the Indian Ocean again, to the island of Diego Garcia, for six months. Lance and I stayed with my mother the entire time, and one of the warmest memories of that visit — which turned out to be my last one — was when we took the donations raised by the newspaper publicity to the orphanage. We bought sixty bunk beds with the funds, and Sister Trong told us that "at least 240 of my little ones could sleep there."

John and I felt good about the help we had given those poor children. We didn't know that we would end up giving them something much greater just two years later — new lives in a new land.

Chapter 16

ℐ looked at the calendar on the kitchen wall and counted the days in February until John would be home from his latest flying assignment. I made a pretty poor navy wife, I thought, because I hated when my husband was away. We had been lucky for the first few years of marriage, because John did all his flying at the naval air station at Johnsville and didn't have to leave home much; then, when he was at post-graduate school in Monterey, we were together almost all the time. Now, however, in 1975, he was assigned to Fleet Weather Central in Hawaii and he was off on long flights for days at a time. I found myself talking out loud to myself at night, when the house was so quiet I could hear the lizards' lamenting calls outside; I slept with a PPK pistol under the bed, a chair propped against the bedroom door, and floodlights burning all night to chase away the dark.

I went back to finish up the last chapter of a Vietnamese novel I had been reading; it was a cheap way to "go home," and by the time I put the book down I had gone to at least a dozen places in Sai Gon and seen many familiar faces as I walked along the streets and boulevards in my mind.

Just before I started out the door to get Lance at his preschool, the phone rang. The operator said, "You have a collect call from Mr. Sagan in Paris. Will you accept the charge?" The name meant nothing to me, and after a little hesitation I declined to accept the call. Moments later the phone rang again, and this time a man's voice with a French accent spoke directly to me — with a startling message: "My Yung, I am your father's friend. I want you to listen to me very carefully."

My hands started to tremble when I heard this man call me My Yung, the name only my father had called me, and that had been nineteen years ago. The caller went on in an authoritative voice. "I want you to arrange for your mother and sisters to leave Sai Gon at once!"

"I've tried to bring my mother . . . ," I began, but he interrupted, his tone becoming more urgent. "You must get your mother and sisters out. The war is going to break out any day now!"

Despite my surprise at his calling me My Yung, I didn't take his words seriously. I thought this might be some kind of scheme to get money from me, because once before when I had tried to get an exit visa for my nephew to leave Sai Gon, a high-ranking official at the Interior Department had made it clear that money would have to change hands before anything could happen. I chuckled a bit and told the caller, "The war has been there ever since you Frenchmen set your hairy feet on our land, and it hasn't ceased since the battle of Dien Bien Phu."

"Listen," he said again, "your mother's life is in danger. You must get her out of Viet Nam as soon as you can!"

"I appreciate your concern, but I don't have 50,000 piasters to buy her visa," I replied.

"Your father's friends will be in Sai Gon, too. It is not safe for your mother and sisters to be there. Do you understand me?" He began to sound angry.

"I understand what you said, but if they are my father's friends why should they harm my family?"

"Don't play stupid with me! You must trust my words. Bring them to the United States, to France — anywhere away from Viet Nam!"

"Can you tell me how to do this?" I asked. "Nobody is allowed to leave the country now."

"Tell your husband to go to Admiral Gaylor, the commander in chief of the Pacific, and ask for help. He is a kind man, a good man for the job, he'll help. You do that, My Yung."

I held the receiver with both hands in front of my chest and sank to the floor. I could hear my heartbeat, feel the perspiration in my hands, and only when I heard the loud dial tone did I think to hang up the phone. I sat on the floor and tried desperately to recall where I had heard the name "Sagan" before.

The phone rang again, and it was another demanding voice: "Mom, why don't you pick me up? I want to go to McDonald's!" I realized then that I was five minutes late picking up Lance from his preschool.

That afternoon I went through all my address books and notebooks, searching for some hint of this stranger's identity. A manila envelope in the lowest drawer of my desk, with a postmark from Paris, caught my eye: The name "Jean Sagan" was written on the left-hand corner. I hadn't known this man, but three years before, he had sent me this envelope containing pictures of my father, my brother Khoi, and my cousins Tran Tu Trung and Thu Van. Some of the pictures had been taken in front of the Kremlin, with snow piled high under overcast skies. There were pictures of my father in Mongolia, pictures of him at tea with Ho Chi Minh, Le Duan, Truong Chinh, and others I didn't recognize. I had been disappointed at the time because the sender had written only his name, not his address, on the envelope. Now this unknown Frenchman had resurfaced in my life, with another message that concerned my family.

For some time I had been confident that I was captain of the ship that was carrying me to my destiny, but after that phone call I felt I had lost control. I stayed awake at night filled with fear and thousands of questions that I wished I could have asked this Jean Sagan. I began listening to the radio and watching the evening news more closely, hoping to learn more about the war situation but knowing I had to discount half of what I heard. The news from Viet Nam in those days was nothing but bad: The South Vietnamese troops lost Ban Me Thuot, recaptured it, then lost it again in a few weeks; Quang Tri fell to the North Vietnamese, and people again fled south by the thousands in search of refuge.

I felt helpless, and could only look up to heaven and ask for protection for the millions of people who were caught in the cross fire. I was ashamed for letting myself feel defeat, but I said to God, "If my country is destined to be in the hands of the Communists, at least let my people live with dignity." I knew deep inside my heart what the Communists were capable of doing once the celebratory period was over.

John returned from his mission in about ten days, but I couldn't bring myself to tell him about the phone call. Every night I tried to get him to watch the news and to think about what was happening in Viet Nam. One evening I asked him, but he just turned the question around to me. Quietly, I told him, "I think we are going to lose the South."

He looked at me in dismay and disappointment. "Honey, you always let me believe that you love and respect the soldiers of your country, and saying that they are going to lose the South at this stage is no respect at all. Have faith in them. They are good soldiers."

I cried, and my heart felt crushed. "John, losing the South is not an easy thing to speak of, but for the first time I have that feeling. I don't know how to explain it to you, but I am scared. I know they are the best soldiers, but only when they are allowed to carry out their mission. We will lose the South because of Thieu, not because the army can't lick the North. How can the soldiers advance when their generals and their president tell them to withdraw? Tell me, you are a soldier: Would you disobey your commander in chief?

"President Thieu is keeping his troops from fighting," I went on. "He pulls them away from the front lines, and the North Vietnamese are advancing toward the South. The map of South Viet Nam is being painted red every day now, John! I believe that Thieu is selling out Viet Nam to the Communists for a price. Ha Noi can have the South without losing a drop of its Communist blood, and in return Thieu gets his gold, his wives and his children out of Viet Nam!" (After the fall of Sai Gon, indeed, Thieu went to London and lived with his family, his servants and bodyguards, and all his money and gold.)

John argued vehemently with my assessment. "I think Thieu ordered the troops to retreat deeper into the South so they can use air strikes. He made a good move by retreating; they will be strong enough to push the North back up. With air support they will make it."

"Damn it, John, we are talking about the most corrupt animal! If Nguyen Cao Ky were in charge, then I could be convinced by military strategy, and believe every word you are saying and go to bed with pleasant dreams. But this is Nguyen Van Thieu that you are talking about. You don't know the man, John. All he ever wants is money and power. Peace for Viet Nam is nothing to him!"

John went to the kitchen to make himself another rum and Coke, and I got the mixer and made myself a Mai Tai. I seldom drink, but I wanted to drink that afternoon. When we came back into the living room, I decided I still didn't want to tell John about the call from Jean Sagan, because I felt he would trust my own instincts more than a warning from a stranger.

"John, would you find a way to get my mother and sisters out of Sai Gon?" I watched his face carefully. He took my hands and said, "Honey, they are mine as well as yours. I'll take care of them."

"Thank you," was all I could say.

"You must be crazy to think that I would leave them there if and when the South is taken over. It is my duty to protect my family," he said, "and it would be my pleasure to see your happy smile when they are here and safe."

For the first time since the telephone call I felt a measure of peace. I decided to tell John about it, thinking that if the information about a North Vietnamese attack had any merit we might pass it on to the navy or to an intelligence agency. That evening, after dinner, I made John a drink and told him, "I must tell you something that I have been hiding from you for days."

"Let me guess — you're pregnant!"

"I wish I were."

"Uh-oh, not another speeding ticket from the Barber's Point police?"

I covered his mouth lightly to hush him, and told him about the call. He was upset that I had waited ten days to tell him about it.

In fact, I had borne the burden alone for about three weeks; I didn't even tell Cuong because she had chosen not to tell her husband about our father's background. Wray was in the army and Cuong worried about his career. We respected her wishes.

John and I talked for a long time about Jean Sagan's message, and what we ought to do about it. John was somewhat suspicious, wondering why a friend of my father's would call with such instructions. The military situation didn't seem that bad to him, and besides, he wondered, why would my father want his family taken out of Viet Nam if he was about to march triumphantly back into the South?

John agreed that telling Admiral Gaylor about the situation wouldn't necessarily be the smartest course; as he said, he could see the eyebrows raising all over the navy if they found out that an officer with top-secret security clearance had a Communist father-in-law. Instead, he said, if the time came when it was really necessary, he would figure out a way to go to Sai Gon and rescue my family himself.

He would watch developments in Viet Nam closely, looking for some sign that the end was really near. The key would be the situation in the Central Highlands, he told me; he had always thought that the best chance for the Communists to win was to attack the middle of South Viet Nam from Cambodia, cutting the country in two. At a minimum, he thought, they would force the loss of the northern half of South Viet Nam; at worst, they could precipitate the final collapse of the South's government.

Sure enough, before long the war began to heat up. The North did indeed attack the Central Highlands, as John had expected, on March 10, 1975; no one was prepared, however, for the news that ARVN forces were going to abandon the whole region with hardly a shot being fired! President Thieu had ordered his troops to pull out and march to the sea, where boats were supposed to take them south — but what boats? The withdrawal turned into a rout; bases were abandoned with bombs and ammunition still in the storage bunkers. North Vietnamese troops took over the bases and turned the ARVN's own abandoned artillery on them and their families as they tried to flee.

John realized that the time had come for him to move, and move fast.

— — —

The next day John went to his office at Fleet Weather Central at Pearl Harbor to ask for a thirty-day leave to make a trip to Viet Nam. The leave was no problem, he was told, but it was against regulations for navy personnel to travel to Sai Gon without official orders. "Just give me thirty days," he said,

"I'll spend them wisely." He came home with the travel destination left blank on his leave order.

While John started checking with the Military Airlift Command at Hickam Air Force Base about flight schedules, I called the South Vietnamese consulate in San Francisco to ask about an entry visa for him. Americans didn't need visas for visits shorter than three days, I learned, but if John was going to stay longer it would take about three weeks to process his application. Well, he would certainly need more than three days to wrestle with the bureaucracy in Sai Gon, but we didn't have three weeks to wait.

John and I talked about whether he should try to go without a visa; no one was likely to know whether he was there for more than three days or not, I said, and besides, who would care after Sai Gon was overrun by a bunch of hoodlums from Ha Noi? John then suggested he could go to Bangkok and run to the Vietnamese embassy there, where he could probably get a visa in less than thirty minutes. "I can do it either way," he said. "It depends on the situation in Sai Gon. I may just get off right at Tan Son Nhut air base in Sai Gon."

That afternoon, John went to Hickam to check on military flights again, and was told that the weekly embassy flight would be leaving the next day but would probably be full. In the navy, John says, if you want something done you find a chief petty officer and tell him the problem. Luckily, there was a CPO stationed at the MAC facility, and John looked him up. "Chief, I have a problem," he began. "My wife has a family in Sai Gon and I have to get them out. I'm on leave, and the air force people are saving all the seats for their buddies. How about some help?"

The CPO stood up in his crisp whites, looking sharp, and said, "I will assume that you have the correct paperwork. You know that there is a new Defense Department directive stating that only military personnel with proper orders can go to Viet Nam."

"Sure, Chief," John replied. "I've got all the paperwork." They both knew he didn't, but John was getting the CPO off the hook — even though that probably wasn't as important to him as helping a fellow navy man. The CPO got John on the waiting list for the next day's flight with a Red Cap priority — the highest one could have on a space-available basis.

At the flight registration desk, the air force sergeant in charge scowled at the Red Cap paperwork, but said nothing about what he was probably thinking. He handed over a computer printout of the flight orders and told John to be at the terminal two hours before departure.

That night, John was really up about his trip. "They can throw me back on the plane if they catch me at Tan Son Nhut," he said, smiling from ear to ear,

No pictures of Yung Krall as a child survive; each photo of Yung included her father, so they were all destroyed for security reasons while she lived in South Viet Nam, and he fought for the North.

My mother, Mrs. Tran Thi Pham, in 1939, one year before the French captured her husband and imprisoned him until 1945.

My mother, brother Khoi, and twin sisters Kim (left) *and Cuong* (right). *This picture was taken to send to my father in the French prison on Con Son Island, 1943.*

My father, Dang Quang Minh, was this young when he left us for Ha Noi in 1954 (photo taken in 1957).

My father was this old when he returned home in 1975.

Hai Van, an honor graduate from the South Vietnamese Air Force, trained in Savannah, Georgia, 1971. (Photo by Terry Morris)

My oldest brother, Dang Van Khoi, in military training in the USSR, 1966.

Khoi when he graduated from the USSR Military Training, 1967.

My father with Khoi (right) and his adopted daughter Thuy Xinh (left), Moscow, 1966.

(Left) *My father, Ambassador Dang Quang Minh, in Moscow, 1968.*

(Below) *On the right is my father, the NLF ambassador to the Soviet Union, speaking to Ho Chi Minh (left) in Ha Noi. The others are members of the politburo, including Le Duc Tho, standing next to Ho Chi Minh, 1964.*

Ambassador Dang Quang Minh (seated, 2d from left) and the NLF delegation at the Kremlin, 1966.

Myself and Lance, Sai Gon, 1973.

Lieutenant John J. Krall, USN, Sai Gon, 1967.

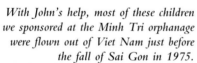

With John's help, most of these children we sponsored at the Minh Tri orphanage were flown out of Viet Nam just before the fall of Sai Gon in 1975.

(Left) *My first reunion with my father, Tokyo, 1975.*

(Below) *My son, Lance, and his grandfather, when they first met in Tokyo, 1975.*

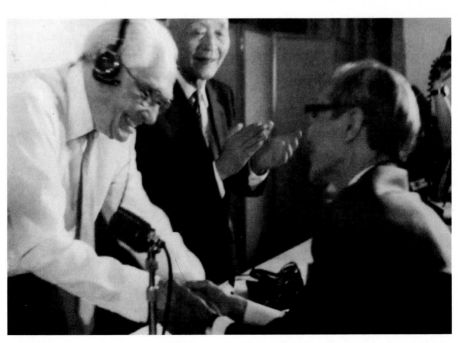

My father the ambassador, meeting with an American scientist at the ban-the-bomb rally in Tokyo, 1975.

Christmas in London, 1977.

Lance with "Grandma" and "Grandpa."

Left to right: *Myself, my sister Hoa Binh, and our father and mother.*

Left to right: *Hoa Binh, John, my father, and Lance.*

My father's last farewell, the morning he said goodbye to us all and returned to Ha Noi.

Hoa Binh's first reunion with our father.

My mother and Minh Tam in the United States.

but he knew he could get a proper visa easily in Bangkok. "So either way, your husband will be in Sai Gon this week."

Then he got more serious. "I need the address of the Minh Tri orphanage — write it down in my notebook. I also need the name of your friend, the army intelligence colonel, and someone who can help me get a Jeep and a pistol in case I need them."

"What for?" I said, panicking.

"Don't you want your orphans to get out if there is a chance?"

"Oh, John, yes," I said, "thank you for thinking of them!"

"Don't 'oh, John' me, just write down those names and addresses for me." Typical of a navy pilot, John's mind had a tendency to work like a clock, and he habitually logged important things down in a notebook.

I gave John the telephone number of my family's old friend Colonel Tran Duy Binh, and told him he would have to see him at his office because I didn't have his home address. I also gave him the telephone number of my good friend George Esper, the Associated Press bureau chief in Sai Gon, and we both agreed that he would be our communications link if we couldn't get through to each other by telephone. I had been introduced to Esper back in 1973 by his competitor, Paul Vogle of United Press International, whom I had met years before when I worked for G-5 in Can Tho.

Tucking his notebook away in his briefcase, John then asked me to write him a letter in Vietnamese. "In case they take me," he said, meaning the Communists, "maybe I'll have something to save my skin." When he said that, I suddenly thought I didn't want him to go at all. "It's best we make plans," he said. "I want you to write exactly what I say." Then he dictated the message to me:

> My name is John Krall. I am here to see that my wife's family
> is safe until Mr. Dang Quang Minh, alias Dang Van Quang, is
> back from Ha Noi. Mr. Minh is my father-in-law. You can check
> with Colonel Nguyen Hoan Phat, originally from Can Tho, or
> with other members of my wife's family such as Tran Van Diep,
> or Tran Van Thuy. I will not talk or negotiate with anyone other
> than those mentioned above.

I shivered as I wrote the note for John. The only compassionate Communist I had ever known was my father, and I hadn't seen him for more than twenty years. This note would be nothing but a joke to them, I thought. From here on, I realized, I would have no control over anything. I could only depend on John's ability, his wits, and his luck.

I left the house to take Lance for a walk by the beach in front of our house. The sky was dark and the city lights from across the harbor shone brightly, but

I was scared. I found myself talking silently to my lost brother Hai Van: *I need your help, Hai Van. You have to help John get Mom and Binh and Tam to me. Somehow I have the feeling that you are still with us and looking after the family the way you did when you were with us before.*

—— —— ——

John has always been an optimist, and even he had to admit that as the plane started its takeoff roll he felt a flood of anticipation. He was going to have to draw on all the confidence he had gained through his years as a naval aviator if he was going to get through this test.

The plane's stopover in Guam was only supposed to last an hour, but for some reason it stretched to three. A longer time to think about what might lie ahead was the last thing John thought he needed, but in fact that delay saved his secret mission.

On the next leg of the trip, John noticed that an admiral had gotten on board, and they both eyed each other's navy wings of gold. John nodded and smiled, but wasn't sure he ought to talk to him since he was treading on awfully thin ice by flying off to Sai Gon illegally. Suddenly the admiral got up from his seat, came over to John, and introduced himself as Admiral Oberg of CINCPACFLT (Commander in Chief Pacific Fleet) staff. They were both going to Viet Nam, it turned out, and the admiral asked John what he would be doing there. John told him the truth: "I'm going to get my wife's family out of Viet Nam."

After a long moment Admiral Oberg pointed out quietly that Viet Nam was closed to everyone except people on official business. John merely nodded in acknowledgment, but said nothing. Another pause, then a smile. "They won't find out from me," the admiral said, "but you'll need good luck." The time for that luck would come soon, he warned John, because the U.S. military police were checking everyone's paperwork extremely carefully at Clark Air Base in the Philippines, where they were about to make their next stop.

As the plane neared its landing, John grew more anxious about the documents check. All kinds of excuses ran through his mind, but he knew none of them would explain his lack of genuine travel orders. Then the miracle happened! Because the flight was so late, having been held up in Guam, all the passengers were told to stay in a secure area near the plane so that it wouldn't be necessary to check everyone's papers all over again on reboarding. John breathed a huge sigh of relief, and as he looked over at Admiral Oberg he got a knowing smile. After only a thirty-minute refueling stop, what must have been a record of some kind, they were airborne again with nothing between John and Sai Gon except a few hundred miles of ocean.

Before the landing, John went to the lavatory on the plane and changed

into a tan safari suit of the kind favored by embassy personnel and other civilians in Viet Nam. With the plane full of people dressed the same, he thought
he might be less conspicuous than he would have been in navy khakis. Still,
when the plane landed, he didn't have a very firm plan for getting past the
army MPs who were screening the arriving passengers. Then, as he was moving up the aisle toward the door, he glanced out the window and saw Admiral
Oberg get into a big black VIP sedan and go whizzing away. An idea burst
into his head.

Stalking down the gangway from the plane, he shouted angrily to the MPs
at the bottom, "Where are they going with my car! Damn! Stop them!" The
soldiers, stunned by the outburst, looked around at the vanishing VIP sedan and
with innocent faces told him that "some navy admiral" had taken it. John
leaped around like a furious bigwig, damning everybody at the embassy and
demanding that somebody get him another car and right then! The two MPs,
cowed by his feigned fury, took off in one direction to find a car and John took
off in the other, fleeing the airport and disappearing into Sai Gon, which he
knew better than a lot of Viet Cong did. No one was going to catch him now.

After taking a U.S. Defense Attaché Office taxi to the Brinks BOQ, John
caught a cyclo and went to my mother's house a few blocks away. Everyone
was thrilled to see him; I had called long before to tell them he was coming,
but they had no idea when to expect him or whether he would make it. They
had a thousand questions about the family in America and about the war that
was drawing closer to them every day. Then he broke the news to them: He
had come to take them out, to take them to the United States.

This news met with a mixed response. While everybody in Sai Gon was
frightened of the North Vietnamese invasion, my mother also thought of the
possibility of seeing Khoi and being with my father again. For years she had
dreamed of one day being able to grow old with her husband in their old village, to take care of their ancestors' land and their graves. Hoa Binh definitely wanted to leave, as did Minh Tam and the maid, but my mother panicked
with another thought: "How can I visit Hai Van's grave?"

That night John called me to let me know he had arrived and was starting
to work on his difficult task. I was so relieved that he had made it to Sai Gon
safely, but I knew the hardest part was still ahead.

By the end of the sixth day I couldn't stand not knowing anything, so I tried
to reach George Esper in Sai Gon. It took several hours and many calls, but I
finally got through. He didn't have any details, but he told me he had seen
John and knew that John was doing everything he could to get my mother
and sisters out.

The time was getting shorter and shorter, as the North Vietnamese advanced nearer and nearer to Sai Gon. There was nothing I could do but listen to the bad news on the radio and TV and sit by the phone, waiting for some word from John.

Meanwhile, in Viet Nam, John had given up trying to go through regular channels to get everyone out. Cuong and I had stood in long lines at the immigration office in Hawaii to file immigration requests for the family, but the American embassy in Sai Gon was so swamped with people who had the same idea that John made no progress at all. He was ready to talk to someone about the phone call from Paris, hoping that would stimulate some special attention.

Before that, however, he looked up Colonel Binh. This time it was my family's turn to help him after all the favors he had done for us. John told him that he saw no reason for the North Vietnamese and the Viet Cong to stop their advance and no political settlement in sight, so he suggested that Colonel Binh make arrangements to get himself and his family out as quickly as possible. We knew they would certainly be killed when the North Vietnamese and the Viet Cong learned of his service in Sai Gon's military intelligence. Colonel Binh appreciated the warning, but he was still optimistic — or perhaps, knowing the fate that might lay ahead for him, just didn't dare think of the possibility of defeat. John asked if Colonel Binh could get him a pistol, and the officer handed him a large revolver; John said a small automatic would be much better, and Colonel Binh promised to get him one in a few days.

John went to the Minh Tri orphanage and met with Sister Trong, who told him that many of the children were getting sick and some were dying. She said that many people were trying to get hundreds of orphans out of the country to a safer place. One of them was Ed Daley, the flamboyant owner and president of World Airways, who had been flying to Da Nang to pick up Vietnamese army and marine units that were evacuating the Central Highlands. He was trying to get the embassy people to let him airlift orphans to safety, but they said no. John, who was hanging around every day trying to get some action on the Minh Tri orphans, heard the embassy staffers talking about Daley as if he were a stupid jerk who was interfering in their business.

John talked to several of the people who were trying to help the orphans, and one of them, Shirley Clark of the Friends Service Committee, told him she thought something was going to happen soon. She was right. A day or so later, Ed Daley took a planeload of orphans out of the country without anyone's permission. For the first time, John said, he thought the U.S. embassy sounded just like the North Vietnamese, calling Daley a "kidnapper." We now know how the Communists treated the American-Vietnamese orphans who remained after their takeover, and it's clear that Daley was a hero: He forced the embassy to start the paperwork to allow more of the children to escape.

In the following weeks, hundreds of orphans in the Sai Gon area were evacuated, including "our" children at Minh Tri. There was one young boy there, however, a blond French-Vietnamese, who didn't make it. Because his maternal grandmother had always visited him at least once every six months, the authorities refused to classify him as a true orphan and so they would not let him join the airlift. The poor woman probably never knew that her love and concern for this little boy sentenced him to stay behind to greet his "liberators."

The Minh Tri orphans made it safely to Australia. A newspaper clipping that we read later described their arrival, saying they were dirty and in poor health, with body lice and patches of hair missing. But there were thousands of Australian families waiting to adopt these few hundred refugee children. John and I both had tears in our eyes when we recalled their happy faces during our earlier visit to the orphanage, when we had brought ice cream and they had tasted the sweet treat for the first time in their lives.

At home, of course, I had no way to know what was happening at the time. One night, on the television, I learned of the tragic crash of a C-5 that was taking 243 orphans and about 45 adults out of Sai Gon. I was angry at a fate that had snuffed out these children's chances at the very brink of freedom. I wished I could cry.

People everywhere were fleeing before the Communist advance. By this time Da Nang was lost completely, and refugees from the Central Highlands flooded into the southern cities. If only those who believe in the myths of Communism, with Marxism and Leninism, could look at this kind of exodus and understand the ugly truth about their doctrines. I thought of those people who live in free societies, including the United States, who flirt with Communism — intellectuals who are naive enough to embrace the philosophy but not dumb enough to leave the societies that nurtured them and allowed them to preach their foolishness. I wondered if any of them ever stopped to wonder why so many Vietnamese were leaving their homes, and even their country. When I was a child in 1954, I saw 800,000 people flee the North for the South, and only 100,000 go the other way to join the Communists. Even at the age of nine I was able to see the difference.

Finally, John called me from the AP office. His voice was tired, and he told me there was no good news, but he promised, "I'm doing my best, Nha." ("Nha" was his nickname for me, from the Vietnamese word for home, something stable, warm, and secure.) He didn't realize that his call alone was good news, because now I knew that he and my mother and sisters hadn't been among the people killed in the C-5 crash. I thought about what a monumental task he had taken on, and in a desperate moment pleaded with him: "John, please don't come home without my mother and sisters!" I heard him laugh, and then realized how stupid it was for me to say that.

— — —

Back in Sai Gon, it was getting harder and harder for John to get into the U.S. embassy, much less to get anything accomplished. The guards had orders to keep out everyone who didn't work there, and he was asked to leave several times by the marine guards, who were polite to a navy officer but had to do their jobs.

But John simply had to get in, so he finally figured out a way. One day he waited outside until a carload of "official-looking" Americans in their safari suits pulled up and started toward the door. John, dressed the same way and carrying a briefcase like all the others, melted into the crowd and waltzed right in with them.

Once inside, he wandered the halls, trying to look as if he knew what he was doing, while he searched out the intelligence analysts' section. He found it, poked his head in the door, and was greeted by a young man named Joe McBride, who asked, "Can I help you?" He certainly could! John startled him with his first words: "I am a lieutenant commander in the navy and my father-in-law is the North Vietnamese ambassador to Moscow."

He went on to tell McBride about the phone call from Paris, and his struggle to get my family out before it was too late. John added something else: He told the analyst that he thought there were probably less than thirty days left "before this embassy becomes a North Vietnamese villa." When McBride agreed, John said later, he knew he had found "not only a good analyst but an honest one."

McBride typed up a report on John's story and passed it "upstairs" to his superiors. After a few more trips and several phone calls, John eventually got a meeting with a ranking embassy staffer, Shep Lowman — whose reaction turned out to be another disappointment. The people in his office hadn't been able to find my father's name in their computers, although they admitted that many files had been destroyed. Even if they had, however, there was nothing they could do to help, Lowman said. His main concern was that John not go around telling people of his prediction that Sai Gon had only thirty days left, because it might "upset the general population." John was astonished! Anybody on the streets knew that the people were already in an uproar, John said. This was the time for action, not public relations, yet the embassy seemed more worried about the "image" of the situation. Downstairs a few minutes later, McBride confirmed John's suspicion; all the briefing papers sent upstairs by the analysts were being edited, he said, to keep them "positive."

Fortunately, even though the CIA station staff at the embassy didn't do much with John's report, they had sent a copy to headquarters back in Langley, Virginia, where someone on the Viet Nam desk recognized my father's name. Things had started to move, although back in Sai Gon John didn't realize it yet.

Time was getting short and John became anxious. Even if he did get permission for the family to leave, things might be so confused in the last days that he wouldn't know where to take them for the evacuation. Nobody at the embassy was talking, of course, so he started going to the bars where Americans hung out. In a short time he had all the information he needed — where the pickup points would be, how people would be transported, and so on. Sai Gon was that kind of place in those days.

John also discovered that the two thousand dollars he had brought along for payoffs wouldn't have bribed a policeman to tear up a traffic ticket at that time. There was more money floating around in the streets of Sai Gon than there was on the tables at Las Vegas, as people tried desperately to buy their freedom. John could almost smell the fear as he walked around.

From the balcony of my mother's apartment, John could see a man on the sidewalk, obviously watching the house. Apparently it was an NLF cadre, with orders to watch over and protect his party leader's family. Considering how dangerous the city was getting to be, John said, "That was OK by me — I just hoped he was good at his job." The Communists had infiltrated Sai Gon in March, and people in the city were already finding ways to leave before a major invasion. The fear of being kidnapped was rampant, too, and it hit my family hard when a Viet Cong messenger appeared at the door and asked my mother to go with him to receive a message from my father. She refused to go.

Once, when John got through to me by using the telephone at the AP office, I was really worried and told him I had seen on TV a report that the Viet Cong were planning to cut off the water supply in Sai Gon, so I told him to fill up the water tank and the bathtub before that could happen. Suddenly the operator in Sai Gon, who had obviously been listening to our conversation all along, broke in and asked if I were sure about the report. I'll bet almost every bathtub in Sai Gon was full that night, along with all the pots and pans in every house.

George Esper was letting John see his people's reports and analyses, and it was good work. The AP reporters weren't the kind who got all their information in Sai Gon hotel bars. The bottom line confirmed John's belief that time was very short. As it turned out, the only reason there were still a few days in which to work was that the North Vietnamese advanced so much more easily than they expected that they outran their supplies. They had to wait for fuel and food and ammunition to catch up with them, and this gave us two more precious weeks.

At last, the U.S. government got moving on the case. Joe McBride told John to call a certain number and speak to a person named Grant Ichikawa, who was with the CIA. After hearing the whole story again, directly from John, the man promised he would be back in touch soon with some news.

About this time, I managed after endless attempts to get through on the telephone to my mother at home. It was the middle of the night there, and I woke them up; that's probably why my mother's voice sounded distant and faint, but somehow it made me feel as if this might be our last conversation. "Daughter, John must go back," she told me. "He did his best and it is no longer safe for him to be here. If something happens to us, at least you have John and Lance with you."

John was staying at my mother's house, so they woke him up to talk with me, and he had an important message. It was time for me to go see "the man," he said — meaning Admiral Gaylor. There was no need to worry about what the navy might think anymore, because the embassy staff and the CIA knew the whole story of the naval officer with the "unusual family." We didn't know what the admiral might be able to do, but at that point we didn't dare leave any stone unturned.

Getting to him wouldn't be easy, of course; with things rapidly falling apart in Viet Nam, the commander in chief of the entire Pacific Fleet was one of the busiest men in the world. I had seen him in his morning press conferences, looking worn out after working fifteen to seventeen hours through the night on the special task force handling the crisis. That morning, after my conversation with John, I saw on television that Admiral Gaylor had left CINCPACFLT headquarters at 6:00 A.M. for his private quarters. I thought I should let him get some rest, so I resolved to wait until 10:00 A.M. to call him.

After getting Lance off to school, I sat by the phone until 10:05, then dialed the number. The admiral's steward answered, but when I told him my name he lowered his voice and said, "The admiral is sleeping, he can't be disturbed." I asked to speak to Mrs. Gaylor, and when the steward said she was busy, I pleaded with him: "Chief, I am a navy wife, and I need help from the admiral. I understand that he's just returned from all night's work, but it would help me so much if I could speak to Mrs. Gaylor."

He relented, and in a moment the admiral's wife came on the line and asked what my problem was. I started right at the top: "I am a daughter of an ambassador to the Soviet Union; my father is in Ha Noi."

"What nationality is your father?" she asked.

"He is Vietnamese. I know this doesn't make any sense to you, but I must ask the admiral to listen to an important message that concerns Viet Nam, and I need his help to rescue my family."

"Calm down," Mrs. Gaylor told me gently. "I'll wake him up. He shouldn't sleep over a matter like this."

When the admiral came on the line, his voice was hoarse from lack of sleep, but on my apology he graciously said it was all right because he had to get up to go back to work anyway. "Now tell me what I can do for you."

"My father is the National Liberation Front ambassador to the Soviet Union," I said. "Someone has told me that the North Vietnamese are getting nearer to the South every day and that my mother will be in danger when that happens." I played a wild card in throwing out my father's affiliation rather than my husband's. Admiral Gaylor was the man who first received American POW's when they were released in 1973 after the Paris Peace Accord. It was an emotional event for him then; now in 1975, I thought the name of his adversary might create a greater reaction.

He was mobilized instantly. "Listen, Mrs. Krall, one of my aides will get in touch with you as soon as possible. I'll see that he gets in touch with you today." Sure enough, within a few short hours I got a call from a Lieutenant Commander Dave Smith, who agreed to come to my house that afternoon.

When he heard the story about Jean Sagan's phone call, Lieutenant Commander Smith was extremely interested, because of course the prediction was coming true even as we were talking. He took down all the information I could give him, then promised to brief the admiral right away. "I don't know what he can do to help you and your family in Sai Gon at this time, but I'm sure he will think of a way."

I believed he was sincere, but at that critical moment I was desperate for something more concrete. I swallowed hard, and played what I knew to be my last card. "Commander Smith, I want my mother out of Viet Nam! I will cooperate with the government if and when I am needed." He looked a bit surprised at my outburst, but said he would pass that offer on to the admiral as well.

Apparently I had said the right thing. Less than twenty-four hours later I was sitting in my living room talking to a tall, handsome, fatherly-looking civilian who had been contacted by Lieutenant Commander Smith. He didn't introduce himself as a CIA officer, but I was sure he was. (In my world then, any American in civilian dress who was interested in helping my mother was with the CIA.) The man, Bob Jantzen, said he had heard my "rather interesting story," but insisted that his main concern at the moment wasn't my Communist father but the safety of my mother and sisters. He told me to give him all their names and birthdates, and he would see what he could do.

Then I dropped the little surprise that John was in Sai Gon, and suggested that it would be a great help if he would notify the embassy of John's presence so they could work something out together. His interest was really piqued by that news, and he asked for John's full name and rank.

"You know that your husband took a great risk by going to Viet Nam at this time," he said, grinning. In fact he knew that John had gone without the navy's permission. Taking a sip of the tea I had made for us, he continued: "Mrs. Krall, I want you to know that we take a great interest in your mother's safety now. We'll do anything in our power to help."

Jantzen was a great communicator, I thought, his words gentle and soothing yet conveying a feeling of great capability and trustworthiness. Later that night I started wondering about him, though. I knew he wasn't a navy man, because he didn't have that "salty" look, but he obviously carried a certain air of authority. Still, since marrying John I had felt that the navy was like a family, and wouldn't send anyone to me who would hurt me in any way. With that thought I went to bed and for the first time in weeks had a good night's sleep.

Later I would learn exactly who Bob Jantzen was, and I began to realize what I had gotten myself into. I had some idea that the U.S. government was extremely interested in their adversary's family. For me, I only cared that they get my family out; I would deal with what they wanted in return later. I never regretted it. As my grandfather had often told us, "There is nothing free on this earth. We even have to work hard for our place in heaven someday."

John's efforts "on the ground" in Sai Gon and the pressures exerted from above by the admiral and by the CIA finally bore fruit. After several more meetings with Grant Ichikawa, John was assured that everything was all set. Grant promised that he would see that my family was flown out — not right at that moment, but plans were under way. "If anyone gets out, they will," he told John — adding that he and his wife would be on the plane, too.

That evening, John had dinner with Grant and his wife at their house near the air base. It was a sad evening, full of "what-ifs" about the American effort in Viet Nam. Grant's wife had tears in her eyes as she wondered aloud about what was going to happen to the South Vietnamese people. At the end of the evening, John was convinced that my mother and sisters were in good hands at last.

John himself wasn't completely in the clear, however. The next day he got momentarily careless and went to the Brinks BOQ, where he was caught by MPs who demanded to see his orders. Of course he didn't have any, so he was told to report to an army colonel at MACV headquarters. The officer was angry that John was "freelancing" in Sai Gon; he ordered him to get out of Viet Nam on the next available plane and said the navy was being informed of John's illegal activities.

At that point, John was in no mood to quibble over legalities. He stood his ground and insisted he did have a reason for being there, a job to do, but that it was classified and he couldn't reveal it to just any old colonel. As soon as his "mission" was completed, he promised, he would be leaving. "I told him I had no intention of being there when the North Vietnamese entered the city anyway," John said. "The prisoner-of-war school that the navy sent me to long ago convinced me that I never wanted to fall into that hell." The colonel still insisted that John leave, but he refused. "If you confine me I will escape," he growled. The colonel just sat down and said weakly one more time, "Be on the next plane," but John walked out with no intention of going anywhere just yet.

Eight days later, on April 10, 1975, when John was confident that all the arrangements were solid and the family would be evacuated safely, he decided the time had come to leave. "If I stayed until the end," he said, "I would only take up a seat that somebody else could use." So he kissed my family good-bye, promised to see them all soon in America, and headed for the airport to hitch a ride out on some plane going somewhere.

As he waited at the airport, John made a courtesy call to the army colonel and left a message that he was leaving the country, but as he says now, "Who knows whether he was still there to receive it?" The final collapse was just days away.

Chapter 17

‎Ↄ will never forget the date — April 23, 1975, the same day President Ford pronounced the U.S. war effort "finished," one week before the fall of Sai Gon — when I got the phone call from Hoa Binh. "We are out of Sai Gon," she said in a tired voice that buried her sadness. Weeks before I had thought I would scream for joy when I heard the good news, but now I felt only a sense of loss. There was a long silence between me and my sister on the line from Guam.

"Are you all right?" I asked finally.

They were, she assured me, and everyone was anxious to see us in Hawaii. I told her they might have to stay there for a few days, until further arrangements could be made, and she said they didn't mind. Still, there was something not right in her voice, and I pressed her for the reason.

"We left everything behind," she burst out, sobbing.

"We have each other, Hoa Binh." I couldn't do much to comfort her over the telephone.

"We lost Viet Nam forever," she cried.

I knew what she meant, and I knew my mother must have felt it even more painfully than Hoa Binh or Minh Tam or me. In one early morning she had left behind years of yearning to be with her husband, her son. She knew that her older brother, her younger brother, her niece and nephew would soon be marching home in victory, but she would never be able to see them again. She wouldn't even be able to continue the weekly visits to the grave of her only other son, Hai Van. I was afraid to think of what she must be feeling.

Hai Van's death had made my mother age twenty years. Now, leaving his grave unattended was the most difficult decision for her to make. We all could envision what the Communists would do to their former adversary's gravesites; indeed, they bulldozed the National Cemetery several years after the end of the war.

As we watched the headlines in the *Honolulu Star Bulletin* and listened to reports on radio and TV, we knew a tragic showdown was coming in Sai Gon. Today, tomorrow, maybe two weeks from now, I knew that Sai Gon would be changed forever. My favorite streets, the bridges over the water, would soon bear the names of Red dictators. I lay in bed and visualized the Communists burning books, the ones I had read and those I had yet to see; I knew the next generation would learn history the way the North Vietnamese wanted it portrayed.

Five days after the first call from Guam, the telephone rang at midnight. It was Hoa Binh, telling me that everyone had just arrived at Honolulu International Airport. I got dressed quickly and phoned my sister Cuong in Pearl City; she got her family up and we all rushed to the airport.

My mother looked a hundred years older than the last time I had seen her. The pain in her face made me stop and wonder if all my effort to get her out had been the right thing to do. They were more than tired travelers, they were refugees from a terrible war. We were separated by the immigration check-point, and when my mother tried to come to embrace me she was stopped by one of the immigration officers. Cuong started weeping, and our children rushed around her and tried to get to Hoa Binh and Minh Tam. Pretty soon the officials gave up, and we all embraced while a customs man went through the luggage.

I looked into the suitcases and suddenly went to pieces. In one of the bags I saw my brother Hai Van's air force uniform, his dress coat, and the drawing book that had belonged to him in the sixth grade. The other suitcase contained a dozen or so books and more pictures. There before her was all that was left from the long life of this hardworking woman, I thought: her daughters, mementos of her dead son, and a few pieces of arts and crafts. I walked away from the crowd, and as people called after me I heard John tell them to "leave her alone for a minute." I stood against a cold glass window until John came over and told me quietly that I should be with my mother and sisters. Somehow that final step to end our long separation was too painful to take; I didn't want to face them, even to ask if they had had a good flight. How could anything to do with fleeing your beloved homeland be "good"?

I was numb as we walked to the parking lot and got into the cars. John and Wray, my brother-in-law, took one car, and the rest of us piled into the other — the children huddling close to my mother, Cuong, and Hoa Binh in the back, Minh Tam sitting next to me in the front. Kenneth, my four-year-old nephew, took my mother's hand and told her, "I'm glad you are alive." Hoa

Binh burst into tears and said, "Me, too, Kenneth."

I tried to see my mother in the rearview mirror as I drove toward our house. "Mom, are we doing the right thing?" I asked her.

"Don't ever doubt that," she told me. "I'd kill myself before I'd let the Communists persecute me, and everybody knows that no one in the South will be left alone when the people from Ha Noi come down."

"I'm thinking about Father," I said.

"He has the party to grow old with. He'll be fine with the 'Liberation.'"

"I have been staying up nights, thinking about his homecoming. It'll ruin him to find that you have gone," I insisted.

"Don't torture yourself," she said. "It is a shame I must leave Viet Nam. But believe me, we made the right decision for all of us — for your father, too — because if I had stayed I would only have continued to criticize his government. I would have embarrassed him and made him miserable when I refused to participate in any of their functions."

Hoa Binh changed the subject by telling us how "lucky" they were to be able to leave Guam so soon. She had helped the immigration officers and flight attendants on Pan Am by interpreting for other refugees and translating their papers, so she had managed to register our family to get on the first flight out.

For the next few days, until Sai Gon finally fell on April 30, we all huddled in front of the television set and felt the taste of defeat in our mouths. When we saw helicopters being pushed off the decks of carriers, our hearts went with them. Aircraft weren't just machines to us, because Hai Van had flown them, some of Hoa Binh's friends and boyfriends had flown them. I even felt a secret bond with helicopters, for some of them carried men who had once destroyed many of the Viet Cong.

When General Nguyen Cao Ky boarded the command ship *Blue Ridge,* the Americans made him submit to a body search, and for the first time I really experienced the bitterness of the defeated and shared the sorrow and shame of those who had surrendered. For a moment a question of honor arose: Was it more honorable to stay behind and take whatever came, or to leave and be subjected to the indignity of a body search? With my family sitting next to me, though, I had to admit that survival was the most important thing, at least as important as grace and honor.

I went to bed thinking of the triumph the Communists must have been feeling in that faraway city. Their red banners would be flying on rooftops everywhere, their soldiers would be marching through the streets, they would be cheering as they eagerly destroyed our past, my past. Many of those who stayed behind would be betraying their friends and acquaintances, hoping to curry favor with their conquerors. It wouldn't work, though. Everyone —

nuns, priests, criminals, intellectuals, prostitutes — would be placed in the category of "reactionaries" and sent off to reeducation camps, and the Vietnamese people's heritage would be tainted forever.

For the first time, I felt ashamed to be an American, because we had failed Viet Nam and its people.

— — —

Four weeks after Viet Nam's ugly end, Bob Jantzen called and invited John and me to come to see him.

His office was a world apart from the offices we were used to. A thick shag rug cast a striking shade of orange. The furniture was heavy and masculine, but fresh flowers lent a touch of gentleness to the room. A large portrait of a Chinese queen hung on the wall, apparently an antique.

Meeting John for the first time, Mr. Jantzen praised him for his rescue mission and added, "Your wife is a courageous lady, too." I didn't feel particularly courageous, and I wondered what he meant — what was so brave about talking to the CIA? Perhaps there was more to it than I knew about. I'd heard all the tales and legends about the CIA, from my Viet Cong cousins, from books and novels, from gossip on the corners of Tu Do Street and in the Le Loi cafes, but tales and legends aren't supposed to be believed.

After all the small talk, Mr. Jantzen got to the point. He asked if I would be willing to meet with a CIA case officer from Washington, who was working on southeast Asian affairs. I was so ignorant about such matters that I had to ask him what a "case officer" was. After he explained that this was a person who handled agents in the field, directing them and getting reports on their contacts and findings, I told him I had no objections.

A few days later my husband and I went back to the office, where we were introduced to the case officer, Robert Hall — or Rob, as we later learned he liked to be called. Mr. Jantzen left to attend a meeting, and we spent some time talking in a kind of mutual "get-acquainted" session. One thing struck me as odd: Mr. Jantzen had told us we were going to meet a CIA case officer, but Rob Hall introduced himself as a military officer.

John and I invited Mr. Hall to dine with us that night in a restaurant in Honolulu. After dinner we drove him back to the Moana Hotel, where he invited us into the bar for a drink. While tourists at one end of the bar were captivated by the hula dancers' show, we sat in a quiet corner while Rob drilled me in the techniques of espionage. When he explained to me about "dead drops," the method of leaving messages where only the intended recipient will find them, I thought that it sounded like a game we had played as children. The night was young, so I suggested we go out right then and there and practice "dead drops."

I took a packet of sugar from the table and said I would hide it somewhere in the shopping center across the street. John was going to be my "recipient," and Rob would have to tail me to see if he could spot where I placed the sugar and get it before John did. Rob just watched and listened with no expression on his face. I could imagine that he was thinking he would have a long, hard road ahead before he would be able to figure out this "navy wife."

As we crossed the street, I whispered to John that I would put the packet of sugar inside a bolt of black cloth in the fabric shop in the mall. He was worried about the chances of finding one bolt of black fabric in an entire shop, but I knew that in Hawaii there weren't many dark colors in the fabric stores.

We separated, and I bought myself a Coke and sat on a bench to drink it; when I finished, I very deliberately placed the empty paper cup in a trash can, then walked off to a gift shop. As I looked back, I saw Rob looking at the trash can, apparently debating whether to poke through it to hunt for the sugar before deciding not to. I spent about ten minutes in the gift shop, handling a lot of merchandise, then bought two postcards and went on to another store.

Finally, I reached the fabric shop, where I looked at various prints, holding them up in front of me, then bought two yards of Indonesian fabric. As I was paying the cashier, I rested my hand on top of a bolt of black linen — and dropped the sugar packet into the cardboard tube inside it.

Back at the ice cream parlor where we had agreed to meet, I asked, "Do we have the prize?" John looked downhearted, as he kept his hands in his pocket. Rob was speechless and motionless. "Come with me, gentlemen," I said.

At the fabric shop, I lifted the black fabric and Rob snatched up the packet of sugar from beneath it. "Bingo!" he said. "You got an A for the test."

The next day Rob and I met again, and he told me he would like to sit down at length to learn all he could about my family — my Communist family. "Try to refresh your memory," he warned me. "I'll be asking you a lot of questions tomorrow." He didn't know that my problem had never been a lack of memories, but too many memories; my mind was like an endless movie, now a documentary, now a tragic drama in which my family's scattered members were the unwilling and unfortunate actors.

The following morning I went to Rob's hotel, and my "service" to the Central Intelligence Agency began for real. We talked for hours, and by noon my case officer knew my family tree almost as well as I did. He learned of my father's political career from the time he was a schoolteacher, through his service as a congressman, all the way to his ascent to the post of ambassador to Moscow. I also told him about my uncles, my cousins, my brother Khoi, and all the North Vietnamese leaders who I knew were closest to my father. That was only the beginning, however; he asked to see me again that evening to talk some more and to set up a routine, what he called "tradecraft." Once again I didn't know the terminology, so when I was back home I looked up the word in the dictionary: "a mark, a footprint left by the passage of a person, an animal, or thing." That didn't help much, but I figured it had something to do with the art of spying, of following a target without being discovered. I didn't know what that had to do with my conversations with Rob Hall, but I went along with whatever he said.

I didn't want my mother to know that I was cooperating with the CIA. For the rest of the time Mr. Hall was in Honolulu, I took her to spend the week with Cuong and her family in Pearl City.

For days I talked and talked and my case officer listened, asking questions now and then to probe some area he was particularly interested in. We got to know each other better, and he became "Rob" to me instead of Mr. Hall. I had no clear picture of what he wanted me to do after our series of interviews, but apparently he had more things in mind. He promised to contact me again if anything came up that he wanted me to do, and asked me to make plans for a trip to Washington for "training." I didn't know what lay ahead of me, nor what to think or feel about becoming an American spy, but one thing was becoming obvious: The simple promise I had made to Lieutenant Commander Smith on that desperate day a few weeks earlier was going to change the course of my life.

— — —

While I had been flooding Rob's mind with everything I could remember, thousands of refugees were flooding into Hickam airport and into Honolulu's civilian airport. Volunteers were desperately needed to cope with the throngs of people, and I was called by the Red Cross and the immigration service to help. I signed on for a day shift, but when we ran out of volunteers I would stay on into the night. For weeks I walked around like a zombie, desperately needing sleep but unable to walk away from my countrymen who were arriving tired, weak, and often empty-handed.

My whole family got involved in the effort. John and I ran an ad in the newspapers seeking used clothing for the refugees, and soon the phone started ringing all day long. People asked for directions to our house to bring donations or asked us to come and make pickups. We ran out of manpower, so John built some wooden boxes and put them in shopping center parking lots and in front of the Fleet Weather Station to spread the collection points. Every night we would drive to all the boxes and pick up the day's offerings.

At the arrival gate where I worked, many people said they had been separated from their loved ones in the confusion of getting out of Viet Nam. Children arrived alone, shepherded off the plane by the flight attendants, and sat by themselves in the terminal. I remember one little boy, about seven, who asked me "Where do I go next?" I asked where he wanted to be, and he told me "I want to find my mother." A plane took him and a hundred others to a camp on the mainland.

Every day I spent all my waking hours amid people who were in tears from their desperation. A few passed through the immigration checkpoint with briefcases or cloth bags containing gold and jewelry, but most came through empty-handed and hurried to the corner where my husband and I had put the used clothing for them to help themselves.

We were living at Iroquois Point at the time, and our three-bedroom house was fully occupied by us, my mother, and Minh Tam. Hoa Binh had left to stay with Kim in her new home in Atlanta, Georgia. I went through those few weeks in a daze, dividing myself into many pieces — one for my husband, one for Lance, one for my mother, a little bit for Minh Tam, and the rest devoted to the refugees. Life was a blur as I rushed from Hickam to Honolulu International Airport, hearing one sad tale after another, offering what little help I could. For a long time, I forgot completely about Rob Hall.

— — —

At about 10:00 A.M. on July 20, 1975, I was getting ready to settle into a much-needed nap — I had just wound up a sixteen-hour stretch of work through the night at Hickam — when a friend of John's phoned from the airport and said he was on his way back to the States from the Far East and had "something interesting" to show me.

At that point, nothing could have been more interesting to me than a few hours' sleep, so I asked if he could come to dinner with us later, say about five in the afternoon. He accepted, so I took the phone off the hook, asked my mother to entertain Lance for me, and dropped off to sleep before I could even think about what to serve for dinner.

Lance woke me up about one o'clock, wanting to go to the beach just across the street from our house. Groggily, I mumbled something about wishing he were old enough to go by himself, but he caught me up short with my own words: "Remember that you always said you hoped I wouldn't grow up too fast?" I got out of bed before he even finished the sentence.

John had been due back from a cross-country flight that evening, but the operations officer from his squadron called to say he wouldn't return until the next morning, so John's friend and I were alone for a while when he arrived for dinner. We got drinks, and as we sat down to enjoy them he handed me a newspaper. It was the previous day's edition of the *Japan Times,* one of the English-language dailies in Tokyo. "Oh," I said, "thanks for the souvenir. I'll read it later."

The man smiled. "Open it to page four, I think you might like to read it now."

On the right-hand corner of page four, a headline caught my eye: "Hanoi, Saigon Groups to Join Ban–Bomb Rally."

"I am a peace-lover, but I don't like antiwar demonstrators," I told him. He just smiled again and motioned for me to continue reading:

> About 80 delegates from 21 countries are expected to partici-
> pate in this year's ban-the-bomb rallies to be held in Hiroshima
> and other cities by the Japan Council Against Atomic and
> Hydrogen Bombs (Gensuikyo) beginning August 5.
>
> The foreign participants will include the five-member delega-
> tion from North Viet Nam and a four-man group from the
> Provisional Revolutionary Government of South Viet Nam. This
> will be the first time North and South Vietnamese delegations
> will both take part in the world rallies against atomic and hydro-
> gen bombs in this country. Gensuikyo reported that neither the
> Justice Ministry nor the Foreign Ministry would raise objections
> to the entry of the Vietnamese groups.
>
> The Ha Noi delegation, headed by Do Xuan Oanh, secretary
> of the Vietnamese Peace Committee, will arrive here around July
> 27 via Peking. The South Vietnamese delegation, headed by
> Dang Quang Minh, member of the Central Committee of the
> National Liberation Front . . .

I stopped, stunned by what I had read. "Hey, this is my father! It's him!" I screamed. "I must go to Japan to see my father," I said without even thinking.

I went back to finish up the article, my heart pounding with excitement. My father was "expected to arrive around July 26 from Moscow." Other foreign delegations were to include ten Americans, including sculptress Ethel Taylor, who was a member of a group called "Women Strike for Peace." The International Peace Bureau was sending two representatives, including the 1974 Nobel Peace Prize–winner Sean McBride.

I fixed us both another drink and asked our friend to give me a few min-utes to read the article to my mother, who was playing with Lance in the bed-room. I wished that she could go to Japan to see him, too, but we didn't have the money or the proper travel documents for her; the immigration form under which she had entered the country wouldn't be sufficient to obtain an entry visa for Japan.

I wish I could have captured in a bottle the wonderful smile on her face when she read my father's name in that paper. She was a bit concerned, how-ever, when I told her about my plan to meet him. "You should inform somebody in the government if you do go to see your father," she said. Mostly she feared for my father and John, and she didn't want me to break the law by being seen with a Communist official. I protested her suggestion, thinking I didn't actually need anybody's permission if I wanted to go see my own father. She took my hands and looked hard at me. "I know how much you love your father and through that love you believe nothing could stand between the two of you, but don't forget that he is not just an ordinary father. Besides, you should ask John when he gets home."

John came home about two in the morning, and I was waiting for him at Barber's Point Air Base to tell him the news. We talked about it all the way home, and in the end he said he'd support me all the way: "One way or another, you and Lance should go to see your father."

That morning, while John was still asleep, I made my plane reservations and called the Japanese consulate; by afternoon my visa was approved and my bags were packed. I wanted to arrive several days before the conference to familiarize myself with the strange city. Before we left for the airport, Cuong and her children brought small gifts for me to take to my father, along with their school pictures and other pictures of my sisters. Mother had stayed up late to write my father a long letter.

At the airport, Lance and I boarded early with other passengers who had children. The plane roared down the runway and soared into the air over the Pacific. I sat back in the seat, trying to comprehend that within a few days, if all went well, I would be face to face with the father who had left me and the rest of his family to serve his political philosophy more than two decades before.

Chapter 18

$\mathcal{J}$t couldn't have been easy, of course; after all that time, it would have been too much to expect that I would be able to fly to Japan and walk directly into a room somewhere and greet my father.

The first problem was that we didn't know exactly when the NLF delegation was coming to Tokyo, or where it would be staying. So Lance and I had to spend several days sitting around our hotel room or wandering the strange streets of the city.

Lance and I checked into the Sanyo Hotel, which was an official U.S. military billet in Tokyo; John had said it would be the most natural thing for a navy wife to stay there.

Every day I bought the *Japan Times* and scoured the pages, looking for some mention of my father or his delegation's arrival. The days wore on, and Lance and I both became bored. We saw *The Pink Panther* three times and a Donald Duck movie twice, and other than that we mostly stayed near the hotel pool, trying to escape the awful mugginess of July in Tokyo.

Shortly after lunch on Monday, July 28, I learned that my father would be arriving on the thirtieth, and would probably be staying at the Prince Hotel. Even though I knew my father wouldn't be in until two days later, I hopped into a taxi and rode over there. At first I wasn't going to stop, but when we came to the entrance drive I got out of the cab, took Lance by the hand, and strolled boldly inside. At the reception desk, I told a young lady that I wanted to make reservations for a party of fifteen people. She looked at her book and shook her head politely: "I'm sorry, Madame, but we don't have room for you. However, I'm sure we will have rooms after August 15." Somehow that convinced me that this was indeed the hotel where my father's delegation was staying — although of course it could have been full for any number of other reasons. I was satisfied, though, so I picked up a hotel business card, thanked the woman and started to leave. After a few steps, though, I stopped and asked her where the rest room was. I had decided to spend a few more moments there, scouting the layout of the hotel, so in the future I wouldn't look lost or like a tourist when I came to find my father.

We spotted another hotel quite near the Prince, one called the Takanawa Prince. Since I wanted the convenience of being near the hotel where my father was expected to stay, we checked in. This hotel's luxuries made Tokyo somewhat less boring to Lance, especially the little refrigerator in the room that was filled with soft drinks. He took advantage of the situation by drinking one after another whenever I was busy.

From the window of our room we could see the hotel's beautiful Japanese garden and outdoor dining area below. Looking down onto that tranquil scene, I couldn't help thinking of my own war-torn country and the upcoming meeting with my father, one of the "liberators" of that land. Somehow I felt that his sacrifice had been a waste; my people in the South really needed to be liberated *now*, to free them from the grip of Ha Noi. For several days the love I had for my father overcame my feelings about the fate of Viet Nam, but now as I sat by this window and let myself think hard about the realities of the situation, I felt different. My father and I and South Viet Nam had *all* lost, I concluded. The excitement and joyful anticipation of seeing him seemed to fade for a while.

On July 30 the *Japan Times* carried a picture of my father smiling and waving the NLF flag as he walked by a crowd of people. I looked at the photo, and for a moment he seemed like a stranger to me. But his exuberant smile made him appear healthy, and I felt good about that. I looked out the window toward the Prince and thought, at the end of that street is my father. Somehow, all those years when my mother had struggled so we could all survive to this day, all the misery and loneliness, seemed to have been worthwhile.

That afternoon I almost went again to the Prince Hotel. I got the hotel's business card out and held it for a long time, debating whether to go there, but my hand started to shake and my throat went dry. I could feel my heartbeat becoming louder and louder in my chest. Lance was taking a nap, and I put a thin sheet over him and took the rest of his soda back to the refrigerator. Trying to get a grip on myself, I fixed a gin and tonic and sat for a while sipping it slowly.

Halfway through the drink, I decided I couldn't see any reason to wait any longer, so I picked up the phone and called the Prince. Talking quickly, as if I were in a hurry, I told the operator, "This is Miss Tran, would you please ring Mr. Minh's room?"

"Please spell the name," she asked.

"M - I - N - H, and the last name is D - A - N - G."

It took more than two minutes for her to check the register and come back on the line, and as I waited I could feel myself becoming weak.

"His room is 421, please make a note of it. I'll ring him for you." Then I listened as the buzzing sound repeated a dozen times. There was no answer.

In a way I was almost glad there was no one there to pick up the phone. My heart was filled with a mixture of excitement, anxiety, and fear. I simply didn't know what to expect of my father. I feared being rejected by him for whatever reason he might have had, and at the same time I yearned to be with him.

Lance and I had an early dinner, and I felt that maybe I ought to give my father a chance to rest up after his long day. I read Lance a book for a while and tried to lull him to sleep. The hands of the clock moved around, and soon it was 9:30. Lance was asleep. It was time.

I picked up the receiver and dialed the number.

— — —

"Allo?" a voice said in sort-of-English, sort-of-French.

I don't know how I knew immediately who it was, but I did. I wanted to call out "Father!" so badly I thought I would burst, but I also wanted to be cautious.

"Are you Ambassador Minh?" I asked formally.

"Yes, I am. May I ask who is calling?" His voice was soft and clear, and somehow I could tell he was smiling.

"You were once Mr. Dang Van Quang, the senator from Can Tho before 1954, is that correct?" I asked.

I heard a little cascade of laughter, and in a friendly voice he replied, "That is correct. Now can you tell me how you know me that well?"

"I used to live in Bien Hoa, near Aunt Khue," I told him, using the term "aunt" in the polite way Vietnamese refer to older persons, not in the sense of an actual relative.

"She is my sister! You must be one of the overseas students who came to meet the delegation at the airport when I arrived."

I couldn't hold it in any longer. With a sharp intake of breath I blurted out, "Papa, it is me, your daughter My Yung!"

There was a terrible, long silence on the other end of the line. "Papa, are you there? Are you all right?" I waited, and then heard the "thunk" of the phone being dropped on a hard surface, perhaps a table. A few seconds passed, and there was a fumbling with the receiver as he picked it up again.

"My God! It is my daughter," he said, and then he couldn't talk for a moment. I could hear him weeping.

When he had regained his composure, I asked, "Is it all right to talk on the phone?" I knew the Communist government spied on their own officials, including my father, and well may listen in on our phone conversation.

"No, it is not wise to do so," he warned. "How do you know I am here, my daughter?"

"You are all over the *Japan Times*. Your picture was in the newspapers," I said, smiling from ear to ear.

"Oh, it is so good to listen to your voice, my daughter." His voice began to choke again with the words.

"Can I come to see you now? I know it is late."

"Are you alone?" His tone turned a little more serious.

"I am with my son, but he is asleep. I'll get a babysitter to watch him."

"Can you trust someone else with him?"

"You already sound like a grandfather," I laughed. "He'll be fine."

He instructed me to come directly to his room, not checking in at the hotel desk, and to watch for anyone suspicious on the way up. We also agreed to maintain a fiction about my identity, even to anyone I might meet in his room later; I was to be an overseas student who had come to visit her country's representative, just as he had assumed when I called. I thought that was an appropriate "disguise," because surely no one would be going up to his room so late except a leftist or a "rusty," an old, worn-out antiwar activist from the 1960s. I was neither, but I would have put on a false goatee and pretended to be Ho Chi Minh in order to see my father that night.

As I hung up the phone I felt pain for my father. I could tell the whole world who my father was, but he had to invent an identity for me and could only whisper his love for me.

I arranged for a babysitter through the hotel and took a cab to the Prince Hotel, forcing myself to relax during the short drive. I was preparing not only to see my father, but to meet a statesman from the government that, in my opinion, had conquered my people. I felt angry when I thought of the South being under the dictatorship of the Ha Noi government, but I wanted to think of my father as a dim light of hope for a better Viet Nam; I hoped that seeing him would give me some reason to be encouraged.

I paid the driver and walked quickly through the lobby, my earlier scouting expedition now paying off. My father opened the door almost the instant I knocked. "Oh, God!" he cried out, and he swept me into his arms and hugged and kissed me for the longest time. It seemed like only yesterday that he had done the same thing when he came home from one of his trips.

He sat me down on the couch, put his hands on my shoulders and looked me over. "My darling daughter, it has been so very long." Tears began to flow from his eyes once again.

I couldn't speak. I reached up and touched his hair, noticing that he combed it the same way he had when I was nine years old, even though it was no longer thick and black as it had been when he was a young man.

"There are not enough words to tell you how much I missed you, and your mother and sisters and Hai Van," he began, his voice choking when he mentioned Hai Van. He had to stop talking for a moment. I squeezed his hands and tried to share the pain with him; I thought I knew how he must have felt because I had lived through the agony of losing my brother five years before. "You would have been proud of Hai Van if you had had the chance to know him, Father. He was a good son to Mother and a prince of a man."

"I don't want to talk about Hai Van," my father said, suddenly looking off into space.

"I don't understand."

"I was told that he was killed by the Americans." Hatred glowed in his eyes as he looked back at me and said this.

"Would you believe the truth, or did you choose to listen to fabrications?" I asked. "I feel bad for starting our meeting this way, but I would sacrifice our precious moment to honor my brother's death and stand up for the truth."

"Let's talk about you, about your mother, and your sisters," he said, shrugging off his anger and smiling once again.

"Mother is fine, and she is very anxious to hear from you. My sisters are doing fine. Kim is married. So is Cuong, who has two daughters, Christina and Teri. Hoa Binh has a son, Kenneth, and she and Minh Tam are learning to adapt to their new lives in America. I think they will find it very exciting. But I think Hoa Binh will miss Viet Nam more than any of the others, except me.

"I am still homesick," I told him. "I still dream about Viet Nam, about being there, and I can still remember the smell of ripened rice fields in my sleep. I see the color of the harvest season, I feel the coolness of our rivers and the warmth of my grandparents' village in my dreams."

"That is good, my daughter," he said, his face brightening.

I got very serious. "Father, I want you to know that nobody killed my brother. He was a warrior, he was a pilot in the South Vietnamese Air Force. He didn't sacrifice his life, he died in a senseless accident. He knew it, and we all knew that it was a goddamn accident. How I wish you could have learned about my brother's death from us, not from a lie from your own Communist people."

He slammed his hand on the edge of a table. "You don't understand," he shouted.

"Do you believe that as his sister I would let whoever 'killed' him get away with it?" I demanded.

"The same people who killed your brother tricked your mother into leaving Sai Gon before I came home," he insisted.

He leaned over the coffee table and poured himself a glass of water, sipping it as if he were trying to cool his temper. For a moment he looked deep in thought, then he smiled and tried to put the dispute away. "You look very close to the way I had imagined my little girl growing up," he said.

"I am sorry that I have disappointed you in the way I think," I told him, not quite willing to let the issue go.

"No, I am not disappointed in you," he said. "The only thing I want from my children is that they love me, and have faith in me."

I put my arms around him and felt closer to him. "I am very happy to hear you say that. Now please tell me about my brother Khoi!"

My father's face lit up when I mentioned Khoi. I could tell he enjoyed talking about him. "Your brother is packing up to move back to Sai Gon. When I go home, I'll stop in Ha Noi and Khoi and I will fly home together. He will ship the household goods. He is out of the army now and he will be working for the television station once he gets to Sai Gon. He misses you the most."

"Not as much as I miss him," I said. "I was miserable growing up without you and Khoi."

"You will come home to visit," my father said softly. It was partly a question, partly a wish.

"No, Father. I had the courage to share the losses with my people through the war, but I don't think I would find any pleasure in having to witness my people in disgrace under the Ha Noi government."

He looked angry again, but managed to say, "I would like to bring your mother home with me."

"My mother wouldn't want anything more than being with you, Father."

"Could you bring Mother to Paris?" I knew that Paris was like a home away from home for the North Vietnamese, and that my father had friends there. Ironically Viet Nam and France had had diplomatic relations for years, through the French Communist party.

"I will try. I will do my best."

"Please try hard for me," he asked.

"I will."

My father looked at his watch, an expensive Omega, and told me I should go back to my hotel and be with Lance. I didn't want to leave, but he seemed tired and told me he had to be up early the next morning to participate in a rally somewhere in Tokyo. I felt rather awkward that someone so close to me would be taking part in a "ban-the-bomb" rally, and I smiled at the feeling. He asked me what my smile was about, and I said, "I just realized how different we are."

"If we were all the same, the world would be one big boring place to live, my daughter." He rubbed my hair with an affectionate touch.

I didn't want another confrontation before we left. He held me in his arms for a long time before he let go. I gave him the telephone number at the Takanawa Prince so he could call me when he returned from the rally the next day. Still, neither of us wanted to part. Finally he said, "I must put a final touch on my speech for tomorrow night's conference with the American scientists. Please come back early in the morning with my grandson. I'll have breakfast in my room, and that way I can spend a little time with you before I have to leave."

"I'll be here," I promised. "What time should I come?"

"About eight o'clock."

"I'll be here at eight."

"Have pleasant dreams, my daughter. I will be thinking of you when I lie down tonight."

Once back in the room I walked over to Lance's bed. He was sound asleep. I bent over and kissed him, and without waking he stirred a bit and raised his arm to wipe off the spot where my lips had touched his face. I wished someone from my family had been there to talk to then, to pour out my innermost thoughts of happiness and pain.

Suddenly the telephone rang. It was my father, calling to see if I had gotten back safely.

"How is my grandson?" my father asked.

"He is sound asleep."

My father had more on his mind than simply checking on my arrival. "Next time when we meet let's not talk about politics," he began. "Let's talk about our family. You can tell me about your mother, your sisters, and my sons-in-law. Our time is so limited, my daughter." He sounded tired, but I couldn't let the matter go unquestioned.

"I'll never have enough of you, Father. You owe me twenty-one years, and politics was the only thing that kept us apart. Our anguish, our suffering, was caused by politics. It kept husbands and wives away from one another, and it separated sons from mothers. Of course we should talk about politics, because our lives revolved around it, Father."

"I remember your being sweet, stubborn, and intelligent, but I don't remember you being mean like this," he said, chuckling. "But I know you love me and that is all that matters to me."

The conversation unexpectedly seemed to take on a life of its own. "Father, it is not you that I am angry at, it is the Communist party, the system and the men who betrayed the revolution that I despise." I referred to the long-past Viet Minh, the patriotic anti-French organization that the

Communists took over after the Geneva Conference.

"I hope I will have the opportunity to show you the positive side of our revolution," he said gently.

"I had no doubts about the motives of the Viet Minh," I said. "I am proud that you were a Viet Minh. I am even proud that you had to go to prison for the cause. But I do not accept the presence of the Ha Noi government in the South."

My father broke into my stream of words. "Then you continue to be proud of your father and trust that your father will do his utmost for the people of the South. We are not the only winners in this war — the Americans won the war, too."

"Perhaps the draft dodgers and a handful of antiwar activists," I said, "but not all Americans. And I am very unhappy that we lost the South."

"It is refreshing to hear you talk," he said, his voice sounding bright despite the harshness of my attack.

"I guess no one dares speak candidly to a PRG ambassador. But I am lucky to be his daughter, and I am sure you know that I am taking advantage of it."

"You can take advantage of me anytime you like, my sweetheart."

"Are you serious?" I leapt at his "offer."

"Yes, I am."

"Then there is one thing I want so very much for you to help me with. Promise me that you will try your best." Already, after only a short time back with my father I was sounding like a spoiled brat.

"I can't promise if I don't know what you want," he replied, sounding exactly like a father accustomed to a spoiled brat.

"You told me that the war is over, correct?"

"Yes, my daughter, the war is over in our country."

"So there is no war, there is peace. Shouldn't it be a time to heal, to love one another, to 'forgive and forget' according to the spirit of the Liberation?"

He sighed, perhaps guessing where I was going.

"Father, I wish to remind you about the American POWs who are still in captivity in Viet Nam." As I spoke of them, I broke out in tears. I hadn't planned to speak to my father about these men, but it seemed the right thing to do. From the time I had heard the news reports about the "last American prisoners" leaving Viet Nam, I knew in my heart it wasn't true.

"My daughter, that is an issue about which I don't have the authority to speak." His voice had suddenly turned formal and distinctive, like a politician making a speech.

"I know, but I am not speaking to some authority; I am speaking to a man whom people love and respect and admire for his compassion to his fellow men, his family, and mankind. I am speaking to a man with a heart and with experience of being in captivity himself, a man who has had his right to fight for his country taken away from him. I want the American prisoners home, Father. I am a big girl now, but I still believe there is magic — magic that can happen through the hearts of men like you."

"Sweetheart, why are you doing this to yourself? This is an issue which neither of us has anything to do with. It doesn't concern our years of separation."

"Father, being your daughter, I have learned what it's like to live without a father, and I also experienced one of the most wonderful feelings when I saw you again. I know how well you understand those feelings, and how special the chance is to feel the feelings you felt when you talked to me. I want so very much for you to help other men, women, and children have that experience."

"I can't talk about this," he said coldly.

"Yes, you can!"

"You don't understand, do you?"

"I understand, but I refuse to accept that my father would not take a chance to bring happiness to others. You should be the one who would smile when a man returns to his family after a long separation. You should be the one who would wipe his tears when he pictured a prisoner throwing away his crutches to embrace his children. That's how I think of my father. If you had not taught me to be selfless, I wouldn't be using this precious time to discuss someone else's happiness. It shouldn't be difficult for you to understand how I feel and why."

"Daughter, listen to me," he interjected, genuine anguish obvious in his voice. "I love you for your unselfishness, but you must understand that before me there is the party. It is not as simple as you think."

"I am not asking you to open the cages and let the Americans go, I am asking you to influence the proper people in their decision. If you can charm the Russians for the PRG, then you can charm Le Duan for the POWs' families, Father." Le Duan, who became chairman of the Vietnamese Communist Party after Ho Chi Minh died in 1969, was one of Father's best friends.

"I don't think it is wise to talk about this on the telephone."

"Please, just think about what I have said, won't you?"

"I will think about everything you have said to me, my daughter."

"I'd like to ask you to think about the wives and children of those missing Americans whenever you think about my mother and me. Your thoughts are important. They will make a world of difference for those in captivity." I started to weep again.

"I love you, my daughter."

"I love you very much, Father."

He changed the subject, trying to lighten our moods before hanging up. "People have told me that your husband is a Yugoslav."

"He is an American of Yugoslav descent. Father, love can be spoken in so many languages, and it comes in different colors, including Red." I laughed, and he laughed with me.

"I am happy to hear you say that. I was worried . . ." He paused.

"You were worried that I married an American for convenience? A Dang wouldn't do that. My mother told us that Dangs are great lovers!"

My father roared with laughter then, and the sound brought back memories of the happy times we had shared when I was young. We said good night to each other five or six times before we managed to hang up.

— — —

A warm, red light fell across the paper on which I was writing my diary. I looked up and realized that I was seeing the rising sun outside my window. It was 6:00 A.M. I had stayed up all night, absorbed in my work. I looked over at Lance, who had kicked the covers off and was resting on his arm the same way his father sleeps.

I pushed my chair away from the table, stood up, and stretched my aching back muscles. There would be no time for sleeping now, because soon it would be time for breakfast and my son's first glimpse of his grandfather. I soaked for a long time in a hot bath, then got Lance and myself dressed and ready.

On the way to the Prince Hotel in a taxi, I tried to explain to my five-year-old son that Ong Ngoai, the Vietnamese name for grandfather, was one of the officials of the new government in Sai Gon, and that he was in Tokyo on business for that government.

"If he is with the government in Sai Gon, he must be a Communist," Lance figured out.

"Yes, he is. But don't forget he is your grandfather, and he wants to see you very much."

"I am not afraid," Lance assured me.

I cautioned him that there might be visitors while we were with his grandfather, and it might not be wise for us to tell anyone that his own father was a navy pilot. I proposed that we make that our private secret between the two of us.

"Did Daddy bomb North Viet Nam?" he asked.

"I don't know."

"You can tell me," he whispered conspiratorially. "I promise I won't tell even if they ask."

"When we get home you can ask your daddy." I kissed his forehead to hide my smile at his effort to sound grown up.

My father must have been waiting at the door to open it for us. He looked happier this morning, and his hair was combed neatly and he wore a fresh shirt and tie. He picked Lance up in his arms while the door was still open and gave him a big hug, while I closed the door behind us. When I saw him kiss Lance's hair, I thought of how he used to do that to me and then say, "Your hair smells like the orange blossoms at Grandfather's home."

He spoke Vietnamese to Lance, and fortunately Lance had become quite fluent during the time he lived in Sai Gon for six months before the final collapse of the South. Seeing them together, I thought they belonged to each other and deserved each other — and why not?

"Can you come to live with me and my mom?" Lance asked.

My father squeezed him tight, but didn't answer.

"My father will love you too," Lance went on. "He told me before we came here."

"Thank you, my grandson," my father said in English.

"I think Ba Ngoai [grandmother] misses you. She wrote you a letter and she cried." Lance crawled down from his lap and asked me to give my mother's letter to him. Dad put the letter in his shirt pocket and kissed Lance's forehead again.

Watching them talk and play together should have been sheer joy for me, but in reality I felt a dark cloud over the whole experience. I couldn't forget the devastation of my country, and the fact that my father was one of those in power there. The loss of my homeland kept me awake at nights and continued to trouble me during the daytime hours, and somehow being here with my father made it even more painful.

I envied my father's ability, as a career politician, to concentrate on a purely personal relationship while putting our political differences aside. He seemed at peace with himself, while I experienced torment inside. I knew that when our time together was over, he would go back to Viet Nam and back to his role as an official of the Vietnamese Communist Party, and I felt that my chance of being heard — really heard and listened to — by that official side of him was terribly slim.

As they played and I thought my sad thoughts, there was a knock at the door. My father looked upset, and the smile faded from his face as he went to answer it. In the hall stood a Vietnamese man in his thirties; my father greeted him with a "Dong Chi" (comrade) and invited him in. "I'd like you to meet someone from my village," he told the stranger, motioning toward me. I took that as a signal to hide our true relationship, so I began addressing my father as "Bac" (Uncle).

The man was my father's Japanese interpreter, and he also spoke French and

English. When he saw Lance he seemed puzzled, and well he might — how could this round-eyed youngster have come from my father's village? He extended his hand to Lance and said, "Bonjour."

"I don't speak French," Lance said as he somewhat reluctantly shook hands. "I only speak Vietnamese and English."

After some chitchat about Lance's age and his school, Lance went for more meaty information: "Are you a Communist?" he asked the visitor.

My father and I were startled and worried by the question, but the man just smiled and said he was indeed a Communist. Lance moved away from him for a moment, but then returned and asked in his most serious voice, "Are you going to hurt my mother and me?"

"Why are you asking such questions, little boy?" the man asked, completely confused by this point.

"I've heard that Communists kill women and children in my mom's country."

The man looked sharply toward me, but I avoided his glance. "Where did you hear such things?" he asked Lance.

"My mom took care of the refugees. They told her how much they were afraid of the Communists. I hope you will not hurt my mother and me!"

My father made a gesture for me to stop Lance from talking before everything was out in the open. I offered Lance a croissant and a glass of apple juice and told him to sit down at the table. He moved from the couch, but even while he ate his eyes never left the interpreter.

After a short exchange with my father, the man started to leave. Lance piped up: "I hope you will be nice to people in Sai Gon. I've been there before and they were very nice to me."

The man looked rather awkward as he walked over to the table. He sat down and took Lance's hand in his. "I will be nice to the people in Sai Gon, don't worry."

"My father is an American, but he was very sad when people got killed in Viet Nam by the Communists."

The man looked at me, said goodbye, and then left without another word. My father shook his head repeatedly. He was upset by Lance's revelations and, I think, a little hurt. "Perhaps when you come back tomorrow, you should not bring Lance with you. In the next few days there will be a lot of people waiting to see me for numerous reasons," he said sadly.

"I am sorry, Father. But remember it took you a long time to teach us to measure our words before we speak."

"When adults poison their minds with such things, children are not to be blamed," he said, sighing.

"I don't think I have poisoned his mind. I tell him what I believe to be true, and it will be his choice to take a side when he is capable of doing so. You raised me in the spirit of revolution, and I made a revolution by recognizing good and evil — and I chose to disbelieve the evil."

"I thought we might have a pleasant breakfast," my father said, hoping to change the subject. We sat down at the table and I saw that, just as he had twenty years before, he still enjoyed his morning tea. I reminded him of those early mornings when he and my mother sat in the kitchen drinking tea before the rest of the family got up. He smiled and some of the happiness returned to his eyes. For a moment the pleasure of the time he had shared with his wife and family came alive in his heart.

"Most of my friends cut all ties with their families when they joined the revolution, leaving them in the cities," he said. "But I was fortunate enough to persuade your mother to come with me into the Liberated Zones. How can I not remember those precious years? And I am happy that you were old enough to remember it. It is important to remember those days, my daughter."

"Father, do you believe that everything I have said to you comes from my heart?" I asked.

"I know that you have been sincere, only you don't understand the complexity of the issues."

Brushing aside his comment, I said, "I wanted to know how much you understand me so that I could ask you something else."

As he waited to hear what I had in mind, I realized how difficult it was for me to continue because I had no idea how he would react. I squeezed out the words:

"As far as Ha Noi is concerned, Viet Nam is totally at peace. Therefore, I want my father back."

Surprised, he covered my mouth with his hand as if he feared we were being listened to. He turned the radio volume louder, then spoke to me softly, almost in a whisper. I knew he wasn't wrong in being suspicious.

"I don't want to hear that kind of talk from you again," he said. "I will forgive you this time for your misunderstanding about your father." I was astounded by the vehemence of his reaction; I had assumed that getting our family together again was a goal we all shared.

"I begin to see that our trains travel on two different tracks," I said. "Our hearts are yearning for different purposes, different causes."

"I will not try to change you," he said, "but I must ask that you not trample on my beliefs."

I cried as I realized that the gap between us was so vast, and our personalities so strong, that I would never be able truly to reach him. "From you I grew to love Viet Nam," I told him. "From you I know the pain, the suffering that our people had. And because of you my heart jumped whenever we saw a dim chance of peace in Viet Nam. I only wish to remind you that there is a time for politics and a time for you to be with your family, for us to have the chance to know our father. As you see, we hardly know each other."

"I am touched by your concern, and it is an honor for a parent to be loved and wanted the way you love me," he replied. "But, my daughter, I want you to know this so you will not repeat yourself. Viet Nam needs all the helping hands it can get to rebuild, to heal, to step into a better future. Let me put it this way: Viet Nam must make progress, must work harder to improve its economy. You said you love Viet Nam, you care about your people; then you should be able to share my dream, the dream to make Viet Nam stronger, prosperous, and independent."

"I hope your dream will come true, Father," I said. But I wouldn't give up my beliefs, either. "My doubt is not about your dedication, but about the system. How can the country prosper when the workers are not allowed to be their own bosses, or lead their own lives, or own their own farms? Their future is being dictated to them by the party; nothing can ever change."

"All I can say is that I'll do my utmost to make Viet Nam prosper." He reached over and shook my hand as a gesture of a contract between us: He would do his job, and I would not be able to make him leave his party.

"How soon can you make arrangements to get Mother to Paris?" he asked as the atmosphere began to grow calmer.

"As soon as I get back to Hawaii I'll start working on it."

"Is your mother angry at me?"

"When we were very young, life was not kind to us, and my mother had to work very hard. Sometimes she said she wished you were there to help her."

"Daughter, do you know that I never made any money to support your mother and the family? As a matter of fact, your mother was the sole support, with the help of your grandparents. I owe so much to your mother. I feel guilty for not taking you all to Ha Noi with me that time."

"But I thought it was Mom's decision not to go."

"It was my fault that I didn't persuade her."

"Do you think if we all went with you to Ha Noi in 1954 I would be a member of the Communist party today?" I laughed.

"It isn't easy to become a member of the party," he said, not taking it as a joke. "Your brother failed after many tries; not even he is a member." Khoi didn't participate in Communist studies or obey all the rules, I learned, and he often spoke his mind, which was different than the party's.

"Does that disappoint you?" I asked.

"No. Your brother never tried hard enough, but I am happy for him that he has a good education, as that is the most important thing to him."

"My mother is very concerned about Khoi. She always wonders how he turned out after living with the Communists — if he is still a good person, if he is still warm and honest, whether he is still the son she once knew before he went to Russia."

"Your mother will have her chance to get to know your brother," he promised.

It was time for my father to leave for the rally. He said he would call when he got back, and we made plans to go shopping the next day; he said he wanted to buy a guitar for Khoi. He and Lance hugged each other, and before we left Lance invited his grandfather to visit him in our room at the Takanawa Prince. "They have a refrigerator in my room, and every morning the maid takes away the empty bottles and gives me new ones. It is really neat! I want you to have a drink with me over there, Ong Ngoai."

I knew my father couldn't leave the hotel on his own, without his Japanese bodyguard and his interpreter, so I told Lance that Ong Ngoai was very busy and it was better for us to come to his hotel.

On the way back to our room, Lance and I both had mixed emotions. Unknown to me, he was thinking in a much more complex way about the situation between me and my father, seeing how it could apply to his own life. Suddenly he burst out, "I won't let my dad live apart from me and you! I'll cry my head off if he goes away!"

"If he goes away for a good cause, you must let him go," I tried to explain. "You must be brave."

"Did you cry when your father went away?" he asked.

"Yes, I did."

"My dad says it is OK to cry, but don't carry on," Lance told me seriously.

I thought about that, and wondered if I had been "carrying on" about my father's departure all these years — and was still doing it.

Chapter 19

When my father had not called by dinner time, Lance and I decided to eat in our room so as not to miss his call. Sure enough, while we were eating he telephoned. He had had a pleasant day, he said, meeting with "old friends," both Japanese and American — people who had been his friends during the war. I often wondered what sort of Americans might have been friends with a man in my father's position while their country was waging war with the people he served.

Since my father sounded tired, I suggested we rest that evening and meet early the next day for our shopping expedition. He agreed, but later, about 10:00 P.M., he called again. There was nothing important, he said, he just wanted to talk. We discussed the family and some of our friends from the old days. I asked him about Uncle Le Duc Tho, his closest comrade from the Viet Minh days, who now had a less important position after the Paris Peace Talks. I found out my father still loved to travel, as he told me about seeing the midnight sun in the Scandinavian countries he had visited. I asked about his trips to Mongolia, which he described as a sad and barren country. I told him I'd like to visit China someday and would love to "return to Mongolia," too. He interrupted: "Why do you use the word *return*?"

"Because somehow I feel that a part of me is Mongolian," I said, laughing.

"Why?"

"When you went away, I had to grow up alone against all kinds of odds. I had to pretend that I was tough, physically and mentally. I read about Genghis Khan, and he impressed me so. I have never met a Mongolian, yet I feel very close to the people and to me they always possess some mystique."

"I think you would be fascinated with Russia," my father said, perhaps dropping a hint but not pursuing it.

The next morning, when we went shopping, the bodyguard provided by the Japanese Communist Party sat in the front seat of the taxi, silent and still as a rock. His eyes, though, were alert and constantly busy, and they reminded me of the eyes of a leopard. He knew Tokyo well, because as I struggled to tell him we wanted to shop for a guitar, he nodded his head repeatedly and delivered some rapid-fire directions to the taxi driver. Soon we arrived in the Ginza area, and we got out to enjoy some of the shops.

As we walked along, I made an effort to study our surroundings by looking at reflections in the store windows. I was just trying out my beginning "spy" techniques, and I was surprised to find that they worked — I spotted a well-dressed Caucasian man at several places, apparently following us. The first time he walked into a guitar shop where we were looking for Khoi's present; he appeared again at another store where my father found just the right instrument and bought it; and he turned up once more at a coffee shop, sitting alone at a table near the entrance. I caught his eye when he was looking at us a few times, and he left without ordering a drink.

When my father next went into a toy store, I discovered that I had an adopted sister. She had been ten when my father arrived in Ha Noi and took her in. He raised her and sent her to a good school, and later she had attended a university in Moscow to study engineering. She now had a son Lance's age, and it was to buy a present for the boy that my father had stopped into the toy store. I didn't have much time to think about my new "relatives," though, because I spotted the Caucasian man there again. This time I moved closer to him and got a better look at him: His eyes were blue, and sharp; he had a pale complexion like a European, and I thought he must be either a Frenchman or a sophisticated KGB agent. His tailored suit, his expensive shoes, and the folded umbrella he carried told me he wasn't one of "us" — the CIA.

When we left the store, I found that my father had seen the man, too. "I think we are being followed," he said.

"Your people or mine?" I replied with a small laugh. It wasn't a good joke at all, because he appeared quite shocked at my question.

Back at my hotel after the shopping trip, I thought about my involvement with the CIA. By now I realized that the American people in general were sick and tired of Viet Nam; my father's statement that the Americans also won the war might have been closer to the truth than I first thought, at least in the sense that they didn't have to wrangle with that troublesome corner of the world anymore. Still, I had hope that my small contribution would do something toward the goal of freeing my people from Communism.

My father had reserved that afternoon for me, so I left Lance with a babysitter and headed for the Prince Hotel once again. In the middle of the day the lobby was almost deserted. Outside my father's room on the fourth floor, the Japanese bodyguard paced the floor. He turned as I came out of the elevator, greeted me politely, and then resumed his pose, hands over his chest to stand guard, as I went into the room.

My father had been working before I arrived, and there was a pile of paperwork on the table next to his leather briefcase. I noticed several pieces of paper that looked like identification cards of some sort, and out of curiosity I picked one of them up. It was an American draft card, this one issued in July 1969 to an eighteen-year-old boy.

At first I thought the cards were part of the belongings of dead soldiers. I had come from a country where men made soldiering their profession and their lifetime commitment, where soldiers were heroes who died for the flag; my own brother had volunteered for service even though he was eligible for an exemption. I asked my father what the cards were.

He smiled and took the slips of paper from me and placed them together with at least a dozen more on the table. "These are draft cards," he said.

"I know that, but how did they end up in the possession of the Ha Noi government?"

"It shows you that the involvement of the Americans in Viet Nam was wrong, not only by our judgment but in the minds of the American people, too. These are a few examples from the Americans who refused to fight for a wrong cause. They sent these draft cards to our mission," he explained earnestly.

I bit my lip to suppress my outrage. It hurt me again to face the fact that my father and I traveled through life on two very different paths, leading quite definitely in opposite directions.

"I hope that you use these only for your propaganda," I said. "To me these men were cowards. Those who turned their draft cards over to the enemy are traitors! They don't deserve a place in your briefcase."

"The war in Viet Nam was wrong and these young men recognized that," he persisted.

"What was wrong about the war in Viet Nam was the U.S. flirting with the idea called 'Vietnamization' — the Americans pulled out and let the ARVN fight the NVA with U.S. military aid. It was wrong because the U.S. government didn't fight dirty enough; they were too civilized, too naive about guerrilla warfare. Ha Noi says that the Americans were wrong to help Viet Nam, but what would you say about the Russians who poured money into North Viet Nam to destroy our people?

"This war was wrong because Vietnamese killed one another," I went on, still steaming about the draft cards and not allowing my father to interrupt. "Because people liked to flirt with socialism and allowed that ill breeze to sweep away thousands of years of our tradition. That is what was wrong with the war in Viet Nam!"

When I finally stopped, my father looked at me sadly and said, "I don't want to argue with you, my daughter. I never want to change your mind. If you are content with your belief then you are happy, and when my daughter is happy I am happy for you. My family is too precious to me, you know that."

"Ah, but the party is even more precious to you than us!"

"The country is more precious to me. You are strong, you are independent, you can take care of yourself. You are OK." He smiled as he said "OK."

"The Vietnamese people were OK, too," I countered. "Your wife and your children are the image of the Vietnamese people. We are no different from them. Our needs, our desires, are the same as those of millions of other people, and we were OK until Ha Noi invaded us."

"I understand their needs, and I promise you that I'll do everything in my power to meet those needs."

We went back and forth about this. Finally, my father looked disappointed and tired. "Can we talk about something else?" he pleaded.

"Yes, let's talk about something else." I got up and hugged him tightly.

He said he had spent half the night just looking at the photos I had brought of my sisters, my mother, and the grandchildren he had never seen. He spoke as if he were thinking out loud: "I would like so much for your mother to come home with me."

We talked on, making plans for bringing my mother to Paris. My job was to get her the proper travel documents when I returned to Hawaii; his was going to be harder — to get an entry visa into France for her. He said he had a friend somewhere in the French foreign ministry who might be able to help.

My father's interpreter called to let him know it was time for lunch. He tried to get out of it, suggesting that his lunch be served in his room so we could talk longer, but he didn't succeed; a group of American Quakers wanted to meet him at lunch and there was no way to avoid it. As we waited for the time for him to leave, I noticed that his thoughts seemed troubled by something. In a moment, he asked, "Are you familiar with the Quakers?"

"I try to stay away from religious organizations," I replied. "God is too superior to be organized by men and women down here, don't you think?" We both laughed.

"During my visit to Oslo a few years ago there were a few men and women who said they belonged to the Quakers in America, and they came to me and offered their help," he told me. "They defied their government and turned to us."

"What could they do for Viet Nam?"

"They were educated people, two were doctors and the others were ACLU lawyers and professors."

"Sounds like a bunch of disenchanted creatures," I said. "They couldn't find God, and they couldn't find happiness — maybe they thought socialism would be more fun."

My father was still disturbed by the memory. "I turned them down," he said. "I told them, 'You take care of your country, America also needs help.' You see, my daughter, when a person is not good for his own country, he is useless for the universe."

"Hurrah!" I exclaimed. "Now I know who you are! I feel the same way you do." I rushed over to where he sat and jumped into his lap. I put my arms around him and wished with all my power that the world could stand still for that instant.

The moment was only a brief one, as finite as the narrow area of agreement we had found in each other. I was grateful for it, however, because it made me feel truly close to my father, and gave me hope and strength to face him again in the future.

— — —

It seemed silly at my age to keep a diary, but things were happening so fast I didn't have a chance to figure them out fully, so I decided to start jotting down my thoughts, my feelings, and all the activities going on around us. Perhaps sometime later, when it was all over, I could go back through the account and come to understand all of it.

Whenever I thought of my father, I caught myself thinking out loud, arguing with him as if he were there. I kept trying to find out what we had in common, what key there might be to a way to draw us closer together. I recalled a poem by Edward Markham:

> He drew a circle that shut me out,
> Heretic, rebel, a thing to flout.
> But love and I had the wit to win:
> We drew a circle that took him in!

Was I the one who had shut my father out? As I prowled through my memories, I remembered that he had wanted peace between us ever since we met again. He wanted to talk only about love and family, and I wanted to open a wound; I wanted and created confrontation. I prepared myself for the likelihood that the sadness between us would deepen — and realized that I was the one who made it likely.

I still had the first letter my father had written to me from Moscow; I had read it and reread it hundreds of times since receiving it in 1972. Some weeks before that was the first time the family had received anything from him: he had sent a package and two-line letter while on an official mission to Milan, Italy, which was passed to us by an old family friend in Paris. I immediately wrote him back with news of the family, and he sent me this longer letter. I almost knew by heart the part where lamented the circumstances of life that had split our family in two:

My darling daughter, I am proud of my wife and children who are loyal and faithful and precious to me. And I am sad for all of us, for your mother must raise six children alone for 18 long years in the troubled times of our homeland. I blame myself mostly for causing my wonderful and devoted wife and my wonderful children whom I love very much to be apart from me. My children with whom I wish very much to spend every minute of my life. And yet I "left" you all in such a challenging situation. I thought you all might never make it, and the fact that we lost Hai Van never escaped me.

I always kept my faith and believed that my wife and my children love me and would be waiting for my return, but I thought I was dreaming when I held your letter in my hands and all that day I wouldn't work, and all night I was dreaming that you came to visit me in Moscow. When I left you were nine years old, Hai Van was six, Hoa Binh was two and Minh Tam was only three months old.

Hai Van was very intelligent when he was small. I remember a time when he was only four; we were rowing a boat one night on the river in front of the house in Ong Deo and we were studying the names of the stars. I showed Hai Van the Milky Way and he pointed at the crescent moon and said, "Do you know why the moon is only half tonight?" I said to him, "Why, son?" "Because I broke it in half," he replied. And when I asked him what he did with the other half, he said, "There, I threw it into the river."

Even then, he showed me that he had a gift for music. I never forgot those small fingers of his picking at the mandolin that grandfather gave you. But I never believed that his life would be so short. I also never would have thought that your brother would choose that direction for his life. Your mother can visit his grave each weekend, she can cry, she can express her pain and her bitterness, and she can burn the incense for him, but I can never do anything about this enormous loss.

Although your letter stated clearly that you had lost your brother, I still imagine his radiant face, full of life and vitality, and realize that I can never hear his laughter.

When my father left us twenty-one years before, he had said he would return in two years, but other people had other plans for him. This time, when he left me, I knew in my heart that it was not up to Ha Noi when or where I could see him again; this time I was in control, or rather, I had the choice to make.

It was clear to me that my father wouldn't ask me to join the Communists, but if I wanted to see him again I knew I would have to learn to hold my tongue when I thought about his government or his party's beliefs. I couldn't possibly cast aside my true feelings, about those who raped my land and oppressed my people, but I would have to be careful not to express those feelings so frankly and so often. It would be a greater tragedy if I were to lose my father once again.

My father called it "going home" when the North Vietnamese flag flew in the skies of Sai Gon. But it was his home; it was no longer mine. Still, I knew that no matter what political system he worked within, he was there for one reason and one reason only — to bring peace to Viet Nam. More than once he had said, "We, the Vietnamese people, now achieve peace. We gained control of our nation and our destiny; it is now time for all of us to heal the wounds of war, to rebuild our fatherland and consolidate peace. This is not a job which is only for the party but is for all peace-loving people in Viet Nam. We must all contribute to the effort, and your father is one of those Vietnamese who have been assigned that task."

I felt sorry for him, because I knew that the independence and peace he thought had been achieved were just mirages, products of his never-ending dream. What Viet Nam faced now was not peace but the beginning of a new war, one of a different type, one in which all Southerners would fight in silence under the yoke of the "liberators."

My father had often asked us to "be my children, believe in me, trust me as you would believe in your country and be loyal to our own people." He never had to worry that we would neglect that duty, but he hadn't realized that trying to honor him and our country, when we had such different beliefs about what was best for Viet Nam, would build a terrible barrier between us.

Before my father left Tokyo, we spent a few happy hours together and I stuck to my resolution not to say anything to make that barrier any higher. In a different way, however, I took a risk that could have made the wall insurmountable: I used my father to "smuggle" a message to my brother Khoi, a message that included an invitation to defect.

He didn't know it, of course, because the message was hidden in an alarm clock. I trusted my father implicitly and knew he would not open a private letter from me to Khoi, but I wasn't so certain about the good manners of his "comrades." When I handed my father the letter, I asked him if they would open his luggage.

He smiled at me patiently. "No, daughter, 'they' will not search my luggage."

Still, I thought I should be circumspect, and so in this letter, the first I had ever written to my brother since I had struggled with my reading primer back in 1954, I reached back into our childhood together for a way to hint to him that there was more to the alarm clock than computer chips and wires.

"Remember when you were six years old," I wrote. "Dad gave you a harmonica. Remember what you did with it that night? I want you to treat this clock exactly the same way you treated that harmonica."

I prayed that Khoi would remember everything about the day he got that harmonica from our father. He had gone all over the house all day long, playing tune after tune on his new instrument; then, that night, he had gotten out of bed and pried it open to find out how it worked!

If he pried open the alarm clock, as I hoped, he would find the message explaining that I had become associated with people who could help him if and when he decided he wanted to leave Viet Nam and go to America. It also told him there would be other messages in the future.

I held my breath when I gave the alarm clock and the letter and the sheet music to my father. I had no idea what Khoi's reaction would be, but worse, I was afraid that somehow my secret would be discovered. If that happened, both Khoi and my father could be in deep trouble — and our renewed contact could be cut off forever.

Still, I tried not to betray my feelings in the last days and hours with my father in Tokyo. The day after he left for Paris, Lance and I flew home to Hawaii and we started looking forward to seeing my father again in Paris — this time with my mother to join in the reunion.

— — —

The first weekend back in Hawaii I spent entirely with my mother and sisters, since my husband was away on assignment and wasn't due back for almost two weeks. I felt as if I had to race with the sun to bring all of those precious meetings with my father back to the rest of the family. I tried not to leave out a single detail. My mother listened raptly; my sisters asked countless questions. Everyone read the letters from my father that I had brought back, and we all had red eyes and happy smiles.

When we talked about arrangements for my mother's trip, we all knew the discussion had more than one layer of meaning. In our hearts, we all knew that this might well be our last chance to be together; it was possible that my mother would decide to accept my father's plea and go back with him to Viet Nam.

She was being presented with a terribly painful choice. My sister Cuong and I believed strongly that it was time for her to make a choice solely for herself. She had given her whole life to her children; she had provided us with love, protection, food, clothing, shelter, our education. She had given us a simple set of rules to live by, and wings to fly with when the time came for us to be on our own. She had given us the independence to explore religion, ideologies, and love. She gave us security, faith, and a strong sense of loyalty.

Now, it was her turn. We knew she wouldn't be eager to give up her freedom in order to see Khoi again and to grow old with my father, but if she chose that we were determined to accept it. Cuong and I promised each other that we would not shed any tears or put any other pressures on her that could impede her decision; we knew she would have enough trouble confronting the thoughts in her own mind.

Dealing with the more mundane aspects of the Paris trip brought back memories of my departure from Viet Nam many years before — going through all the hassles a bureaucracy can require just to get a few simple pieces of paper. At the Immigration and Naturalization Service office in Honolulu, an officer advised me it would take about four weeks to get the "Refugee Travel Document" that my mother required. My insistence that we needed it much sooner got us nowhere. So we went through the long process of taking pictures, taking fingerprints, filling out endless application forms — and then I went home and called an immigration officer who had known me when I was helping out with the crush of refugees at the end of the war. He took down all the information, and I was able to pick up the travel papers exactly two weeks later.

With that document I went to the French consulate in Honolulu to apply for an entry visa. The French woman who worked there looked at the application and asked, "Vietnamienne?" I was offended, as I always was when a French person expected every Vietnamese to speak French. Perhaps there was a scar that had never healed, even decades after the French had been defeated and driven out of my country. Then the woman asked, again in French, if my mother was a legal resident of the United States.

"I don't speak French," I told her.

"You are Vietnamese, Mademoiselle, and you don't speak French?" she said incredulously and, I thought, somewhat haughtily.

"You are absolutely correct," I shot back, probably too testily. "I am

Vietnamese. And I speak Vietnamese. I don't have to speak French in order to survive any more!"

"Mademoiselle, you don't have to be so sarcastic!" the woman responded, somewhat shocked.

I realized that I had just created a negative impression in someone with whom I would need to do business, but I hadn't been able to hold myself back. Still, the storm seemed to blow over. The woman looked at my mother's travel document for about five minutes, checked some books, then told me my mother would need two sponsors in France and that the application would take about four to six weeks to be investigated. Another roadblock!

On the way home, my mother and I talked about the problem. She had a friend whose children were working in France as a doctor and a teacher, so she thought we would have a good chance of getting the sponsors. As for the time element, I decided to write to my father and see if the NLF had any useful connections with their left-wing friends in the French foreign ministry. In the meantime, I asked my CIA case officer if the agency could do anything to speed things up; to my surprise, he said it was "beyond my power." So I kept thinking, trying to come up with a way around the obstacle.

Suddenly, I remembered that in Tokyo my father had given me the name of a colleague who was acting ambassador in Paris; if I had any trouble before he arrived from Moscow, he had said, perhaps Mr. Phan Thanh Nam would be able to help. I got on the phone as quickly as possible and gave him a call. Because he was younger than my father and below him in rank, I addressed him as "Uncle" rather than as "Mister." Sure enough, he said he thought he could get help from a "close friend," and he asked me to go ahead and submit the application to the French consulate in Honolulu and to send him a telegram with all the particulars.

Two and a half weeks later, the French woman called me from the consulate to say that the visa was ready. She was more surprised than we were at the quick action. "You must know somebody very high up in the foreign ministry to be able to get it so fast," she said when we went to pick it up. "It is the French turn to work for me, don't you think?" I replied with a wink. "Bon voyage," she said — to my mother.

John wanted me to leave Lance home with him while my mother and I went to Paris. Considering his excessive candor when he spoke to the interpreter in Tokyo, we thought it would be best not to put Lance into a situation that would force him to lie, or at best withhold the truth, about his family. After all, he was only five years old. We made arrangements with a friend, the wife of another navy pilot, to watch Lance during the day while John was at work.

When I called Rob to let him know I had gotten the visa, there was a long pause on the phone; I think he was caught by surprise at the quick action, and perversely may have been a little upset at my good luck as an "operative." More than that, he didn't sound as if he wholly supported the idea that my mother might decide to stay with my father. He told us to stop in Washington on our way to Europe to meet him, because "we need to discuss a few important matters before your family meets with your father this time."

I understood his feelings, because I didn't really want my mother to leave either, although for different reasons — I'm sure Rob simply thought he would have one less bit of leverage to use if she was with him in Viet Nam instead of with me in the United States. The day after our phone conversation I wrote him a letter and asked him not to discourage my mother from going, if that was the way she was leaning. I told him to respect her logic and judgment; whatever she decided, it would be the choice she would live with. I didn't expect him to understand my mother, but I was determined not to let him make her decision any harder than it already was.

Rob's reservations were mild, however, compared to Kim's reaction when I called her in Atlanta to tell her and Hoa Binh about the upcoming trip. Considering how she and Cuong had always felt about our father's leaving Mother, it was natural that Kim should be livid at the prospect of Mother going back to Viet Nam with him. She said she and Hoa Binh would fly to Washington to meet us before we left for Paris.

The weekend we spent together in the capital was a rough one. Neither Kim nor Hoa Binh had the heart actually to speak up and try to stop my mother from going, because we all knew that she belonged to my father; on the other hand, none of us wanted to encourage her in any way to go to Viet Nam, because we all knew what was waiting for her there. Even Khoi had sent her a letter telling her clearly that she should not return there. Through it all, however, my mother maintained her perspective. Before she made any decision, she assured us, she would have to talk to our father a long time about the conditions in which his government would allow her to live. "I have always wanted to be with your father," she told us one night, "but my decision must be based on how his government will react. I must know the truth about that 'liberation,' how they will treat the people in the South. I don't want to depend on the newspapers or the radio or anyone else's opinion about that government. I must know from the government itself — and that is from your father. And when I make up my mind, that will tell your father and his government how people feel about their revolution."

Even as the wife of an ambassador, my mother would have to attend the Communist "reeducation" classes if she returned to Viet Nam, my father said.

Khoi later told me the southern people suffered greatly during this period, losing their homes and being forced into prison camps in North Viet Nam. One writer whose father was a Communist went back to South Viet Nam in 1975 to try to save his son. He failed; his son, the anti-Communist writer/ paratrooper Phan Nhat Nam, spent fourteen years in prison, along with his brother-in-law. His sister killed herself because she couldn't endure the humiliation by the North Vietnamese.

This was more than a family affair by now, of course — it had become a very important part of a certain CIA case officer's business. As I had suspected, Rob told me that if my mother went back to Viet Nam we might lose touch with her.

Almost as soon as I had gotten to Washington, Rob took me to a farm in Virginia for a meeting with his supervisor, Jerrie Parker. The "boss," as Rob called him, said he had wanted to take the occasion to welcome me to the intelligence community, but it pretty quickly became clear that he was far more interested in Khoi than in me. I had reported what I had learned about Khoi from my father — that he had been educated in Ha Noi, then spent three years in Beijing before going to the Soviet Union, where he attended a military academy and came home with a degree in engineering and a specialization in guided missiles.

What attracted the CIA to my brother wasn't so much what he was doing with all that training — after all, there wasn't any high technology at the television station, and it had been built by the Americans for the South Vietnamese anyway — but just the fact that he was my father's son, that he was still located "inside," and that he might be willing to help them in order to get out.

They knew the last part was a possibility because of something else I had told them. In the late sixties, a close friend of my father's had sneaked back into Sai Gon when he came south to run a clandestine operation. One day he visited my mother and brought news of all the family members in the North, telling us that my father and Uncle Diep were well, that our cousin Thu Van was one of the best Vietnamese students in Ha Noi, that our cousin Trung had the potential to become a model member of the Communist party. Then he bent closer to my mother and whispered that he was worried about Khoi, because he showed no ambition to follow in my father's footsteps and serve the Liberation cause.

I'm sure he must have thought he had given us the good news first and the bad news last, but the word that Khoi was not fitting into the Communist "system" was a glimmer of hope for us, a reason to believe that Khoi had remained the same good-hearted, free-spirited, gentle man he had been as a youth — and that one day he might want to return to us.

I don't know how much the CIA wanted Khoi to leave Viet Nam, but I know that my mother, my family, and I dreamed of the chance to see him again. After the door to freedom had been shut tight following the U.S. airlift of refugees in April 1975, it had taken several years for Southerners, including many former Viet Cong, to see the truth about the "wonderful, equal, everybody the same" Communist regime. We hoped that Khoi had come to see it as well, and would want to escape if given a chance.

That dream was a nightmare sometimes, as we realized the hardships Khoi must be enduring, especially if he was not considered a true "revolutionary." But we comforted each other by remembering that we had survived the war and the scorn of my father's comrades who were mad as hell at my mother because she allowed her daughters to marry "American imperialists." We had come to America, had begun contributing to this country, and had become a part of this great nation; perhaps we could still hope that Khoi would do the same.

Because my brother was a musician, my dream for a long time was for him to be invited along with other Vietnamese artists to play in a cultural exchange in a neutral country. If the Communist government would let him out, then all he would have to do is walk away from the group and go to an American or other Western embassy — defect. I had heard of people escaping on this kind of "first-class ticket" on the luxury train to freedom. I realized then that the ticket on the freedom train would have a price. I was greatly worried, however, about the risk to my brother and to his relationship with our father. We may all disagree with the path my father took, but none of us would ever do anything to hurt him, and that included Khoi.

In my opinion, I thought the work I was doing for the CIA ought to be enough to "earn" my brother's ticket out. Because I knew the Communists and could parrot their nonsense, I could work hard, be productive and be one of the most effective intelligence agents the CIA had — without endangering my father's position. I didn't know if Khoi could or would do that, but I was willing to help find out if it would speed the day when we might see his face again.

— — —

My first duty after arriving in Paris with my mother was to check in with Rob, who had arrived separately. He had checked into the Paris Sheraton ahead of us. I used my usual procedure of riding the elevators up and down, and on one floor found Rob waiting when the doors opened. We ignored each other, but when we got into another car and found ourselves alone, he handed me a matchbook, said "Welcome to Paris," and got off at the next floor. In my room, I opened the matchbook and found Rob's room number written inside.

A few minutes later I was in his room. "Good work," he told me. Then we talked about our expectations for the days ahead. There was little for us to plan, because once my mother and father met, everything that happened after that would depend on them and on the Communist officials.

Back in my own room, I asked my mother if she was ready to go and meet my father. "Not yet," she said, smiling but looking a bit nervous. Still, despite her anxiety, I could see a radiant look in her eyes and a glow on her face that seemed to make her look younger. I noticed her newest *ao dai* was pressed and hanging on the hook by the bathroom door. At that moment I couldn't think of myself or the rest of the family; I found myself hoping that my mother would just melt into my father's arms and say, "Yes, we should go home," because I knew that would make him happy and from the look on her face it could bring her joy, too.

I sat on the edge of the bed next to her and asked what she was thinking.

"I'm thinking how sad this is!" she said. "Your father and I have twenty-one years to make up, yet only a few hours away from seeing him again I have nothing but contempt for his party, his so-called socialist party. He knows I love him, and he pretends that I also love his party."

"Mom, the most important thing is for him to know that we love him as much as we hate the system he represents. I believe he understands that."

She frowned and became even more serious. "My son, my only son, is now in the claws of the Communists. If I must go home it is because of your brother, Khoi."

"You can't do anything for him," I warned.

"But at least I will suffer with him," she said, beginning to weep.

"Mom, let's try to concentrate on Father, here and now. He needs to hear some kind words from you. Don't disappoint him, please, Mom."

"All right. I am ready to see him," she said, shaking off her tears. Still, there was an unmistakable air of uncertainty in her voice and in her eyes.

I placed a call to the Provisional Revolutionary Government headquarters — PRG was the official name used by the NLF in diplomatic circles overseas — and spoke to Mr. Phan Thanh Nam, the acting ambassador who had helped us with the visa. My father was there, having arrived on September 14, and was eager to hear from me, he said. When my father got on the line, he immediately asked me to give him the hotel address so someone from the mission could drive him over to pick us up. I asked if he could stay with us at the hotel, but he said he couldn't; "I must stay in the government quarters, according to the rules."

Half-jokingly, I told him, "It is healthy to break the rules once in a while, Dad."

He laughed and said he and Nam would be right over. I was a little sorry that "Uncle" Nam had to come along, because I would have preferred that our meeting be just the family, but I also realized that I needed to meet as many officials as possible if I was to "penetrate" the mission once my father had returned to Viet Nam.

When they arrived in the lobby, I went down to meet them and was introduced to Nam. He was nothing like what I expected of a Southerner; he was rather short but well built, with a dark complexion and fingers turned yellowish-brown from the cigarettes he smoked. I got quite a shock when he shook my hand and said, "So you are the young lady who talked to me on the phone. Quite an operator you are!" For an instant I thought my "cover" had been blown — until he saw my look of confusion and added, "I was surprised to receive your call."

"You mean no one calls you from the United States?" I asked, recovering a bit.

"Oh, yes, there are people who call me from America, but not from . . . ," Nam seemed troubled as to how to finish the sentence. I helped him out: "From someone who is not a Viet Cong?" And we all laughed.

I was also introduced to Pham Gia Thai, a North Vietnamese who was said to be a student. He must be a "professional student," I thought, because he was obviously in his early forties. Thai wore thick glasses, and behind the lenses his eyes seemed to be crossed; he had feminine gestures and a soft, limp handshake, all of which combined to make me underestimate him at once.

On our way upstairs, Nam suggested my mother and I move to the mission that same evening, and the next day Thai could drive us to the PRG's villa in Verrieres-la-Buisson in the suburbs, the villa the North Vietnamese had used during the Paris Peace Talks. I was anxious to see the place, but had no desire to sleep under the same roof with a lot of Communists. I didn't want to owe them any debt, because I knew the "interest" they would want in return would be too high a price to pay. More important, I needed to be accessible to my case officer, and that would be impossible if I was "locked away" in the PRG's own lair. Grasping for an excuse to say no, I told Nam that I didn't know if the Vietnamese government would object to having a guest who was a U.S. citizen, but I thought there could be a slight problem if I stayed there. I said I would remain at the hotel but come to visit my parents during the day.

Nam looked uneasy and Thai seemed rather surprised. My father pinched me in the back. Still, Nam responded, "Whatever suits you best, My Yung." He warned that they wouldn't be able to provide regular transportation between the hotel and Verrieres, but I assured him I could find my way on the Metro.

We reached our room at last, and the door opened. My father and mother looked at each other — and both burst into tears.

Sadly, they had to restrain their emotions as much as possible, and to speak almost formally to each other, because of the presence of these other people. In the Vietnamese culture, it is considered impolite to be outspoken and direct, especially for a woman. I wanted to ask Nam and Thai to step outside for a while, but there was no way I could say that to my father's comrades. So the first moment my father and mother shared after twenty-one years — a moment that should have been a warm and joyous reunion — was made stiff and mundane by the presence of the same Communists who had kept them apart all that time.

After only about fifteen or twenty minutes, Thai had to go back to the mission for a meeting and Nam had engagements, so they had to leave. My father would have stayed longer, but he couldn't be alone without an escort — such is the kind of "privilege" that goes with high rank in the Communist system. My mother said she preferred to stay at the hotel that night, so we made plans for Father to pick us up the next morning to go to the villa.

After they left, I went to the lobby to call Rob, following his advice to assume that the phone in our room might be monitored by almost any intelligence agency, including the French. I met him in his room to give him my report. He was disappointed that I had turned down the offer to stay at the villa, seeing it as a good opportunity for infiltration. "You don't understand the Communists," I told him. "Today you are a guest in their house, tomorrow they will ask more than the price of a presidential suite at the Paris Sheraton. I'm not going to trade anything with them if I can help it."

The next morning, Thai came over with my father to pick us up. Instead of going directly to the villa, we were asked to pay a visit to the PRG mission; the people there were eager to meet my father's family, we were told. My mother whispered to me that she was reluctant to meet "any Communists," but we agreed to go just to please my father.

The mission was located at 44 Avenue de Madrid in Neuilly-sur-Seine. Thai had said that Nam would be busy meeting some "friendly Americans" who had come to see him, but in fact we found him in his office, his nose buried in a thick hardback book entitled *Inside the Company: CIA Diary*, by Philip Agee. I had heard about the book and the furor over its publication, but had never read it. I came over quietly to Nam's desk and put my finger on a page; he looked up, like a little boy caught stealing candies, and hurriedly put the book into a desk drawer.

"Doing your homework, Uncle Nam?" I teased.

He shook his head. "No, just practicing my English." He smiled, but looked rather embarrassed by my question. He quickly ushered me out of his office and we found my parents in the living room.

When the servants had brought tea, Nam ushered his staff into the room to meet us. Among them was a young woman, Nhu Phi, who was introduced as a secretary. I later learned that she was married to a French nuclear physicist, Mr. Kaplan, who worked at the French National Scientific Research Center. We met a Mr. Thanh, and later found out that he was hardly the ordinary chauffeur that we were supposed to believe he was; he was an intelligence officer and Nam's right-hand man.

Other officials were introduced as diplomats, who told me they were working under my father in the foreign service. One man told us with considerable pride that he had taken care of my father when he was convalescing in Paris after an illness he suffered in Moscow in the winter of 1971.

I couldn't help feeling like an outsider, even though everyone made every effort to bring me into their circle. When my parents went into my father's room to talk, finally being left alone for maybe ten minutes, Thai took me on a little tour of the mission. He gave me an NLF flag, which he said was the flag that regularly flew in front of the mission, and I realized I now owned a small piece of history. Later, I gave the flag to Rob as a souvenir of my penetration of "enemy territory"; he told me that his section chief hung it on the wall behind his desk for several days, almost like a hunter's trophy.

All the attempts at friendliness and warmth collapsed, however, a few moments after my tour. I had asked to use the rest room and was shown to a guest bath upstairs. When the light came on, I was struck cold. There on the floor was a flag of the Republic of Viet Nam, being used as a toilet rag; another lay on the floor in front of the commode as a mat. I sank to the floor and tried to pick up the "mat," and found it heavy because it was soaked with water. In my mind I remembered this same flag covering my brother's casket before he was buried, the same flag covering the bodies of my classmates who had been killed in combat. I choked back tears, and fainted.

I don't know how long I lay on the floor, unconscious, but it must have been long enough to cause concern to the people outside. I came to hearing my father's voice outside the door, calling to me. Struggling to my feet, I opened the door and yanked him inside with me.

"Look," I pointed at the flag and lowered my voice to an angry hiss. "This is uncivilized! I'll make it up to them! I vow to you right now, I'll make it up to them." I pushed him back out into the hall, then picked up the wet flag and stuffed it into my purse. That evening, back at the hotel, I wrapped it carefully in a plastic laundry bag and put it into the trash can, only wishing I had known how to give it the proper treatment for disposal.

I was driven into a fury by what these people had done to my country's flag. My love for that banner had been instilled in me as a child by my grandfather, and even now, as a grown, married woman with a son of my own, I still felt a loyalty and responsibility to it. That night I told myself many times, "All right, Yung, now you know you must be a good spy. You will unveil the face of these monsters. From now on you will learn to talk like them, to be as ruthless as they are, to be like a chameleon — and you will persevere until you have accomplished your task."

Rob was disappointed with my contact report on that day at the mission, because it was filled with my anger and frustration over the disgusting treatment of the flag. He was only interested in facts, and after he read the report he asked me to draw him a floor plan of the PRG headquarters. Perhaps my temper, my prejudices, and my stubbornness weren't good qualities for the kind of work he wanted me to do, but I did have determination and an "elephant memory" that would serve us both well. I sat down and drew a very accurate diagram of the layout of the mission and turned it in to Rob, and he looked very pleased.

My career as a spy was under way.

Chapter 20

On the evening of our first visit to the mission, my parents and I were invited to dine at a Vietnamese restaurant in the fifth arondissement of Paris. The owner was a Vietnamese man named Thanh, a longtime resident of Paris; his wife, Simone, was a French woman who seemed to have married not only a Vietnamese man but his country, his Communist associates, and his culture as well. My father introduced us to the couple, and I got the impression he had known Thanh and Simone for a long time.

Simone brought a glass and a full bottle of Johnny Walker Black Label for Nam; when she took our order, my father said, "This is a special occasion, so I will have a drink tonight," and asked for a bottle of Cote du Rhône. My mother has always believed that "nice girls don't drink," so I have always abstained in her presence. When Nam insisted on pouring me a glass of wine while she had gone to the powder room, I told him that "we will have many chances to drink together when my parents have left." He smiled mischievously and agreed to leave my glass alone that night. Thai turned red after his first glass of wine, but Nam finished half the bottle of whisky and still handled himself well, although his face looked a little blue.

The dinner was a sumptuous one, dish after dish of authentic Vietnamese cooking; the style was Southern, because Thanh, the owner, was from Tra Vinh province.

Up to this point Rob had given me no specific instructions on what to look for in our "targets," the Vietnamese Communist officials; all he had said was "keep your eyes and ears open." So during the dinner I watched my parents' reunion, but I also kept my attention on Nam and Thai.

My vow to stay in character as a sympathetic daughter slipped once, when

Nam praised my effort in locating my father in Japan. That was no great feat, I responded, reminding him that in free countries ordinary people could easily get access to information because of the free press; I had read about the arrival of the NLF delegation in the open pages of the *Japan Times*.

Everyone at table fell silent. My father gave me a disapproving glance, and my mother kicked my foot slightly under the table. I realized that I hadn't obeyed my aunt's old teaching about speaking out: "Before you speak you must consider three things — are your words kind, are your words necessary, are they true?" In my heart I knew they were true, and I felt they were necessary, but they may not have been kind under those circumstances.

Nam was an aggressive person, and I knew I would have to be alert and careful in my conversation with him. He asked me how I came to America in the first place. I didn't have to lie to tell him that "I thought the USA was a home of opportunities, a free country that might bring me closer to my father someday."

"What did you do in America, then?" he asked, while Thai moved closer to hear the discussion.

"Oh, I taught Vietnamese to the American servicemen in Fort Bliss for a while, and then in Monterey, California."

"How were you chosen to teach for the U.S. government?" Nam asked.

"Perhaps you remember Colonel Pham Ngoc Thao, who was killed in the coup d'état in Bien Hoa? His wife was the . . ."

Nam interrupted me by adding, "Madame Pham Thi Nhiem, the younger sister of Pham Ngoc Thuan, correct? They are our people, My Yung."

"At least I hoped so," I told him, "because Mrs. Thao gave me the job when I needed it."

"Although you are away from your father's direct guidance, I am glad to hear that you were close to the right kind of people," Nam said with satisfaction.

"Nobody should expect my father's children to go astray," I said with a smile, and a bit of satisfaction of my own at the role-playing.

"When you taught the American servicemen, what did you tell them about the war in Viet Nam? Did you tell them it was wrong for them to be there?"

I knew Nam had to be aware of the Viet Cong infiltrators in various language schools in the United States, so I decided to try a little white lie. "I wasn't trained to recruit the young GIs to desert the Army," I said, "but I was aware of the operation where Vietnamese instructors, both male and female, became very close 'friends' with their students in order to persuade them to desert. They also succeeded in bringing down the morale of these young soldiers by planting misinformation about the situation in Viet Nam to scare them off before they actually engaged in combat. This was a sophisticated operation, and I didn't have the knowledge or the privilege to be involved."

"Well, the war is over, My Yung," Nam said, "but your chance to make an important contribution to our country is still awaiting you if you want it." He studied my face to gauge my reaction.

"If I want? Of course I want, Uncle Nam," I said with as much eagerness as I could feign.

"You and I will have to spend some time together after your parents go back to Ho Chi Minh City — for your information, Sai Gon is no longer the name of the capital."

I wanted to throw up in his face at his sneering remark about the name of my old home city, but I kept my cool; I reminded myself that a chameleon isn't supposed to give itself away so easily.

As we were about to leave I asked my father if I should pay the bill; Nam overheard and said, "Don't worry, it's on the house." I didn't realize that the Communist tradition of one cadre helping another was still alive even in the heart of Paris, far from the jungles where I once grew up, where my mother had worked day and night at her sewing machine to support our family and to help all the men and women who came to our house "on their way to build socialism."

On the way back we talked about that a little. Nam told my mother and me that their "friends" in Paris, merchants as well as intellectuals and workers, had always been enthusiastic with their contributions; they donated time, money, and effort to build the revolution, and it was only natural that each participant give to the cause according to his ability. A restaurateur feeds the Communist officials, a dressmaker sees that everyone is warm in winter, a blue-collar worker gives part of the money he earns at a factory, and so on. As I listened to his lively description of the many ways of being useful to the movement, I couldn't help but wonder what the revolution wanted from me.

— — —

The next day, instead of going to see my parents in Verrieres, I just had to test the system to see if I could get through the gates of the PRG mission with only my father's name as a "ticket." Before I left the hotel, I told Rob that "if I don't come out of that headquarters by midnight tonight, I want Phan Thanh Nam hanged upside down in the chief of station's office at high noon, you hear?" My joking always made Rob a little nervous about my safety, and I was glad; I didn't want him to get so confident of my ability that he put me into a risky situation when he shouldn't have. After all, I had been operating so far with no formal training from the agency — I was just trusting my instincts and hoping I was "born to be a spy."

Rob asked if I really felt secure about going into the mission by myself. "Why," I laughed, "do you want to come along?"

"If you don't feel comfortable, then don't go in," he said. "I mean it."

"I'll never be comfortable with a bunch of uncivilized Communists around, but I have to try my best," I told him. "Just wish me luck."

"OK, good luck, then. You be careful, kiddo."

For all his concern about me, Rob had managed to overlook a detail or two — such as making sure I knew how to use the Paris Metro. Actually, I had very little idea. With the help of the hotel concierge I found my way to the station at Montparnasse, but I tried in vain to figure out from the signs there just exactly which was the closest station to Avenue de Madrid. Eventually I just picked a train that went in the direction of Neuilly and got on. At my destination, I didn't want to waste any more time, so I hailed a taxi and let the driver find the way to the address.

From outside the high wall one couldn't see much inside the mission's grounds. The door was locked and there was a call box at the gate. I pressed a button on the intercom; there was no answer, but I saw a person looking down from an upstairs window where Nam's office was. Then the door clicked open.

Mr. Thanh, the "chauffeur," came down to meet me just inside the gate, then took me to the formal living room and asked me to wait. I was alone for a few minutes, and noticed how Communists seemed to enjoy flirting with capitalist-style luxury. A beautiful Persian rug covered much of the floor, and the room sparkled with its crystal chandelier, elegant vases, antique satin drapes, and a Limoges china tea service. I remembered the days when my father tried to raise silkworms to help produce our clothes, and grew his own ginseng to nourish his body when he had only an unbalanced diet in the jungle. This room was quite a contrast from the meager life we had endured when my father was defying the French colonial government in our country.

Phan Thanh Nam was surprised to see me, but he must have thought my visit was a golden opportunity to work on recruiting me to the cause. We left the living room and moved to the small dining table in the kitchen where Nam said it would "allow for more private talk."

Without wasting any time, Nam plunged into questions. He asked about my husband, and I wondered if he knew I was married to an American; I decided to tell him so, and from his expression I could tell it wasn't the first time he had heard about it. He asked lots of questions, even about John's ancestry. When I told him John's grandparents had come from Yugoslavia, Nam was delighted: "Then he's not a stranger to us."

"What do you mean by that, Uncle Nam?"

"Yugoslavia is our ally," he said.

I wanted to say, "You damn fool, didn't his grandparents' journey to the United States tell you anything?" Instead I just smiled and said, "I'm sure people are proud of their own heritage."

Nam cleared his throat and looked serious. I knew the chitchat was over. "What does your husband do, My Yung?" he asked without actually looking at me.

"He has a master's degree in oceanography and meteorology. He is a weatherman," I said, leaving out the name of his immediate employer — the U.S. Navy.

Nam looked toward me with a greedy expression. "If you asked your husband the right questions, he could be very useful to our country, My Yung."

"Can you be more specific?"

"Not now. I'll have to do some research, but later I'll have some questions for you to ask your husband." He leaned over the table and gave me a piercing stare: "Do you love your country, My Yung?"

"I'll bet I love my country more than you do," I said, drawing myself up straight in my chair. "I was born there, raised there, fell in love there, and witnessed an awful lot of sadness and tragedy there. While you lived in Paris, you read the news in the newspapers and perhaps saw the war on television." I ground each word into him. It was a mistake.

"I was in the army back home," he said quietly.

"I didn't know that," I replied, embarrassed now at my outburst.

"Like your father, I sacrificed my personal life for the freedom of our country," Nam told me. "I have never had the opportunity to live for myself or to even think of settling down with a wife."

I tried to salvage the moment with a little joke. "You didn't miss much, Uncle Nam. A family is just an obstacle to an ambitious man like you, and a wife would just be an extra piece of luggage when you have to run."

"As a matter of fact, those are only a few reasons," he smiled. "How do you know that anyway?"

"Don't forget where I came from before I went to America."

That seemed to bring Nam back to his business at hand. "Did you try to persuade your mother to go back to Viet Nam? You know it is the only right thing to do now."

"In my family we make our own decisions," I told him. "I will support her no matter what she decides."

"Sometimes old people can't think clearly for themselves," Nam insinuated.

I gripped my hands tightly together to keep from slapping the table in my anger. "Uncle Nam," I said carefully, "you might know my father very well, because you two are comrades. Let me tell you about my mother so you don't underestimate her. She's married to my father, and she kept the family together for the entire period of his absence. She is far more than a liberated woman, she is intelligent, a good mother, a strong person — stronger than you can imagine. And she is not 'old people,' she is only sixty years old. If my father could live again twenty-five more times, he would never be able to find a woman to share his way of life the way my mother did. And she will never love anyone the way she loves him. So why should I try to make her go or stay?"

"Why did she leave Sai Gon in the first place?"

"I brought her out for her safety. I thought it was going to be another bloodbath in the end."

"You actually went to Sai Gon and brought her out?" he asked, his eyebrows rising.

"I wish I had had the privilege. No, it was my husband who went to Sai Gon to rescue my mother and my sisters."

"Your sisters should go back to Viet Nam, too," Nam leaped at their mention. He spoke slowly and seemed to be studying my reaction.

"Again, it's up to them, Uncle Nam. We were raised in a democratic family. Nobody makes anybody do anything against his or her will. Besides, my brother and sisters are likely to raise hell if I even attempt to make them do anything my way."

"My Yung, perhaps you have forgotten that it is their duty to go back for your father's sake. Don't you see how bad it looks for your father when all of his children are in the enemy's land?"

"We shouldn't discuss this matter now," I protested. "Please. I don't have any influence on my sisters' decision."

"After your mother has left, I certainly hope you will talk your sisters into going back," he persisted.

"Why, Uncle Nam?"

"Your father is a very well-liked and well-known ambassador in Moscow. Our Russian friends have already granted your mother an entry visa to their country. They have already invited her to visit Moscow on her way back to Viet Nam. They have already offered a free ride on their Aeroflot flight from Paris to Moscow. Don't you see how they honor your family?"

"I can see what an honor you and my father must feel with such treatment from the Russians, but that is his cup of tea, and his pedestal. It means nothing to me."

"It will be a victory to us, and to Viet Nam, when your mother leaves the United States for Viet Nam."

"Who cares where my mother lives, Uncle Nam?" I asked. "She is only one among the hundreds of thousands of refugees in the United States. Now, if Nguyen Cao Ky were to ask for political asylum in North Viet Nam, he certainly would make headlines in every newspaper in the world, but my mother? Or my sisters?"

"My Yung, you are wrong," Nam insisted. "Your mother is not just anybody. She is the wife of the PRG ambassador, a kidnap victim of the CIA. They tried to embarrass us by taking her to the United States. Your mother's return to Viet Nam now would serve as a slap in the face for Gerald Ford and the U.S. government."

I was furious when Nam called my mother a "kidnap victim of the CIA." This suggested he didn't believe me when I said that we ourselves had brought my mother to America. I excused myself to go to the rest room and cool off. When I came back, I found that Nam had had beer served, but I told him I didn't drink beer.

He was ready with a new line of questioning — he wanted to know about Hai Van. I really didn't want to talk about that; I had nothing to hide, but I thought this man didn't deserve to hear about anyone as noble and good as my brother. He was persistent, though, and he struck a nerve when he said, "You should never forget those who put an end to your brother's life. You must make the people who killed your brother suffer as much as you and your family have suffered," Nam challenged me.

I became impatient with his clumsy scheme to make me hate the Americans. "My brother's death is our family's tragedy, Uncle Nam," I said.

He had an answer for everything. "Your father's family is our family, My Yung. We care and our sorrow goes deep, especially since we have had a chance to meet you and your mother."

What could I say to a Communist who was trying so desperately, and so stupidly, to plant a seed of hatred in me? All I could do was lead him on and learn more about him in hopes that I would know how to deal with him, how to act like him — and perhaps someday lead him into his own trap.

"I am very glad to have met my father's comrades," I said. "I need all the teaching I can get from you, because being my father's daughter I at least should be able to understand his work, his goals, and his needs in order to help him, if I am ever allowed to do so."

"I will be happy to guide you when your father is absent," Nam said proudly. "You can do so much to help rebuild our country, using the Americans' technology to do it. It is only fair that they rebuild our country one way or another."

"Last night I overheard you and my father talking about 'war compensation.' How much do you believe the Americans owe Viet Nam?" I asked.

"According to the Paris peace agreement, they owe us 3.5 billion U.S. dollars," he said.

I ran out of patience, and even though I knew my next statement could cause trouble, I said it anyway and planned to plead stupidity if necessary: "The Americans may remind us that according to the peace agreement, the North Vietnamese government was not supposed to invade South Viet Nam. What do you say about that, Uncle Nam?"

"You are very naive. We didn't invade the South; rather, we liberated the South from the Americans and their puppets!" He chuckled with a look of satisfaction on his face.

"I forgot that," I mumbled.

"When you go back to America, you must rally the people there to demand that their government live up to its agreement in Paris," he said.

With whom should I rally? I thought, a smile flickering on my lips. The antiwar activists? The deserters in Canada? Senator George McGovern? Nam noticed my expression and asked what was on my mind.

"I was thinking about someone I might rally with, or deliver your message to, and whether that person would be good enough to urge the U.S. Congress to act on the issue."

"Who is it?" Nam seemed anxious to know.

"Senator McGovern," I laughed.

"I have studied U.S. senators," Nam said in all seriousness. "McGovern is one of the few who is liberated, and who is enlightened enough to understand."

God! I prayed that I would never be called "liberated" by the Communists. If that ever happened, I knew, it would be because I had made myself useful to them, capable of dancing like a Russian's puppet. I wondered if Senator McGovern had ever done anything for Ha Noi, so I asked Nam, "What makes you think McGovern is liberated?"

"The most obvious thing is that he opposed the war in Viet Nam."

How simple Nam was, I thought. "As I said, Uncle Nam, I still have a lot to learn from you." He didn't catch the sarcasm.

At that time a servant came into the kitchen to prepare lunch. As much as I knew I ought to stay and talk to Nam as long as possible, I felt I had to get away. I had lied too much, spoken too much doubletalk, and I had begun to feel ill because of it all. Nam asked me to stay, but I made some excuse and said my goodbyes.

As soon as I had set foot outside the mission's walls, I started walking as fast as I could. A short distance away I caught a taxi and went directly to the hotel.

I felt dirty, as if my exposure to Nam and his oily efforts to subvert me had somehow contaminated my person. The first thing I did when I reached my room was to take a bath, shampoo my hair, and toss the clothes I had been wearing into a laundry bag.

Chapter 21

The window of my room at the Sheraton looked out over the Montparnasse cemetery. As I stood there after my bath, gazing out over the city and trying to relax a little after my unpleasant morning, a funny thought came to mind. Were the dead men lying before me some of the casualties from the battle of Dien Bien Phu? Even the beauty of Paris could not overcome my memories of the ugliness of the French colonials in my country, and my distaste for France grew more vivid each day I stayed there. Even the brass handrails in the hotel lobby made me think of the empty artillery shells I used to find lying all through the countryside when my father and the rest of the Viet Minh were trying to free our land.

I shook off my thoughts and went out for lunch, studying the Metro map the whole time. Eventually I figured out which stop would put me closest to the PRG's villa, where I was going to see my parents. When I reached the station in the suburbs, I was happy to find several taxis waiting, so I hopped into one and gave the driver the address, 49 Rue Cambaceres.

"You are going to the Viet Cong's headquarters, yes?" he observed. When I told him in English that I was, he asked if I spoke French, but I had to say no. Then he pulled down his polo shirt from his neck to show me a tattoo on his shoulder that said "Viet Nam." He told me he had been there in 1952 and 1953.

"Do you speak English?" I asked him. He made a sign with his thumb and forefinger to indicate "just a little," and I remarked, "So the Viet Minh shipped you out, huh?"

"Are you Viet Cong?" he asked, ignoring my taunt.

"No, I am a nationalist Vietnamese."

"Oui, oui!" he said, smiling and going back to his driving.

When we got to the villa the old soldier refused to give me change after I paid him, claiming as taxi drivers do everywhere that he didn't have any small bills. I got angry and would have made a fuss, but at that time I saw my father and mother standing on a balcony on the second floor, and the feelings I had seeing them together overcame my irritation. I dismissed the driver and started for the door.

My mother disappeared into the room, and I thought how much her movement reminded me of the time we lived in the second-floor apartment in Sai Gon. Mother often waited on the balcony for us to come home from work, and as soon as she saw us she would run inside to open the door to greet us.

An elderly man, apparently the housekeeper, met me at the door and said with a sincere expression, "It is my pleasure to have you here, Miss." I greeted him in the old Vietnamese fashion, my hands in front of my chest and my head tilted forward, but the housekeeper bowed to me. I addressed him as Mr. Cac, but my father later told me I should use a more friendly term and call him "Uncle Cac."

The weather in Paris in late September probably seemed pleasant to the French, but it was much too cold for a Vietnamese who had known only her own country and Hawaii; my mother was standing by a small lily pond, wearing a thick sweater and a red wool scarf over her head. The housekeeper showed us all into the living room and brought some hot tea, then left us to prepare dinner for the three of us. Because it was a special occasion, he said, he was going to cook for us himself; he warned us, though, that he was not very good, but said the mission had also sent two members of its staff — which it called its "association" — to help out.

After he left, my mother and I looked at each other, and without speaking a word we agreed that having all these people around wasn't really helping. What she needed most was to be alone with my father, to talk to him, to get to know him again after twenty-one years. She needed to know the truth about the "liberation" in her country, and she needed to be able to confront him directly to find that out.

My father went out of the room for a few minutes, and I asked her how things were going. Tears came to her eyes as she answered: "I want you to know one thing for your peace of mind, and that is that your father sincerely wants me home with him. But his government — and the Russians — want me to leave America for their propaganda purposes. Your father didn't spill it out, he didn't dare, but I could see that they are making a big issue of us."

"Mom, I talked to Phan Thanh Nam today and I got that feeling, too. But I don't care about them. I just want to know if you would be safe if you went back."

"John risked his life and his career in his attempt to save me and your sisters," she broke in. "You risked your husband when you urged him to get us out of Sai Gon. There is not enough of a reason for me to throw away all your effort."

I shook my head vigorously. "It was our duty to do what we thought was right at the time," I insisted. "Forget our effort. That's the past. I am talking about you and Father at the present time. Are you going back with him?"

Before she could answer, my father came back into the room and said he wanted to give me a tour of the historic villa. He had his reasons for being proud of it; after all, it was there that Le Duc Tho, Madame Nguyen Thi Binh, and the others stayed while they were making history at the Paris Peace Talks. There wasn't much to see, however. The villa was being renovated, and furniture was piled up in various rooms, but I made a show of being interested and enthusiastic as we walked around the building.

Even as we talked about the villa, I detected a certain sadness in my parents' eyes. I felt frustrated, because I knew that only they could resolve their dilemma; there was nothing more I could do. When we were living in Sai Gon my sisters used to call me "three heads and six arms," because I was such an enterprising person I could usually fix any situation. Now three heads and six arms weren't enough; this situation could be resolved only by two hearts.

My father was happy that we were all together, despite the uncertainty of it all. "We are alone at last!" he said as we walked through the rooms.

"Father, I dreamed so long for us to be together," I said.

"I must say that a big part was because of you. You made it happen for your mother and I to be able to sit here together in one room," he said, beaming.

"You can't chase your father halfway around the world just so you can be with him for a few days, or a few weeks, all behind his party's back," my mother said with some bitterness. "It is time you should know the conditions in which the two of you can meet." She apparently was thinking that I might have to obey the Communists in order to get them to allow us to see my father; I have to admit that I wasn't sure, either.

"It takes time for personal matters," my father reminded her.

"In Japan you denied her being your daughter in front of your 'comrades,' and I don't like that," she grumbled.

I made a signal to her to calm down and stop attacking my father on my behalf. It was true that I had felt hurt in Japan, but it had been necessary for him to conceal his personal life from the Communists in order to have even the limited freedom to travel around that he did. If the party found out that his children were living in the United States and would always try to meet him, that freedom might be curtailed.

Dinner was served, and once again I enjoyed another delicious, authentic Vietnamese meal. I ate with such gusto that my parents asked if I had eaten any lunch.

When Uncle Cac and the two women from the mission disappeared after serving dinner, we talked and talked about our family, and about old times. My parents discussed all the children, our good qualities and our failings. When my mother praised me — something she seldom did — she said the children (including me) took after her; she has always been quite modest, and that surprised me. When she criticized me, saying, "This one here gave me a lot of gray hair before she got married and settled down," she looked at my father and said, "She must be your daughter!"

My father laughed and commended her for raising "independent children." My mother chuckled and told him, "Thank God they are independent enough to find their own path."

When my father spoke of Hoa Binh I could see sparkles in his eyes. "I still remember Hoa Binh and the times when the weather was good and we would eat dinner by the dock in Kim Qui," he said, looking at me. "She would fall into the water on purpose, and you would jump right in to save her."

"If I had let her swallow some water once or twice she probably would have stopped doing it," I said.

"She just wanted attention," my father recalled.

"She wanted attention from the whole family, even from our dog!"

"Yes, I remember our dog — he always guarded her when she slept," he said, laughing gently.

"Father, remember the time you experimented in making *nuoc mam* (the strong-smelling fish sauce that Vietnamese use much like Chinese use soy sauce)?"

"What a stinking hobby you had!" my mother chided.

We all roared at the memory, and Father asked my mother what ever happened to the two barrels of *nuoc mam* he had made. "You'll never believe it," she said, "but there was another family who came to buy those two barrels. Maybe they needed flies for their back yard!"

"Be honest, now," my father insisted. "Wasn't the *nuoc mam* I experimented with better than the one you could buy at the store?"

"Right, it was. And your own silkworms produced more silk. Your kids were the best kids in the Mekong Delta, your cucumbers were bigger than the ones your friends grew, and your sugarcane was sweeter than the ones your brother planted," she teased him, recalling all the things he had always taken pride in and wanted credit for.

Those brief moments of relaxed happiness that we shared were precious to me; it was wonderful to hear them laughing together about the old days. I felt so lucky, and I didn't want to believe that it might be the last time. I resolved I would never give up trying to find a way for them to be together.

That day at Verrieres a man from the Paris embassy of the Socialist Republic of Viet Nam (SRV) came to see my father. While his driver waited outside in the Mercedes — another example of the Socialists' remarkable ability to endure living in a capitalist country — the man and my father went into the formal living room to talk privately. Because of the renovation, there were no chairs or tables, so they stood by the window and chatted for some time.

My mother had gone off for an afternoon nap, so I decided to take advantage of being alone and do a little exploring on the second floor. In an office next to the room my parents occupied, I found shelves and shelves of old files, crammed with yellowed papers. I ran my fingers across the dusty folders and had a sudden thought: There must be a lot of material here that would be of value to the U.S. government; I should read through the files and make copies of the important ones to take to Rob. The light in the cold room was dim, however, and the simple camera I had with me was useless in that situation; I wished Rob had given me the right kind of equipment.

I decided to see what I could find anyway, so I closed the door and started looking around. I didn't want to turn the light on, because the driver in the Mercedes outside could have seen it from the driveway. I opened one of the drawers of a desk in the room, and from the papers I found there I realized it must have belonged to Madame Nguyen Thi Binh, the PRG foreign minister! I pulled out the chair and sat down. A strange feeling came over me to know I was sitting at the desk of this very formidable and striking person. As I read through some of the papers, however, I felt shame that she was also a Vietnamese woman like me.

One of the letters in the desk was from an American, who sent Madame Binh her best wishes as the Paris Peace Talks seemed to be making "positive progress toward peace." The woman praised Madame Binh for her "peace-loving nature." Then in the last paragraph she pleaded with Madame Binh and the Ha Noi government as well as the PRG to release the American POWs in North Viet Nam. She wrote that her nephew had been "forced to fight for the South Vietnamese puppets" and had become a POW.

Madame Binh had written a comment at the bottom of the letter: "This woman is desperately crazy. Do not reply."

The second letter I saw was from the mother of a young soldier serving in Viet Nam. She identified herself as an "antiwar activist" and begged Madame Binh and the SRV government to bring an end to the Viet Nam War — and she asked if she could do anything to help the NLF in order that she might get her son back home.

I couldn't help but utter a word of contempt under my breath when I finished reading that woman's letter. I knew that my brother would never have allowed my mother even to have such feelings, much less to beg the enemy to put an end to the war so her baby could come home to Mommy!

Madame Binh's note on this letter was for her secretary to send a response: "This woman will tell her son to claim for his benefits once he comes home, but don't mention it in our reply. Tell her to rally the neighborhood and rally against her government's policy in Viet Nam. Agree with her that her son's place is at home with her and not in Viet Nam."

A third letter was from a young American girl who expressed her admiration for Madame Binh and "the effort you have shown toward peace in your homeland. I am ashamed to be an American in this era, for Viet Nam has been the only nation that demonstrates a positive gesture toward peace." The letter revealed more about the insecurity of the writer than she might have intended: "I wish through you and the Vietnamese people that one day I may have the opportunity to see light after these darkest days of my country, and furthermore that the USA will soon learn the lesson that even a superpower must work for peace."

Madame Binh's instructions to her secretary in this case were to "continue sending this girl literature and have our people in America contact her. Valuable resource!"

I wanted to read more, but just then I heard my father calling for me. I peered out the old-fashioned keyhole and saw him in the hallway; when he went into his room and the coast was clear, I slipped out and tiptoed downstairs, then walked back up as if I was coming in from the garden.

I teased him about his frequent interruptions to receive guests, and then in an effort to keep my investigative work going I asked, "Who was that wicked man who came to see you?" He knew I was quoting the term the South Vietnamese often used to refer to Communists, and he smiled. "It was an official who came to pick up your mother's travel documents in order to process her entry visa to Viet Nam and Moscow."

I didn't know whether he knew it or not, but I had my mother's travel papers locked safely in a deposit box at the hotel. The issue hadn't come up, however, because he said he had told the man that my mother needed more time to think. I realized it must have been terribly difficult for them to have to deal with something as concrete as her passport and travel arrangements, because it destroyed the illusion of togetherness they had been able to enjoy at the villa. My father looked troubled, and my mother seemed disgusted. I glanced toward her and started to say something, but she interrupted: "I don't like to be put in this position — and don't try to force me to go back."

"Who is forcing you?" I asked.

My father left the room without a word. I let him go and sat down on the edge of the bed next to my mother. She shook her head several times and said, "That man came here to inform your father about a flight that had been reserved for him and me to Moscow and Ha Noi this weekend." That was pushing things far too quickly for her.

The situation reminded me of an old story I used to read when I was a child. It was about heaven and hell, and there were caretakers in hell who come up to earth to pick up people and take them "down there." One day a caretaker came to an old woman who was lying sick in her bed and said, "Go, woman, it is time for you!" The woman raised her feeble body and shouted back, "Go away! It is time for you, but not for me. I am still waiting for my sons to come home from the war to get married and bear me grandchildren!"

I smiled to myself as I thought about how my mother refused to go yet. I comforted her as best I could and asked her to try not to take her frustration out on my father. As far as I knew, I reminded her, he had always allowed her to make up her own mind about everything.

— — —

I tried to call Rob several times after I got back to my hotel shortly after 9:00 P.M., but couldn't find him, so I decided to work on my "intelligence report" about my visit to the villa. It was a long report, and I ran out of the special paper he had given me the day before.

I wished Rob would come that night and pick up the report, because I didn't like having it in the room. It would have been embarrassing — more than embarrassing, potentially dangerous — if French security forces or even the KGB had broken into the room and found it. I looked all around the room for a safe place to hide it for the night. The walls were solid and the carpet was wall-to-wall and firmly tacked down; in the closet, though, I noticed that the three rods on the clothes rack seemed to be hollow. They were, so I used my fingernail file to pry off the plastic cap on the end of one of the bars, rolled the papers into a tight cylinder, and slipped them into the tube. I tapped the plastic cap back into place and went to bed, feeling a little more secure.

The next morning Rob called. On the telephone we pretended I was just an old friend visiting Paris and Rob was coming to take me to lunch. As a precaution, when we spoke on the phone we always set our rendezvous times twenty-four hours later than the time we actually intended to meet.

About ten that morning Rob showed up, and I handed him my report with a feeling of great relief that it was out of my hands. He seemed surprised that it was ready so soon — or maybe he just wasn't ready to do business that early in the day. He folded the report and tucked it away inside his sports jacket.

"If you get mugged," I warned him, "give them your Rolex and your Metro tickets but hang onto that report!"

"Very funny," he said.

When I eagerly recounted my "penetration" of Madame Binh's office, Rob looked startled and asked me not to go back there again. It wasn't that he was worried about my safety; later I learned that the CIA wasn't all that interested in the Viet Cong and their activities anymore. Since the end of the war the NLF's star was in decline and the SRV had stepped into the spotlight. Now the focus was to be Phan Thanh Nam, who was moving on from the PRG to the SRV, and the SRV embassy; the old ghosts of the NLF had become useless to American intelligence.

For the three days I had been in Paris, I had seen little but men in dark suits — the uniform of Asian Socialists in the West — trying to play their games to seduce me to their cause. I thought I should get out to learn more about the city so I would feel more comfortable after my father left and I remained to poke around in the Vietnamese community there. I told Rob not to wait for me, since I had no plans for that day; I couldn't decide for myself when to see officials of the SRV embassy, but mostly had to wait for a proper excuse to arise.

We both thought it would be a good idea to try to get to know Pham Gia Thai a bit better. Even though he had been introduced to me as a "student," his relationship to Nam, the acting head of the mission, seemed to be quite significant. I had his home telephone number, so I resolved to call him later in the day. Rob suggested I not try to do too much too fast; he often reminded me to "dust yourself before and after your meetings with Phan Than Nam or any SRV officials," meaning to get rid of any people who might be following my movements. I knew he was trying to protect me and the operation, but sometimes his constant warnings made me nervous.

That morning I took the Metro at Gaite and went to St. Michel, where I walked along the boulevard and enjoyed the sidewalk book stalls and thousands of other things for sale; for a moment I thought I was back in Sai Gon on Le Loi Street. I began to feel good, walking in the fresh air in a beautiful city. Hearing everyone around me speaking French, I remembered my French teachers in high school and wished I had been a better student during those seven years. I could read and understand most of what I encountered, but I felt like a mute immigrant as I moved through the city streets.

After a late breakfast in a cafe across from Notre-Dame, I decided to try calling Thai. He lived with his fiancée's family in Meudon, a suburb of Paris.

When his fiancée's mother answered, she told me Thai was working that day at the SRV embassy. Aha! I thought, a new piece of "intelligence" already. Clearly Thai was not just a student, but had some role in the government.

I thought that if I identified myself to this woman, she might volunteer some more information, so I told her my name and that I was in Paris to visit my father, Mr. Dang Quang Minh. "I know Brother Minh," she said. "My family is very fond of him. How nice of you to tell me." I almost felt guilty for trying to use her when she sounded so friendly. I didn't know what else to say, so I just asked her to tell Thai that I called. She gave me the SRV embassy number and suggested I call him there to have lunch with him. I said I didn't want to bother him if he was working, but she insisted. "Thai will be delighted to see you. Perhaps he'll want to take you to the association and introduce you to the chairman." She meant the Vietnamese Union, a leftist organization in Paris.

How could I refuse when that kind of opportunity seemed to fall right into my lap? I jotted down the number and thanked her. Still, I decided not to call the embassy right away. I didn't know if I was being watched by French security or anyone else, so I thought the best thing to do was to go on being careful. I joined the throngs of tourists outside Notre-Dame, took a few pictures, and toured the famous cathedral.

Later, in a department store on Boulevard Haussman, I found a public phone and called the embassy, asking for Thai. A man who answered said he would get him if it was an emergency, but that Thai was with the ambassador at the moment. That was another good piece of information — that Thai deals with the ambassador on a personal level. I was pretty sure then that anything Thai said to me would probably reflect the ambassador's opinions and ideas, so a contact with him would indeed be useful. I thanked the man on the telephone and said I would call later.

I felt lucky, but as I walked around sightseeing my thoughts gradually returned to my parents' situation, and clouds covered my blue sky. After a while I took the Metro back to my hotel and called my father. He sounded happy, but then he always tried to make me feel good when I talked to him. I asked if he wanted to take a train into Paris with my mother so the three of us could go shopping together, but he reminded me that he shouldn't go anywhere without "my people from the mission" — that is, his bodyguards.

On the telephone, my father promised that he would have Thai come out the next day to bring him and my mother into town to go shopping with me.

That afternoon I stayed in my room and watched the movies on television. Oddly, the French-language films made me feel homesick for Viet Nam. My brother and I had gone to the movies often in Can Tho, and we always tried to follow the French dialogue, then hurry to read the Vietnamese subtitles when we stumbled over something we didn't understand.

I wrote up another "intelligence report" with the little I had learned about Thai, and gave it to my case officer when he came to see me that afternoon. He was happy with it, and we agreed that a trip to Meudon to meet Thai's fiancée, Mimi, and her family could be very helpful. I shouldn't push that, however, just wait and hope for an invitation. Rob thought it would be better if I appeared to be passive, because that might encourage Thai to want to teach me about his world of socialism.

Rob said he would send my report to Langley that night, then lightened the mood a bit by suggesting that we celebrate our progress with dinner at a great restaurant he knew in the city. We had to take precautions going there, of course; we went separately, he from the embassy and I from the hotel, and met on the Metro platform at St. François-Xavier. We had a great time, although I drank far too much before eating. Later I thought I should go back there sometime and try the food sober, because Rob bragged about it for a long time afterward, but I just couldn't remember much about it.

Back at the hotel the concierge handed me a message slip: Thai had called while I was out. Good, I thought, they are interested. I slept like a baby that night, and woke up the next morning eager to spend the day with my parents and happy that I miraculously didn't have a hangover.

— — —

As soon as Thai called from the lobby, I rushed downstairs to join my parents and the four of us went off on a shopping trip. We went from store to store, looking and talking about the things we saw. My father bought himself a movie camera, but when my mother suggested we should go to a men's store to get him some shirts, he wasn't very interested because, he said, "I have everything." Actually, I knew that he only owned four shirts, but if a man needs only four shirts then he probably believes he has everything.

My father had never been a very materialistic person, although even during the years we lived virtually without anything except basic necessities, he always found a way to get the few things that he thought were important. He used money with which we had intended to buy soap to purchase strings and rosin for his and Khoi's violins, and then made "soap" from coconut ashes for us to use instead. He also traded my mother's water buffalo, the one and only helper we had to plow the sugarcane fields, to buy a bigger boat so we could all be comfortable when we had to travel for long distances.

After much begging, my mother got him to try on some shirts, but he refused even to look at trousers for himself. He did pick out two pairs of pants and two shirts and some underwear to take back to Khoi. When I saw that,

I have to admit, I was jealous for a moment of my older brother. Even at his age, he still enjoyed that kind of loving attention from our father. For a split second I thought that if I went my father's way, if I stopped singing my anti-Communist song in his ears, then I might be able to have him the way Khoi did. It was only for a second, however. I knew full well that I would never be able to sell my soul to the devil, even if I could "buy" my father for that price.

It was on this shopping expedition, during a moment when my mother and I were alone, that she let me know she had made her decision about her future. She and my father had had a long talk, and had come to an understanding that it would be best for her to go back to America with the children. I didn't have time then to talk to her about reasons, because Thai was seldom out of earshot. I could only be thankful that they had come to a decision, even though I knew it must have been a painful one for both of them.

When we finished shopping, Thai surprised us with an announcement that Phan Thanh Nam wanted to see my mother and me at the mission. We had no great desire to see him, but we couldn't very well refuse, because Thai was driving and there was no way we could be candid about our feelings.

When we arrived at the mission, Nam's attitude seemed quite changed from the cheeriness he had exhibited the first time we met. He seemed almost indifferent toward my mother, not even bothering to put on an artificial smile. I think he must have been losing patience, waiting for her to make her decision. He greeted her with a cold, iron face.

As soon as we came in, Madame Nhu Phi, the woman who was married to the French scientist, asked my father to come to her office on the second floor. She needed some advice, she said, about dealing with the Canadian government regarding a ship that had sailed to Canada after the fall of South Viet Nam. The ship was loaded with valuable antiques from the South, and the new government wanted it returned to them.

Thanh, the "chauffeur," was in Nam's office with him as my mother and I sat down. I could tell by the look on her face that she didn't want to talk to this "little dwarf," as she called Nam, but she waited silently while Nam and Thanh exchanged glances. Then Nam cleared his throat, as was his habit, and asked her bluntly if she had come to a decision yet about leaving Paris and going to Viet Nam.

"I have finally made my decision, Chu Nam," she said. "Chu" is a term of address used in speaking to younger people and to inferiors; I'm sure my mother meant only to reflect her seniority in age by using it.

Nam and Thanh looked at each other, their faces brightening somewhat, then looked eagerly back at her for her answer.

"I will leave Paris very soon," she said calmly, "but I will not go back to Sai Gon."

The shock was evident in their expressions. Both of them sat without moving or making a sound for what seemed the longest time. Finally Nam managed weakly: "I don't understand."

"Let me explain to you, Chu Nam and Chu Thanh. My husband and I serve our motherland in two separate ways. He made a revolution, and I raised his children. Neither one of us can switch places or quit our duty at this stage."

Thanh interrupted. "But your children are grown now, and peace is restored to our country."

"Please let me finish, Chu Thanh. I still have two young ones. And although there is no fighting in Viet Nam, there are other wars that my husband and the new government must fight to bring the country together. I am older than you two, I've been through many wars and many peacetimes. It is not as easy as you think.

"Without me," she continued, "my husband will have more freedom to devote himself to the effort to restore peace. With me, my two young daughters will have a stable home in a strange land. I only ask you two to reflect my feelings as well as my reasons to the responsible people in Ha Noi."

The two Communist officials sat quietly, trying to digest this news. I looked up at the portrait of Ho Chi Minh on the wall, and at the sign below it which said, "There is nothing more precious than independence and freedom." Uncle Ho should like my mother, I thought; she has always been an independent person, and now she had just chosen the system that would allow her the freedom to express and enjoy that independence.

My mother turned to me: "My daughter, we shouldn't waste Chu Nam's time." Nam and Thanh, of course, wanted nothing more than to "waste their time" with her; they had arranged their schedules just so they would have plenty of time to concentrate on her "issue." While they went into another verse of their sales pitch, I excused myself and ran upstairs to see if my father was finished talking to Nhu Phi. The secretary told me he was in the guest room, and I went in to find him standing at the window, staring out at the September sky.

I walked over and put my arm around his waist and followed his gaze outside. The chestnut tree in front of the mission was brown, its leaves swirling from the branches with each gust of wind and scurrying away down the sidewalk.

"What are you thinking about, Papa?" I asked.

"The autumn in our country, my daughter, and the harvest at my father's land when I was very small." There was a trace of a nostalgic smile in his face as he spoke.

"I can close my eyes and imagine my grandmother's golden rice field when the rice was about to be harvested," I said.

He rubbed my hair gently, and reminisced a bit. "I visited my sister a few months after I came back from Ha Noi. One morning I got up and walked about the land. The morning air was so sweet, I could hear the bell in the air and see sparkles on every leaf of the trees, and I thought how lucky I was to be there once again at my birthplace. I rubbed the soil between my hands and wished that I could share those moments with my own family." His mind seemed thousands of miles away.

"It's funny," I told him. "Each time I smelled the burning rice straw in the fields I was filled with indescribable memories, and I got all tangled up inside. The only way I could express my feelings was to cry. Why does it hurt so much to love somebody?"

"I don't know how to answer that question either," he said.

"When I was much younger, each time my feelings hurt and I cried it hurt in the back of my jaws. I didn't know why people always used the word "heartbreak," because it never hurt me in my heart — the real hurt was in the back of my jaws. That bothered me for a long time, but I didn't know whom to ask."

He knew I meant that I didn't have him to ask. "I missed the best time of my life," he said, "the time to watch my children grow. I missed the chance to share the growing pains, the happiness, the hopes and disappointments with you all and maybe answer some of your silly questions."

"Were you close to your father?" I asked him.

"He loved me more than his life, but our relationship was rather formal. I called my father 'Thay' [master]," he said, smiling at the recollection. "But my mother was unlike most Vietnamese mothers. She wasn't shy about showing affection to us, even to my father."

"It bothered me for a long time that I had to be a Tran in order to be safe from the Cong An under Diem's regime," I told him.

"In your blood and in your heart you are my daughter, and that is all that matters to us, my darling."

"Nobody can take that away from us," I insisted, "not even the Kremlin, and I want you to know that."

"No, not even the Kremlin," my father said, laughing with me. Then he turned serious. "My daughter, take care of Mother for me."

"I promise."

"I promise you that I'll do my utmost to deliver peace and prosperity to our people because I know it is also important to you."

I could see that another long separation was about to begin, and I was sad.

"I want so much to be able to share a morning walk with you, to hear that bell in the air, and taste that sweetness in the air of my grandparents' home," I told him, squeezing his hand.

"I'll be there when you come home for a visit," he promised.

"Viet Nam to me now is like a lover one can't have," I said. "It hurts, you know." I began to say more: "Last night I compared my feelings now with your feelings when Viet Nam was occupied by the French, and I was sad for you. . . ." Then I stopped, as I remembered where I was and realized that the walls there might well have ears. I couldn't express my true feelings to my father in the house of his own people.

My parents and I had been invited to have dinner with Ambassador Vo Van Sung and his wife at the SRV embassy that evening, but having reached her decision, my mother wasn't in any mood to spend time with North Vietnamese officials. When Nam told her the purpose of the dinner was to celebrate my parents' reunion, she was even more adamant that it would be inappropriate now that they were about to separate again. Nam seemed reluctant to have to break the news to the ambassador, so he pleaded again: "The ambassador is anxious to meet you and your daughter." Her decision was final, however. She had chosen not to spend the rest of her life with Communists, and it seemed just as well to start living with that choice right then. In the end Nam gave up. It would have taken someone much more persuasive than the "little dwarf" to change her mind at that point.

— — —

That afternoon Thai drove my parents back to the villa at Verrieres le Buisson, and asked me to ride along with them. I would have come anyway, even without his invitation, because I knew that my opportunities to be with my parents together would soon become close to zero. I wanted to enjoy that wonderful and fleeting feeling just as long as I could.

There was little pleasure in the trip, however. We couldn't discuss our personal affairs because Thai was in the driver's seat, sharply attentive to our every word. We talked instead about our shopping trip. We had gone to the department store called LaFayette, and we reminisced about seeing the store's catalog years ago at home. During the French occupation many well-to-do people in Viet Nam ordered goods by mail from LaFayette, and it may have been better known there than it was in France.

As we rode through town on the way to the suburbs, I noticed the street signs in blue with white letters, and remarked that they reminded me of the signs in Sai Gon. I shouldn't have said that, because it sent Thai off on an endless speech about how the "liberation" was going to be changing all those signs. Street names, cities, townships, even precincts will get a "facelift," he said. "We will get rid of everything that would remind you of the French era, and the American imperialists' footprints, too."

I asked if he knew what would happen to the American embassy in Sai Gon. Sure, he said. "The American embassy will be the place to display the criminal acts of the American imperialists in our country. It will show our courageous victory, the victory of the people who were determined to overcome the world's greatest superpower!"

Thai went on and on with his sloganeering about American imperialism and praise for the Liberation Movement. It had been only five months since the fall of Sai Gon, yet he spoke already about North and South Viet Nam's "reunification" program, saying he thought the sooner it could happen, the better.

I noticed that my father remained silent during most of Thai's diatribe. A few days before, when I was alone with my parents, I got the distinct understanding that reunification of North and South was at the bottom of his priority list. In fact, the kind of rushing ahead reflected in Thai's words caused him some concern. He believed the South needed more time to rebuild and strengthen itself before any reunification. He thought it was the job of the NLF and the PRG to bring the South together with the North, rather than vice versa.

As I listened to Thai rave on about how the North was going to solve everything, I couldn't help but look ahead to the day when my father would go back to resume his duty as he saw it and once again face disappointment — this time not from his wife, or from his long-lost children, but from the government he had trusted and the party he had served his whole life.

Shortly after she announced she would not go to Viet Nam, my mother decided she wanted to return to the United States as soon as possible. Tensions were growing between her and my father, but more important, there were frequent visits to the villa by unidentified persons, and she was getting scared. Sometimes she feared that the SRV would force her to go to Viet Nam to save face for their own government.

The day before her scheduled departure, I went to the villa to get her belongings and take them back to the hotel with me. At the last minute, she said she wanted to go back with me then, instead of waiting until the next day. She said she just didn't want to endure any long goodbyes with my father, but we all knew that wasn't the real reason; my mother actually wanted to make certain that she left France on a plane headed west and not one headed east.

She got off all right, and flew to Washington to spend a few days with an old friend of ours, Hoa Burke. After that, she was going to Atlanta, where she would visit with my sister Kim and her husband. Hoa met her at the airport in Washington. My father stayed in Paris a few more days, saying he wanted to spend a little more time with me. He moved back into the PRG mission, saying he didn't like staying at the villa alone because it was too upsetting to remember the time he had spent there with my mother. He was hurt, frustrated, and deeply saddened to have lost her again. I believe he knew he had lost her to an ideology, to a system that allowed her to make her choice. I wondered, though, whether he really understood that she was making that choice by herself, and not at the dictates of a government or anyone else.

It was the knowledge that, if she returned to Viet Nam, she wouldn't be left alone by government that finally pushed her to her decision, I believe. When she asked him what the government would do when she got to Viet Nam, he didn't answer right away, she told me later. After a long walk alone by the lake he came back to her and said to her, "As you already know, you let our daughters marry the Americans while I was away. You are the target of much gossip and criticism at home. You would be meeting with the responsible people to explain your position."

My mother would have none of that. Besides, she had been affronted by his own words. "I will always love him and I salute the strength and the dedication he displays, but I will not forgive him for saying 'You let our daughters marry the Americans.' After all, the Americans he mentioned are the fathers of his grandchildren!"

Time is a magic medicine. My mother and I can talk freely now about that time in Paris and even laugh about some of the funnier moments. But that first year after she met for such a short time with the man she loved was the most painful year in her whole difficult life.

Chapter 22

When it was time for my father to leave Paris, Thai and I took him to Orly Airport. Thai was still circling around the parking lot looking for a space when we went inside to check in at the Aeroflot counter. I couldn't help but smile when I heard my father speak Russian to the Russian woman who was examining his travel documents and his ticket. Thai had wanted to book the flight on Air France, but my father insisted on Aeroflot. It reminded me of how Rob had told me I should always fly on a U.S. carrier if possible.

We stayed with my father in the passenger lounge until his departure. When the airline representative called his row number for boarding, he didn't move. He held my hand tight and didn't want to let go.

"Take good care of your mother for me, daughter," he said for one final time. Then we stood and he held me for a long time. At the last moment, he released me, shook hands with Thai, and disappeared into the aircraft.

Once again I felt like an orphan. I stood there and stared out the windows at the plane that was going to take my father away. Thai stood a few steps away, waiting patiently for me. I had nothing to say to him at that moment.

Before I left Paris, Phan Thanh Nam took me to meet the SRV ambassador, Vo Van Sung. Nam advised me to call the ambassador "Chu" (uncle), and I was happy to oblige; it would help me in my effort to play innocent in front of the fox.

We had tea in a cozy room in the old SRV embassy, and I listened to all the ambassador's questions. "Is your husband a good American?" (To the Vietnamese Communists, a good American is an antiwar activist.) "What does he do?" (The most favorable position to the Communists is one that can do them no harm.) I could have lied to them, but I had long ago decided there was no way I would lie about my husband, so I disappointed both Nam and the ambassador with the truth.

"My husband loves his country the same way I love mine," I said. "What I found out, and am content with, is that he has empathy for the troubles of Viet Nam." They were a little more encouraged when I told them he was a meteorologist and was working at the Pearl Harbor weather station. "It is a fine profession," the ambassador immediately remarked. "Someday your husband could help your papa when he is needed."

The ambassador was straightforward and didn't waste much time in chitchat. He asked if I had ever been involved with the Front, and I told him as I told everyone that my whole family in the South had always been very much involved — the Front had used my grandparents' land for their operations, and my youngest cousin had been killed for the cause. I knew all that meant nothing to him, though; he wouldn't have been truly satisfied unless my blood had mingled with the blood of his adversary and I had appeared before him as a one-legged war casualty. He was willing for me to start now, however.

"I have a very good friend in America," he told me. "He lives in San Francisco. I want you to see him when you get back." I wondered if this high official of the SRV had ever studied a map of his enemy's land; didn't he know that the distance from Hawaii to San Francisco was no short jaunt? Still, I asked for the address of his friend and wrote it in my small address book. Then it occurred to me to ask him to write a few words on the back of his business card to introduce me to his friend, and he did. I then had everything I needed to make the SRV ambassador to France my assistant in gaining access to the Communist network in the United States.

The person he wanted me to meet in San Francisco turned out to be the longtime president of the so-called Vietnamese Patriots Association in America, and I did indeed meet him a year later. I asked the ambassador if he had any friends in Honolulu for me to contact, and he replied proudly, "Perhaps we have our people in Honolulu, but they are undercover for a certain duty which I don't even know myself."

I left Paris for Hawaii with confidence that I would always be welcome in the Vietnamese Communist community there, and certain that the future would hold many meetings between Nam and Thai and me. I didn't make any promises before leaving, but my doubletalk led Nam to believe that he had me under his little Red thumb. The day I came to say goodbye, he told me, "I'll see that your future contribution for the Liberation will be known by the responsible people back home. And that will make your father very happy!"

— — —

After my trip to Paris, I had looked forward to some time to relax with my family in Hawaii. The CIA had other plans, however: They wanted us to move to Washington, D.C. For several months it seemed that most of my contacts had been with victims of the Vietnamese Communists, not the people who were the perpetrators of the crime done to my country. It was time, however, to start spreading my net. I decided to start with a man Thai had introduced me to, Mr. Huynh Trung Dong, the chairman of the Vietnamese Union in Paris. He had asked me to come back to talk with him sometime, without Thai's company, so I took him up on the invitation and returned to Paris several months later.

Dong was a strange man. Every time I met him I had the idea that he was there, but not really there; he had a sort of "thousand-mile stare" like a soldier suffering shell-shock. He also had a habit of not talking in a normal voice, but always in a sort of whisper.

The morning I went to see him alone, he showed me a copy of the journal *Doan Ket*, which meant "United," published by his union, and promised to send me the bimonthly issues if I would give him my home address. I suggested it would be best to send it to a post office box I kept in Washington.

Something occurred to him, and he fished around in the "USA" file until he found a dog-eared card; reading from it, he asked if I knew a Vietnamese woman named Nguyen Thi Ngoc Thoa, who lived in Washington, D.C. I told him I had only just moved to Washington and hadn't run into her. He looked back at the card for a while and then told me about her.

"This person is married to an American, but he is our friend. She was actively involved in the antiwar movement in the early seventies."

"I was a sleeper in the late sixties and early seventies," I said, sticking to my cover story.

"I would like you to meet her," Dong said. "Make friends with her, and see what goes from there."

I wasn't too thrilled by what was apparently just a "fishing expedition," but I remembered Thai's advice to be patient, so I nodded and kept my mouth shut.

During that visit, Dong took me on a tour of the union headquarters. There was a library in the basement filled with books on "Communist studies," and a group of young people listening to a lecture from a woman who used all the colorful but meaningless Communist terminology to interpret what was in the book they were all reading.

In a glass case near the entrance hall on the main floor, Dong proudly showed me "the pen that signed the Paris peace agreement." Then he picked up a piece of white metal on which was engraved a picture of a female cadre, pants rolled up to her knees, a machine gun slung over her right shoulder; she had a rope over her other shoulder, dragging along a piece of twisted wreckage. "This was the body of an American B-52 bomber," he boasted. He handed me the picture to look at more closely, but I just quivered and kept my hands in my pockets. Thoughts of the American pilots, and all the other American servicemen, suddenly popped into my mind, and I was upset because I couldn't say anything on their behalf.

Dong gave me a stack of literature to take back to America, most of it propaganda magazines in English and Vietnamese. I thanked him for them, although I knew I was going to turn them all over to the CIA, along with the address of the antiwar activist in Washington, Nguyen Thi Ngoc Thoa.

The three weeks I spent with the Vietnamese community in Paris were the longest and most trying of my ventures into the "spy world" so far. Not a day went by when I didn't have to go to meetings, to talk to the leftists either in government or in the French "network," and to act and speak as if I, too, were a pro-Communist.

I made all the contacts with the right people we could have hoped for, and now over a cup of green tea or a glass of wine I could pick up all kinds of information. There is nothing for nothing, of course; the price I ended up paying required my sitting through endless, boring Communist study sessions in the union's basement. The strain of having to work in this reversed political environment was beginning to tell on me, however. I was sick of Phan Thanh Nam, of the so-called Liberation. I was sick of the French and their rude waiters and cashiers who didn't accommodate American visitors. I was exhausted, body and soul.

Being away from my family was difficult as well. I missed my son, even though he sounded happy enough when I talked to him on the phone: "What did you get me from the toy store?" I knew my husband must be tired of the frozen casseroles I had made for him before I left on the trip. I even missed the traffic jams on I-95 to the Pentagon, and the hamburgers at McDonald's.

I told Rob I needed a break, a chance to be alone and to recuperate. He understood, and he got a green light from Langley, the CIA headquarters, for me to take a few days off — in the location of my choice. He suggested Stockholm, but I decided I would rather go to Copenhagen. The trip turned out to be therapeutic for the relationship between Rob and me as well as good for my spirits. He and I had long had a personality clash of sorts, a kind of power struggle, perhaps. He always played the role of official representative of the world's most powerful intelligence organization, and while he flattered me with talk of how valuable and sensitive the information I gathered was to the agency, he always insisted on keeping me in the dark about what they would do with it. I didn't even know what he said to them in his reports on my activities or when I didn't want to do things his way, but I did know that he held all the cards and the key to Langley. As for me, I had the key to the people the agency wanted to know about. I had the connections and the sources, and as a double agent I could go places and do things the case officer couldn't. I'm sure some genuine "super spook" — CIA talk for a great spy — came up with this kind of system, but it had the effect of exaggerating the friction that often cropped up between Rob and me.

The trip to Copenhagen was a bit different, however. For the first time in three long weeks, I think neither of us wanted to be in the other's shoes, or even our own. Neither of us had the energy or the desire to "shoot down" the other. For the first time we ate dinner without mentioning Thai and Nam or even Madame Binh and her downfall in the SRV government.

I even made peace with Rob by lending him my silk scarf to use as a necktie when the maitre d' at the restaurant told him that gentlemen were required to wear ties. As we chatted over our meal, he told me I still had "class" even though I didn't share his love for ballet, and I told him he was "not so bad after all" when he said he liked Roger Whittaker and Yves Montand, two of my favorites.

Rob sometimes seemed to like it too well when I told him how much I regarded his expertise on Viet Nam, but it was true. He has an amazing memory, remembering in intricate detail all the names and dates and events regarding SRV activities that I reported to him. Having to work with someone with that kind of ability was a challenge to me, I told him, because it meant I had to be even more careful about being knowledgeable and correct in the information I gave him.

The day after we came to Copenhagen, Rob had to leave for a family emergency, but we parted on good terms, and I spent three wonderful days seeing the city before going back to Washington, D.C.

There, sadly, the bloom of the newly relaxed relationship between Rob and me wore off, and rather suddenly. The issue was my feeling that we ought to take advantage of what Dong had told me about SRV agents working in the United States. I thought I should try to make contact with them, especially the woman Nguyen Thi Ngoc Thoa, as Dong had suggested — but he was dead set against the idea.

"Counterintelligence is not our job," Rob said, "it is not the CIA's responsibility." I didn't disagree over the rules, but I was adamant that "somebody has to know about this." He said it was the FBI's job to catch spies in the United States, but I argued that the FBI wouldn't know anything if we didn't tell them what I had learned.

"It is the trash in our own back yard," I insisted. "If we don't clean it up, what good does it do for America if we run around the globe collecting information?" I pleaded with him to share my findings with the FBI, but he said there was a technical problem in the way: The CIA was not allowed to recruit American citizens to operate on American soil without specific permission from the Justice Department. "Then spill our guts to the Justice Department," I wailed.

He wasn't eager to do that, observing that at times he wished I were not a U.S. citizen, because that would "make everything easier for me." He also didn't seem to have much respect for the FBI, referring to them as "the police" — such as when he told me that "we don't want the police to identify our super star," meaning me.

Still, he promised to think about my plea. "In the meantime you just sit tight." Perhaps I should have, but I wanted to make him understand how serious I was about this. "If you don't inform the FBI about this Vietnamese woman, I will," I declared. "If I can't, I'll ask my husband to transfer my message to the right place." That would probably have been easy, because by this time John had gone to work for Naval Intelligence under Admiral Bobby Inman, working in the Foreign Liaison section of Admiral Inman's staff.

"If you do that, I'll fire you," Rob said. He was as serious as I was.

I just laughed. "You would have to hire me first before you could fire me," I said. Even though for nine months I had been supplying the CIA with information, I was still doing it on an unpaid, volunteer basis. I had clearly not chosen this line of work to "bring home the bacon."

My statement jogged something in Rob's mind. "OK, maybe you and I should sit down and talk about employment," he said.

"Fine, that will give you the authority to fire me whenever things don't go your way. Spying is not always as smooth as the last three weeks have been, you know. I can be very pleasant to work with, but I am a skunk when people try to step on me. Maybe you should try to remember this secret about this bad quality of mine."

— — —

In Washington, we continued to meet at least weekly — sometimes in the Marco Polo restaurant in Vienna, Virginia, for lunch, sometimes at the McDonald's in Springfield for breakfast, sometimes just in the parking lot of a shopping center near Fairfax for a quick talk. We discussed future dealings with Thai and Dong and the others, and we worked on details of plans on how to use Dong as a bridge to meet the SRV foreign minister, Pham Duy Trinh, and the prime minister, Pham Van Dong, when they came to Paris on a visit that was scheduled soon. That visit would be important to the SRV, because it was trying to restore good relations with France, and of course it would be of interest to the CIA as well.

At one meeting I brought up the issue again of "cleaning our own back yard" — informing the FBI about the SRV cadres and associates in the United States and trying to infiltrate their network. Rob must have been thinking about it long before I asked him the question, because he said, "I couldn't agree with you more. Of course it's important. But the answer is no."

I couldn't accept it. I knew that the presence of Vietnamese spies in America was harmful to my adopted country, and I thought something ought to be done about it. The Vietnamese spies were the force behind the antiwar movement in the 1960s, and even though the war was over they could and would still recruit Americans to work for them. They could steal national secrets, including industrial and technological secrets, and infiltrate the CIA, FBI, and State Defense Department. Another strategy of theirs was to give misinformation to the press, to divide the cohesiveness of political organizations, create mistrust among minority communities, and create racial tension. Further, they could disrupt relations between our allies by knowing exactly our words and thoughts on top-secret communication. Then, if a war broke out, they would know almost all.

That night I discussed the issue with my husband. I told John I appreciated Rob's concerns about "the police," Rob's derisive term for the FBI, but I really wanted a second expert opinion. I wanted to know what Admiral Inman, a real "super spy," thought about the issue. John agreed wholeheartedly that the counterintelligence people ought to know about the cadres on American soil.

Very soon, John met with Admiral Inman, who said he would check out the situation. To my heartbreak, a few days later the word came back that "they're not interested." I couldn't believe it. I could feel it in my bones that something wrong was being done to my adopted country, and I was in a position to do something to help. I wrestled with my thoughts for weeks, and then again asked my husband to help — I wanted him to arrange for me to meet Admiral Inman personally. Maybe I could make my case better in a face-to-face encounter.

John set up the meeting, and the two of us met with Admiral Inman in his office at the Pentagon. The admiral listened carefully to my story, then promised that he would talk to FBI director Clarence Kelley about it.

I don't know exactly how things happened after that, but just a few days later Rob announced, "You're now legal" — meaning the Justice Department had given permission for me to be used here at home. Soon I would meet an FBI agent who would be my contact in those activities.

He also had some other news, something not quite so rewarding. "They are going to send me to a special school," he said, "and you'll have to work with a new case officer." From his tone, I knew that something was wrong — that there must have been some kind of problem or difficulty surrounding my case, and that Rob wasn't just being sent off to a "special school" to further his education. I asked him to tell me what was wrong, but he only responded bitterly, "You wanted an FBI agent, now you'll get one. What else do you want?"

For all our clashes, I was worried about having to work with a new CIA case officer, someone I didn't know and who didn't know me. I asked Rob what the new man was like, and his description wasn't encouraging: He didn't know much about the Far East, and he was mostly looking forward to an upcoming assignment to a new post in Bangkok. I told Rob I didn't want a messenger, I wanted an experienced officer from the Viet Nam desk, but he responded that what I wanted was about to be sent away.

Not long after that I was introduced to my new CIA case officer, Bill Reardon. He was a sweet gentleman in his forties, a quiet man who never asked questions in all our meetings. He simply had no interest in my project, because as he made clear to me he was mostly waiting for his transfer to Bangkok. He actually fell asleep a couple of times as I read him some letters I had received from my sources in Paris and tried to explain what they meant.

I realized there was no reason to work very hard to cultivate a good working relationship with a man who was determined to be a short-timer in the position. I liked him as a person and admired his love for his family, and I thought we might have worked well together if he had been interested in the project, but that was not to be. We met occasionally for lunch just to keep in touch, we exchanged vegetables from our gardens, and that was all.

One hot day in June of 1976, I was introduced to my new "domestic" case officer, FBI Special Agent William Fleshman. A clean-cut, quiet man about my own age, he sometimes had a kind of Robert Redford look, but mostly he reminded me of a history teacher. As I got to know him, I came to respect him greatly as an agent — honest, precise, cooperative, open for suggestions. He had the rare quality of being able to admit that he doesn't know everything and being willing to ask questions to learn. He seemed mild-mannered and a little bookish, but I came to know that he had the "right stuff" to be an FBI agent.

Bill Fleshman was, and is, a patient man, one with a lot of common sense. He and I agreed that in real intelligence work there are plenty of times when we have to deal with boring details and endless research, but we were willing to do it. It wasn't glamorous and sexy and fun, like in the spy novels, but it was critically important, and we knew it.

My first contact with the American-based cadres was to be Mrs. Thoa, the woman Dong had told me about in Washington. I suggested that the FBI cover my meeting with her, because I didn't have the slightest idea what this new target might be like. I wasn't expecting anything in particular; at that point she was just a name. I could not have dreamed that she was going to be the entry point into what would turn out to be the most important case I would ever work on.

— — —

Armed with Dong's letter as my entrée, I went to see Mrs. Thoa in her second-floor apartment in the 1300 block of 18th Street N.W. in Washington. There was a Vietnamese man visiting her when I arrived, but as soon as I came she showed him to the door and cautiously welcomed me in. She told me he was a refugee who had come to her for help in finding a job.

Thoa was a small, thin woman, quiet and rather reserved toward me. I tried to break the ice a bit, telling her I should have come to see her earlier but had been busy moving into my new house. She didn't say anything at first, but looked at me from my head to my toes a few times. Finally, she said, "There are many people who came here and told me they are on our side, but later we found out they are reactionaries."

"I believe I know what you mean. You wondered if I was real or not, right?"

"I am sorry, but I must be careful," she said, still looking at me doubtfully.

"I am glad you practice that rule," I assured her. "I am sure we will get along just fine." Then I took out my trump card, the letter from Dong (a copy was in the FBI's hands), and gave it to her. She read it through, then put it back inside the envelope and shook my hand, apparently satisfied.

We didn't talk about very much that first time. I told Thoa that I made frequent trips to Paris and would be happy to do anything there for her that I could. She thanked me, and indicated that she might ask me sometimes to "carry things" to Paris for her.

We went to lunch together for our second meeting, not long afterward. Thoa had picked the Old Stein on Connecticut Avenue; I told the FBI ahead of time, and they had people watching while we ate and talked.

Thoa showed me a monthly newspaper she put together called *Nguoi Viet Doan Ket*, meaning "The United Vietnamese." I say "put together" because that was literally what she did; instead of writing articles she simply reprinted articles from Communist newspapers published in Ha Noi and elsewhere. I wondered where she got the money to print and mail out nearly 5,000 of the papers each month, because they were circulated free. She didn't tell me, although she did mention that she got quite a bit of help from a Vietnamese Catholic priest, Father Tran Tam Tinh. He lived in Canada, she said, and she traveled there to visit him from time to time.

Thoa was a hard-working, dedicated, and level-headed woman. She believed totally in the Liberation government and was proud that she had played a role in it. She certainly displayed none of the materialism of the capitalists; she worked, ate, slept, and conducted all her political activities in her tiny apartment. She slept on a mattress laid on the floor, the light in her room was poor, and she pasted up her newspaper on a table that was so rickety she had to hold it steady with her legs while she worked. Her clothes, she told me, came from the Salvation Army. None of that bothered her, she said, as long as she had "the health and the opportunity to serve the Liberation."

I may be wrong, but I think the way I described her dedication in my second contact report caused a few frowns in the agencies; but I couldn't ignore someone who was obviously a talented star, even if she was on a quite different stage.

Thoa never liked to carry on a conversation on the phone. After we had gotten to know each other, her calls to me were usually cryptic and brief: "Hi, it's me. Can we meet tomorrow at the same time and same place?" That meant 10:00 A.M. at the Old Stein; after a while I began to develop quite a taste for kosher food. As an active member of the Vietnamese organization during the antiwar movement, Thoa had recently begun to feel that her work was being forgotten by the revolution. I was her link to the SRV people in Paris and Viet Nam; she wanted me to listen to her, then convey her thoughts and feelings to Mr. Huynh Trung Dong, chairman of the Overseas Vietnamese Organization.

According to Vietnamese custom it was rude of me to dine with this girl often without ever inviting her to my house, but we both kept our personal lives out of our relationship. The only things she knew about me were my telephone number and the fact that my father was a member of the NLF. I never asked her about her husband, because I didn't want her to ask about mine. Besides, her comrade in Paris, Mr. Dong, had already told me that Thoa's husband was a "good American." My husband certainly wouldn't rate that description by the Communists' definition, and I didn't want him or anything else to come between Thoa and me.

Through many conversations with Thoa I learned quite a bit about the Vietnamese leftists in the United States. Their organization was very limited, but they were strong, very dedicated, and mostly highly educated. Many of them were former students who had avoided the draft under the Thieu regime by not returning home after earning their degrees. Almost all of them had joined the antiwar movement during the sixties and seventies.

One student to whom Thoa introduced me was a young man named Truong Dinh Hung — whom she said was Truong Dinh Dzu's son. Back in

Viet Nam, the name Truong Dinh Dzu was quite well known. Rich people had known him as a famous lawyer, but everyone else came to know him when he ran for president against Thieu in 1967. His campaign became a tragedy for him, since Thieu threw him in jail for daring to oppose him. Despite the fame of the Truong name, however, I didn't make any connection right away when I met his son.

We had run into Hung on the staircase at Thoa's apartment, and she pulled me over to introduce us. At first he didn't even look at me, but when she said the magic words, "My Yung comes from Brother Dong in Paris," he suddenly became a warm and friendly person.

That autumn I was to make another trip to Paris for the CIA. A week before my departure I told Thoa I was going, and she said she had some things she wanted me to take there for her. She didn't think it would be wise for me to keep them in my house for any length of time, though, so she asked if I would pick them up just before I left. I respected her position, although I knew the FBI and CIA would like to have as much time as possible to look them over while they were in my possession. There was nothing I could do, however. I didn't want to jeopardize my relationship with Thoa by giving her a hard time about her simple request. Anyway, I figured our intelligence agencies had the reputation of being supermen, so they should be able to cope with the task on short notice.

A couple of days before I left, I drove to Thoa's place to pick up her "things." Hung was never present when I met with her, but this time he was waiting for me. I parked the car out front and then gasped when I saw what Thoa wanted me to take to Paris — two large and terribly heavy boxes loaded with pages of testimony from hearings in Congress and dozens of hardback books, ranging from political and technical volumes to one entitled *Jimmy Who?*. Before I left, Hung handed me a sealed envelope. It was addressed to a Mr. Nguyen Ngoc Giao, but Hung asked me to deliver it to Dong when I gave him the books. I was learning that false names were a way of life in the spy business.

Two hours later, the FBI and CIA were at my house, poring over the contents of the boxes and listing all the titles in their records. Because of the short notice, and perhaps because the wheels of any bureaucracy turn slowly, we didn't have time to get legal permission to open Hung's letter, so we had to live with the unknown and deliver it to Mr. Dong as he had requested.

Two rather important changes occurred before I made this trip to Paris. The first was that I found myself working with Rob again, and oddly enough it was at my own insistence.

In April of 1976 I had written to Mr. Nguyen Van Luy, the chairman of the

Vietnamese Patriots Association in the United States, the man Ambassador Sung had said he wanted me to meet when I had spoken with him in Paris. Luy replied that he wanted me to come and visit him in San Francisco and meet with members of his organization's board. He also wanted me to go down to Christianburg, Virginia, to meet "clandestinely" with his "two most active members," young people who were attending Virginia Tech. I knew that Luy operated his left-wing organization under the direct supervision of the foreign ministry of the SRV, and I wanted to have input and advice from someone who was more interested and involved than Bill Reardon, who was still dreaming of Bangkok.

I took a chance and called Rob's boss, Mr. Roger McCarthy, and asked for a meeting. He agreed to meet me for breakfast at a McDonald's in Vienna, Virginia (as I noted, the business isn't always glamorous).

When he arrived, Roger bought a cup of coffee and walked over to my table. As the breakfast crowd milled around us, I told him my concerns about the operation being stalemated because Bill Reardon was in transit to another post and because "he treated this matter like a cold sore." I told him that if things were going to go on that way, then I wanted out.

Roger reassured me that he would do something. Before he left, however, I thought I should take what might be my only chance to speak directly to someone in the agency about the difficult relationship Rob and I had had. We didn't get along well on a personal level, I told his boss, but "as professionals we respect each other." For the sake of the agency and the operation, I was willing to work with him again, "but that doesn't mean I'll get along with him. You must know that for me he's a pain.''

Roger smiled and pointed at his balding head. "He's the reason I lost most of my hair," he laughed. I believed it.

Soon Rob was back in the lead seat of our operation. And that led to the second change in my situation: I finally became a paid spy.

— — —

I was terribly busy during the month of December. Every Friday was set aside for meeting with the FBI and CIA officers to report on my activities with the Vietnamese left wing. Since John was now serving as a liaison officer to foreign military attaches, we were invited to lots of embassy parties, including big affairs put on by the Russians, the Australians, the Pakistanis, the Thais, the Swedes, the Koreans, the South Africans, the Yugoslavians, and the Filipinos.

At home, though, I had to get ready for two far more important parties that month. One was Lance's sixth birthday on the ninth, for which we had planned a get-together for twenty-two of his first-grade friends. The other was my mother's sixtieth birthday, which is called *luc tuan* in Vietnamese.

Under the old custom, it would be only the third birthday celebration since her first birthday and her month-old birthday. Hoa Binh had come up with a list of guests, including mothers of our friends who were refugees in the Washington area and a girl who had been our next-door neighbor in Sai Gon, and we were keeping everything a deep secret. When the big day came, on December 16, it was wonderful to see the surprise on my mother's face as old friends and new ones came to help her celebrate.

By the first week in January my energy was gone. I told my sisters, "If the dirty Communists call, tell them I am on strike, no meetings this month."

That kind of break was unlikely, however. For one thing, I heard there was a rumor among the Vietnamese women married to Americans in Reston and Sterling, Virginia, that a woman named Thu Novax was going around asking questions about "a daughter of the Viet Cong ambassador to Moscow." At this time not even my close friends knew about my father, so I only heard about the woman by accident from a friend.

I telephoned Truong Dinh Hung and asked if he knew of anyone named Thu Novax. He did, and advised me not to associate with "such a character." He and Thoa told me that this woman was using her close relationship with the SRV ambassador to the United Nations, Dinh Ba Thi, to boost her own image, and that her openness about her association with the left-wing Vietnamese could do harm to "our" efforts. I told Hung I still needed to get in touch with her to stop her from making such inquiries in the Vietnamese community, to avoid any possibility of my secret leaking out. Hung then told me that Novax was associated with the Vietnamese Patriot Association head-ed by Nguyen Van Luy, the man I had corresponded with, and he gave me her telephone number.

When I called her and identified myself as the person she was looking for, I was surprised to hear her say that she had recently visited the UN ambas-sador, Mr. Thi, and "he asked me to look for the daughter of Ambassador Minh." I asked what had made him think Thu Novax could find me, and she said the ambassador thought it was only natural that "the daughter should be associated with the group since her father is who he is." I thanked Novax for passing on the message, but asked her never to mention my name to anyone in the association or to any of the Vietnamese wives in the area. "I have good reasons to keep a low profile," I told her.

Novax said she would like to meet me because she was sure I could teach her so much about socialism. I wondered if that meant the leftists were final-ly beginning to realize that Communism is not an inherited illness but a social disease. I never intended to meet her, although she was a rather ambitious member of the patriot association and her name was often heard in unfavorable references among members. Hung and Thoa were uncomfortable about her frequent visits to the UN mission.

After my talk with Novax, I excitedly told my case officers that there was a good chance I could get inside the SRV's mission at the United Nations, since the ambassador was looking for me. The CIA was flatly against it, mostly because Rob just didn't want me to expand my services to the FBI any more than I already had. Naturally, though, the FBI thought it was a great idea. I suggested I call the ambassador first to see if we could learn more about what he had on his mind, and then determine where to go from there.

When I phoned Ambassador Thi in New York, I called him "sir," but he quickly corrected me: "Call me Uncle, I am your father's friend." He said he had recently made a trip home and heard people in the foreign ministry talking about "Dang Quang Minh's family in America." He didn't invite me directly to come and see him, because it might not look right to have a woman visiting him personally, but he did suggest I simply make a visit to the UN mission. "It would be right if you can visit us, the sooner the better," he said. "We are your father's friends, and after all we are compatriots."

I would have thought the intelligence agencies would all leap at a chance like this, considering how hard they work at keeping up with the Soviet bloc countries, but again the CIA didn't seem happy. In fact, Rob threatened to "fire" me if I went to New York. Reluctantly, though, he allowed me to tell Bill Fleshman about the invitation. I told Bill that this conflict was something the two agencies would have to work out, and that I was just waiting for a green light to go. I finally got permission, but I'm sure the CIA and the FBI met and fought long and hard in my absence before they came to a final decision. I don't know if they fought over me — since working for the FBI would mean I couldn't continue working undercover for the CIA — or simply fought because the agencies generally don't work together or even like each other.

Although I was eager to see Ambassador Thi for the U.S. government, another part of me wanted personally to see a man who had been part of the peace talks in Paris, a man who was much loved by Thai and Mimi, his fiancée, and many others in the Vietnamese leftist community in France. I also wanted to meet some Communists other than people like Phan Thanh Nam and Huynh Trung Dong; perhaps I was searching for a light in the darkness, for some humanity among the tyrants and martinets.

Before leaving, I spread my net out once again to see what kind of fish I might catch. I called Truong Dinh Hung and asked if he had anything for me to take to the UN mission. Indeed he did, he said — an envelope that needed to reach the ambassador "in a hurry." I drove to D.C. and picked up the envelope outside a restaurant on Connecticut Avenue, with the knowledge of course of the FBI and the CIA.

I called the ambassador to tell him I would be flying to New York on January 19 and would come to see him that same day. I wouldn't be able to contact the intelligence agencies for the three days I was there, because the ambassador had insisted I stay at the mission rather than in a hotel. I was to call my family, however, and arranged with the FBI and CIA that if I didn't make that call by the third day at the latest then they should assume something had gone wrong.

I wasn't really expecting any trouble, however, and was even more relaxed after I met the staff of the UN mission. There were just five men: the ambassador; his personal aide Pham Ngac, who had been with Thi during his tours of duty in France and Switzerland; Pham Duong, an economic analyst; Mr. Hung, a housekeeper and cook; and Mr. Van, a driver and bodyguard.

The last two were clearly not diplomats. Mr. Hung never left the apartment for anything except in the company of one of the other members. He didn't speak English and he hated the "American imperialists" with a passion. He hated the winter in New York, the television commercials, and the department stores. The driver, Mr. Van, seemed somewhat like a cross between an Asian and a British farmer. He smoked cigars, ate, drank, and drove the car while wearing a little flat cap as if behind the wheel of a sports car. He enjoyed being in New York more than in Moscow, because "it is a challenge to drive in the city of New York," he bragged.

We all ate lunch together on the first day of my visit, and then everyone disappeared to take their midday nap. Mr. Van let me use his room and he took his things to sleep in Hung's room. Although the apartment was quiet and I had two hours to myself, I couldn't sleep; I had lost the pleasant habit of taking a nap in the middle of the day since coming to America. So I was sitting up reading the *New Yorker* when Ambassador Thi got up from his nap. He brought a chair into the room and sat down to have a chat.

"I didn't get a chance to ask about your mother. How is she?"

"She is physically fine," I replied, "but my parents' situation is a dilemma. She misses my father and Khoi very much, but she also knows in her heart that she would not be happy if she went back." I'm not sure why, but I felt I could be honest with Thi. Apparently, I was right.

"This is just between Uncle Thi and you," he said. "Your mother is right that she would not have the chance to be as happy as she is now in the United States. There are still very hard feelings toward your mother and you girls."

"You mean because my sisters and I married Americans?"

"That, too," he said. What he left unstated was the embarrassment my mother caused the government by leaving Sai Gon before the Liberation.

"When I told my father that an American citizen is the father of his grandson, I also told him that love exists in many languages besides Vietnamese, and he was happy for me," I recalled. "He accepted my husband. If I married a Russian, would it make me a better Vietnamese?"

"Things like this will need time to make people understand," Thi said gently. "Don't force the issue."

That afternoon the ambassador took me on a tour of the UN complex. As we went through the international gift shop, I felt truly sad to see products from many, many countries but nothing from Viet Nam. I pointed that out to him and asked, "How long would it take to bring our country back to normal?" He looked at me and then quickly turned away, unable to answer.

The next morning they all went to work, but Pham Ngac returned to the apartment about eleven, and we talked about the Vietnamese community in the United States, both refugees and those who sympathized with the SRV. Until this day, twenty years after the refugees had to leave their country to avoid death or imprisonment, the two groups still harbor hatred toward each other in the United States.

Pham Ngac said he had a friend who was his "bridge for my twenty-five-mile zone." Members of the UN delegation were restricted to travel only within twenty-five miles of New York City, so he used other people, including members of the Vietnamese Patriot Association, to make contacts for him beyond that. His special friend, he said, was an American woman. "She is great for us not only because she is an intellectual and a liberated woman but because she has friends who are millionaires," including a man who owned a nationwide chain of women's clothing shops.

Ngac had another question for me. He held up a letter from the AP journalist Peter Arnett, who wanted permission to travel to Viet Nam.

I laughed and told Ngac that "most American newsmen are like the American politicians — they stay away from unpopular issues. So if Arnett supported the war in Viet Nam the readers will never know. I do know that he covered the war for a few years in Sai Gon."

"So he must know Viet Nam very well, don't you think?"

"How can a white man know our country 'very well' when he has only touched the surface of the thirty-year war?" I asked. "Most of them looked for what the American taxpayers wanted to hear. Others wanted to touch the bleeding-hearts. Some wrote home about the fascinating war, the ugly human suffering, the poor, underprivileged Vietnamese. Many Americans only know Viet Nam through the paintings that newsmen painted for them. Many think Viet Nam is a vast jungle full of disease, mosquitoes, swamps, and bad water.

And they think Vietnamese are beggars, pimps, prostitutes, shoeshine boys, and innocent peasants in the liberated areas. You don't have to know his political background, he probably cast that away when he received his press card anyway," I concluded.

"You don't like newsmen very much, do you?" Ngac said.

— — —

On the second day of my visit, when everyone headed off for their midday nap, Ambassador Thi said he would stay up to chat since I wasn't going to be sleeping. I was glad we had a chance to be alone. I wanted to probe his feelings about the new SRV government and his position in it; that was, after all, my main purpose in coming to New York.

We talked about the dreams each of us secretly had about our country. "I lived half my life away from my wife and children," Thi said. "My dream is to have a small house with a garden plot to grow our own food and raise our own chickens — and maybe a pig!"

"Where would you like to have your dream home?" I asked.

"In Thu Duc. I went to the South to many beautiful places, but I fell in love with Thu Duc and the Dong Nai River. When I build that house in my head, I can see the chickens run at feeding time, my sons coming home from work in Sai Gon on their new motorcycles, and we watch the sun set by the river in front of my house." Thi was smiling, but his eyes were all red.

I couldn't hide my feelings, either. I put my hand on his and said, "I hope your dream will come true soon, Uncle Thi."

"I hope so, too, before it is too late," he said. "My wife is not well and I have been asking our government to allow her to come here to seek medical help."

"When will she come?"

He shook his head. "The request went to the highest place, but the answer hasn't come back yet. There are faults in each government system, you know that, and one of ours is the lack of trust. The wife is not allowed to join the husband when he serves the country abroad."

"I notice that rule is also practiced by the Russian diplomats and those from other Communist countries," I observed.

"Can you imagine that a man like your father would defect to a capitalist country if he were allowed to serve outside Viet Nam with your brother with him?" Thi laughed at the absurdity of my father defecting for any reason.

His comment stirred an idea in my mind, though, and I decided to try it out on him. "Do you think it is possible, if my mother asked the government, that she would be allowed to see my father and my brother?"

"Tell your mother to write to Chairman Le Duan, and I'll deliver the letter for her," the ambassador offered. He was referring to the chairman of the Communist party in Ha Noi, the successor to Ho Chi Minh.

"Twenty-three years is a lifetime for a mother to be separated from her oldest son!" I exclaimed.

"If our government can't fulfill a humble dream such as your mother's, then it will fail its people. Tell her I'll do my very best to help her."

"Now I know why people I met in Paris told me that you are special, different from others," I said, feeling a genuine respect.

"Don't doubt my loyalty to Viet Nam and the road I chose for our country," he warned, "but socialism or Communism, whatever it is, if it doesn't allow us to make our people happy and bring our country forward to a promising future, then we have to step back and look at it and ask ourselves why. Because, my dear, I am separated from my family to serve our country, but if my sacrifice doesn't bring happiness to anyone then there is something not right within the system I serve."

"Mr. Phan Thanh Nam interpreted the party differently from you," I said.

"You are talking about Nam at the PRG permanent mission in Paris?"

"Yes."

"Phan Thanh Nam is a Southerner, too," Thi said, shaking his head in what must have been disappointment. "Nam is a military type. He changed jobs later."

"I had many occasions to talk with him about 'doing something constructive for Viet Nam,'" I recounted. "On two occasions he told me to ask my husband to steal valuable U.S. government research materials. Then he said, 'If you want to see Papa again you should prove your loyalty to Viet Nam.' He promised that he would make sure the responsible people back home know that I work for him."

The calm and peaceful look on Thi's face vanished, and he became visibly angry. Taking a deep breath, he said, "Perhaps your mother knows Mr. Do Muoi, but I am sure you wouldn't because you were too little then. Mr. Do Muoi is your father's longtime friend, and he didn't like it when he heard about your association with Phan Thanh Nam. It is not that Nam is a bad person, but Mr. Do Muoi knows what he is doing." (Do Muoi, I learned later, had been a close friend of my parents in the Viet Minh days and was now in Vietnamese intelligence.)

He continued, "Listen to me, My Yung, you are Papa's daughter. Viet Nam is your country. You don't have to do anything for Mr. Nam to earn an entry visa. If he approaches you again, let me know. He is doing his job well, but sometimes he can be ruthless."

I changed the subject, wanting to find out more about his connections among the Vietnamese in the United States. "Have you met Truong Dinh Hung, in Washington, D.C.?"

"As a matter of fact, he and his friend Thoa were the hosts of my visit to Washington. Why?"

"I have some indication that Hung is involved with Phan Thanh Nam, and I am seeing Hung from time to time now that Thoa is not as active as she used to be." I didn't say it, but Thoa was not as active because she was being cast aside by the SRV now that it no longer needed people like her — people who had been anti-Diem and anti-American during the war, but didn't have the proper Communist political background. While the fighting was going on, the NLF and the North had used everyone and every group they thought would help their cause — students, Buddhists, and so forth. Now, though, the war was won and the only people who were going to be prominent and favored were the true believers in the Communist cause. Thoa had been a "dominant figure" in the antiwar movement, but now the SRV preferred people like Mr. Luy, the head of the Vietnamese Patriots Association, who had been their foreign agent in the United States as far back as the fifties. There had been a power struggle between the two of them, and Thoa had lost. She was ordered by Dong in Paris to join Luy's organization as a member, and Dong asked me in a letter to advise her to go back to school and try to build a new life for herself. Now I was going to be dealing directly with Truong Dinh Hung.

"I know Hung," the ambassador mused. "He is very ambitious, and he strikes for whatever his goal is. He volunteers; let him be. But you don't have to if you don't want to. Speaking of Hung, when you see him tell him to keep sending the same stuff that he has been sending up here."

"Will he understand that?" I asked. Thi just nodded. I wondered if the FBI and the CIA would.

On my last day in New York I wanted to take Mr. Thi out to dinner with me, and since he said he liked ballet I was willing to suffer through it so I could spend time with him away from the others. After he agreed, I made reservations at a French restaurant. I was sure I could reserve tickets by phone for the ballet, but since I needed to get out of the mission to call the FBI's New York office to tell them of the evening out, I told Mr. Thi that I would have to go out to pick up the tickets.

I was almost ready to go out when the ambassador came back to my room and told me, with great disappointment, that we would have to change our plans. "Mr. Duong doesn't think it is wise for us to go out alone," he said. Thi may have been the ambassador, but obviously Mr. Duong had considerable clout.

"Why not?" I asked. "The places we will go tonight are within the city limits."

"The FBI and the CIA will take our picture, and the press will spread ugly rumors about 'Dinh Ba Thi and Vietnamese Woman Wine and Dine in New York City,'" Thi said, drawing a newspaper headline in the air with his hands.

"What about all of us going out tonight, then?" I suggested.

"It would cost too much money." He smiled to cover his white lie.

"It is too bad you allow the FBI and the CIA and the American press to keep you hostage," I said a little scornfully.

As an alternative, he suggested that Hung and I go to Chinatown and buy the ingredients for a good dinner at home. So the cook and I went out with Van, the driver. I asked Hung to get the ingredients to make Mr. Thi's favorite meal, and also to stock his pantry with items like Chinese mushrooms, *nuoc mam,* rice, noodles and other dried food that would keep. I paid for everything.

Life at the mission, as I observed it, was a little strange and terribly dull. The members skipped breakfast for "economy" reasons, Mr. Thi explained. Lunch and dinners were small, but he insisted they were prepared carefully to ensure a well-balanced diet. If I were asked to write a song that would capture the atmosphere in which these five men lived and worked, it wouldn't be music — it would be the sound of the three television sets that played constantly throughout the apartments.

The most exciting times in the day were news times. They watched "Good Morning America," midday news, evening news. Monitoring the radio and television was one of the most important jobs for Hung, Van, and Pham Ngac. They taped anything they thought was pertinent for transmission back home.

There was no time for play. There wasn't even a deck of cards or a Chinese chess set in the place. Mr. Thi said, "We don't have the luxury of relaxation. We must work because we were sent over here to work."

But they almost never went outside the mission. The view of America that the SRV's United Nations mission sent back home was almost entirely the view they saw while trapped in their apartments, guarded by invisible eyes, hemmed in by their own rules and regulations. They were judging the "American imperialists" almost entirely from what they saw on television. Yet they were accorded all the respect and dignity that went with their post in the United Nations. Now, twenty-two years after the Geneva agreement, I got an inkling of what my grandfather had meant when he used to laugh at the UN peacekeeping force in our country. "The UN peacekeeping force can do one thing in Sai Gon — that is to inflate the price of housing and servants in this poor country." My great-uncle put his view of the United Nations in even more basic language: "Those UN people can't do shit."

For all my sense of the absurdity of the way the mission was carrying out its roles, though, I came away with good feelings about Ambassador Thi. Before the long talk we had privately, while everyone else was taking a nap, I had had a notion of trying to study him carefully to see if there might be one small chance that he might want to stay in America and thus might be persuaded to defect. But I was ashamed of myself after I talked with him that afternoon. I knew that if he were offered the Golden Gate Bridge, the Kennedy Center, and an Aspen ski resort for not going back to Viet Nam, he would turn them all down. I said aloud that I hoped he would have a chance to live the life he wanted with his family in Thu Duc near the Dong Nai River. He smiled when I mentioned his dream.

His return home and his final days were to be nothing like his dream, however — and it would be thanks to me and my work as an American spy.

— — —

More than once during my months with the CIA, Rob had raised the issue of my taking a lie-detector test. I didn't know why they wanted me to do it; I didn't think they should have any doubts about who I was or why I was with them. Besides, how could a machine with its wires and sensors tell more about me than the case officer who had traveled with me, worked with me, and talked to me for hundreds of hours in every kind of circumstance? Rob always told me he thought it would make our relationship easier, but that I didn't have to give my consent if I didn't want to. I didn't; I was strongly against that method of assessing someone's allegiance.

A time came, however, when the "requests" became much more insistent. When I returned from New York and handed in my reports on my visit with Ambassador Thi, Rob made it clear that I was going to have to take the test "or else." Someone must not have been altogether happy with the fact that I had unabashedly expressed the admiration I felt for this "enemy" official; I don't think the intelligence agencies could ever understand how, in my mind, I could separate human beings from their ideologies and governments. I felt somewhat betrayed by their reaction to what I knew were my honest opinions, and I asked myself whether I would do anything differently if I were to visit Thi again. The answer was no; the only way I knew how to do something, whether it was for the U.S. government or the South Vietnamese army or my own family, was to go all out, and I couldn't pull punches just because some people might misunderstand.

Rob and I had had lunch with Bill Fleshman shortly after I returned from New York to talk about my report to the FBI. Bill seemed pleased, and that balanced things a little in my mind. As soon as he left the parking lot, however, Rob started in on me again about the lie-detector test. "I have to do it once a year," he said, stressing that it wasn't anything unusual.

"You can do it twice a year and it still doesn't mean crap to me," I said, still angry about the whole idea. I started to get into the car and Rob held the door open.

"Hey, kid, be reasonable. I want you to treat this matter with more respect. For your information, even the highest guys in the agency agree to take the lie-detector test when they are asked to."

"If ten thousand men do it, that doesn't mean it is right, Rob." I stuck to my guns. I didn't remember ever seeing a greater look of disappointment on anyone's face.

The issue wouldn't die, however, and after a long ugly argument a few weeks later I finally relented. Well, I told myself, the agency's rule is the agency's rule, and if the big boss does it and the officers do it and my case officer does it, I guess I can, too. "If it makes the technician happy," I told Rob, "I will allow him to wire me up." He looked like he wanted to turn cartwheels at the news.

After all the fuss, the test didn't really seem very momentous, either to me or to the CIA, although I did give them one scare, just for meanness. Among all the rather silly questions they asked was one significant one: Besides the CIA, did I work for any other intelligence agency or organization? "Yes," I said, and Rob and the machine operator almost went through the roof. Then I chuckled and added, "I also cooperate with the FBI." From their expressions, I couldn't tell for a moment whether they considered the FBI friendly or not; then they looked at each other and grinned with great relief. "Besides the agency and the FBI, do you work for any other intelligence agency or organization," the operator rephrased the question.

"No, I don't."

And so the CIA had its "proof" that I was their spy and nobody else's, not the KGB's, not the NLF's, not the SRV's. They should have known that from our flesh-and-blood contacts, but if it took a machine to reassure them, that was OK with me.

Chapter 23

My case officer, Rob, and I made yet another trip to Paris after my parents' reunion. I arrived in Paris in the middle of the dreary winter. No snow was on the ground, but there was lots of cold rain and slushy sidewalks. People were bundled in layers of clothing, and the "rummies," or homeless, used the Metro platforms and tunnels to seek shelter from the wind and blowing wetness. The gypsy beggars cursed Mother Nature as they dragged their little ones out of the Metro stations to try new panhandling spots. I gave one little girl five francs and the rest of them ran behind me; I shook my head at them and they all pouted at me.

When Rob had asked me in Washington if I would again register at the Sheraton, I told him I thought it might be best not to become a familiar face at any one place, so this time I checked in at the Hilton. After a short walk and a bite to eat, I was ready to get down to work, so I called the PRG mission to speak to Phan Thanh Nam.

Nam was anxious to see me, but I told him I had some business to take care of first. "What kind of business?" he asked. I told him "I need to place my order as soon as possible so my china can get to Washington." That established my cover with him, and he asked no more questions about my boring "profession."

I also called Pham Gia Thai at the home of his fiancée, Mimi. The girl's mother said Thai could be reached at the Hotel Lutece, a boardinghouse that had been owned by the South Vietnamese government before the end of the war. Now it was SRV property, and Thai was running it as housing for university students.

After making my first two contacts, I took a nap and then got dressed to go out to meet Rob, as we had planned earlier. I remembered that he had warned me to be extremely careful because I had been seen in public on my first trip in the company of SRV officials, and it was possible that French security agents might recognize me if they saw me again. "Dust yourself to and from the hotel, no matter where you go, even to a beauty parlor," I repeated to myself.

This time I decided not to leave my key with the concierge when I went out and not to check in person for messages, all to make it harder for anyone to spot me if they were looking. I could see the pigeonholes for each room anyway as I walked past the front desk, so if there was a message for me I could call from my room to get it.

Rob knew where I was staying, of course, but I never knew where he was. I thought it must be an agency rule, or perhaps just the case officer's own precaution. It was true that we had only known each other since June of 1975, and whenever we worked together I spent half my time with people from the other side, but for a moment I felt a little hurt that perhaps he didn't trust me. Frankly, though, if I had been in his situation I would have slept with a Korean "throwing star" for my protection.

That first day when I started out to meet Rob, I spotted two suspicious-looking Frenchmen sitting in chairs somewhat apart from each other in the hotel lobby. I didn't know if they were agents or not, but I didn't want to take a chance on dragging a tail as big as those two men through the streets of Paris. So I played tourist for a while, stopping to ask the concierge about package tours of the city. I picked up a brochure and walked by the first man with my nose glued to the tour schedule, and when he looked at me I glanced at him and tried to memorize his face. I wasted five minutes in the lobby gift shop, hoping the men would leave, but they sat like lumps in their chairs.

I was determined not to take a chance, so I decided to go into a hair salon. One hour, one shampoo, and a blow-dry later I came out, paid the cashier, and looked down into the lobby. The chairs were now occupied by two Arab women. At least they looked like Arab women; what was under their veils had to be left to chance.

As I walked toward the Metro station, I suddenly spotted the two Frenchmen from the hotel, walking along behind me. I decided to slow down and let them catch up with me, thinking I would have only one chance to "burn" them — that is, to ruin their surveillance. As they drew near, I turned around and took a good look at them, then asked for directions to Printemps, a big department store.

They looked shocked and angry that I had stopped them. One of them brushed me aside and said gruffly in French, "Go ask the police, don't waste my time!" I shot back in English, "You two are the biggest assholes in French intelligence!"

They turned in a hurry and stepped into a puddle on the slushy sidewalk as they left me alone at the gate of the Metro station.

Even though I was already forty-five minutes late for my rendezvous with Rob, I still wouldn't risk being careless. I took a train part of the way to my destination, got off and waited for the next one. Then I got off at Trocadero and walked toward the Museum of Modern Art where Rob would be waiting for me. Our arrangement was that if he was reading a newspaper and smoking a pipe, it would be safe for me to approach him; otherwise, it would mean he had spotted someone tailing me and I should just keep going and ignore him.

Rob was sitting on the steps of the museum, leisurely puffing on his pipe and leafing through a French newspaper as I walked up. "You are clean, kiddo," he smiled. "What took you so long?"

I told him about the two mysterious Frenchmen and he nodded. We walked to a small cafe where the locals gathered, most of them old men playing games at tiny tables. We had Coca-Colas, which cost the equivalent of a dollar each. After a short chat to bring ourselves up to date, we left, Rob going on foot toward Pont D'Iena and I taking a taxi back to the hotel where I had a bottle of Johnny Walker Black for Phan Thanh Nam.

Nam seemed pleased to get the gift of his favorite whisky. He put it in a closet and led me to the kitchen, where he reminded me of my promise to have a drink with him when my mother wasn't present. He opened a bottle of rosé and poured it into two glasses. I noticed a cigarette box in his shirt pocket; he smoked Dunhill, a brand that had always been well-liked by the "bourgeois" Vietnamese.

As I had gotten out of the taxi, I had noticed that the NLF flag out front had been replaced by the red flag of the SRV. I asked him what had happened to the NLF banner, and he gave me a disapproving look. "My Yung, the role of the NLF has reached its achievements. Our country is now unified in one most important task, and that is to stand together as one nation, one Viet Nam. It is time to reunify the North and South." His words sounded more like a lecture than conversation.

"As a former official of the NLF yourself, Uncle Nam, do you sincerely agree with the plan for reunification of the country so soon?"

"Why wait?"

I repeated what my father had told me in October. "To give the NLF time to introduce socialism to the Southerners, because the sudden change by the SRV may result in a misinterpretation by the people of the South."

"What do you mean by that?"

"As you know, our people are not politically minded people," I said. "Most of them only know the NLF, but few people believe the NLF liberated the South. The Southerners feel that they were victimized by the Liberation, and that if the government in Ha Noi goes ahead with the plan to reunify the country, the North Vietnamese cadres will come to the South to govern the Southerners. That will put more fear, more rejection in the hearts of the people in the South. They will take it as an invasion by the North rather than being liberated."

Nam took a long drink of his wine, poured another glass, and looked at me with a dull stare. "You are being brainwashed by the reactionaries, by the unliberated opinions of the capitalists. It is not what you think."

"What I think couldn't be sold for one Ho Chi Minh note, Uncle Nam," I told him. "What people think in the South is what counts. The future of our country is in the hands of the people you govern, not in your hands."

"Listen, My Yung, this talk is just between you and me," Nam said, lowering his voice. "I advise you not to let your opinion float freely. Other people may misunderstand you."

"But you understand me?" I asked, trying to sound eager.

"You have been associated with the wrong type of people while your father was absent, but I expect more from you from now on."

Nam picked up his glass and made a gesture to touch mine in a toast. "To Viet Nam as one independent nation," he intoned. I felt awkward about making that toast; I touched his glass, but didn't drink the wine. I placed my glass on the table and tried to avoid eye contact with him.

Nam walked around the table and sat facing me, rather than next to me as he had before. He seemed a bit more businesslike. "Tell me, My Yung, did your husband ask any questions about your last visit here?"

"He was sad for my parents' situation," I said.

"Did he ask who you met, if you met anyone in the mission?"

"He asked if I took my father and mother out to dinner. He asked where we stayed. He asked if my father asked about him and our son."

"What does he think of the Liberation of our country?" Nam wanted to know.

"Last time he asked me to convey a message to my father, that he sincerely hopes peace will really come to the lives of our people in Viet Nam."

"Don't you two talk about politics?" Nam was incredulous. "What does he think of socialism?"

"We talk a great deal about war and peace in Viet Nam, and he knows that every bone in my body aches for that devastated, war-torn country, that I yearn for a peaceful Viet Nam. And I think he has great empathy for all of us. He respects my father and admires my mother."

Nam got to the point. "Do you think he will help us if and when he is needed?"

"What kind of help?"

"His expertise is vital to Viet Nam," he explained. "The fishing industry in Viet Nam needs scientists like him who know the ocean the way he knows it. He could help our research teams to discover a great many of our natural resources. Through him we may learn more about how to defend our coastal region from the enemy. There is information about antisubmarine warfare —"

Suddenly Nam stopped, as if he had made a gross mistake by being too eager, too greedy. This statement was probably going to be worth a thousand hours of study by the Paris station and the analysts back at Langley. So this little man was gathering information for the SRV government, including information about antisubmarine warfare. I sat there and wondered what in the world Viet Nam could do with that kind of intelligence — trade with the Soviets, I guessed.

Our conversation went off in other directions, but Nam was anxious to get back to the subject of my husband. He wanted me to find a way to tell John that he "would like to obtain information that was done by researchers of the oil companies in America," to learn where they had detected signs of oil deposits off the Viet Nam coast. The second thing he wanted was a map of the coastal natural resources that had been done by the Navy and the government's oceanography experts. The studies involved fishing techniques and the habits and activities of the fish schools in the area. When Viet Nam had all that information, Nam said, "we will have a gold mine in our hands."

He wasn't quite finished. "One more thing, My Yung. Since he is now in the Washington area, perhaps he can help find this one particular piece of information for me. This is for me, because I have been truly interested in it for a long time. The U.S. Navy antisubmarine warfare — what they do and how they do it to compete with the USSR's navy?"

I had to wonder what Nam thought of me while he sat in front of me and asked for all of these things. Perhaps he thought that I loved my father so much I would do anything he asked; or perhaps everyone who had come to him in the past, including Americans, had always been eager to do everything he asked. I said only that I would talk to my husband when I returned home.

After giving me his "shopping list," Nam became rather possessive of his new recruit. When I told him that Thai had taken me to the Vietnamese Union to introduce me to its chairman, Mr. Huynh Trung Dong, Nam protested that I shouldn't be seen with members of the Vietnamese left wing in Paris or elsewhere, "to protect your father as well as our relationship." Nam said I wouldn't be doing much for the country by joining the Union. "All you would be doing is wasting your precious time at meetings," he insisted. "Besides, you can contribute far better when you work with me."

"There are many patriotic Vietnamese in Europe, in the United States, and in other countries who don't join any association, but they are Viet Nam's most valuable contributors," he said. He warned me to be careful from then on what I said to "capitalists" about Viet Nam. "There are people who shouldn't know where you stand in the political arena, and there are people who don't have any business knowing about your background. You should even pretend that you are anti-Communist," he instructed.

It was becoming clear that Nam and Thai had quite different ideas about how to "recruit" me to the cause. Thai wanted me to become involved with the leftists in America to rally support to Viet Nam's side; Nam wanted me to get inside information from the U.S. government. One course would have required me to espouse my "pro-Communist" sympathies openly, the other demanded an "anti-Communist disguise." I, of course, wasn't interested in doing either.

When I submitted my contact report on that meeting, I told my case officer that my husband had a right to know about the parts of the conversation that involved him. I wanted Nam's proposal on the record, and also the fact that John was going to be made aware of it. And, because of Nam's obvious hunger for every kind of American intelligence about Viet Nam, I even suggested that I be allowed to furnish "misinformation" to him. That idea, I knew, would have to be made at the highest level in Langley, the CIA headquarters, perhaps as high as the seventh floor — where the director sat.

Soon people started coming into the mission from various duties at the SRV embassy and elsewhere, and a cook came to prepare dinner. Nam invited me to stay and eat with them, but I told him I had an engagement with some people I did business with. I did indeed, although it had nothing to do with Wedgwood and Spode; I was eager to tell my case officer about Nam's hungry questions.

— — —

I opened the door to my hotel room, walked in and stopped dead in my tracks. Everything was gone! There was not a trace of my belongings anywhere; the wastebaskets were empty, the toilet had been "sanitized."

The concierge on duty was the one who always refused to speak English to me, even though I was certain he could. "Look," I said, "I want to know what happened to my room and to my belongings!"

In his usual arrogant manner he did not reply, but another concierge came rushing out of the back office and pasted a big artificial smile on his face. "May I help you, Mrs. Krall?"

"I want to know what you people have done to my room. Everything is gone!"

"There must be some mistake, Madame," he fumbled. I demanded to see the manager if he couldn't help, but he said the manager wasn't in the hotel at the moment. "I'll check with my staff."

"Please do that," I said. "I am very tired and I need my room back with my things in it." I told him I'd be in the coffee shop. I couldn't make up my mind whether I wanted a glass of milk or a cognac to calm me down. I would have been upset in any case like this, but the fact that I couldn't know whether this was merely a simple, honest mistake had me really shaken.

Half an hour later, when I returned to the front desk, the concierge scurried from behind the counter with a pathetic look on his face. "Madame, we are so sorry that we made a mistake. You see, there is a guest who didn't pay his bill, and instead of throwing him out our chambermaid took your belongings by mistake."

It could have been true, I suppose, but I didn't believe a word he said. "That is unforgivable. I still would like to see the manager."

"Perhaps tomorrow afternoon, Madame, Mr. Charrière will be here. In the meantime, your things are back in your room ready for you now. And we are truly sorry for this rather stupid mistake."

"Please have your Mr. Charrière call me when he comes in tomorrow," I said sternly. Turning away, however, I didn't feel as bold as I had sounded. I felt like running to my room, but I was sure somebody was watching me.

I locked the door behind me and wedged a chair under the knob. Checking to make sure all the windows were locked tight, I drew the drapes and then started going through my suitcase. In a moment I stopped, realizing it was a waste of time; anyone who had gone through my belongings wasn't interested in stealing anything but just wanted to know who I was and what I was doing in Paris.

At least I knew they wouldn't have been able to find any of the rough drafts of my reports to the CIA; every time I finished a report, I would burn the drafts immediately in the sink, then flush the ashes down the toilet.

I had made one mistake, perhaps. I had left in my suitcase one letter from my father, my favorite letter that he had written to me from Milan, Italy, in 1972. Well, I thought, then he could have shared a few tears with his partners.

That night I was so scared I didn't even dare to stand under the shower. When Rob came and I told him what happened, he asked if I wanted to change hotels. I lied: "No, don't worry about me. I'm fine." After he left I wasn't fine at all; I got up the next morning exhausted after a sleepless night of fear.

I had to pull myself together, though, because on this day I was finally going to see Mr. Chau, the son of the Nhuans with whom we lived in Sai Gon when

I was a child. He had come to France for cancer treatment through the special effort of PRG president Tho. My visit was both business and private. In addition to finding out anything useful about what was going on in Viet Nam and among the expatriate community, I wanted to see Mr. Chau for myself and for my mother. She had asked me to visit him to send her regards, and I wanted to see if he was still the man I had had sort of a crush on when I was twelve years old.

At that time, Mr. Chau was the prince of his family, a petroleum engineer working for the Esso Oil company. His job hadn't meant much to me at twelve; I just knew that he was important, worldly, and sophisticated. His villa was smaller than his parents', but it was a modern home. I also knew from Grandfather Nhuan, his father, that "Uncle Chau supports your father."

After getting breakfast at a restaurant — I didn't want to eat in the hotel coffee shop that morning — I bought a few magazines and newspapers to take along as gifts and got a taxi for the Rue de Savoie, where Mr. Chau was convalescing at the home of his father-in-law, Mr. Coa Minh Chiem.

Rue de Savoie was a small street, with far more traffic in dogs and cats than in cars. The lack of activity made it easy for me to realize that I was being followed as I walked toward Mr. Chiem's address. Each time I turned a corner I saw a man behind me; he would disappear into alleys or around the corners of buildings, but then a minute later I would pick him up again.

I didn't want to lead him to Mr. Chiem's house, because this man had been a pioneer revolutionary in my country and I was sure that members of the Vietnamese Communist community came there often, even though I also knew that he was more of a socialist than a true Communist. Mr. Chiem's involvement with Ho Chi Minh dated well back into the French-Indochina war, but he had not wanted to go to Ha Noi at the partition of Viet Nam in 1954. Instead he stayed in the South and organized the Vietnamese People's Self-Determination Movement to fight the Diem regime and the American involvement in his country, using his writing as his best weapon.

He was finally deported to Ha Noi by Diem in 1965, and shortly after that the SRV sent him to Paris to use his talents as a bridge between them and the intellectuals there. He wrote their propaganda and seemed to be "one of them," but in fact his heart had been broken when he saw the atrocities committed by the North when South Viet Nam fell.

Worried about his security, I kept on walking, right past his house, and went into a delicatessen I found on the next corner.

I knew I couldn't hide out there very long; people don't just loiter around in delicatessens, they buy something. I "browsed" for a moment, keeping half an eye on the window, until I saw my "shadow" pass by. The saleswoman got a little impatient and asked me what I wanted. Glancing around, I settled on yogurt and told her to give me two of them. I left a moment later and ate the yogurt as I strolled slowly back up the street. When I was sure the man was no longer in sight, I went quickly to No. 15 and knocked on the door.

A tall, handsome Vietnamese gentleman opened the door and invited me in. "So, you have come to visit Uncle Chau. Let's keep this visit a normal one," he said in a warm voice, laughing a bit. "Don't talk politics to me, I have had enough of it all morning with this sickly person." Even though he was being friendly, I sensed something not quite right in his laughter.

Mr. Chau was lying on a bed in the small studio apartment; oddly, he had covered himself up to his chest with a camouflage blanket, the kind I used to see displayed at the flea market in downtown Sai Gon — the kind that had belonged to the U.S. military. I bent over and clasped the hand he held out from beneath the blanket.

"Papa, this is My Yung, Brother Minh's daughter." Mr. Chau introduced me to his father-in-law who had come to the door.

"Well, now, there is hope for me here," Mr. Chiem said, laughing strange and loud again. "A Communist's daughter is not supposed to say anything bad about Communists in front of an old friend, right?" I assumed it was a joke between Mr. Chiem and his son-in-law, and I didn't try to respond. (Sometime afterward Mr. Chau explained to me that they often argued about the Communists in Viet Nam, and even though he was certain Mr. Chiem's true feelings agreed with his, as a professional he had to defend the people running the SRV. There was no life, after all, for a Communist defector.)

A moment later Mr. Chiem reached for his coat and hat and said he was going off to the store. He asked if Mr. Chau needed anything, but the ailing man said, "If I need anything, she may be able to help me."

I locked the door behind Mr. Chiem after he left and turned back to the man on the bed. My spirits had been high as I was on my way here, looking forward to seeing this person who had touched our lives, whose family had done so much for mine in our time of need. But seeing him now was heart-breaking. He lay on a bed in a tiny apartment, surrounded by old pots and pans, an electric double-burner hot plate, a bottle of old cooking grease, and a tin can that held chopsticks and cooking utensils. Except for the kitchen table and four chairs and Mr. Chau's bed, there was no other furniture, and still the little room was crowded. I counted in my head the number of rooms in Grandmother Nhuan's villa and was sad to see how far her son had sunk.

I was struck, too, by how much Mr. Chau reminded me of his father — except that he looked a hundred years older than when I had last seen him. Suddenly I quivered as I remembered a terrible coincidence: Grandfather

Nhuan had suffered from colon cancer for years, and had died after surgery; now his son had the same illness and had had surgery. So far, though, Mr. Chau was still alive, though he barely looked it.

The room was quiet, except for the sound of water beginning to boil in a kettle I had put on the burner to make tea. I broke the uncomfortable silence: "I have the feeling that Mr. Chiem tried to avoid me. Did I come at a bad time?"

"I was just thinking about him, too," Mr. Chau said. "Yes, he avoided you, as he avoids all of us who were lucky enough to survive the first few years of 'Liberation' and brave enough to tell it like it is."

"It was difficult for my father and me to be together without expressing our differences, too," I told him.

"Speaking of your father, he was one of those I care most about who have been on my mind since I came home from the hospital. He will not fit in with that system," Mr. Chau predicted. "One may argue with me about that, but there has been a great change in the Vietnamese Communist Party since the death of Ho Chi Minh. The Ha Noi communists suppress our people in the South. They are trying to take away key functions in the government from the members of the NLF. They betray the NLF because they listen to the Russians." He struggled to sit up, and placed pillows against the headboard to support his back.

"My father will never speak his mind," I said.

"I had the chance to know him, and I agree with you. He will never protest because 'disagreeing' in that system means 'betraying' the system. Your father will never give up his dream of bringing happiness to his people. He will try in his own way until the day he dies."

"I respect my father for that," I told him, "but from time to time I don't believe it is fruitful. One should have the courage to stand firm for his beliefs, and one should have the serenity to remove himself from his association if it no longer serves his purpose. My father knows damn well that the Ha Noi government will steal and cheat and rape the South as soon as it finishes singing its revolutionary ballads, yet he still 'tries to do his best for the people.' What a lonely and thankless job!"

"Look at me," Mr. Chau said, indicating his dissipated body. "Your father's political situation can be compared to my terminal cancer. Eventually I'll die, but should I commit suicide or should I try to live my life to the fullest each day with people I love? A day is a wonderful period in life, and I began to value each one. I spent most of my money to find the best medical care there is to stay alive so I can see my children, my wife, my mother a little longer, although I live in pain. Sometimes life seems meaningless when I can't eat the things I like, I can't go to the bathroom the way a normal human being could even if he were blind and deaf — but I want to stay around longer.

"As for your father," he continued, "if he speaks out about his disillusion-ment with that system it means an act of suicide. They will put him away in a place for the 'mentally unfit.' And what could he do for people he cares about, then? Now, he still has his influence, and his input into certain deci-sions does wonders for people in the South. Don't ever underestimate your father. He has the serenity to understand the needs of the Vietnamese people and the determination to fulfill those needs. You can't ask more of a man."

We sat quietly for a while and sipped the tea I made. Mr. Chau told me that my father had helped him leave Sai Gon to get better medical care in France, although the biggest help of course came from President Tho. Tho had also promised to speed things up so that Mr. Chau's wife and children would be allowed to leave Viet Nam and join him in Paris. He hoped that his mother would be allowed to come, too.

All of them had lived a horror story in the days after the war, Mr. Chau said. After his father had died, a few years before, Mr. Chau and his wife and chil-dren had moved into the villa with Grandmother Nhuan, and they had been happy there. But the "honeymoon" ended in late autumn of 1976.

A squad of North Vietnamese cadres known as the "Liberators" in the newly renamed "Ho Chi Minh City" had stormed into the house. All the family members and the maid were ordered to sit in the dining room, guard-ed by men with AK-47's, while the rest of the squad ransacked the entire house. When they didn't find what they were looking for, the head of the team started questioning Grandmother Nhuan, demanding to know where she had hidden her gold and money. He wouldn't listen to her insistence that there wasn't any money there, and finally pushed the 70-year-old woman off the chair and began to browbeat Mr. Chau and his wife.

The search went on late into the night, and Grandmother Nhuan was taken away "for further questioning." The rest of the family was thrown out of the house, and were allowed to stay the night in the adjacent servants' quarters. The cadres told Mr. Chau that the villa would be sealed off for the necessary search and that no one would be allowed in but "Liberation officials." Late that night, Mr. Chau's youngest child began crying for her bottle; his wife begged the soldiers to let her go into the villa to get it, but they denied even that — food for a crying baby.

Mr. Chau's expression was pained as he told me how he had been unable to find out any information about the whereabouts of his mother for a whole week. During that time the house was stripped of its antique furniture and everything else. After that the family was allowed to go back into the empty villa, but a few days later the Liberation officials sent a letter saying it was too big for Mr. Chau's family and "suggested" that it be "donated" to the government.

It was then that Mr. Chau first went to President Nguyen Huu Tho, who was an old friend of his parents, to ask for help in locating his mother. Tho pulled a few strings, and a month after her arrest he found her in a jailhouse in Can Tho province, almost 400 kilometers from her home. President Tho went to Can Tho personally to get Grandmother Nhuan out of the jail and brought her back to Sai Gon. When she got there, Mr. Chau found out that her "Liberators" had forced her to sign over all her properties in the Mekong Delta, her rental houses in Bac Lieu, her rice mills in Can Tho, and everything else she owned. All of it now belonged to "the people."

"I can bear the loss of our properties," Mr. Chau told me. "After all, my family was in the process of signing over many of my parents' properties to the government already. But the humiliation that my little children had to witness caused more pain in my heart than I can stand. The cadres shouted at Grandmother, pushed her off the chair, called my wife names, denied my baby her milk. The kids will never be able to forget that." I looked away for a moment, so he wouldn't be embarrassed by my seeing the tears in his eyes.

Mr. Chau had a confession of sorts to make to me. In April of 1975, when my mother was getting ready to leave Sai Gon, she had come to see him and Grandmother Nhuan and asked if they wanted to get out, too. At that time, he said, he told his family that "she allowed her children to marry his adversaries. She has every reason to leave, but we should stay to enjoy the fruits of Liberation." He knew better now, although he said that in a way he was almost glad they didn't leave at that time. Because his children had seen the ugly truth that followed, he said, there was no chance that they could grow up to be fooled by "any of those SOBs" again.

Leaving the sad, personal things behind, we began to talk about conditions inside Viet Nam — the currency exchange rates, the price of gold, the cost of rice and fresh meat and produce. Everything had been skyrocketing in the past few months, he said. Without saying why, I asked if he would mind if I wrote some of those things down in a notebook. He not only didn't mind, he encouraged me. "You should share this information with the U.S. government, if not the press. It is about time the West knew how stupid and naive they were during the Viet Nam War. Henry Kissinger should bury his head in the mud for participating in the Paris Peace Talks; it was in the control of Ha Noi almost 85 percent of the time."

Lunchtime was approaching, and I offered to go out and get some food at the market and prepare a meal for him. He declined, however, suggesting instead with a chuckle that we both go out. "I'm going to die anyway, let me sit in my favorite place in St. Michel with my compatriot for one last time." He crawled out of bed and drew a curtainlike partition between us so he could get dressed. I tied his shoes for him because it hurt for him to bend down. Then I helped him into a heavy coat and we walked to a cozy little restaurant, Mr. Chau holding onto my arm for support.

We had a long lunch and a bottle of his favorite wine. We were near the Sorbonne, and Mr. Chau said it was in this neighborhood that he had really developed his own interest in communism, even though his parents had been sympathizers. He had later married a woman who shared his convictions; she had been jailed by the Thieu regime for supporting the NLF, just a few months before the fall of Sai Gon.

A broken soul inside a broken body, Mr. Chau walked alongside me back to the Rue de Savoie. We stopped in at a bookstore, a record shop, and an art gallery on our way back. The sun was hiding behind the gray sky; the cold, dreary day seemed to reflect the sadness of the story I had just heard and all the pain that afflicted my country. I wanted to go back to my hotel and close the door to the world and try to wash the whole sorry business out of my mind.

With the help of President Tho, Mr. Chau's mother, wife, and children were allowed to leave the newly liberated Viet Nam a couple of months later and join Mr. Chau in Paris. He died less than a year after he was reunited with his family.

— — —

The hotel room door slammed against the wall with a great crash and bounded back toward me again. I had thrown it open as hard as I could on purpose, hoping to scare anybody who might be inside. But all was normal; my suitcase still sat in the same position I had left it. I walked in, still a little cautious.

Flowers! A huge bunch of fresh flowers sat beautifully arranged on the coffee table. I knew it wasn't my birthday, and Ho Chi Minh's birthday was still three months away, so what could be the occasion? Next to the crystal vase was a card addressed to me; it was from the hotel manager, Andre F. Charrière, who wrote, "Avec les compliments, vous souhaite de continuer trés agréablement votre séjour au Paris Hilton."

It was either a genuinely kind gesture, or the manager was cooperating with whomever had taken my belongings out of my room. I didn't know what to think. While I was standing there trying to figure it out, my case officer dropped in unexpectedly. After I told him where the flowers had come from and what had happened, he made a gesture not to talk.

Then Rob examined each and every one of the flowers, petal by petal and stem by stem. When all the flowers were out of the vase he emptied the water in the sink and peered into the bottom of it. At first I was holding my breath, waiting to see what he would find, but by the fourth stem it had become comical. I couldn't help it anymore, and I burst out laughing. When he had finished, I asked, "What were you looking for?"

"You might be bugged," Rob said softly. He wasn't laughing.

I filled the vase with water and put the flowers back in, although I was sure my arrangement wouldn't fool anybody who was looking for changes in the room. Just then there was another knock at the door. Rob had been so preoccupied looking for microphones in the flowers that he had forgotten to tell me that his boss from the Paris station had decided he wanted to meet Rob's "superstar."

It was with considerable pleasure that I met Dan Andrew, the station chief; I knew that the U.S. government wouldn't have sent a man of that rank to meet an agent if the agent wasn't trusted. Yes, I still wondered from time to time if I was completely trusted, not only by the agency but even by my case officer. To my surprise Dan Andrew handed me a bottle of Christian Dior perfume and said, "Happy Valentine's."

Our meeting was short. Andrew said his particular interest was Phan Thanh Nam, and he wanted me to complete a target "profile" on Nam as soon as possible. A few days before Rob had brought me this standard form, which contained many blanks where the agent was supposed to fill in details about the target's physical characteristics, personality, habits, and activities. At that time I had jokingly said it would be easy to describe Nam: "Short, strong cheek bones, heavy drinker and smoker, often talks about women, especially European women. Comment: dirty tricks are highly recommended against target. Note: target doesn't drive a car, reason unknown — perhaps afraid to be caught DUI."

In fact, when I filled out the form for Andrew I included most of those same things, although I went on to a full extra page with details. My final report included my recommendation of some kind of action against Nam.

Chapter 24

$\mathcal{H}$ome again, I returned my focus to Ambassador Thi in New York, and his mention of the "stuff" Truong Dinh Hung had been sending him. I was more certain than ever that Hung was deeply involved in smuggling some kind of information to the SRV government, first through Nam in Paris and now through the UN mission in New York.

I wanted to learn much more about him, so I needed to get closer to him. I thought one avenue might be another "task" I had, one that had been given to me by Mr. Dong in Paris. He had in mind that I might be able to start a Vietnamese American Association, so as a start he wanted me to study the structure as well as the nature of the existing Vietnamese Patriot Association in America. In order to do that, he urged me to mix in with the members of the Patriots' chapter in the Washington area.

When I mentioned Dong's intentions to Hung, however, he had a negative reaction. In the tone of a brother giving advice to his little sister, he said, "If you want to get ahead in this business, don't let yourself get mixed up with people in the association. They are a bunch of opportunists and troublemakers."

Unlike his friend Thoa, Hung had removed himself from association activities, and had said things to make the members believe that he had an important mission working directly for the SRV government. He told me, in fact, that he was not on good terms with the chairman of the association, Mr. Luy of San Francisco, but that didn't bother him because "I deal with different people in higher places." He still had friends within the organization, though, people who would report to him on its activities, gossip, and any other developments. More than once, Hung tried to advise me not to "mingle" with the association, but just to "stick with the tasks that Nam gives you." I think he thought I was serving as Nam's spy, perhaps keeping an eye on him as a cross-check of his activities.

Well, I "mingled" just the same. I ate with members of the Washington chapter, met with them on weekends and late into many weeknights. The chairman began to be a little uncomfortable about me because he couldn't control me; he repeatedly sent me applications to join his group, but I repeatedly refused. I wrote and told him that I supported him and would assist the association whenever I could, but that it would be safer for his organization and me if I didn't join, because I directly contacted people in the SRV embassies and their "agents" overseas.

Luy didn't give up easily, but when I finally asked Dong to advise him diplomatically that he shouldn't worry about my independent status, he wrote to me that "I finally understand your position." He went on, though, to say, "Your contact with us is vital. Please keep in touch and we hope to meet you on the West Coast soon."

Because I let Mr. Luy know that my duty to Mr. Dong in Paris was to report to him about the association in America, I got red-carpet treatment when I visited him. It also automatically made me record at each local meeting I attended, since the members believed I was sent by Paris to inspect and spy on the association.

Ironically, the more I learned from the members of the Vietnamese Patriot Association, the less important it seemed to be. It was an ailing organization, hampered by many power struggles among its leaders and branches. The D.C.-area chapter, for instance, was not on good terms with Mr. Luy and the West Coast chapter. On my first visit to San Francisco in autumn of 1976, Mr. Luy brought me into a meeting at his house with the entire board of this organization, and they tried to draw me into the fight between them and the Washington chapter. I made a few innocuous comments about the D.C. group, such as "They're waiting for your direction, the soldiers are there but we don't have a leader." They pumped me for more substantive things they could use against their rivals, but I declined to get involved.

Despite its internecine battles, the group was a good source of intelligence for the American agencies. The association was a political tool for the SRV, trying to recruit American scientists and others who could be helpful in getting badly needed technology or other benefits for Viet Nam. Because Luy believed that I was reporting to Ambassador Sung and to Dong about his activities, he always put on a "show and tell" performance every time I saw him. He told me the names of people involved with the organization in other parts of the United States, and about various projects that were under way to drain technology from America.

On one trip to San Francisco, I got a chance to see close up the fruits of some of the association's efforts to recruit sympathetic Americans. Luy threw a party at his house in honor of one Dr. Edward Cooperman, a physicist from California State–Fullerton who had been persuaded by association members to form something called the U.S.–Viet Nam Science and Technology Committee, a group of about seventy people that sponsored visits to Viet Nam for people who wanted to work in medical research and educational institutions there.

Cooperman had just returned from a trip to Viet Nam, and at the party it was announced that he was going to have a slide show afterward in an undisclosed location. I wanted to let Bill Fleshman, the FBI agent, know about this, while I observed the way the association conducted its clandestine meetings, so I looked for a way to get a message to him. There was a young man who had come to the party in a classic old Thunderbird, so I feigned interest in his "cute little car" and asked if he would give me a ride. He did, and while we were driving along the waterfront I asked if he would stop at a drugstore. There, I paid a clerk a dollar to let me use the telephone, and I told Bill what was up. Since I didn't know where we were going, I said, his people would have to use a helicopter to trail the group. "No problem," he said. Besides, he added, agents were already watching the party from a van across the street from Luy's house and they would also be watching to see where everyone went.

At 9:30 Luy told everyone to get into designated vans and cars — not their own — and head off to the slide show. I climbed into the front seat of a van in which Dr. Cooperman was already sitting with a young Vietnamese man, apparently friends for a good while to judge from their conversation. I spotted the FBI van behind us, but after a while I didn't see it anymore. The helicopter did keep the motorcade in sight, however, and directed the agents on the ground to the high school auditorium where the program was eventually held.

There was nothing exciting or glamorous about spy work that night, as I sat through Dr. Cooperman's homemade slide show of his trip. The only good thing about it from my point of view was that it seemed that his escorts had only allowed him to photograph the positive side of the Liberation, so I got to see my country green and beautiful and my people with smiling faces.

The doctor gave a short talk about his meetings with the scientific community in Ha Noi and promised to do more for Viet Nam with the help of his American associates.

When we left the auditorium I was surprised to see "our comrades" the Iranians, about six of them, acting as guards outside the big double door. Luy told me that it was extremely difficult for his group to have meetings without disruptions — fist fights, rock throwings, or even baseball-bat beatings — by "reactionaries," meaning South Vietnamese students and supporters. For that reason, they needed bodyguards.

I saw the kind of confrontation he described once, when a fight broke out at San Jose State during the showing of a movie I had brought back from Paris, a propaganda film entitled *The Spring Victory*. Halfway through the show, a South Vietnamese refugee threw a smoke bomb into the auditorium. As the place began to clear out, a big Iranian bodyguard whom Luy had assigned to protect me quickly took me by the arm and led me out the back door where a small army of his countrymen stood waiting. It was then I discovered the strange relationship between the leftist Vietnamese community and the Iranians in America; as my protector told me that day, "You people protect us from the Immigration, we protect you from the hoodlums."

For all Luy's hatred of Americans, he left a definite impression on me that was not all bad. Out of the memory of his mother, who he believed was still alive in Ha Noi, he owned and ran a rest home in Montana, California, for old people, caring for them as if they were his own parents. He carefully planned their menus and cooked for their special diets, and he listened carefully to their problems and did everything he could to solve them.

Luy greatly disliked and distrusted Truong Dinh Hung, to the point that he whispered to me that he believed Hung might be engaged in espionage for the "other side," and that I had better be careful not to get in trouble because of Hung.

Hung was engaged in espionage, but it was wholly in the service of the SRV. One of the reasons Luy didn't like him was that Hung was virtually untouchable because of his direct connection with the intelligence people, and that bothered Luy, whose ambition was to be able to control every leftist Vietnamese in the United States.

After Thoa succumbed to the "weeding out" process of the new leadership of the Liberation and moved to Santa Monica where her husband lived, Hung and I started to meet more frequently. He showed considerable interest in my "import and export business" — my cover for spy work — and at one time he pressed me to know what kind of resources I would need to start such a business and where I got the money. I told him I had needed a lot of money for initial capital, since china and crystal are expensive, but my husband's grandmother had left her only grandson a lot of money when she died so we were able to go into our venture. After I told him that I only wished it were the truth!

Hung must have had some doubts about me, or perhaps it was just his nature, but he frequently asked me quite pointed questions about myself and my activities. That became an advantage to me, though, because in return I could ask him some things rather directly as well. Once I held out what I suspected would be a tantalizing prospect to him: "How would you like to be something equal to the chief of the CIA station when we [the SRV] have normal diplomatic relations with the United States?" I was curious to know just how ambitious and confident he really was. Of course I couldn't offer this to him, but Hung had become so desperate to find an important position for himself in the new government that he became careless.

"I know how to operate in this country," he bit eagerly. "I could be effective!"

"I promised Phan Thanh Nam I would show him the town when he first comes here," I said, meaning that I wanted him to meet the agents and sources I worked with in the Vietnamese community.

"That is one reason you and I shouldn't get mixed up with the association," Hung reminded once again.

— — —

By the spring of 1977 I was deeply involved in a working relationship with Truong Dinh Hung, who I learned was better known in the United States as David Truong. After delivering the big collection of books and papers to Dong in Paris for him and his friend the previous year, I had brought back a letter from Dong to David Truong. Both men now considered me to be a reliable courier.

In mid-March, Dong wrote me a letter brimming with good news. He had just come back to Paris from Ho Chi Minh City, where he had been accepted into membership in the Communist Party of Viet Nam. His tone was bubbly, and he wrote that "in the history of the Vietnamese Communist Party, up until this day, I am the first and only overseas cadre leading the Vietnamese Union to receive this honor." This news meant more to the CIA station chief in Paris and the CIA analysts at Langley than just the fact that Huynh Trung Dong was now literally a "card-carrying Communist"; it told them much about the importance of his position, his duties, and tasks and how he and his organization fit into the hierarchy in Viet Nam.

In the same letter, Dong asked me to try hard to come to Paris in May for a meeting with delegates from Vietnamese organizations all over the world, including London, Rome, Tokyo, West Berlin, and the United States. One of the attractions, he said, would be the possibility of meeting Premier Pham Van Dong, who was coming to speak to the representatives of the worldwide network. He asked me to tell David Truong if I could make the trip.

I didn't have to ask Rob and Bill twice; they thought it would be a fruitful trip for both the CIA and the FBI. I started making plans to be in Paris by April 22.

The same day I talked with the agents I went to see David Truong with the news from Dong's letter. I studied his face to gauge his reaction, but I could tell he already knew about Dong's acceptance into the party. He also knew about the premier's visit to Paris, but more important he knew of a meeting that would be held there soon between a U.S. delegation from the State Department and a group from Ha Noi. I didn't have to pretend to be surprised at hearing that report, because I hadn't known it before.

Over lunch that day, David told me that he was going to give me some materials to ferry to France, and he carefully instructed me that I was to "deliver the stuff to Dong, not to Nam." He also dropped another little bombshell. In Washington, he told me, it's easy to operate in the intelligence business as long as you make the right connections; his connection was "a man who has a pass to the seventh floor at the State Department — he can get anything he wants."

This piece of information kept FBI director Clarence Kelley and Deputy Secretary of State Warren Christopher busy for months to come, and eventually led to the culmination of my career as a spy catcher for the United States.

Three days before I was to leave for Paris, I drove my Ford Bronco into D.C. to pick up the "stuff" that David had asked me to carry. I pulled up curbside at our prearranged spot in front of his workplace on K Street; three cars behind me was an FBI surveillance team. David handed me a large sealed manila envelope, heavily packed with papers, the material intended for Dong, and a business-size envelope for Nam. The following day he phoned me and asked me to meet him again, "same time, same place," to pick up another package. He said he didn't want me to have too much material in my possession at one time, but I knew that he was being cautious — there was something in that second manila envelope that he didn't want me to have any longer than necessary before my trip.

And so at 12:15 on April 21 I drove back to K Street, this time in my little Datsun. I was being cautious, too, because I didn't want all of David Truong's associates to know me. Earlier he had told me that he had met a Soviet on the steps of Capitol Hill and that "the Soviets are too demanding." I assumed, therefore, that there was a Soviet somewhere in his life and that the packages he wanted me to carry contained some of our national secrets. "Don't ask me why or how I know they're our secret documents," I told Bill Fleshman when I handed the two big envelopes over to him, "my gut feelings tell me they are."

The FBI didn't want to rely on gut feelings, so as soon as they got their hands on the packages they began working to get permission from the Justice Department to open them. On the morning of April 22, however, a disappointed-looking Bill Fleshman returned them to me, still sealed; there had not been enough time for the legal process to be completed.

"I could postpone my trip," I suggested. "Who says I have to leave tonight?" But Bill said I had better stick to my schedule, so at 4:45 that afternoon I was at Dulles waiting for my plane. Suddenly I heard my name being paged on the public-address system, asking me to come to the Pan Am ticket counter. I walked there and saw Rob standing in line, with no baggage in sight. I got in line behind him, and without looking at me — in fact he was looking down at his watch — he mumbled, "Cancel your flight. Take a taxi home."

Back at the house, he and Bill told me that my suggestion of delaying the trip had been accepted. I gave them back the "stuff" and off they went. Their "superstar spy" then spent most of the day Saturday attacking dandelions in the back yard and planting an oak tree in the front of the house.

At 2:00 P.M. Rob called and said Bill would bring the packages back soon and that I should plan to leave that afternoon on the 6:20 TWA flight. When Bill came, I stopped him at the door and asked him not to tell me if the envelopes had been opened.

Because I had to make my reservation on such short notice, all the economy seats were booked and so the agency had to fly me to Paris first class. I teased Bill that the FBI would probably have to make up the difference with the CIA, and he smiled and said he would buy lunch for me and Rob when we got back.

It was a chilly Sunday morning when I arrived in Paris, and for the first time in my life I felt guilty as I went through customs. Ahead of me, almost all the passengers except a few senior citizens were having to open their bags for the customs inspectors. As they waited for me to open my heavy suitcase, my mind raced along, trying to come up with clever stories in case they asked me to open those sealed manila envelopes which I was sure were filled with secret American government documents — I am a student of political science; I am studying anthropology, and Vietnamese are my subjects. Nonsense, I thought; no matter what story I tell, they'll throw me in the slammer! I had a telephone number to call the CIA in an emergency, but we had never even talked about this kind of emergency yet.

All my sweating was for nothing. The only thing the French customs officer wanted to see was my receipt for the Black Russian cigarettes I had bought in a duty-free shop as gifts for the ambassador — they were his favorite brand.

I checked in at the Intercontinental Hotel, an impressive place that was a world apart from the other places I had stayed. A lavish brunch was being served on the Terrasse Fleurie, and I could smell the coffee as I walked by on my way to my room, but all that would have to wait. I needed sleep.

— — —

My "slave driver," Rob, woke me up around 1:00 P.M. and asked if he could come over to my hotel to see me. We met for about twenty-five minutes, and then my workday began. I grabbed a quick lunch in a little cafe on the Rue de Rivoli and took a taxi to see Phan Thanh Nam.

I wasn't carrying the packages of secret documents around with me. Before I left the room I had searched for a safe place to hide them. As it happened, the hotel was undergoing renovation and my room was not quite completed; in the back of the closet there was a small door that led into a dark space, apparently a temporary access for electricians. I doubted that any workers would be there on Sunday, so I put the two envelopes behind the door and hung my clothes in front of it.

I surprised Nam when he answered the doorbell. I know it wasn't good etiquette to drop in unannounced that way, but I wanted to find out what Nam did on an ordinary Sunday afternoon. Perhaps he wouldn't be there, I thought, and the housekeeper might be able to tell me something interesting. No such luck; Nam was at the mission, reading "Communist studies."

He was delighted when I gave him the letter delivered from David Truong, but he didn't waste much time on pleasantries. Mostly he wanted to know if I had made any progress on recruiting someone he had mentioned to me on my last visit — a high-level State Department official who was married to a Vietnamese woman whose aunt was the famous NLF army general, Vo Thi Dinh. His idea was to get the woman to contact her aunt in Viet Nam, and then Nam's people in Washington would move in on the target, perhaps trying blackmail of some sort since the official's sister-in-law was still in Viet Nam and married to an NLF officer.

Nam hadn't known it when he talked to me about this "project," but that official and his wife happened to be my friends. The man had served a tour of duty in Viet Nam and had been one of the last Americans to leave in April 1975. I had of course passed on Nam's "creative" idea to the State Department. I only told him that it was a difficult task and that he would have to be patient. He said that some of his people had driven by this couple's home and had taken some pictures of their children, but had been unable to identify him and her yet. When he said that, a cold shiver of fear ran down my spine.

The next day, when I arrived at the Vietnamese Union headquarters, things were strangely quiet, even though there were more people than usual in the reading room. The old, yellow mutt that hung around the offices was nervous with so many strangers on the premises; he didn't bark, but he stood stiffly at the door, blocking my entrance, until the old housekeeper kicked him in the ribs to run him off.

Dong took me into a room where I saw four men dressed in identical dark suits, all wearing Ho Chi Minh pins in their lapels; they were obviously officials from Ha Noi. I was introduced only to a Ms. Van, who was described as Madame Binh's personal aide who had been with her during the Paris Peace Talks. Van was now serving in the NLF foreign ministry, spending most of her time in Cuba and Paris.

My instinct told me that all these mysterious people were waiting for something significant that day; their expressions were anxious, full of anticipation. I suspected that what they were waiting for was me — or, rather, the material I was bringing from David Truong. I handed Dong a hotel laundry bag containing the two manila envelopes and said, "I've got a present for you." He took out the envelopes and said, "You've come in the nick of time." One of the men at the table reached hungrily for the materials, and as they began to open it like kids at Christmas, Dong led me off to his office.

As we left the room I heard Ms. Van remark, "This will take at least five hours to translate!" I wondered to myself, "Would you rather the State Department's translators handle that for you next time?"

Dong took me to lunch and praised me for bringing the materials. "The right people back home" would hear of my contribution, he promised.

"So when will our delegation meet the Americans?" I asked.

"Soon, soon. And it should be to our favor this time. We'll know ahead of time what they want to talk about. That's why your timing is so great." He was absolutely pleased with me and the information.

"What are our people going to talk about with them?"

"The same issue, that the United States must keep Nixon's promise." He referred to the Communist claim that President Nixon had made a secret promise of $3.5 billion in aid after the end of the fighting "to heal the wounds of war."

I couldn't help but think as we talked that while Phan Thanh Nam used me like I would use a lemon for juice, Huynh Trung Dong cultivated me like a fruit tree. There was goodness in Dong, love for his country and its people. He bore pain and disappointment, too, after his return to Viet Nam, where he had seen the suffering caused by wrongdoing by some of the revolutionary soldiers and high-ranking officials.

Dong had come from a wealthy family in the South, the son of a city councilman in the French era. His ailing father had been robbed of his wealth, and his sister, who was a widow, had been forced to give up her house as a "donation" to the Liberation and move in with her father. When Dong's father had been sick, he had been unable to get proper medical care until Dong took advantage of his position to write to some "big shots" in Ho Chi Minh City for help.

Dong told me he would get me a security pass so I could ride the bus with the Vietnamese group to Orly Airport to greet Premier Pham Van Dong when he arrived for the big meeting. I wasn't crazy about that idea, but I was looking forward to attending the big reception at the new SRV embassy, and Dong promised to get me an invitation soon. "You can't go near the embassy that day" without it, he informed me.

Later that week, however, when I saw Nam again, he asked me not to go to the airport and not to attend the reception. Still thinking about using me as a spy and recruiter in the United States, he said he didn't want the American informers who would certainly be present to see me and identify me. "I don't want you to become a familiar face in this community," he cautioned.

I didn't go to the airport, because Nam had told me not to, but I thought it was important for American interests that I get a close look at the ailing premier, Pham Van Dong, regardless of what Nam wanted. So rather than attending the reception with an official invitation, I simply stood in a long line outside the embassy for an hour and a half with all the other common people, going through a body search at the entrance, to see his public appearance. He joined the group for only about fifteen minutes, so there wasn't much to see or report. I did find the crowd interesting, though — many Vietnamese, some old French colonialist soldiers, a few Corsicans with their Vietnamese war brides. The meeting was a display of the kind of patching up of old differences and forging of a new friendship between France and Viet Nam that the premier had come to Paris to establish.

I spent eighteen pleasant spring days in Paris, working from ten in the morning until midnight meeting and talking to people, then staying up well after that writing reports on what I saw and heard. Some of the people I met with were old NLF supporters who had become disillusioned when they saw what was happening after the "liberation." Those meetings usually ended with sadness, tears, and frustration when the questions about the future of our country under the Communists couldn't be answered.

— — —

While I was away in Paris, the FBI had gotten busy finding out more about David Truong and his "friend with a pass to the seventh floor of the State Department." Beginning an operation that became known as "Magic Dragon," they began tapping Truong's telephone, and several hundred calls were intercepted. Many of them were in Vietnamese — including some conversations with me — and so the FBI's interpreter had a heavy load of work.

It only took a couple of days, however, to hear the one conversation the FBI really wanted to hear — one in which Truong asked a man named Ron to meet him at his apartment. The FBI was watching when the man showed up later that night, May 13. They followed him when he left David's apartment and trailed him to the offices of the U.S. Information Agency (USIA). By checking the register at the front desk, they found out that he was Ronald Louis Humphrey, a USIA official. He had top-secret clearance.

All this was happening without my participation, or even my knowledge, but I later found out that the operation had really gotten serious when the FBI found out that one of Truong's contacts had access to material classified top secret. Attorney General Griffin Bell gave them authorization to bug Truong's apartment, and with President Carter's permission a television camera was hidden in Humphrey's office.

Meanwhile, I returned from Paris with a letter from Nam to David Truong. Judge Bell got President Carter to let the FBI open it. Nam had written, "I applaud your business plans. . . . Very often there are efforts to swindle and deceive one another." I don't know exactly what that meant to Truong, but when I delivered the letter to him later he smiled to himself as he read it.

Truong smiled more broadly when I told him I thought he had done something significant by sending his two packages of materials to Paris in time for the meeting between the American and Ha Noi delegations. I told him that Dong had asked him to keep working hard, but had advised him to take good care of himself.

Suddenly David gave me a piece of advice. He asked if I had a lawyer, and when I said I didn't he suggested I retain a good one right away. I don't know if he had any particular reason to be worried about things, but he told me that in our line of "work" it was wise to have a lawyer handy.

Along about this time, David invited me to his apartment for tea for the first time. It was Father's Day, so John took Lance fishing with a friend near Quantico, and I went into D.C. to the apartment on F Street. The place was neat and clean, full of books and magazines and stacks of newspapers, but it was almost too clean; there were no flowers, no plants, almost no colors. The room seemed lifeless.

As I looked around at the sterile place and I thought of David Truong's rather meaningless existence as a committed agent, I thought of my brother Hai Van and the good life I know he would have led if he had not died. At that moment, part of me wanted to jump up and grab David and tell him that the game was over. Get your parents out of Viet Nam, I wanted to say. Get out of that mailroom and get a real job, use your education. Wake up from your dream, David, or it will turn into a nightmare!

He startled me out of my thoughts when he placed the teapot on the coffee table in front of me. We drank our tea and enjoyed some idle conversation. I didn't really want to talk, and I didn't want him to say very much either, because I knew the FBI was listening and that every sound we made was being heard.

Shortly before this meeting my husband, John, had received orders to go to London. I had told David I was going, and so during my visit to his apartment, we made plans for me to pick up some more "stuff" before I left to take with me and carry on to Paris when I had a chance. School was out for the summer by then, so on the day I was to pick up the documents I took Lance with me. I pulled up in front of David's workplace on M Street at the appointed time, but there was no sign of him. I drove around the block three times, but he still didn't show up. I couldn't linger there much longer and risk being noticed by the wrong people, so I left.

As we crossed the Memorial Bridge, Lance was sitting on his knees in the back seat, looking out the rear window. "Mom," he told me cheerily, "I think we're being followed."

"Don't be silly," I laughed.

"Really, there's been a white car and a blue car following us since you were driving around over there. Look!"

"I can't look now, Lance. There are all kinds of white cars and blue cars, honey." I was almost dying from trying to suppress my laughter. I knew the FBI agents who were driving those two cars, and I also knew they wouldn't be happy to know that a six-year-old boy had been able to pick up their tail so easily.

At Arlington Cemetery, I stopped and the two agents joined us and I told them about the missed connection. For the rest of the day I tried to call David, but it wasn't until 10:30 that he got home. He insisted that he had just gotten the date of our rendezvous mixed up, thinking it was supposed to be the following day. We set another date, and then perhaps to convince me he really had made an honest mistake, he informed me that "today at noon, right at that time, I ran over to the Congress to get a package of that stuff." Knowing that his phone was tapped, I panicked for a split second; somehow I was still worried on his behalf.

That evening, we met in the parking lot of the Hecht Company store at the Landmark Shopping Center, and David took a shopping bag stuffed with papers out of his car. I took the bag and promised I would deliver it to Dong as he requested.

He suggested we have a cup of coffee, so we stopped into a small shop in the rear of the mall and chatted for a while. As we were about to go our separate ways, David extended his hand and wished me well in London. Suddenly, out of a feeling of compassion for a young man who was my compatriot, even if he was a spy, I hugged him and almost went to pieces. "Take good care of yourself, Hung," I told him. "Promise me you will take a vacation. Go to Boston and see your friends!"

I ran to my car, and he stood there staring at me. He must have thought I was not as dedicated as he was.

I felt an uncomfortable inner conflict when I pulled out of the parking lot and saw the FBI surveillance car and some familiar faces leave right behind me. I burned up the road to Springfield, then turned into the parking lot in back of a Holiday Inn. There, Bill Fleshman and several other agents I knew were waiting for me. I handed Bill the brown shopping bag of documents and in my strange mood I said, "Do whatever you want with it, I don't want to see it anymore." Everything was blurry in my eyes as I drove away from them.

Chapter 25

It was now time to concentrate on the move to London. Being a navy wife, I was certainly accustomed to moving, but this was a little different. My biggest concern was the safety of my family if we were living outside the United States; another was the higher cost of living in European capitals. When I mentioned those two things to Rob, he insisted I had nothing to worry about on either count. If I continued to observe the kinds of safety precautions I had always done, then John and Lance and I would be as secure as any other navy family living in London, he said. And as for the money problem, "You will get an extra five hundred dollars a month to cover the high cost of living," he promised.

As usual, when it came to money, things weren't as simple as they seemed. Some time later, when our plans were well along, I was discussing details with Rob and happened to ask how I would get paid while I was in London and he was in Washington. "I will deposit your seven hundred dollars in your account at the Virginia bank each month," he said, "so don't close that account when you leave for London."

The CIA must have spent a lot of time training its people in psychological warfare in Viet Nam and Laos, because Rob seemed unable to stop trying to play mind games with me now. When I corrected him, "You mean twelve hundred dollars," he came back with an entirely new story. "It is impossible that you ask for that much raise at one time. I can get you a step increase, which is fifty dollars more than you get now, and that is the best I can do for you."

Of course, I had asked for no raise at all; my current salary was seven hundred dollars a month and Rob himself had volunteered the number five hundred dollars as the cost-of-living differential, and in anybody's system of arithmetic that adds up to twelve hundred dollars. I realized that there was no point in getting involved in the game, so I demanded to see his finance officer or someone higher up who could give me a straight answer. He thought about it for a moment, then said, "I don't care who you talk to. You are not getting a five-hundred-dollar pay raise."

"I have not asked for a raise. I only reminded you of your commitment. I didn't agree to move to London because of that miserable five hundred dollars, but that five hundred dollars will help me to pay a higher rent, food costs, fuel costs, and other necessities. I do not like it when you bend my words. Stop playing games with me, Rob," I pleaded. "This is not the Viet Nam jungle, this is America!"

He wasn't happy, but the next day at a CIA "safe house" in Crystal City, Virginia, I got to meet with a man described to me as "our finance officer." After all the stormy argument with Rob, I was surprised to find that this man asked me practically no questions at all — but agreed to the cost-of-living differential figure that Rob had given me weeks before. Considering how important and meaningful the work was that we were doing for the U.S. government and the American and Vietnamese people, I could never understand how the CIA could be so petty over something like a few hundred dollars' pay for someone who was trying to help.

By the middle of July 1977, we packed for London. My husband had gotten his new assignment with CINCUSNAVEUR (Commander in Chief U.S. Navy Europe) there, my sister Hoa Binh moved out into an apartment of her own in Alexandria, my mother and Minh Tam went to Atlanta to live with Kim, and Lance's dog Moon Joe went to live with our friends Thuy and Bruce Stader in Herndon, Virginia.

John and I found a lovely house that belonged to a British Air Force officer who was serving at the British embassy in Washington, and we happily arranged to rent it. About a week after we moved into the house at 8 Regal Lane, I had a dream that Rob and Bill Fleshman came to London together to see me, and Bill asked me if I would testify in court if the Justice Department decided to prosecute David Truong. The next morning I told John about the dream and we both laughed over the idea that I was becoming a spy even in my sleep.

A week later, Bill appeared at my front door.

"Don't tell me," I said. "You came to tell me that they want to arrest David Truong!"

He looked stunned. "Gee, Yung, you made it so easy for me. I've been up half the night trying to find the right words to tell you."

After we sat down at our small dining table, Bill explained that the Justice

Department had sent him and Rob, along with two attorneys from Justice and the CIA, to talk to me about the possibility of cooperating in the prosecution of David Truong and the American at the USIA.

This first, formal meeting was brief, and Rob and Bill arranged for another meeting in a safe house to meet with the two lawyers and get into some serious discussion. I asked Bill to wait until the next morning, so I could have time to pull my thoughts together, and he agreed.

That night I was still awake at two o'clock in the morning, worrying about a choice that seemed tougher than me. I knew that if I testified at a public trial, it would mean the end of my undercover work. The Communists would learn that I had been fooling them about my interest all this time, and all those doors that my father's name had opened for me would slam shut. I knew, too, that it could mean the end of Rob's career as a case officer, if he had to testify and reveal his name and face to the world. Mostly, though, I was concerned about what might happen to my family. The Communists had my father and Khoi, and I could only imagine the horrors they could inflict on them if they chose. I took a sleeping pill and finally dropped off, still not certain what I should — or could — do.

The next morning at the Reeve House, the CIA safe house in London, John and I were introduced to Tony Lapham, the chief counselor at the CIA, and John Martin, an attorney from the Justice Department Criminal Division. In so many words, Martin let me know quickly that the government really needed my cooperation. It was my choice, he stressed. They couldn't force me to reveal my undercover role, but without my testimony they would not be able to prosecute the criminals.

I couldn't make a commitment on the spot. I sensed that all four men wanted a quick decision, saying they had only a day or two in London, but I had a lot at stake. I asked for another day to think about it.

Years before, when the VC cadres had come around and pressured Hai Van and me to join them, I used to ask my grandfather to tell me what I should do. His reply was always the same: "Do what your heart tells you." Over lunch after the meeting with the lawyers, I asked my husband what he thought I should do in this case. "Lady," he said, "you will have to live with this decision for the rest of your life. Therefore it isn't fair for me to make it for you. But whatever you decide, your husband will be behind that decision one hundred percent."

As I wrestled with my doubts and fears that afternoon, I remembered back to the first time, months before in Virginia, when Bill Fleshman had asked me, "Hey, Yung, would you testify for us if and when any of these cases goes to trial?" My answer was short and sweet: "Hell, no!" Wouldn't it be great, I thought, if I could just come out and tell everyone "Hell, no" when they showed up at my house the next morning? That way I might still be able to see my father again, and perhaps someday my mother might be able to see my brother, and the bloody Communists would never know how much I wanted to destroy their bloody system.

I lay awake once again that night, staring blankly at the truth that if I did say "Hell, no," then David Truong would get away with his wrongdoing and would probably continue to do a lot of damage to the United States of America. CIA agents who worked undercover outside of the States would be identified; in particular, Vietnamese spies who used to work with the CIA but were still unable to escape Viet Nam would be in great danger. I was the only person who could stop him, the lawyers had said. Could I refuse that responsibility?

I needed time. I needed to see my father once more, to ask him once again if he would ever consider leaving Viet Nam. I wanted to ask him to retire and spend the rest of his life anywhere he liked, but outside Viet Nam. If I was going to go public at a trial and close the door to the other side forever, I wanted one last shot at getting my family together.

Perhaps even more important, I pleaded with John Martin to delay the trial until my brother could escape from Viet Nam. I thought my father would probably get through the turmoil that would result when the SRV government found out I was a spy for the CIA, but I worried about what they might do to Khoi to try to prevent his baby sister from testifying against their agents and exposing their spy network.

I proposed that we send Khoi some money so he could buy his way out of the country, as so many other people had done; in those days the going price was three thousand dollars. Rob said the CIA would help, and so the only problem remaining was to figure out a way to get the money to my brother without anyone knowing about it.

Luckily, Huynh Trung Dong had told me that he was going to be traveling to Viet Nam within a couple of weeks. In fact, he was calling me every few days, asking me to get to Paris to bring him the package of letters and other information that David Truong had given me in front of the Hecht Company store before they became "outdated." We all decided that a trip for that delivery would be a good excuse to go to Paris to see about speeding up arrangements for my father's trip to the West, and would also allow me to use Dong to pass the money to Khoi — if I could figure out a way to conceal it.

Tony Lapham and John Martin returned to Washington with my promise that I would in fact testify — but only after I saw my father and only after I could make certain that my family would be protected from any possible consequences of my cooperation. When the lawyers and agents talked about my answer they called it my "conditions" more than my cooperation, but I wasn't offended; I knew these people were just watching out for their own behinds. It was ironic, in a way. In the beginning I had had to fight with my CIA case officer to bring the FBI into the case. I was the one who insisted it was our duty to "clean up our own back yard." Now they were grumbling about having to work harder to meet my "conditions."

One always faces obstacles before reaching the end of the road. You can either walk over them, or trip over them, but I knew that none of the obstacles on this particular road could bring me down. And that was all I needed to know.

— — —

The CIA case officer asked my husband and son to accompany me on the trip to Paris to help with my cover, as a businesswoman and her family taking a leisurely trip across the channel. There was certainly no objection on their part to a free visit to Paris, although Lance was a bit disappointed on the first day that I couldn't go sightseeing with him and his father. I had to lie to him, telling him I had to "take care of my import business first." Of course, it wasn't china and glassware I was hoping to "import."

My first stop was the SRV embassy. Ambassador Vo Van Sung had treated me kindly up until now and was also very fond of my father, so I hoped he would be able to help in the difficult job of persuading his government to allow my father to visit us in London. I told him the story we had decided upon earlier: that my mother was in poor health, and we thought my father should come to see her quickly, because this could be the last opportunity. To my delight, the ambassador promised to relay my request, and I returned to the hotel with high hopes that things were under way.

When I came back to the hotel that evening, the concierge gave me a message: Phan Thanh Nam wanted to see me at once. I checked the room and Lance and John hadn't returned from their sightseeing, so I left them a note and went out again.

At the former NLF mission, I told Nam right away that my husband and son were with me in Paris. I didn't know whether he already knew that, so I thought it best to be clear I wasn't hiding anything from him, even apparently innocent details. He said he would like to meet John someday, but "perhaps next time when we can make better arrangements."

Nam's urgent business was a letter he wanted me to take to David Truong when I returned to Washington. It was addressed to Tam, the phony name he usually used for letters to Truong. Just after giving me the letter, however, it dawned on Nam that I would be traveling back to London with my husband before I went to Washington to "deliver chinaware to the stores," as I had told him, so he asked to have it back. He ripped the envelope open, went to his desk, and came back with a plain envelope addressed to an American woman at an address on S Street in Washington.

He looked a little uneasy when I read the address on the letter. I don't think he wanted his various "assets" in the United States to know about one another. "Please put an American stamp on this and mail it for me as soon as you get back to the United States," he instructed.

"Will this lady know what to do with this letter?" I asked.

He nodded.

"I assume it must be an important letter," I said.

"All my letters are important," he smirked.

"In that case, I should hand-deliver it to her," I suggested, testing him a bit.

"Don't, don't do that!" He leaned over to me suddenly and looked as if he wanted to take the letter from my hand. "I mean, you don't have to do that. Just drop it in the mailbox for me." In a moment he recovered from his agitation, and went on to explain: "You shouldn't be seen with this woman. Don't ask me why, but I have my own reasons for not wanting you to meet this woman." He looked at my handbag, where I had put the letter, a doubtful look still on his face.

I realized I not only shouldn't push any further, I ought to get out of there before he changed his mind and took the letter back. I looked around at the room, absolutely quiet at this hour of the day, Uncle Ho smiling down at us from the wall.

"What is our next war in Viet Nam, Uncle Nam?" I tried to put an innocent expression on my face as I asked this "antirevolutionary" question.

"The war is over, my child. It is time to rebuild the war-torn country. People like you are our country's treasure."

"I will do my best," I said stoutly.

Nam took me to the entranceway and we shook hands. The wooden gate closed, and I left behind his world of lies and darkness, as dark as the lives my people now led in Viet Nam. I felt nauseated.

— — —

During my whole time in Paris, I never stopped thinking about how I might disguise the money I wanted to send to Khoi and use Dong as my "courier." In the hotel room one day I happened to pick up a picture of my husband, one that I had long ago made into a decoupage plaque when I had the luxury of free time to enjoy hobbies. Suddenly the answer flashed into my head! I could make a new "antiqued" picture, one of my mother and father, and send it to Khoi — but not before splitting the board in half, hollowing it out, and hiding the money inside.

When Rob came to the hotel for a report one evening, I sat down and told him my idea. Because I planned to put a picture of my father on one side of the board and a picture of my mother on the other, Khoi would think it was stupid — if he displayed either picture, the other would be turned to the wall. I was sure the absurdity of it would catch his attention, and I could let him know cautiously in a letter that there was more to the plaque than it might seem.

Rob loved the idea. He also told me that "they" had decided to send Khoi ten thousand dollars, rather than the three thousand I had mentioned, to increase his chances of getting out. If he failed in his first attempt and was jailed, he would still have enough money to buy his way out of prison and start another trip. I thought ten thousand dollars would surely be enough for Khoi to escape. I went to bed happy that night.

Before Rob sent the picture to be put in the frame with the money, he asked me to write a note to Khoi with a short, urgent message: "Get out of Viet Nam now."

Gradually, over several letters between myself and Khoi and my mother, we had worked out a sort of code system for communicating in open letters. One of the things Khoi had told me was that if I wanted to let him know there was something particularly critical in a letter, I should draw a picture of the head of a water buffalo on it. So I asked my seven-year-old resident "artist" to draw me four pictures of water buffalo heads on a piece of white construction paper. Lance spent twenty minutes on the task, thinking he was showing off his talents to his grandfather and uncle, but he was actually playing a much more important role.

In the letter I told Khoi, "You don't need any more guitar strings, and you asked for Mom and Dad's pictures, so here they are. The drawings were done by Lang." Khoi called Lance "Lang," but Lang was also a code phrase for my associates — the CIA. I was sure that all of this together, the back-to-back pictures, the water buffalo drawings, and the coded phrases, would be enough to prompt my brother to break open the board and find the money.

Before leaving Paris and returning to London, I gave Dong the picture, and he carried it back to Viet Nam along with four bottles of vitamins and a pair of pajamas my mother had made for my father.

This was the last effort the CIA and I made to contact my brother, and for more than three years we never knew if he had figured out the trick and found the money. Finally, my mother received another letter from "Xuan Mai," the girl's name Khoi used to write to her. "Thank my sister for me for sending the picture frame, but I broke it in half by accident," he wrote. I was happy that he had gotten the money, but only God knows why he didn't use it to escape from Viet Nam. My family would still have to wait another eleven years to see the son and brother we had "lost" more than twenty years before.

— — —

Rob Hall and Bill Fleshman came back to London a few days later to find out whether there was any news on if and when my father would be coming. There wasn't, but I reassured them that I was sticking to my commitment to testify in the Truong-Humphrey case. That wasn't any thrill to Rob, of course, but Bill was glad to hear it.

I showed them the sealed envelope Nam had given me and suggested to Bill that if the FBI couldn't get legal authorization to open it, the Bureau should at least make an effort to identify this new asset. I suggested they have an agent hand-deliver the letter, pretending to be from one of the messenger services in the D.C area. Bill liked the idea and said he would talk to his supervisor about it.

Autumn came, and still no word from Ha Noi about my father's trip. Lance started school again on September 8, and just two days later we were asked to go back to Washington to meet with the FBI and John Martin from the Justice Department to talk about the upcoming case. I spent two traumatic weeks there, moving from meetings with the FBI to sessions with the CIA, checking with my contacts among the Vietnamese Communist sympathizers in the D.C. area, and meeting with David Truong. In addition, my mother flew in from Atlanta to accompany us back to London, so I had to help get her visa and make all the travel arrangements.

When we got back to London, my mother hadn't even had a chance to unpack when we got a call from Ambassador Sung in Paris. Ha Noi had spoken, he said, and the answer was that my father would be allowed to come only as far as Paris — not to London. He wanted to know if we could afford to fly my mother to Paris, and I said we could try but I had to check with her doctor to see if she was well enough for the extra travel. Before the conversation ended, the ambassador hinted that we might be able to get the foreign ministry to change its mind if we sent a letter saying that the doctor thought that going on to Paris would be risky to her health.

I trusted his advice, but I also thought we should go ahead with plans for any eventuality. I remembered that Dong had said once that in the history of the Vietnamese Communist Party he had never known of any man, even one in the highest position, being allowed to travel outside Viet Nam just to visit his family. I had responded, half-jokingly, "My father may break the record if we try hard enough." So we got my mother's visa for a trip to Paris, if it came to that, and I wrote my father a letter telling him she was in London and we were all anxious to see him. I sent the letter to Huynh Trung Dong so it would get to my father sooner by traveling via diplomatic pouch.

My temperament could have sizzled the damp October weather in London. I went to bed in terrible anxiety, woke up with nightmares, and went about my business during the day haunted by the prospect of going into court some-day soon to tell "the truth, the whole truth and nothing but the truth, so help me God." I felt the weight of the enormous question of what my father would feel when my true convictions and loyalties were revealed. I didn't doubt the right and wrong of my course, but I worried about what it would do to my family.

The pressure from the Justice Department never let up; they wanted my father's visit to get settled so they could move forward on the case and count on my testimony. Yet I couldn't do much of anything except wait. I tried to think of ways to crank the wheel of the bureaucratic machine a little faster, and finally I settled on the idea of going right to the top to get around all the small-er cogs that turned so slowly. Le Duan, the chairman of the Vietnamese Communist Party, had been my father's comrade since I was in diapers; I decided to write directly to him, as well as to the foreign minister, Nguyen Duy Trinh.

Dong was opposed to the idea, insisting that I shouldn't bother men in such high positions, so I couldn't use him to deliver the message. I thought back to my good relationship with the UN ambassador, Dinh Ba Thi, and decided he would be an even better avenue to the top. I waited for everyone in the family to go to bed, then I tiptoed back downstairs to put down my thoughts. By dawn I had three handwritten copies on onionskin paper ready to go to Le Duan, to Nguyen Duy Trinh, and to my father. While I made breakfast for John I read him the letter I was sending to all three men.

Dear Uncle Le Duan, Uncle Nguyen Duy Trinh, and my beloved father:

My mother's health is deteriorating due to kidney infection, as my father was informed by me earlier. I have stayed awake many nights, and I couldn't help but think, what if my father comes too late?

The last days in my mother's life should be the best days in her life, and that means to be with my father. I am asking all of you to create an opportunity so that my mother can see my father soon.

Father, from the day you married my mother until the day you went to Ha Noi in 1954, you may remember that she never asked from you anything beyond your ability, but this time on behalf of my mother I ask your superiors one favor. With all my heart I believe she deserves to be with her husband and her son.

You two [Father and Le Duan] had been sharing your hopes, your disappointments, as well as enduring together the darkest days of Viet Nam, and sharing your triumph together at the Liberation. I do believe from the bottom of my heart that you [Le Duan] will not deny my father and his family when you know our need, and because of that I am sending you this letter.

Father, I am sending each of you a copy of my letter. I am expecting to see you soon. I have the money for the round-trip tickets. Please advise me on where to send the money or tickets to you.

Your daughter, Dang My Yung

I sent the letters off to Ambassador Thi, along with a letter to him from my mother, adding her own plea that she be allowed to see her son, and the long wait continued. On November 13, I got a letter from Dong, who had just returned from an official visit in Viet Nam. He said he had met my father, but there was no news concerning a visit to London. He reminded me again that there was no precedent for a trip of that sort. Dong also had some thoughts of his own about the matter. He wrote: "Your mother's letter already reached the very top people in the party. Of course, the decision is up to the chairman and Mr. Nguyen Duy Trinh. As I learned from my trip, the government would allow your mother to visit Viet Nam, and she could stay as long as she wished."

My mother read Dong's letter and snorted, "I won't set foot in Viet Nam as long as the Communists are in the country. And don't even think of burying me by your father's side, either, as you had the idea to do before!"

Dong's letter continued: "But the problem of letting your father visit your mother is being discussed and measured by the responsible people back home. In writing I can only tell you so much, but I hope you give this matter a lot of thought in order to understand me. Papa is very concerned about your mother, for the fact is that if and when he visits her he must come without your brother Khoi. Because in no way will the party allow your brother to leave Viet Nam. Your father knows the rules but he is afraid that you and your mother will not, and he is concerned about your mother's feelings toward this matter very much, Yung."

He went on to suggest that I write the foreign minister and lay out all the details of my mother's illness, and include an affidavit from her doctor saying she was too sick to travel any farther. "Do not worry about a long letter as you can tell him all he needs to know," Dong wrote. "About your mother's situation, tell him that your mother can't walk because of her kidney infection and so forth." He told me to send the letter to Ambassador Sung in Paris, and to ask for his support at that end.

My mother was so anxious for some results that she wanted to go the "doctor's affidavit" route. She not only thought that might speed up the process — she hoped that if the statement from the doctor were dire enough then the officials might change their mind and allow Khoi to come as well. I was sympathetic to her feelings, since I knew that Khoi was the one she really wanted to see most. And I thought that getting the affidavit would be no problem. I thought, however, that since I had already been in touch with both Sung and Foreign Minister Trinh — which Dong didn't know — that the best thing to do was to wait and see if those efforts bore fruit rather than push too hard before we had even gotten a reply.

Later I wrote to Dong and told him I had been somewhat offended by the suggestion that we needed some sort of proof from a doctor. Bitterly, I wrote, "When my father was asked to leave his wife and children to go to Ha Noi, he was promised that he could return in two years. We trusted and waited for him, and no one asked for a written guarantee of his return." Still, I thanked Dong for his efforts in our personal affairs — although considering how much work I had done for him as his "agent" in Washington I thought I had certainly earned all of it.

Shortly afterward Dong called and pressed once again for the affidavit. I told him I'd write back, and I did: "Brother Dong, I agreed with many things you have said to me, but being my father's daughter I do not and will never believe in a doctor's affidavit of sickness, because we are the people of Viet Nam, a country that should be ruled by the people, people from all walks of life. I shall not copy the French or any bureaucrats to produce that document. The people's words should have greater impact than the words of a bureaucrat. I would like very much to take this step as a liberated Vietnamese."

In the next letter, Dong apologized for having made a suggestion that offended me; he said it had merely been the last recourse he could think of to help me get my father and mother together one last time.

— — —

Life in London could have been as pleasant as a cup of afternoon tea if the FBI and CIA hadn't made such frequent visits to ask me when something was going to happen. By mid-November Rob Hall and Bill Fleshman were back again. I wasn't sure of the purpose of this visit, and wondered if they were really checking up on me to make certain I was going to remain available to them. When they surprised me at the front door I told them, "I can't skip town because the next town is either the U.S.A. or the U.S.S.R." Bill smiled as if I had read his mind correctly.

There was nothing much for them to do on this visit, because everything depended on the decisions being made in Ha Noi. They went sightseeing and shopping, visited their favorite pubs, and met with me a few times over dinner. After five days they went back to Washington, still empty-handed.

Once again, I called Dong. He informed me that Ambassador Sung had passed on my request to the Foreign Ministry. I startled him then by telling him I hadn't waited for that, but had written Le Duan and the foreign minister myself. He didn't sound too happy about it. "Well, that is the highest you can climb so I guess I can't help you any more from this end." I assured him that I would indeed need his assistance again, and I tried to ease his concern by telling him I thought my forwardness would help, not hurt, our goal.

I don't know what miracle may have happened between the time I spoke to Dong and the next day, but I suddenly got a phone call from Ambassador Sung's office in Paris, telling me to get in touch with the SRV embassy in London right away.

Dozens of times Rob had told me that "whenever you make contact with a new member of the SRV, I must be informed before you meet with them." But the only telephone numbers I had were supposed to be used strictly for emergencies. This didn't seem like an emergency, so I went ahead and called the SRV embassy on Victoria Road.

Business must have been slow at this nest of socialists, because it took only the two words "My Yung" for the man who answered the phone to recognize who I was and what I wanted. He asked me to come to his office to discuss our "affairs."

At the embassy, the man met me at the gate and identified himself as Lai Xuan Chieu, the "information officer." I had to suppress a smile at the contrast between the man's name and title; his position is classically a cover for an intelligence officer at SRV embassies, but his name sounded like a pen name used by a poet in my country's olden days.

Lai Xuan Chieu told me he had been advised that my father would be coming to London to see his family after an official visit in Moscow. Hooray! We had won the whole battle, at least as far as my father was concerned, although we had apparently gotten nothing from the Communists regarding Khoi.

"Our mission here would be delighted to assist your family in any way we can," Chieu said. Then he looked me in the eye and asked, "How do you plan to pay for Comrade Minh's trip? Perhaps you should know ahead of time that our government can't pay for it."

"Perhaps there has been a great misunderstanding," I replied, "but I only asked the chairman and the foreign minister to encourage my father to go and to give him permission to go. I didn't ask them to pay for the trip; this is not a case of charity."

"In that case," Chieu said, looking down at his hands, "we don't have a problem as far as the cost is concerned."

"I guess we don't have any problem," I said, a little angrily.

"For your information, I would like you to know that we will be the host when Comrade Minh comes to London," he went on.

"Mr. Chieu, I thank you for your generous offer, but my husband and I would be my father's hosts. We would like to make it a family affair."

"You don't understand, sister," Chieu protested. "Comrade Minh's safety in London is our responsibility. We are instructed to assist your family in any way we can. And," he added, returning to a subject that must have been important to him, "as for your father's airplane tickets, how would you like to handle it?"

"I have the money for it whenever needed," I assured him, puzzled at his concern.

"We know how to get the tickets at a better price," Chieu said.

"I should not want to impose on you with a small matter like that," I told him. "I have already checked with Aeroflot. The trip would cost about 900 pounds. I can pay for it here and my father can pick up his ticket in Moscow."

Chieu wouldn't give up. "You can give me the money, preferably in U.S. dollars. I'll notify the Foreign Ministry and they will purchase the tickets for Comrade Minh from Ha Noi in Vietnamese currency. That way we don't have to spend any dollars."

It was embarrassing to listen to a representative of the government that my father served telling me how he wanted to try to make a buck for their empire by manipulating a few hundred pounds worth of currency. I wanted to end this uncomfortable conversation as quickly as possible, so I just said, "Whatever you say, Mr. Chieu." Before I left he managed to get in one more reminder to bring the money in U.S. dollars.

A week later I called Chieu and made an appointment to see him in the afternoon. I had $2,000 in cash, but I had no intention of giving him American dollars. I made it a point to change the money into British pounds before going to the SRV Embassy. "Don't ask me why I'm going through all this trouble," I remarked to my husband. "The Communists aren't going to have any 'green' in their hands if I can help it."

I informed Rob and Bill by letter of all these developments, and they arrived within a few days. All of the details had been worked out with the government, including a very special request I had asked them to make to Attorney General Griffin Bell: to make it possible for my father to come to the United States if my family could persuade him to "retire" and not go back to Viet Nam. Bill told me the request had been approved, and Rob told me a plane would be available to fly my father to the United States if he agreed to go.

For the first time in months the four of us — Rob, Bill, John, and I — could share hope and laughter under one roof.

I wanted so much for my father and mother to be together, and with these developments I suddenly became a very optimistic human being. My mother and I talked about where they might make a new home together; I wondered if my father would be happy to live with us, or whether he would like to live with just my mother and Minh Tam, our youngest sister whom he had known only for the first three months of her life. We made endless plans, right down to silly details like my suggestion that we ought to get an electric blanket for my father.

I thought about the family that had been divided so long and soon might be reunited. My father had loved all seven of his children, although each in a different way. Khoi was his first child, a link to my mother and to those wonderful years they had shared before he went off to Ha Noi. Kim resembled him most in her tenderness, her sensitivity as well as her insecurity. My sister Cuong was his eternal challenge because she used to argue with him endlessly, even in casual conversation. I had his heart, and his caring for others, but he knew that my God was different from his. My father loved and respected Hai Van, who had all the talents he had and an intelligence that surprised him; he still didn't know, however, how to deal with my brother's decision to become a helicopter pilot in the South Vietnamese Air Force. Hoa Binh had a unique place in our father's heart, because for some reason she had always been his special baby. When I talked to him about her, his face became radiant and he listened raptly to every word. He compared his love for her to "an endless spring with trees in blossom and clear blue sky and nothing to worry about." He only knew Minh Tam for three months, and those three months were the busiest time of his life as he prepared to leave for the North. He changed his first name to Minh, after Minh Tam's name, shortly after he left, and I always thought he did it out of guilt over not having had the chance to watch her grow.

Thinking of my father's feelings for all of his children, I asked Hoa Binh if she could take time off from her work at an engineering firm in Washington to come to London to see him. She said she would try to get permission from her boss, and I talked to Bill Fleshman about it. He thought it was a fine idea, because he welcomed anything that might help our operation; he sent word to FBI headquarters to do anything necessary to help Hoa Binh get the travel documents she would need on short notice.

Things were looking up on the FBI and Justice Department side of things, and I think Rob Hall felt some disappointment because he could see the end of his operation coming. One night the four of us went out to dinner, and the frayed edges in the relationship came loose.

We had been having a pleasant time at the Whaler restaurant, enjoying seafood and the best wine in the house. We talked about places we had seen in London, from Soho to Piccadilly Circus, and the plays Bill had been seeing. The conversation ranged from pigeon droppings at Trafalgar Square to the "birds" in the pubs, and laughter rang out all around the table. Then suddenly a verbal battle sprang up between Rob and Bill, sparked by some nasty remarks Rob made about what he considered the FBI's inferiority as an intelligence agency.

Things turned a bit sour after that. A while later, Bill said he felt ill and went off to the men's room. When he left, Rob turned to me and started what must have been one of his "child psychiatry" games with me, asking me if I was still writing my "book," a reference to something I had once told him about the story of my childhood that I had been writing since I was still in high school. Because of my employment with the CIA, I had been told, I would not be able to publish any articles or books without the agency's clearance. We were all a little silly at that moment of the evening, so as a joke I told Rob I had finished my "book" and it would be published pretty soon.

Rob suddenly looked serious — perhaps panicky is a better description — and started asking questions about how far I had gotten in the story and whether our operation was included in it. I gave him no answer. Then, irritated, he threw out a silly story that he had written a book that would be in paperback and would sell for "a buck a piece," and the first printing would be 500,000 copies. John picked up on my joke and told him, "Yung is going to sell her book for a buck-sixty-five a copy," and he winked at me.

Rob wasn't joking, however, and he kept hammering at the subject until Bill came back from the men's room. He didn't look good, so the conversation ended there. I was glad it did, because I thought everyone had said far too much, perhaps because we had had too much to drink. At that moment, as we left the restaurant, our friendship felt like the leftover wine in the bottom of our bottle.

Chapter 26

December 9, 1977, was my son's seventh birthday. I got up earlier than normal to put frosting on cupcakes for him to share with his classmates. Lance had no idea, but he was my salvation in these tense times, the person who helped me keep my sanity in place. The chance to take a short walk with him to Regent Park and throw a Frisbee back and forth was a blessed relief in between meetings with the FBI and the CIA.

My poor mother wasn't as fortunate, because she couldn't lose herself that way. She sat at home for weeks and waited for events to unfold, the suspense nearly unbearable. We were 99 percent sure he was coming, but how soon? That was what the Justice Department wanted to know, too, and Bill Fleshman must have asked us that question almost every day.

This morning, after I dropped Lance and the birthday cupcakes at school, I wasn't going back home. Bill had called the night before and asked John and me to meet him and Rob at the Reeve House the next day. He didn't say what the subject would be, but I could tell from his voice that something serious was afoot. When we arrived, we found out just how serious it was.

Bill opened with a dramatic announcement: "The purpose of this meeting today is . . . , well, since we last saw you two at the Whaler the other night, we sent a report to Washington. They are worried about your statement, Yung — the statement you made concerning your book."

I couldn't believe what I was hearing, and I stood up quickly from the couch. "Bill, Rob, I expect more from you two than that! You should be ashamed of yourself for sending such a report to Washington. And Bill, I am disappointed in you. At least you are more sensible than this one here" — I gestured angrily at Rob — "you shouldn't have supported such an idea."

"Yung, I am not concerned, but some very important people are worried,"

Bill responded. "We only reported what you and John said, although we don't believe it was true. But they have a right to know what's going on here."

I felt stupid just to be there, involved in such a farce. If this incident had happened years back, before I was married to John, I would have walked out of the house and told everyone including the Justice Department to shove it. But with John there beside me I thought I should show my good side instead.

"Rob, did you tell them where and when that book business took place? Did you tell them that we talked over five bottles of wine on government expense? And Bill, did you tell them that Rob said he is also publishing a book? This is childish! When I publish my book your 'important people' in Washington will be advised, you can count on that."

"How far along is your book now, Yung?" Rob asked, still deadly serious, a pen and notebook in his hands.

"Goddamn it, Rob," I snapped. "We were drunk that night. There is no such book yet! And it is none of your business anyway!"

"It is my business when you are working for us," he retorted. "Do you write about our activities and your involvement with the agency?" He looked like a legal stenographer ready to take down my statement.

"Yung is still writing about her childhood," John said. "She is still in grade school."

"How far along is your book, Yung?" Rob asked again, his voice hardening as if he were interrogating a prisoner.

"Rob, I respect your professionalism. You are one fine operator. But as a person, a friend, I find it hard to respect you and I find your approach to human beings rather stupid. Let's close this subject. You are wasting my time and you have made me very angry." I got up and paced around in the tiny room. Then I sprang my surprise. "By the way, gentlemen, you can tell your 'important people' in Washington that my father will be leaving Ha Noi for Moscow tomorrow. We shall see him soon." Ambassador Sung's office had told me the news when I called there again that morning, but the two men had started in so suddenly on the nonsense about the book that I hadn't had time to tell them.

Like a wave of a magic wand, though, my words filled the room with a harmonious air, and the tension vanished. Bill smiled, Rob blinked his eyes. John lit a cigar and passed one to each man. They started talking about what plans we'd have to make, and someone suggested we go to a nice restaurant somewhere to celebrate. I wasn't interested; I didn't want to eat another meal with Rob unless I had a tape recorder by my side, I thought. When we left the Reeve House, John and I had lunch at the American embassy cafeteria alone.

As I queued up for the bus to go back to Regent Park, a couple of women in black robes and veils over their faces pushed me aside to grab places on the bus when it arrived. I watched the bus pull away, and decided a walk to the next stop would probably be a good idea anyway. I needed a chance to think.

I was filled with an inexplicable feeling, the feeling that I had become a victim of my own trust, my own convictions. Somewhere along the road from my childhood to maturity, I had learned to be accountable, and to love and to cherish my country, my parents, and my comrades. With deepest sincerity I believed I had learned those lessons well, yet my efforts didn't seem to serve anyone and my own associates had betrayed me.

I walked across the street and looked into the windows where Selfridge's had displayed Christmas decorations, and thought about what a sad time holidays had been for me for most of my life. When my father had been fighting the French in the Liberated Zone, we couldn't afford to celebrate Tet, the biggest holiday in the Vietnamese calendar. Then, after he left us in 1954, the NLF people told us every year that "he will be home this Tet." For the next nineteen years, Tet came and went, the promise made and the promise broken. My mother's hair turned gray and her face became wrinkled; I ceased to have that butterfly feeling in my stomach as the holiday approached. The weather still turned cool, the cherry blossoms still bloomed, the boys and I went out and cut them to make New Year decorations, but Tet became little more than a symbol of disappointment and betrayal to us. I got tougher over the years of hearing "he will be home for Tet" whispered again and again, but holidays were never again completely happy times for me.

I looked for a church and went in for at least forty-five minutes. I can't explain it, but I believed that God gave me strength and serenity to overcome my troubles. I thought it was always good to visit God in his house. Even though I knew that he was often at my house, perhaps at his I would get better treatment because I was his guest.

That afternoon I called the Vietnamese embassy and told "Comrade Chieu" that my father was leaving Sai Gon on Saturday. Chieu was flabbergasted that I had the information before he did, and I took advantage of his shock to tell him that I would pick up my father at the airport. He didn't like the idea: "It is our job to pick up our officials at the airport. We don't have our own transportation, but we will rent a car."

"Why go through all that trouble when I can simplify things by driving my own car to pick up my own father?" I asked. I didn't want to be unreasonable, but from experience I knew it was best to win every little war with Communists, lest someone like Chieu get me by the nose and force me to do everything "according to the rules." There was a silence on the other end of the line, but I just waited.

Finally, he mumbled, "It doesn't fit in with the rules . . . I don't know what to say."

"I promise, I'll bring the ambassador home safely," I jumped in. "I will call you the minute we get home. Now, may I have the telephone number of our embassy in Moscow?" I didn't want him to dwell on the previous question.

"Don't you have it?" Chieu asked.

"You can save me a lot of time if you kindly give me the SRV telephone number. I would like to confirm my father's travel arrangements from that side."

After another moment's hesitation, he read me the number from his directory. I had won that little war, at least.

— — —

Rob and Bill gave us another surprise the very next night. As soon as I had told them that my father was going to be leaving Ha Noi, we all agreed that from that day on neither of them would come to our house. This was a firm understanding among all of us, because we all knew that the SRV's people could well start watching our house as part of their responsibility to protect their ambassador while he was in London — not to mention making sure he didn't defect. Obviously, it wouldn't have served our purposes well if they spotted two "G-men" coming in and out of the home of my father's "loyal" family.

I also told Rob and Bill that from my experience with them, the SRV agents had one characteristic that made them better intelligence officers than ours — they didn't always do things by the book. They were likely to make "casual" visits to our house while my father was there, and so it would be a terrible mistake for the FBI and CIA to come anywhere near the place.

Everyone was in solid agreement on this, so I was astonished when Lance answered a knock at the door and called out, "Daddy, Rob and Bill are here to see you!" I was livid, and let Rob know it.

"What if the SRV people were here?" I demanded.

He looked at Bill, but didn't have an answer. Instead he started telling me that he was not comfortable with the idea of being "shut out" of day-to-day activities at our house at this critical time, and he told me he wanted me to give him a "face-to-face daily report" from then until the end of my father's visit. That was clearly a near-impossible demand. I would be dealing with my father, my family, and perhaps even with SRV officials, and trying to find a way to sneak away from all those people to make a "face-to-face" report would put the whole operation, not to mention my family, at great risk. I suggested that since my husband had to leave the house to go to work each day, he could meet with Rob and Bill and tell them what was going on.

Rob violently opposed the idea, saying that I was the one who worked for him, not John. I knew that his greatest interest was in flying home with a very important defector by his side, and I told him that was my hope, too, but he wouldn't be able to obtain his defector by coming to my house and waiting, any more than a little kid could make Santa Claus come by waiting at the staircase. His position was absurd and childish, I told him, and the discussion degenerated into a shouting match.

"Look, Rob," I told him, "when I give you an inch, you want a mile. It is not going to happen when my father is here. I'll make every effort to see that you and Bill are kept informed, but don't give me that ultimatum. From now on I am in charge, and I will take full responsibility and all the blame."

"Goddamn it, Yung," Rob shouted. "It is an order from your case officer!"

They left with the matter largely unsettled. I grew up overnight after that confrontation, I think. I had worked well with these two men for the most part, but I always thought of them as my coworkers, not my bosses. I knew my role and I respected their positions, but as far as I was concerned we were involved in teamwork, whether it was collecting information from the SRV in Europe or spotting foreign spies on American soil.

"Hey, John," I asked my husband after they had gone, "if I want to set a record straight with our government in Washington, what do I have to do?"

"You write them a memorandum," he said.

"How do I send it to the right people?"

"Write it and give it to Rob and Bill. Have them transmit your letter to whomever you want."

"What if they block it?" It seemed kind of doubtful to me that the very people I was going to complain about should be the conduit for the complaint.

"They wouldn't dare," he assured me.

And so I sat down and wrote out a "memorandum for the record," and addressed it to my case officers "for your information and for relay to Admiral Stansfield Turner, director of the CIA."

As the time counts down to the day my father gets here, the pressure is increasing on all concerned, both here in London and in Washington. I realize the importance of keeping the concerned parties in Washington well informed and that is our intention. We all have the same goal and mutual interest in seeing that our project ends successfully. To date, we can be proud of our planning and the execution of our planning as we are close to achieving our goal.

We are especially grateful to the Justice Department for making possible the time to allow my father and hopefully my brother a chance for a life outside Communist Viet Nam. The Agency has been very helpful also and considering the sweet and sour position they are in, they indeed receive my sincere thanks.

The purpose of this memorandum is twofold. The first and most important thing is to thank everyone responsible for their energies that made possible the close approaching event, namely that my father is coming to London, second to make you aware of the pressure your representatives in London are placing on me and my family at this time, i.e., Mr. Robert Hall and Mr. William Fleshman.

A meeting at our house on Dec. 10 developed into a shouting match when they tried to place a firm and absolute commitment of a daily face-to-face progress report to be made by me to them during the time my father is here.

After explaining to them that it may not be possible for me personally to get away from my father and to go out to report to them, they both said they want to hear everything my father said and that meant everything and they only wanted to hear it from me, not my husband. Hard words were passed by Mr. Hall. Mr. Hall said that he will not be satisfied with the reports coming from my husband due to the possibility of "mistranslation." The excuse doesn't make a lot of sense to me and the discussion that followed degenerated further into more hard words and obscenities. Please understand that the first several days of my father's visit are so very important to me as my father may not have already decided to come to the U.S. My husband is perfectly capable of passing on information as he and I share one mind.

My memorandum also recounted the confrontation over my "book" that had taken place a few days before. After explaining how John and I had merely been playing along with each other in response to Rob's game-playing criticisms of the FBI, I assured everyone that there was no lack of concern on our part about security or the need to go through proper procedures for clearance of any writing about my experiences with the agency. "The way it was reported is of concern to us," I wrote. "As we know and understand their cable to you, the publishing of the book was reported with an estimate that was probably not true. There is no need for an estimate or a probability, for we are very much on your side.

"If the question was asked as to the truth of the book story, we would have most certainly responded with the truth that I have been writing a book since long before we began our partnership and it still hasn't reached the stage of our partnership." I wanted the top people to know that neither my book nor I was any threat to them. "The point is that there is no need to speculate on our motives or actions, for they are an open book that you are most respectfully privileged to know."

Then I turned to the question of the sudden arrival of Rob and Bill at our house after we had agreed they would not come. "If my father was here the event of their arrival would have possibly been a major problem as my son and my mother were home, my son opened the door and announced 'Rob is here.' Again, this points out the pressure they perceive, real or not. Please be patient and please transmit this feeling of patience to them. The pressure that Mr. Hall often puts me under has been accepted, but at this time it is counterproductive."

I asked the officials to give me "freedom of action at this time and minimum supervision," and I put in one more good word for Rob and Bill. "As both of your men here are basically good people and furthermore are our friends, perhaps the pressure they are reflecting is that pressure that you are placing on them from Washington. Please at this time be as wonderfully patient as you have been and the results will be the same fine results as the last two and a half years. A miscalculated move at this time may give me a life of sorrow. Please trust me and my husband as you have done in the past. This fairy tale can still have a wonderful ending."

— — —

With the telephone number Lai Xuan Chieu had given me, I put in a call to Moscow. A Russian woman answered the phone at the SRV embassy, and when I asked in Vietnamese to speak to an embassy official she said something to me in Russian. I made the request again in English and she answered, "No." Then I asked if she spoke English, and the phone went dead.

I dialed again and when the same voice came through the receiver I asked in French, "May I speak to a Vietnamese, please." She understood that, but wasn't much help; she told me to call the "welcome committee" at another number.

This time a Vietnamese answered the phone, and I told him I was calling from London. "London, where?" he asked. When he realized I was calling from England he sounded excited; he didn't ask who I was but why I called. I told him I was trying to locate Ambassador Dang Quang Minh, and he said, "Ambassador Minh went ice-skating this morning with friends. You can reach him later at the guest house," and he gave me yet another number.

The man had no idea about my father's itinerary when I asked, but it finally occurred to him to ask who I was. I was hesitant at first to tell him on the phone, but then I said to myself, why not? I am his daughter and for almost two decades I wanted the whole world to know, but I was unable to do so.

For years during my days in high school I used to look up on the red roof of the principal's office and wanted to climb to the very top and tell the whole city who my father was. But I never did. They would have thrown me in jail, locked me up, and the whole city would have never heard from me again. But today I could tell the president of the United States who my father is, so I can certainly reveal that fact to any person who wants to know.

"I am Mr. Minh's daughter," I said to this unknown man in Moscow. God, it felt so good.

Later, I placed another call to the welcome committee to find out my father's arrival time in London. Another man answered the phone, and he was much more cautious. "May I ask with whom I am speaking?" he said politely.

"I am Mr. Minh's daughter," I said again.

There was silence on the phone, although I could tell the man was still there. "You said you are his daughter? And you are calling from London?"

I said I was, and he asked again, "His real daughter?"

I laughed and said, "Real — I am not adopted."

He must have believed me at last. "I was your brother Khoi's classmate here in Moscow. We were very close friends. I'll be going home pretty soon and I'll see your brother." He was making statements, but something in his voice made them sound like questions.

"You are certainly luckier than I, for you can see my brother but I can't," I said.

He asked my name, and I told him. "Ah, you are the tomboy sister!" Then he remembered where I was. "I know it is long-distance, I shouldn't carry on the conversation. Your father is out ice-skating with some of his Russian friends. Would you call back?"

"I need to know when he gets in," I said.

"I don't know his flight number, I only know that he will leave Monday afternoon," the man told me. That information was good enough for me. I thanked him and sincerely wished him happiness in Viet Nam.

Aeroflot's London office told me there was only one flight leaving Moscow for London in the afternoon, and it would arrive at Heathrow at 9:00 P.M. Since I had already made two calls, enough to keep the KGB busy for a while, I thought it best not to call again. John and I decided we would go out to the airport and meet the flight on Monday night, and if my father wasn't on it we would just try again until he showed up.

On Monday morning I called Aeroflot again to confirm the flight schedule. I knew their rules prohibited confirming a particular passenger on a flight, but I tested them anyway by giving them a British name. They wouldn't say anything.

John went to work that Monday morning at his usual hour, and that evening after dinner we left Lance with my mother and took a taxi to the airport. We waited there forever, as the flight from Moscow was two hours and fifty minutes late. There was another thirty-five minutes of delay at the gate before the passengers all filed off. My father was not on board.

— — —

On Tuesday, December 13, we were back at Heathrow, and the Moscow flight was again two hours late. John and I watched with falling hopes as the passengers from the Aeroflot plane straggled through the customs checkpoint. Virtually all of them had come past the barrier and we were about to give up when I spotted a familiar figure, a man in a blue suit and a felt hat I had seen in Paris the year before. My father was the last person off the plane.

Everything else about the airport terminal was blurry after that. I focused on my father and on the possibility that he would take the one step further that would take him to a happy home life with my mother outside the Communist world.

He had stopped and was looking around in the building for a familiar face. I grabbed John's hand and pulled him along, and just then my father spotted me and dropped his leather briefcase on the floor, spreading his arms wide to greet me. He hugged me warmly, then turned to embrace the son-in-law he had never seen. "My son," he said in Vietnamese. Then he turned to me.

"Where are my people?" he asked.

I knew perfectly well whom he meant, but I couldn't resist: "These are your people," I told him, pointing to John and me.

"Where are my drivers and the cadres from the embassy?" he clarified.

"I told them not to come," I said. "I said I'd take good care of the ambassador." I was disappointed that he seemed to care about them.

He made a gesture of disappointment or frustration. "You shouldn't make that decision. I had the embassy in Moscow notify London. My people here should meet me at the airport, my daughter."

"Papa, you are not here on official business, you are here on family business." I tried to change the mood, putting my arm around him and leading him toward the baggage-claim area. "You are my guest, comrade!"

As we walked, my father spoke Vietnamese to John like a diplomat who prefers to use his native language with foreigners. "I want to thank you for loving my daughter and my grandson, and I especially want to thank you for taking care of My Yung's mother for me." He spoke slowly and distinctively.

John responded to me in English. "Please tell your father that it is an honor to be a member of your family, and loving you and Lance and Ba Ngoai is my pleasure. I thank him for having such a sweet daughter, too. And I am looking forward to getting to know him more." My father listened carefully and smiled at John's words, but he seemed preoccupied by something else.

He looked at me, his brow wrinkled with questions. "Will your mother be disappointed to see me without your brother Khoi?" he asked.

"Mother will be happy to see you, Papa, but I hope that you are prepared to answer her questions when it comes to that subject." I squeezed his hand as I responded.

"I'll explain to your mother why your brother is unable to travel with me," he said, looking down at me.

"You may need an ally," I teased. "Would you want me there with you?"

"You don't need to save me from your mother, she is the most understanding woman on this earth. I only wish I could have the chance to make her happy." His eyes seemed to be looking at something far off in the distance, perhaps a remote village where he had shared his life with my mother and the revolution.

"Papa, you would have that chance once you retire from the party," I said. I had blurted out what John and I had agreed I wouldn't talk about until the right moment, but somehow I just felt I had to say it then. Time is something my father and I have never had, and something inside me told me to grab any chance that came along, take short cuts or even steal him as I had stolen him from the SRV officials in London that night.

I may have miscalculated. The twinkle in his eyes died out immediately and he cleared his throat and spoke to me almost formally: "Daughter, this is not a matter which you can make a joke out of."

I was in too deep to back out. "I am not joking," I told him. "I am deadly serious when I ask you to retire so you can spend the rest of your life with my mother. I wanted to say this to you the first time we met in Tokyo, then again in Paris, but I thought those were not the right times because you needed to see our country after the 'Liberation.' Today you have seen it, you have had your triumph, your happiness about Viet Nam, as well as your disappointment for the Liberation that has gone astray."

He looked disappointed at me, not about the Liberation. "There will never be a right time, my daughter, for you to ask me such a thing. I wish you had never mentioned it!"

"That is like saying you wish you never loved me or wanted me," I said, crestfallen.

He softened a bit, and kissed my forehead. "That is not loving me!" he exclaimed.

"This trip is the first and only one like it that anyone in the history of the party has ever made," he told me. "The party trusts me, my comrades in Ha

Noi have made it possible for me to leave as early as I could since you made them believe that the matter was quite urgent. Our family situation is not a simple one," he went on. "Please do not attempt to think of anything that might result in a great disappointment to that family. I am touched, deeply touched, and I am very happy to know you love me and want to be with me, but please don't ever ask me to retire from the party. It hurts me when my daughter thinks that way for me."

I could never take no for an answer. "You can't have it both ways," I told him. "You can't have my mother and the party at the same time. At this point in your life you either have your whole family or your place in the party." I felt compelled to keep fighting to make him see it my way. "You know, you gave your whole life to the party. My mother gave the golden years of her life for the cause. But I doubt that the party ever wanted to share you with the people you love and who love you. For forty-six years the party had you to help make it strong. Now this family needs you to keep it together. I guess you are disappointed in me because my desire is rather selfish."

"We all are selfish to an extent," he said. "We are allowed to be selfish, my daughter."

John had gone off a moment before to check on the luggage, and just then he came back and told us to sit down for a while because it would be delayed. We found a couple of chairs and sat down, and I plunged back into my pitch like a salesman trying to keep his foot in the door even though the housewife was slamming it shut.

"A few years after you left, I was big enough to remember my thoughts, and I remember that I realized that Communism is great as long as you are reading it like a fairy tale. But when it comes to a true test, it fails the people. I was very sad at my own discovery — sad for you, Papa, because in my heart I knew my father, I knew how much and how sincerely you wanted peace and prosperity for the people of Viet Nam. Your friends, my mother's friends, my aunts, my sisters often told me about you and they led me to believe that you dedicated your life to people, not to the party alone. Then in one letter you wrote me soon after the reunification of Viet Nam, you said, 'One swallow can't bring back the spring,' remember?"

My father was disappointed in the way the Liberation turned sour for the southerners, but he was determined to try his best to make small changes for the better. He admitted his lack of individual power; he needed his comrades to think and work with him in his direction.

He sat and listened quietly, letting me rave on.

"How can you lead a country or bring prosperity to a nation by one book that was written by one man, Lenin, and he was a white man, as white as a

Frenchman and as white as an American? Somehow I know that you are experiencing great difficulty after the Liberation."

There was rage in his eyes, even though he was holding his tongue. Once again John arrived just in time to cool us off before things got out of hand. He had the luggage with him, so we went out into the night air and grabbed a taxi for the ride home. As we pulled away from the terminal, my father looked straight ahead, then took his glasses off and toyed with them. He was nervous and badly upset by my obviously premature proposal.

After a few uncomfortable moments of silence, he asked me: "Are you finished?"

I nodded.

"First, I would like to tell you that I appreciate your generosity to offer me a home with you," he began in a steady, measured tone. "Second, I would like you to remember this for the rest of your life — that I love you dearly. Khoi and Hoa Binh are my favorite children, but you are my pride. I am very proud of you and your caring, your love for our people. You are candid, you are strong, but you are also tender, and all that makes you a special woman. I love you for your compassion toward our countrymen, even though you are now a U.S. citizen, a wife of an American officer, and the mother of an American. But I still feel there is love for Viet Nam, for the Vietnamese people, within you. I am very happy about that and I would never dream of changing you in any other way.

"I only wish to remind you of one thing," he said, looking at me and finding a smile somewhere deep in his heart. "Be happy that your father still has the energy and the will to try to deliver a lasting peace to our country."

John sat next to me and had been listening to our conversation, understanding probably half of it. He spoke up then: "Be sweet to your father, Nha. Let's talk about Mom, about Khoi, ask if he had a good rest in Moscow, ask how his skating went last weekend, ask if he's ready to see Mom. To hell with Viet Nam and all that bullshit politics. It is not the time, not now!"

He was right, of course. I regretted not having saved all that for later, but I still felt the pressures of time on me and my father. There was always an old, invisible, bearded man who cranked the clock faster than my heart beat, stealing the time that I needed with him, and I felt that if I didn't tell him what was in my heart as soon as I could, I might never have another chance. I spoke more softly, so that only my father could hear.

"I scratched, I reached out, I crossed the Pacific Ocean, then the Atlantic Ocean, yet I can't have you. Perhaps my last resort is to kidnap you."

My father was truly shocked by that. He shifted away from me in the car seat and looked down the road. "How soon before we get home?" he asked.

"About twenty more minutes," I answered.

"It is quite late," he observed.

"Mom would stay up if it takes all night for us to get home, Papa."

He sat quietly for about five minutes, still fiddling with his eyeglasses, pre-occupied, impersonal. Finally, he spoke up again. "My daughter, I hope you understand the position I am in. Tonight after we get to your house, see your mother and hold my grandson — I should leave."

"I don't understand," I whined, and turned to John to translate. He waved his hand to indicate he had followed the words, and told me to listen to my father.

"If you are willing to listen, then you will be able to understand," he continued. "I am a senior diplomat. I am one of those who make the rules. If I don't live within them, I can't expect my people to follow them. And the rule is rather simple, that I must return to the embassy after a business day. During my visit I will spend all my days with you and your mother, but I should return to the embassy at night." He said it as if it were the most natural thing in the world, a veritable law of nature.

I understood perfectly what he meant. I was still mad as hell.

"Do you know why the governments of Communist countries have to make such a stern rule for their foreign diplomats? Because they are insecure about their own system, like a jealous husband who keeps his wife in a closet for fear that if she were free, she would run away from him!"

My father only chuckled. He understood me, too, but his mind was made up.

We got home about 11:30 P.M. My mother opened the door as soon as we pulled up to the front of the house and turned on the front light as she came out. Her face was radiant. She was wearing a new *ao ba ba,* a traditional Vietnamese blouse, that she had made a few weeks before. She looked younger and more alive at that moment than I had seen her in years.

When we went inside, John and I delicately eased into the kitchen to leave the two of them alone in the living room. John whispered to me, "Your mother is supposed to look sick; she shouldn't go to the door to meet him like that!"

I could smell the soup my mother had made, so after a decent interval I walked back into the living room and asked my father to go into the kitchen with me. As we entered, I told him to close his eyes. He took a deep breath: "Ah, my favorite soup!" he exclaimed with glee. "Sliced cooked liver, chopped green onions, too!"

I carried the soup to the dining table while my father went upstairs to wash up. From the bedroom upstairs I heard Lance's sleepy voice call out: "Hello,

Ong Ngoai. What took you so long?"

"Give your Ong Ngoai a big hug and go back to sleep. I'll be here in the morning."

Later, after a light meal, my father opened his suitcase. "I brought you something from home. There isn't much, but it is your flavor from Can Tho." He smiled, and I grabbed up everything I saw — sweet rice paper, rice cakes, tamarind candies, coconut candies, and other treats that made my mouth water.

In the middle of our fun, I looked at the clock; it was 1:30 in the morning. With some trepidation, I told my mother for the first time that Father wouldn't be staying nights with us, but would have to go to the SRV's residence. Her reaction was nothing like mine had been. Quite matter-of-factly, she began to repack his suitcase and suggested we take him there before it got too late, more concerned about his getting a "good night's sleep" than about missing a chance to spend more time with him. Clearly, this was a woman who was fully accustomed to separations from her husband.

After my father made a call to the residence to tell them he was coming, John and I put his briefcase and one of his suitcases in the back of the car and headed off into the night. The residence was only about five minutes away. John waited in the car while I took my father's suitcase to the house, a sleepy Comrade Chieu coming to answer the door in his unexpectedly cute "jammies."

The thermostat in the building must have been set on at least 80 degrees; it was unbearably hot inside. After Chieu showed us to the guest room and said goodnight, my father asked me to open the window a bit to let in some cool, fresh air. He took two of the three blankets off the bed and put them away in the closet.

"See," I joked, "if you slept at my house nobody would try to roast you like this!"

"My old bones are used to the weather in Moscow," he said, "although the winters there are always miserable. Don't let your husband wait too long out there. Pick me up after breakfast; I need time to discuss a few matters with the staff over breakfast here."

He turned to me as I started toward the door. "Before you go, I want to tell you that I am happy for you, my daughter. You have a fine husband."

"I am glad you approve," I said. I embraced my father and went out into the winter night, leaving him firmly ensconced in the hands of his Communist friends.

— — —

On our way back to the house, I looked up into the dark night and thanked whoever was up there behind the clouds. I was disappointed that my father wasn't going to sleep at our house, but I knew I should be happy that he had been allowed to come at all. I had to count my blessings.

I had grown up in a situation I wouldn't want to wish on anyone else, but somehow along with all the hardships had come values I was proud of. Some of my grandfather's strength had been instilled in me, and I had fought for my own principles, my rights, and my existence in a society in which I believed I fully belonged. At the same time, my grandfather had taught me to recognize the needs and rights of others, poor as well as rich. He never taught me, though, to accept the fact that two people who loved each other as much as my parents did should have to live apart, even for a "cause." As a grown woman now, I still couldn't accept it.

That night I needed to talk to my mother about our difficult past, our frustrating present, our uncertain future. But when we got home she was already in bed. I tiptoed into her room and looked at her lying on the bed, her back toward me; she was perfectly still and silent. Somehow I had the surest feeling that she had not waited up because she didn't want to face the talk she knew I would want to have.

I felt like a small fish swimming upstream; events were rushing past me like a current I couldn't withstand. The thought of my father going back to Viet Nam for good this time filled me with fear.

Over the next few days, my mother and father spent almost all their time together. He followed her to and from the kitchen, from upstairs to downstairs, to the carport when she went to get more coal for the fireplace. They talked endlessly, about friends they had known from their old days in the Liberated Zone. They laughed, they sat silently pondering who knows what, perhaps the disagreements that cropped up from time to time. Through it all, though, they both looked ever so happy.

I thought it was quite tactful of my father not to mention the obvious fact that my mother didn't appear to be sick at all, despite my reports of her impending demise in my letters to Le Duan.

Two days after his arrival, I left my parents home alone and took Lance to "do some shopping." Actually, I wanted to get out to see Rob and Bill, who I knew were dying to know what was going on in our little house. There wasn't much to tell, of course — everything that had happened so far had been quite personal, and I couldn't offer any encouragement about a possible defection. They were disappointed, as I was, that my brother Khoi hadn't come. Still, the atmosphere seemed to have improved from the tension we had experienced together not long before. Perhaps the arrival of their loved ones had something to do with their softer edges; the FBI and CIA had told them their wives and children would be able to join them in London for Christmas. Thank heaven, I thought, for creating a wife in the beginning.

Lance stayed home from school so he could spend time with Ong Ngoai, even though Christmas vacation was coming up in a couple of days. I was amazed at the way he just melted into his grandfather's arms. Normally he wouldn't be still for two minutes, but now he sat seemingly for hours between my parents while they talked. He played with his toys or drew pictures for Ong Ngoai, and now and then my father pulled his grandson closer to him and gave him long kisses. Lance even asked if he could bring his grandfather to school for show-and-tell on Thursday; I had to explain what show-and-tell was, and my father asked Lance, "What will you tell your friends about your grandfather?"

"I'll tell them that you are in the government of Viet Nam and you are my mom's father."

"If I didn't come, what would you take to show your classmates?" my father asked.

"I'd bring my Tinkertoy helicopter," Lance replied, showing off the aircraft he had built from the wooden toy pieces.

"Take the helicopter," I told him. "It's too cold for Ong Ngoai to go outside."

Later I told my father that when we had been in Tokyo, Lance had told a woman at the American embassy that his grandfather was "a good Communist from Viet Nam." My father enjoyed that a lot.

I can't describe the feeling of wonderment I experienced when I shared laughter with my parents after all those years. I looked at myself in the mirror, touched my face, smiled, and said quietly, "It is real, it isn't a dream."

They talked about everything, including the loss of our loved ones; I saw my father wipe my mother's tears when they talked about my brother Hai Van. They also argued as well, their classic dispute not about personal matters but about politics. These two strong people, one a dedicated Communist and the other a determined non-Communist, could not avoid the subject that had kept them apart for so long. I thought their argument was healthy for both of them. My mother needed to express to him the feelings and thoughts that had been locked up for two decades; he needed to hear what a non-Communist feels when she loses her land and everything else to the Communists.

She questioned him closely about the fate of the South. He responded that "it takes a longer time and more effort to rebuild than to destroy; Viet Nam needs time to heal."

She wasn't satisfied with promises. "How can you deliver peace when your Communist Party makes war against the people? My people had plenty, and the South prospered until your party imposed socialism!"

"I must admit the South had plenty," he said, "but only a small number of privileged people had plenty — the others had nothing."

"For thousands of years, there were always rich men and poor men in our history," my mother reminded him. "I can guarantee that your party will make history by stripping every man and woman to equalize the society, and in return the party members will be equally rich."

He put his hand gently over her mouth. He shook his head, and I could see his eyes begging her to stop the argument over their differences and use their precious time just to enjoy the things they had in common.

At more peaceful times, he would sit next to her and watch while she mended his shirts, made him pajamas, sewed on a few loose buttons. That picture lives in my heart even now. A few times when I caught the twinkles in their eyes and the big smiles on my father's face, I said to myself, "If I were to die today, I'd be one hell of a happy angel."

Chapter 27

The next Sunday, December 18, the family proposed a ride into the countryside near London and a picnic to give my father a chance to get out of the house and enjoy a little fresh air. To my surprise and annoyance, he didn't seem to want to go. He urged us to take Lance and to have a good time, but he preferred to stay at home.

I couldn't understand why he was refusing our suggestion, and rejecting the opportunity to spend time together in a family activity. Finally my mother took me into her room and explained it to me. On our way home from the airport, when I had joked with my father about my last resort being to "kidnap" him, he had been startled and could not decide how seriously he should take my words. Now, when we were talking about going out into the countryside, far from the "safe haven" of the SRV embassy, he was worried that I might have meant it literally.

I must confess that although I felt guilty for making my father feel uncomfortable at the idea of being alone with me and the family, the idea of keeping him from returning to Viet Nam was quite strong in me. Each time I thought of it, my heart pulsed faster and faster. However, nothing like that was behind the picnic idea, and my mother talked and talked to my father until she finally persuaded him to go.

He went, but he never relaxed throughout the whole trip. When we stopped near a pasture we had selected for the picnic, he didn't want to get out of the car, and probably would have refused to budge if Lance hadn't taken his hand and pleaded, "Ong Ngoai, I want to sit with you."

His eyes constantly searched the open fields throughout the lunch, apparently watching for squads of kidnappers he expected to burst out of the underbrush at any moment. I wished I had never mentioned the word "kidnap," but had only waited until the right time and the right place to do it if I could. When I said that to my mother, she scolded me: "There would never be a right time and a right place to do that to your father."

We cut the outing short because of my father's obvious anxiety. The tension of the day must have worn him out, because the moment we got home he excused himself and went to lie down on Lance's bed for a rest.

I felt great remorse that my words had had such an impact on him; they had made his entire visit, not just the picnic, a difficult time for him. I thought back over the long life of trouble and hardship my family had experienced, and remembered how difficult it had always been for us to cry together. We could share learning, happiness, hope, and even disappointment, but when something went wrong we always fought each other to shoulder the blame and worked hard on self-punishment. On this day, it was obviously my duty to take the blame for my father's mood. I told my mother how sorry I was that it had happened, and she asked me to apologize to him.

I went into Lance's room, where my father lay motionless. He looked at me, but didn't speak.

"Papa," I began, "maybe I was desperate when I said those things to you. Maybe I am stupid enough to chase a rainbow, to build sand castles, or to insist on the fact that I love you and my mother. But no matter what, forgive me for saying such a thing to make you feel uncomfortable."

He squeezed my hands between his. "You are forgiven," he said, but he didn't want to talk about it anymore. He turned his pillow to the cool side and lay back as if to sleep some more. I left the room and told John I needed to take a walk.

The wind whipped bitterly across my face as I stood on the bridge at Regent Park. An old British couple walked arm and arm across the bridge, the woman supporting her steps with a cane. The old gentleman tipped his hat to me as they passed by. I tried to imagine they were my parents, growing old together, but it was hopeless. I stared at the old couple until I lost them when they turned a corner.

On my way back to the house, I stopped at St. Mark's Church, looked up at the rose windows and asked, "How can it hurt so much to love my father?"

My father was up and reading a solar energy journal when I got back. "When will Hoa Binh get here?" he asked. I told him she would arrive on Friday, and he counted the days on his fingers and smiled.

For the next five days, my parents spent their time together at home, John took a few hours here and there from work to entertain my father, and Lance had his whole two-week vacation to join them. Each night after dinner we gathered in the living room by the fireplace and enjoyed each other's company, until it was time for my father to go back to the SRV residence for the night. All during that time I looked forward to Hoa Binh's visit; I hoped desperately that she would be the catalyst that would change his mind about staying.

Finally Hoa Binh arrived. I went to the airport alone to pick her up, and on the way to the house I gave her nonstop advice, the classical big sister's admonition to "do as I say, not as I do." I asked her to be her old sweet self, "Don't criticize the Communists, don't tell him to give up Viet Nam — I already made that mistake." I wanted her to understand that he needed to hear kind words, to know that the only thing we wanted was to be able to love him. It was hard to explain to Hoa Binh, but I felt she understood my meaning.

My father was in high spirits when Hoa Binh came into the house. The tension eased, the whole house filled with a harmonious air. Hoa Binh cried as she buried her face on his chest. He closed his eyes tight and caressed her hair, saying quietly, over and over again, "My daughter, Hoa Binh." Holding her out at arm's length and looking at her through teary eyes, he spoke: "I named you Hoa Binh with the hope that our country would achieve peace. Now our country is at peace and we're finally together, for a short while."

While they talked I thought I would slip out of the house to check in with Rob and Bill, but they were nowhere to be found; their wives and children had arrived from Washington and they were enjoying a family Christmas, too.

The next evening, Christmas Eve, was like every Christmas Eve with a young child; it took countless repetitions of "Good night, Mom," "Good night, Dad," "Good night, Lance," before he finally went off to sleep "so Santa Claus can come." My father stayed much later with us that night before going back to the SRV residence, and he smiled when I placed a glass of milk and a few cookies on the dining table "for Santa."

Later, on our way to the residence, he said, "I envy your mother for having the chance to raise my children. I could only grow with my children in my imagination, with my best thoughts, and with the most beautiful picture I painted in my mind about you, all of you." I ached to tell him that it wasn't too late for him and for us, but by now I knew that words like that from my heart would only displease him.

That night I lingered at his guest room longer than usual. I wished there had been something I could have said or done to change his mind, or that the magic of Christmas would have done it for me. But with my father, there never was any such thing as magic. There was love, there were obligations, there was our country, and there were our adversaries. His life knew war, peace, hope, pain, joy, and sorrow, but not magic. I fixed his bed for him, gathered up his dirty laundry to take home, and puttered around until there was simply nothing else for me to use as an excuse for staying. I must have looked very obvious, because he asked, "What is on your mind, daughter?" I just shook my head and kissed him good night.

The streets in Regent Park after midnight looked like a scene from a mystery movie. The fog was low in the trees, and here and there a streetlight cast a cone of misty light toward the stone houses. As I drove along, I was angry at myself, at the world, at the circumstances that put my family in this position. Months before, my mother had asked what I would do if he turned down our invitation to come and live with us. "I can't answer that question," I had told her. "Like I can't answer the question, how would you feel if you fell off a twenty-five-story building?" I should have just said to her, "I would like to be in God's hands when that happens." Was I in God's hands? I would like to think I was.

Back at the house, I ate the cookies and drank the milk that I had left out for Santa, and went to bed. I thought that perhaps the magic of Christmas had done all it could just to bring my family together here in London under one roof. From then on it would be up to my father, and it would take more than magic to overcome his idealism, his deepest sense of loyalty to his cause.

— — —

Hoa Binh's arrival touched off a round of sightseeing in London, a flurry of photographing members of the family standing before Buckingham Palace, Whitehall, and the Thames. At Westminster Abbey I sat in the car with my mother while Hoa Binh and my father got out to pose for yet another shot. Watching him smile from ear to ear, his arm wrapped tightly around Hoa Binh's shoulders, my mother commented, "It is good to see your father smile."

"Hoa Binh can make him smile," I said. "I hope she can make him stay!"

"Just be grateful for this day, my daughter. Don't make it any harder for him."

"Sounds like you are giving up already."

"He loves you, he loves all of us — don't ever doubt that — but a man has his own cause."

"I'd like to try one more time to ask him to reconsider, Mother," I admitted.

"Your father is honored by what he has done so far," she told me. "He believes that they still need him, but most of all that there won't be a 'good life' for him in America. He will die inside if he ever becomes a man without a country. You can, I can, many of us can survive even though Viet Nam went down the sewer, but your father would never be able to survive outside that system. Let him be," she pleaded.

That night after dinner, my father and I had a long talk in private. We sat on Lance's bed, face to face, our legs crossed like Buddhas. I held his hands as I poured out my heart to him.

"Father, I would like you to know that you have brought us the best Christmas ever in our lives. You brought back those big smiles on my mother's face and the sparkle in her eyes. I want to thank you for sharing yourself with us and allowing my son to know his grandfather. I want to thank you for loving him. I know you do because you accept his father as part of our family."

He listened seriously, then said, "I must thank my family for having me here."

"How I wish this moment could last forever," I said. "I would love to hear your laughter and continue to see that radiant look on my mother's face."

His eyes gazed at something a thousand miles away: "I must go back to my country," was all he said.

"Papa, you gave more than your fair share for the cause, for the Communist Party. Wouldn't it be right to give yourself to your family? Share it with my mother, show her your love that you had long been putting in your most sacred place for her?"

"I want the same thing you want," he insisted. "My needs are not different from yours or your mother's. You have my love, your mother has my loyalty, my faithfulness from a husband to a wife. But what you ask me I can't deliver, for I'll not walk away from my party." There was anger in his eyes that I had brought the subject up once again. "I taught my children to be loyal, to be trustworthy, and I would like to be a living model for my own teaching."

"I don't ask you to betray them. I ask you to share your life with us, grow old with my mother, and to hell with politics, to hell with the Communist Party," I whined.

"You have asked me to leave my country, and to seek refuge in a country which happens to be the country of my adversary. Think about it, my daughter," he said calmly.

"I have thought about it, long and hard," I insisted. "I am not asking you to live in America. Pick a country! A neutral country, any place that allows you to love your family, any place where we are able to be ourselves."

He interrupted: "I am a Vietnamese. I was born in Viet Nam and I shall die in Viet Nam with my people."

"Papa, I am not talking about dying, I am talking about living, sharing your life with people who long for your presence like the earth needs rain, like the fish need water!"

He softened just a bit, and leaned over to kiss my hair lightly. "I am honored by the love that my children have for me," he said.

"I wish for one moment you could be me so you would know why I ask you to join us, Father," I told him.

"I don't have to be you to understand your feelings. There were times in my life when I needed my children, your mother . . . times when I tried to visualize how my little ones grew, what they did, what they were like, whether life was good to them. Those times were most difficult for me when I was away from you all, but my duty to Viet Nam had to come first."

"It is an honor to be your children, but it is also very hard to live up to your expectations. I thought the war is over, that it has already become the past, and I thought we could reclaim our ownership and you would be ours." I gave him half a smile, all I could muster.

"We can make our relationship richer, stronger with an unselfish attitude," he argued. "We can help one another to face the fact of our family situation and be able to understand one another."

He looked a bit wistful, and told me of his return to the South at the end of the war. "When I reached home after Sai Gon was liberated, not a single friend had the heart to tell me that my wife and children had left for America. Then I went to Can Tho. When I walked through the village center, old friends of the family greeted me but no one said a word about your mother. Then your Aunt Bay told me that your mother had gone because you girls asked her to leave. For a few days I was a broken soul. I am ashamed to admit that I felt somewhat a failure — I failed my wife, my children. Somehow I became thankful that my family was still within my reach."

Just then my mother and Hoa Binh came into the room, and my father moved to make room for them on the bed as he continued.

"When I was sixteen years old, as a young revolutionary I realized that protecting my country is not a job or a career but an honorable duty. And during that critical time of our country, being a revolutionary was more important than anything in my life. One must be a believer in the cause, one must be strong from within, and therefore family was most essential in life. One needed to have a strong family to be by his side and to support him in many different ways.

"I had lived with that and I set as my goal that the woman I shared my life with should be someone who would be my partner, would be able to keep my spirits high and my morale strong, who would bear me children and bring them up to be fine people and teach them to love their country the way she and I did. I kept looking for that woman. I thought I would grow old without a wife. Then when I was twenty-six I met a younger sister of my comrade, fell in love with her, tried to get to know her. And like magic she had the qualities that I needed in a wife. I told my parents that with her genes and ours we would make fine children. My father didn't waste any time in formally asking your mother's family for her to become my wife."

There was pleasure in his eyes as he relived these younger years. Hoa Binh and I wept, but my father just smiled and went on with his story.

"The situation in our country didn't allow me to be side by side with your mother, but she was and still is the closest person to me throughout my struggle. I could sense her love, her loyalty. I looked into the reflection of a quiet river and I felt that I wasn't alone. When the French put many of us in the prison, the biggest fear that obsessed my comrades was that their children might be abandoned and their families might not stay together. But deep down inside me, I knew that my family would survive and my children would be taken care of by their mother. So you see, my daughters, we are so fortunate to have your mother."

Mother got up and took the two of us out of the room and closed the door behind us. We followed her downstairs and into the kitchen, where she confronted us with the realities of life.

"You two hurt your father, and I don't like that. You can't change anything for Viet Nam and the people we left behind by criticizing the Communists in front of your father. Don't punish him because of the pain you experience, together with the people of Viet Nam. It is not only him but the whole system that can do nothing good for the people there, and that's the way it is. Nobody can salvage Viet Nam, not even the United States.

"Let's concentrate on our little family here," she said, "and I don't even think that we can salvage our own problem. You didn't grow up with your father, maybe you think he is still young. In your mind he is the memory, a young father, a French-fighter, but he is no longer a young man. Let him go back to Viet Nam with happy memories from this visit, because this is going to be our last time. Please, for me and for your father, I want you two to go back in there and tell him that you are sorry. I know you are, and you should let him know that."

I was always known in this family as the one who was "stubborn like a water buffalo," but after my mother pleaded with us, I sank to the floor and was ready to go back upstairs to beg my father for forgiveness. She looked out the window and continued, "I know you two hurt, but you are young. Time will heal most scars for you, but your father doesn't have that precious time."

In Lance's room, my father lay on his side on the bed, his back toward the door. I looked carefully at him, noticed his bony shoulders through his thin white shirt, and thought that my mother was right about our impression of him. I didn't remember ever seeing my father in any way except the vigorous, vital man in my life and the lives of the many others he touched. I saw him now, skinny and gray-haired, and for the first time the reality of his age struck me. It didn't create the effect my mother had been suggesting, however; it made me want even more to keep him with us, not to let him return to Viet Nam.

When I was small I used to hear my mother wish aloud that she could have been able to take care of him, to cook him good meals, to mend his clothes and iron his shirts. She wanted to share the happiness with him when Hai Van received honor certificates at the end of each school year, and to have him go to see the principal when she got a note complaining about my misbehavior at school. I had been too occupied with my own problems, wanting my father home with me so I could prove to my friends that I was not a bastard child. I still needed him for my own reasons, even as an adult, but at that moment when I walked into the room I felt the need to take care of him, not only his physical well-being but his spirit as well.

Suddenly, I felt as if I were walking on an extremely fragile surface; one wrong move and I might shatter that whole small world that encompassed me and my father.

I touched his arm and he turned around. With the strength he always had, he looked at me as if no harsh words had passed between us just a few moments before. He was calm, and there was friendliness in his expression as he looked at Hoa Binh and me. He got up from the bed quickly and embraced both of us at once.

"I am so very sorry for what I've said to you, Father," I told him.

"I forgive you," he said. "Please don't repeat that conversation in front of your mother. You made her very sad." He looked at my sister. "Hoa Binh, I am sorry that I haven't had the chance to be with you when you needed me most. I missed you so very much. I often tried to picture you growing, and I smiled when I saw your face glowing in the sun. I pictured you with long black hair, and sometimes I saw you race home from school with your brother and sisters, and your hair flowed in the wind.

"My daughters," he asked, "let's spend our time wisely together while we can. And before we change the subject, I want you to know that I am proud of the job your mother has done to bring up my children. Although I had hoped that my children would try harder to understand my beliefs."

"You mean that you had hoped for us to agree with Communism?" Hoa Binh asked.

"Yes, but it doesn't matter to me anymore, as long as you love your mother and you love our family. That makes me very happy. I can't ask for more from you."

Hoa Binh wept again. "Papa, we tried in our own stupid way to let you know that we love you. For myself, I am trying to crowd twenty-five years into one short visit, and in my desperate way I put the burden of the entire country of ours in your lap, and I spoiled everything for you and my mother."

"Let's go downstairs to see Lance's new toys," my father said. "Let's see what Santa Claus gave him last night." He straightened his clothes and took Hoa Binh's hand to join the rest of the family in the living room.

I stayed there for a moment, lying on the spot where my father had rested, and thought out loud. "Not twenty-five years ago, not now, then when, Papa? You left me when I was 'too young to understand,' but even now I am still confused about your purpose and your mission."

For the first time I had a feeling that I might just give up on everything, and somehow that idea seemed to lift my spirits. To hell with the FBI, the CIA, the Justice Department, and even Attorney General Bell, who was counting on my testimony. I was tired of being accountable. What a lonely route I had chosen! I was even tired of trying to convince my father that it was his turn to enjoy his own family.

On the wall of the room where I lay, my mother had hung a picture of the Virgin Mary with the baby Jesus. Mary looked at me as if she wanted to remind me of something, and with my mind racing I turned away from those accusing eyes. Perhaps she was trying to remind me of my own words just a few months before, words I had said to the FBI and CIA case officers right there in my house: "I'll testify in court if and when the Justice Department needs me, but only when I know that my action will not jeopardize my father's and my brother's position as well as their safety. I give you my solemn word. It is not a promise from me to the authorities, but it is from my belief, a belief that we must stop Truong and the American from stealing U.S. secrets. It is my duty. I started the project, and I should finish it clean."

That was then, and this was now, and nothing seemed to matter much anymore. If I called Rob and Bill that very night and told them I had changed my mind, what difference would it make to history? Who would care? The world would not miss one more spy case in court, the lawyers would find other clients, the taxpayers wouldn't have to feed another mouth in a federal prison, I said to myself as I lay on my son's bed.

There was a small mirror on the windowsill next to the bed, and I looked over and saw my face in it. I stared at the image for a few moments, the image of a woman who was trying to convince herself she could be a quitter. It wouldn't work. "You care," I said suddenly. "And you will live with this decision for the rest of your life."

— — —

That night, December 25, Hoa Binh and I drove my father back to the residence. It was about 10:30 when we got back to the house, and John and Lance were in bed but hardly asleep. I could hear them bargaining about who was going to rub whose back that evening.

"If you write the alphabet on my back from A to Z, I'll walk on your back for two minutes tomorrow night, Dad," Lance offered.

"No, you walk on my back first, then I'll write the alphabet after," John countered.

"But you always fall asleep when I walk on your back, and then Mom says 'Let your father sleep, Lance,'" he complained.

"Please," his father asked in a mock begging tone.

"How long do I have to walk?" Lance asked.

"As long as you like."

"OK, then I'm done!"

The chain of laughter from upstairs reminded me how lucky I was. Since Lance had come into our lives I often wished that I had been able to give my parents the joy he gives us, but there were too many of us, and my mother had to work so hard to provide for us, and it seemed her endless efforts always came in the front door and went right out the back.

Hoa Binh and I found my mother sitting by her bed and looking out the window at part of Regent Park Road and the light from Camden Town shining on the roofs of old buildings. She held a small picture in her hands — it was the most recent picture of Khoi that my father had brought for her. She handed the photo to Hoa Binh. Our brother was wearing a long-sleeved, white shirt and dark trousers; the picture had been taken at Tan Son Nhut air base where he was standing in front of an American-made C-130 cargo plane. He looked healthy and as handsome as I always remembered him.

"I wonder how your brother lives, whether his family is still important to him," my mother said, tears spilling from her eyes. "I have so many questions about him, what the Communists have done to him, to his soul, his good nature."

"Mom, he lived with you for seventeen years of his life. He was a fine person and I don't believe that the Communists can break or destroy a basic foundation of anyone unless that person wants it to happen," I told her.

"The drive to survive can be greater than righteousness when that sickle hangs around your neck for twenty-five years," she said. She took the picture back from Hoa Binh, looked at her son once again, and then slid it into a small frame and propped it on the windowsill.

The little room became uncomfortably silent, and the old storm started building up in me again. Tonight I knew my mother must be wondering whether she would ever see Khoi again. Hoa Binh knew, too, and was angry about the whole situation. She left the room to get a glass of water, and I could hear her cursing under her breath.

In the beginning, I had handled my problems as if they were many tangled yarns, able to separate them into distinctive patterns and colors; but as time wore on and things became more complex and difficult, they became tangled again like a bundle of angel hair. I wished my grandfather would come to me in a dream and give me some answers to the questions that plagued us.

I knew Hoa Binh was going to have some adjustments to make after seeing our father. I had been big enough when he went to Ha Noi that I still had solid pieces of memory to use in thinking of him all these years, but for my younger brother and sisters "Father" had been little more than a shadowy figure in their imaginations, a dim picture they tried to flesh out when my mother talked to them about him.

When I walked along in the green fields at my grandparents' home, I was often reminded how youthful and vital my father had been when I had seen him last. At harvest time, when the field was a golden ocean of ripe rice, I wanted to share the "lucky" feeling of the time with him. When the workers burned off the fields to prepare for next season's planting, I remembered that he had once said the smell of that smoke "brings me closer to my father's home," and I missed him and Khoi immensely.

I told Hoa Binh that if our father's love for us wasn't growing, at least it wasn't dying, either, and we should know that, just as we should realize that our parents' love is immortal and unconditional. I had said to myself many times that it wasn't easy being my parents' child, because one had to want very badly to see through the complexities in the relationships between them and among all the family's members. We had to understand and accept things as they were, because otherwise we would go through life building walls that would keep our loved ones away forever.

That night, after John and Lance had fallen asleep, my mother and Hoa Binh and I went downstairs to talk about my father again. I was surprised that my mother's attitude seemed to have changed; she supported him and asked us not to say anything that would hurt him.

I thought quietly for a while, and then for the first time since my father's arrival I brought up the subject of my connection with the intelligence agencies.

"The CIA will fly my father to the United States right now if you give them your consent," I said to my mother. "Rob told me that."

"Your father would kill himself if you did such a thing to him," she warned me.

"I think I should tell my father about my involvement with the CIA," I said suddenly. My mother shook her head in panic. I tried to explain: "I thought he should know before he goes back. Don't I owe it to him? Don't I have to warn him?"

"You do what you think you have to do, like your father. Don't feel guilty because you work against his party. Your involvement with the CIA won't ruin your father's credibility," she told me. "It will hurt your relationship with him, though," she added.

"I don't know, Mom."

"I do. I also know that he doesn't want to know. What he doesn't know won't hurt him. I know that I can't stop you from working for the CIA, just as you can't ask your father to leave the Communist Party. You know what loyalty can do to people." She pointed her finger at me. "You can appreciate that more than any of us here in this room."

"I am grateful for your candor," I told her, "but I still think I owe it to my father."

"The truth?" she asked.

"Yes."

She spoke to me firmly. "You put all your effort, your mind, your heart into this project. You wanted to catch yourself a spy, and you are very close to being successful. You don't want to lose him now, do you?"

"Of course not," I insisted.

"Then don't tell your father. He will not try to save Truong Dinh Hung, but he will save Mr. Dinh Ba Thi. He will try to save the Foreign Ministry from embarrassment. He'll do anything to safeguard his government's interest. You and your FBI and CIA friends may just sit there and cry on each other's shoulders."

"I thought if I told my father the truth he would think differently about the whole situation," I explained. "He might stay!" When I said that, I made a face and gritted my teeth, because I was ashamed even to have thought it.

"Keep your secret to yourself," my mother advised. "Your father won't have to lie or hide anything about his daughter. He must remain innocent for his own good, do you understand?"

I looked at Hoa Binh for her opinion, but her face wore an expression of helpless wonder. "Don't look at me," she said.

"Somebody once said, 'The truth shall set you free,'" I said.

"That somebody wasn't a Communist, I can tell you that," my mother replied with a chuckle. "But even if Ho Chi Minh said it, it doesn't apply to your father when he goes back to Viet Nam." She looked serious again. "Don't you see how careful your father is? He never asked what his son-in-law does, he never asked what rank John is, even though you volunteered that John is a naval officer. He asked me about Kim's husband and Cuong's husband — he asked if they are good to his daughters, but he never asked me what they do for a living, if they're rich or poor. Like a POW, your father is better off if he only knows your name, your age, but nothing else about you."

She tried to smile, and half-succeeded. I thought her ability to maintain a sense of humor in these circumstances was wonderful. I looked at her and made a promise: "All right, Mom, I'll listen to you. I hope you are right about this."

She seemed satisfied with that, and went off to bed happy.

— — —

My father was going to leave on Tuesday, the twenty-seventh, so on his last full day he asked me to take him to the SRV embassy. He wanted to thank the staff for their hospitality, but he also wanted me to go along to meet some of the people who had served with him while he was a roving ambassador to the Scandinavian countries earlier in the 1970s.

The embassy didn't have an ambassador yet. Mr. Tran Hoan had been appointed to the job, but according to "Comrade Chieu" the Foreign Ministry hadn't come up with adequate funds to support him in the post.

After we arrived at the embassy, my father met privately for about forty-five minutes with Mr. Thi, who was the head of the mission while they were waiting for a full-fledged ambassador, to discuss some official business. Then, over breakfast, the two of them reminisced over their days in Oslo and Copenhagen, bringing each other up-to-date on the whereabouts of close friends and comrades in Viet Nam and abroad. I was thankful that Mr. Thi was diplomatic enough not to ask too many questions about my mother's health, because he of course had been informed that she was "seriously ill."

Both he and my father encouraged me to make more frequent visits to the mission and to get acquainted with the people on the staff even after my father returned home. "We are your family," Mr. Thi assured me. I said I would certainly take him up on his hospitality, and he promised that when the mail started coming regularly from Ha Noi he would have newspapers and perhaps even some films from Viet Nam to share with me.

Just before noon my father and I left so that the staff could close and go back to the residence for their lunch break and their afternoon nap. We began walking under a gray London sky, but soon the light rain and bitter wind forced us to look for a taxi. As we stood on a corner watching dozens of occupied cabs whiz by, I held my father's hand so tight that I hurt his thumb, the one that had been broken by the French interrogators so many years before. While we waited, I wanted to talk to him about my feelings one more time.

"Papa, I never told anyone, but when I was twelve I was very curious about God, and I used to compare God with you. I said to myself, 'Though he can't be with me, his thoughts are with me, like God is with people all the time.' I overcame our separation and felt close to you, even at 1,600 kilometers away."

He smiled and seemed to take satisfaction in my words. "I want you to understand something for me," he said. "I still am responsible for many people in Viet Nam, including your brother. If you make me stay here, I'll rot here, I'll die with shame. What good can I do for my children?" Once again, even though he was speaking to me, his eyes seemed to be looking at a place a world away.

As if plagued by a terminal illness, I could not escape the anger his consistent refusal brewed in me. I suddenly wanted to hurt him just to hear his feelings. "Maybe you never wanted us all along," I lashed out. "Why didn't you say so?"

"I didn't say so because it isn't true," he shot back. "Look me in the eyes and hear this and remember it for the rest of your life — and repeat it to your sisters and your children as well. Your father loves you and he loves your mother and your brother and sisters. I always did and I always will. For more than forty-six years I served our country, and I shall continue to serve her until she no longer needs me. If I don't go back to Viet Nam, what will I be but a defector to a capitalist nation? Would you be proud of me then?" He stared at me, waiting for my answer.

"I don't ask you to defect," I insisted. "I only ask you to retire and live with your family. Let others play politics in that arena!"

"Allow your father to put it this way: What would you and John say if I asked you two and Lance to come to live in Viet Nam today? I will not ask you to join the party, just work for us. We need John's expertise in the solar energy field. We say that he will get good pay and the three of you will get a villa and have maids and servants at the snap of your fingers."

I froze at the horror of his suggestion, and he knew he had won.

"Then you understand my feelings," he said. "We are not different, we are both Dangs and we all live with our own principles." He looked at me and the pain and anger left his face. "Smile when I go back to Viet Nam and know that your father will do his utmost to deserve your trust. I'll take good care of our people."

I rubbed my face against his shoulder to wipe the tears that were beginning to freeze against my cheeks. "The hopes, the fears, the desperation of the people in South Viet Nam are my hopes, my fears, my desperation, too, Papa," I stuttered.

"I understand," he said quietly.

At that moment, just as the rain began coming down more heavily, a vacant taxi pulled up. We got in and headed toward my house. My father wiped the raindrops from his hair with a new handkerchief my mother had given him as a Christmas present.

— — —

On that last evening together, my mother made us promise that we would not mention politics, Viet Nam, Communism, capitalism, or anything else that would turn the occasion into another argument. She spent half the afternoon in the kitchen, preparing my father's favorite dishes, while he played with Lance in the living room next to the fireplace. He was teaching Lance more about drawing, and after making a sketch of him he sat for Lance to draw a picture of his grandfather. When Lance had finished, John looked at the portrait and told him, "You have your grandfather's hands, Lance."

My father wasn't going to return to the residence early on his last night with his family. He called to tell the housekeeper he would be late, and then stayed well past midnight; I think the harmonious atmosphere that prevailed thanks to my mother's "orders" to Hoa Binh and me kept him longer with us.

My father got sad at one point when he told of an event that had taken place soon after the Liberation in 1975. One day while he was still staying at the Majestic Hotel in Sai Gon, the front desk informed him that a woman was in the lobby, asking to see him. He came downstairs and the desk clerk pointed out an elderly woman sitting nearby. "Who is this old lady?" my father said he wondered to himself.

The minute the woman saw him, she stood up and opened her arms for him. He was stunned by the gesture. "Who are you, may I ask?" The woman burst into tears and rushed over to embrace him: "My brother! This is your sister." It was his sister, my Aunt Trong, about ten years younger than he, who had come to Sai Gon to find him. He had not recognized her at all, and he told us that he had been surprised to discover that the people he had left behind had grown much older than he had expected. Despite the tender sadness of the story, we were gladdened a bit because it showed he still felt like a young man.

My father and Hoa Binh discussed Shakespeare after dinner. I left the room to do the dishes with Mom, and later they came in to join us. In this private family gathering he talked for the first time about Khoi and his problems with the authorities in Ha Noi a few years back.

Khoi had been a constant presence in my father's mind, but he must have been a constant problem for him as well, even an embarrassment from time to time. While in Ha Noi, he said, Khoi had consorted with a great many women, causing a lot of raised eyebrows and whispers among the top officials, my father's comrades. The higher-ups had tried to get him to reform, to "better himself" so he could be accepted as a member of the Communist Party, but he had turned them down, and that put my father in an odd position.

The worst was yet to come. My father told us that sometime during the war, a female secret police officer began spying on Khoi, pretending to be his lover and even going to bed with him. One night, after an intimate encounter, Khoi fell asleep and the woman planted microphones under his bed and by his desk. Suddenly Khoi woke up, caught her in the act and hit her in his anger. The authorities hauled him into court on charges of "insulting a government agent." Fortunately, the judge was a friend of my father's and he believed Khoi's insistence that he had had no idea the woman was an agent, so his striking her was not a political act.

The story was a little shocking, but my father couldn't help laughing a bit as he told it. "Your brother is a big boy," he said. "I can't dictate to him. But no matter what he does, he is my son. I can't stay angry at him."

His love for Khoi was obvious in the way he spoke of him, forgiving all the trouble he had gotten into and the embarrassment he had caused my father. Perhaps there was a reason even my father wasn't aware of: Khoi might have been the only breath of fresh air in his life, the closest thing to a real, ordinary person in that pretentious and artificial socialist system. Khoi is at heart a capitalist — a human being who yearns for freedom, for a life of his own, like a fish needs water and a tiger needs the forest. My father knew that perfectly well, but my mother and I sensed that he would never let Khoi go to find that freedom in the West.

There were no tears when my father left the house that night. He spent a long time in my mother's room, talking with her. They hugged each other in the kitchen and said goodbye; then he hugged her again in the living room. He kissed Lance and held him tightly for a long time. He embraced John and said, "Thank you, my son. When conditions between our countries are more favorable it will be my turn to host your visit to my country."

In the last moment, before he was preparing to go, my mother spoke up with her last request to him. "Help Khoi find a way to see me," she pleaded.

My father said nothing. He took a bag from her hand abruptly, then turned and walked out the door, not even looking back. Hoa Binh and I went out after him and helped him into the car, and I drove slowly back to the SRV residence.

The street was silent and still at the late hour, almost one o'clock in the morning. Hoa Binh sat in the back seat, her hand reaching forward to rest on his shoulder as he sat in front next to me. I glanced at them, and saw his hand holding hers. Under his feet was the bag he had taken from my mother. It contained two sets of new pajamas, two shirts, and a few pairs of shorts she had made for him — and two new shirts for Khoi.

We woke the housekeeper, who let us in but quickly disappeared back to his bed. Hoa Binh and I went to the guest room with my father and offered to help him pack, but he said he would prefer to do it himself. "I've packed my own bags for so long, I might not be able to find anything I need later," he said.

It was typical of him. His lifestyle was set in a mold, everything done by certain rules, everything restrained by a certain limit. That kind of orderliness made him comfortable with himself and any situation. Thinking of it I wondered sadly whether my father would even be able to function in freedom if the chance ever arose — whether he could reach out and grab freedom, whether he would spread his wings and fly if Communism weren't there to hold everyone back. I thought I should know his feelings, so I sat on the edge of the bed and took his hands in mine.

"Papa, this is not the right time or the right place, but I would like to know something."

"Ask me," he said.

I took a deep breath and dived in. "If I opposed your government openly, would they do anything to you?"

He looked troubled, swallowing hard before replying. "I am part of the government that you just mentioned," he reminded me.

"I oppose your government, not you," I insisted.

"You are you, and I am me," he said coldly. "I am not responsible for your actions."

"In other words, if I openly oppose the Communist government in Viet Nam today, you would not be blamed? I must know for sure, Papa!"

He looked angry and just shook his head. "Well, it is getting late," he changed the subject. "I must get up early in the morning since I have a conference at the embassy to attend to." He got up from the bed and put his arms around Hoa Binh and me, trying to put a warm tone back into his voice.

"Take good care of your mother and Minh Tam for me, my daughters. Hoa Binh, I am so very happy that we had this chance to see each other again. You have a good life, and always be sure in your heart when you find that man in your life." Then he turned to me. "My Yung, I want to thank you and John for making it possible for me to see your mother. You have a good husband and a wonderful family. Cherish it, my daughter. And in your life, whatever you do, do it in the spirit and with the honor of a Vietnamese."

He kissed my forehead. Hoa Binh wept in his arms as he walked us out of the house. I can't remember my exact thoughts as we walked to the car, but the pain was deep, and the wounds are still bleeding today.

Chapter 28

The visit was over.

We had seen my father and had asked in every way we could think of that he come back to live with his family, and he had refused. My mother had made her special plea that she see her son again, and it had been rejected. There was nothing more to do or say.

Hoa Binh left for the United States the day after my father left for Moscow. Bill Fleshman went back to Washington, eager to get things going from that end for the prosecution at the trial in which I would now have to carry out my end of our bargain. Bill had the air of a winner as he departed, and for the first time Rob and I felt we were on common ground — our projects, our goals were about to be wiped out by the publicity of an open trial. I wanted to say something to him, to let him know I shared his feeling of loss, but I couldn't find the words. An enormous emptiness surrounded us when we met for the last time at Reeve House.

In a taxi going home, I forced myself to turn away from the past and focus on what lay ahead. I thought of David Truong, trying to imagine the look of shock on his face when he was arrested, then the smile when he realized the television news crews would be taking pictures of him as he was being taken off to prison as a martyr to his beliefs. And I pictured my father deciding to take a day off and remain in solitude in his villa when the news reached Sai Gon.

We left London on January 12, 1978. In many ways it was a perfect day for a departure: The heat in our rented house had broken down again, while snow covered the mews and the sun remained hidden behind clouds, where it had been for days. The air was cold and so was my mother's mood. Even the vacuum cleaner wasn't cooperative; it broke down just after the movers left and I had to return the house to the landlord's son in a messy state.

It snowed all the way to Heathrow Airport. From somewhere my mother drew out her eternal sense of humor and talked about how I had missed a great opportunity during my stay in London. In normal times, she said, I would have joined all the other navy wives for a tour to Moscow "to stand in line for an orange" so I would appreciate America more when I went back.

Appreciating America is a subject we speak of quite often at home, as often as we talk about freedom for Viet Nam. More than just the great store of opportunity in this country, my mother is impressed with the democratic form of government and the liberty everyone enjoys to be himself. From her home in America today she constantly wishes that it could happen to Viet Nam someday.

— — —

It's a good thing that our gypsy souls allowed John and me to survive so many moves and changes. When we came back to Washington, we had to stay in a hotel for a couple of weeks while we looked for a new place to stay. The Justice Department advised us not to take our household goods out of storage, because we might have to relocate after the trial for our safety. When we finally found a house to rent, we had to rent furniture for the entire home and go off to the PX to buy pots and pans and all the other miscellaneous essentials a family requires. My mother went to stay with Hoa Binh at her apartment, while John went back to work, and I spent endless hours in meetings with anxious Justice lawyers and CIA people.

As I waited for the case to crack and for the Justice Department to set a date for the arrest, my mother was looking at the calendar, too. Even though she believed deep down that Khoi would not leave Viet Nam as long as my father was there, she still hoped that Justice would stall things a little longer just in case a miracle might happen.

It didn't, of course. Bill Fleshman finally told me that the arrests would take place on January 31. The night before, I brought my mother to our house to stay with us on that fateful day.

When I came to tuck Lance into bed, my mother was just finishing buttoning his pajamas. She looked up at me and asked, "Will you be sorry after tomorrow?"

"Mother, I don't like this any more than you do," I told her. "I worked with this guy, I pretended to be his comrade, his coconspirator for almost a year. I ate breakfast with him, I ate lunch with him, I had tea at his humble home, I even lent him five miserable dollars when he had nothing. I'll be sad for him as a person, but we shouldn't forget that he is an ambitious man. He wants to prove to the Communists in Viet Nam that he is worthy, and he will do anything to gain from them.

"Mother, this is our new land, our new home," I continued. "I feel strongly that it is my duty to protect America any way I know how. We did nothing for South Viet Nam, many of us just used the land, and that is why we lost the South."

"You don't have to give me any lectures," she said, a bit angry.

"Please don't make it any harder for me. I have been going through hell in the past few months since the Justice Department came through our door."

"You had the chance to say no to them," my mother reminded me. I knew she didn't mean every word, but she went on. "I am useless in this family now. Maybe you should let me go to Atlanta to be with your sister Kim and Minh Tam."

"I'll make arrangements for you to fly down there," I told her. "But I want you to know that you are wrong to say that you are useless. I always need you, Mom. It is just that I made my bed, and now I have to lie in it. I'll be responsible for all my decisions."

My mother kissed Lance goodnight and turned off the light. He looked up at me in the darkness and asked, "Are you arguing with Ba Ngoai, Mom?"

"No, we are discussing something."

"I think Ba Ngoai is angry at you," he said seriously.

"No, she isn't."

"Good," he said, his mood changing as only a child's can. "Please rub my back and write from A to Z!"

— — —

I stayed awake most of the night, unable to stop thinking about the upcoming ordeal. About 6:30 in the morning I gave up trying and went into the kitchen. The back yard was covered with layers of snow, an icy pack from the days before and a fresh powdering that had fallen during the night. It was so quiet I could hear my heart beat.

Perhaps the idea of my mother going to Atlanta was a good one after all. For the first time I had begun feeling strangely uncomfortable when I was near her; I panicked when I heard her footsteps coming into the kitchen. Making coffee and cleaning the counter, I tried to avoid talking to her.

"I didn't sleep well last night," she said finally.

"Me either. I thought about Truong Dinh Hung all night long."

"If it hurts you so much, then why do it?" she asked.

"Because I have to." I had no other way to reply.

That morning, after Lance went to school and John went off to work, my mother returned to her room, drew the curtains, and lay on the bed. I took out some clothes that were still in suitcases and ironed them all, seeking some kind of busywork to take my mind off things.

John came home about 10:30 A.M. He was supposed to be working, but I was so grateful he had come back to rescue me from the awful silence and waiting. We decided to go to the commissary to do some shopping, but my mother said she would stay at home. A little after noon, as we were coming back, I turned on the radio and heard the news of the arrests of Truong and Ronald Humphrey. I had never known Humphrey — Truong had only described him as "a man who has a pass to the seventh floor [of the State Department] and he can take anything we want."

Instead of relief or pride, I was swamped by a feeling of remorse. I held my eyes wide open to keep tears from going down my face. John took a piece of tissue from a box we had just bought and handed it to me.

"I understand, honey," he said. "I expected you to feel this way. That's why I came home."

"Damn, it would be easy not to do the right thing."

"No, it wouldn't. How could you live with yourself now if you turned down the Justice Department at this point? You would feel like an ass."

"There are a lot of asses out there," I said, laughing through my tears. "One more won't do anybody any harm."

"Don't you talk like that," my husband said sternly. "You underestimate yourself. What you do is very important. In time you will understand what you have done for the country."

"It sounds corny as hell, John. I feel like a sucker to do a corny job for the government."

"You'd better stop it right here before I get angry at you!" he said. He sounded like he was already angry.

My mother watched the evening news at 6:00 P.M. and gave me the silent treatment. I didn't watch. Instead I went upstairs to read Lance a book. I wondered what I would tell this little guy if he heard on the news that I was involved, or saw my picture in the paper during the trial. Until that day he had thought his mother was just a buyer for a chinaware import business.

The news broadcast told how Truong had been arrested at his work place, the mailroom of a business on K Street N.W. in Washington; as he had once told me, it was "an inconspicuous place to maintain my low profile." Humphrey was arrested in a slightly more prestigious location, the U.S. Information Agency. There were other conspirators named in the indictments but not arrested: Huynh Trung Dong, the chairman of the Vietnamese Union in Paris; Phan Thanh Nam, my old "friend" from the Paris mission; Nguyen Ngoc Giao, a professor at a university in Paris who was one of the people who had collected material that came from Truong to Paris and turned it over to Nam; and Ambassador Dinh Ba Thi, the head of the SRV mission to the United Nations in New York.

At this point, the government was still withholding the names of the agents who had been involved in the investigation of the espionage ring, including me. No one from the Communist side had any idea that I was partly responsible for the arrests. In fact, my disguise had been so convincing that Truong's old associate Thoa sent an express letter to my address in London, advising me not to return to the United States and suggesting I retain an attorney "just in case." She told me to burn all our letters and correspondence and anything else that could connect me with her and Truong and the Vietnamese organizations. At the end of her letter she stressed again, "Don't come back to the United States."

Dong sent a cryptic postcard, too, asking me to destroy all letters or other items that would "connect you with us." He ordered me to "stay away from the embassy, the association and all members. No one must know that you are his daughter."

As a double agent, I took all these warnings as quite a compliment for my performance; after all our meetings, there was not a trace of suspicion in anyone's mind that I was a "capitalist" or a "reactionary." The chameleon had indeed blended in with her surroundings.

It was not until March 17 that the news media learned the identity of "Keyseat," the code name for the government's star witness, when Truong's lawyer filed a motion in court for information about my background and my motives. In his motion, I was identified as living at 8 Regal Lane, Regent Park, London, the last address Truong had had for me.

Lance came home that day and told me that his teacher had read the newspapers and asked if "Keyseat" was his mother. He said it had to be, because "there is only one Yung Krall who used to live at No. 8 Regal Lane in London." We spent the whole evening trying to explain to my seven-year-old son about his mother's activities during the last two years. He listened carefully, and in the end said, "So you work for the FBI. I thought Bill Fleshman looked like an FBI man!" I don't know how much he understood, but we made a special effort to impress on him the importance of being very careful from that day on. We told him never to leave the school yard or go anywhere else with a stranger.

A few days after that conversation, someone broke into the house while we were out. I came home to find a light over the dining room table shattered, and glass everywhere in the dining area. The word "traitor" was scrawled on our writing table with a black marking pen.

I was outraged. I called my husband, then called Don Marsland, supervisor of the "Magic Dragon" operation. Within minutes John had rushed home, the FBI agents had arrived, and the police came roaring up. My home became a public place, as detectives took fingerprints from doorknobs, tables, and chairs. I answered all their questions, knowing it was useless. Mostly I was concerned about Lance, and I asked the men to try to finish their work quickly, before he got home from school.

That afternoon I lied to my son, telling him I had accidentally broken the light while I was trying to shorten the chain so his dad wouldn't hit it every time he sat at that end of the table. Lance bought the story, and even teased me: "Now you have to save your allowance to pay for the light, Mom!"

Don Marsland talked to my husband about having agents stake out our place around the clock. He thought the invaders might come back. I started seeing a car parked on our street with two agents sitting in it day and night. Another agent was assigned to keep an eye on Lance in the school yard during recess. I kept asking myself "what the hell is going on?" but there was neither time nor space to sort out the answer.

For a couple of days I walked Lance to his elementary school a few blocks away. On the third day, though, he protested: "I'm a big boy, I can walk to school by myself." I decided to let him do it; I had already passed on enough of my anxiety to this poor little guy, and I hated the thought of his having to look over his shoulder all the time, even when he was walking to school.

A week after the incident at our house, Lance didn't come home from school on time.

I waited as patiently as I could for about fifteen minutes, then flew out of the house and rushed along his usual route. When I got to the school, I searched the playground, the boys' rest room, the principal's office. The janitor helped me look for him. There was not a trace of him, not even his Spiderman lunchbox.

I thought I would lose my mind. I ran back home, hoping against hope that I would find him sitting on the couch and watching cartoons on TV, but when I arrived the house was still empty. I called the mothers of two of his playmates, but they hadn't seen him. It was exactly one hour and fifteen minutes after school had let out. I forced myself to calm down before calling my husband. He said he would come home immediately, so I left the house unlocked and went back to the school to search the area once again.

The playground was a lonely place at that hour of the day. I walked all around it, my chest pounding and my head spinning. The janitor saw me and asked, "Can't find him yet, huh? Why don't you call the police?" I dreaded getting involved in that terrible process, listening to officers asking me if Lance was a problem child, how often he ran away from home.

All of my energy was used up. I walked back to the house in despair. On top of the television in the living room, I saw the picture of Lance that had been taken when he was a student at the American School in London, a photo of a toothless wonder. I held the picture in my hands and sank to the floor, thinking about the last time I had seen him. That morning I hadn't been able to give him toast because we were out of bread; he had asked for apple juice but I had given him hot chocolate instead because "it will keep you warm." He had asked to sleep for five extra minutes, and I hadn't let him. All I could think of was how I had disappointed my boy. "Come home, Lance," I cried aloud, "come home and you can have all the toast and apple juice and anything else you want!"

Suddenly the door kicked open and there he was, looking as if he had jumped out of the picture I gripped tightly in my hands — the same corduroy jacket, the same white shirt, the same toothless smile.

"Hi, Mom!" he said cheerily. For a second I was furious, but I quickly swallowed it and rushed over to him. He must have had no idea why I picked him up and hugged him so tightly, laughing and crying at the same time. He was full of news that told me why he had been late. "I found a new kid, his father is in the air force. He lives right behind our house. You see that gray house? That's his house. They unpacked today and we went through his toys. I had a fun day, Mom!"

I certainly hadn't.

I made him soup and managed to calm down enough to tell him that it was extremely important that, from that day on, he must come straight home from school every day, and I had to know where he went and whom he played with. I tried to hide my feelings, to keep him from becoming upset, but my anxiety was too obvious. "What's wrong, Mom?" he kept asking. Finally I told him that for a whole hour I had thought I would die because he hadn't come home. It made him feel bad, and then I was even more disappointed. Freedom and independence are important for little boys, too, and I didn't want to take those away from him; somehow I would have to find a way to guarantee his safety without robbing him of his freedom.

When John rushed into the house a few minutes later, Lance was sitting in the living room, innocently watching TV. John was angry, as I had been, and he switched off the TV set and gave him a severe scolding. Lance's eyes showed his bewilderment — he had already put the incident behind him, as young kids will do — but he promised his father that he would return home directly every day from then on. He never failed to live up to that promise.

— — —

Hoa Binh came home from work a few days later and found a postcard slipped under her door. The handwritten note on it was a warning to her sister not to testify in court against Truong or she would face "consequences." On the other side was a picture of Arlington Cemetery.

In mid-April a letter arrived at our house, addressed to me. I opened it and read the short message inside:

Dear My Yung,

I asked a friend to mail this letter to you. Unfortunately, I can't see you in person to discuss the matter more deeply so you understand where we stand (the responsible people back home).

As a daughter of your father, at least you ought to be aware of it. The honor and the interests of our fatherland must be put above all things. When you go to court to testify, that is the action of a traitor, and you must study history to know that we punish traitors by execution, not only of the traitor himself but his next three generations.

You have yet your mother, your uncles, your aunts, your brother and your sisters. They will be the victims of your foolish crime.

Though you still have time to stop this unfortunate matter. I will not make any more contact. You must not show this letter to the Americans and I do hope that you take time to think it over thoroughly and come to your senses and not go through with it.

It was signed only, "a friend of your father."

I turned the letter over to an FBI agent and translated it for him.

There was no question now that we had to find some way to protect Lance more than we had in the past. Helping my country was not worth exposing my son to threats of that sort. John and I decided that the best place for him would be with my sister Cuong and her family. Her husband, Wray, was stationed at Fort Huachuca, Arizona, at the time, and I thought base housing would probably be the safest place in the world — maybe safer than the White House.

We explained to Lance that I would be very busy testifying in court and his father would of course be at work, so we thought this was a good opportunity for him to get to know his cousins better. Kenneth was Lance's age, and Cuong's daughters were four and five years older. He accepted the suggestion with glee. Bill Fleshman and Don Marsland liked the idea as well, and even arranged for an FBI agent to meet us at the airport in Tucson to drive us to Fort Huachuca, about two hours away.

Lance's mood was bubbly as we drove through the sunny Arizona day. He raised his arms into the warm air and shouted, "What a wonderful sun. It's warm, but it's beautiful! Goodbye, London, goodbye, Virginia!" The FBI agent must have gotten tired of all of Lance's questions — "Are there any poisonous snakes in the desert? Can you really eat cactus if you're lost in the desert without water?" Not to mention his personal queries: "Are you from the FBI? Why don't you wear a gun? Mom's friend Bill Fleshman wears his gun all the time, but he didn't wear it when he came to London." Halfway to our destination, he mercifully fell asleep.

Cuong and Wray and their children were excited to have Lance come to stay with them, and he blended in naturally with them. We went off to the elementary school to register him the next morning and he observed, "This is my third school this year, but I still like it."

I told Lance I would have to return to Washington, and he took it well but asked me to call him once a week, "on Friday afternoon after school." He reminded me, "I don't have the money to call you, and I think it isn't right to use Uncle Wray's telephone to call long distance, so you better call me." I gave him my solemn promise I would.

"Mom," he asked, "did you go away from your mom and dad when you were seven years old?"

"No, not until I was nine years old."

"Did you cry?"

"I don't remember," I said, "but it is OK if you cry."

"Don't worry, I'll be fine here," he assured me, looking at Kenneth.

I told him his grandmother would come to visit while he was there, and he was happy about that. "Oh boy! She will tell me *an di* [eat] all the time." He laughed at the thought, then remembered something important. "By the way, ask Dad to go to Seven-11 to check for new Star Wars cards for me. You can put them in the mail to your own son, can't you?" How could a mother say no to a plea like that?

I don't like to look back on a decision I have made and say I wish I could have done this or that, but during this period I did a lot of second-guessing of myself. I asked, "Is it worthwhile for my family to go through all this and all the money the U.S. government has spent on Magic Dragon just to put two worthless spies in jail?" I wasn't sure, but I knew for certain I was paying a high price when I kissed my son goodbye before I left for the Tucson airport.

— — —

The trial was set to begin on May 1. At that time, we moved out of our rented house, and the Ramada Inn on Seminary Road became our new shelter. I called Lance every Friday afternoon, as promised, and cried for hours after I heard his voice. My mother had arrived in Arizona, and she asked me not to call too often. Lance was really doing well there, she said, but after I called he would excuse himself and pretend to go to the bathroom or to take a nap; he would tell his cousins, "I don't want to be bothered, I think my cold is getting worse."

On Mother's Day I called my mother, then spoke to Lance. He finally complained about our separation.

"Mother's Day is stupid when my mother isn't here," he said, crying into the phone.

The next day, after John went to work, I was alone for a while in the hotel room. I lay on the bed and looked up at the speckled ceiling, the monotonous hotel decorations, the paintings nailed to the wall, the table lamps nailed to the table, the TV nailed to the floor — just like me, I thought, nailed to the Justice Department. I heard my heartbeat, I felt my pulse through the pillow. I saw my mother's expression, her disapproving look. I saw my father's bony shoulders, the gray in his hair that represented years and years in the life of a Vietnamese revolutionary.

I wondered if he would have the ability, the serenity, to understand why I was doing these things. I hoped the party wouldn't sell him the idea that I had done it for money, as it had sold him the lie that Hai Van had been "killed by the Americans." Surely after knowing me again he would know that money could have been no motive for his daughter. He loves me, he had said. He asked me to do things "in the spirit and honor of a Vietnamese." I felt I was no longer a Vietnamese. Tomorrow I'll step into that courtroom and words will come out of me, truth will come out of me, the Vietnamese spy network will be unveiled — and I will do it all to protect the interests of my father's greatest adversary. I will do it in the spirit of an American.

I needed more time to think. I got up and put the "Do Not Disturb" sign on the doorknob and went back to bed.

I thought of Bill Fleshman's visit the day before. He had taken me out to lunch, and even though he didn't say much I could figure out that the attorney general had asked him to check up on me and my attitude. When he dropped me off at the hotel I said to him, "You can tell Judge Bell that Keyseat is still here. There is no place to go, Bill." He smiled and looked embarrassed that I had known what they were all thinking.

My sister Cuong had perhaps helped me the most in dealing with my dilemma. When I left her and Lance, she had taken me aside and told me, "Do what your heart feels is right. Don't do it for the FBI, and don't do it to hurt our father. Do it only when you believe it's the right thing to do. You're the one who will have to live with this decision for the rest of your life. I can't tell you what to do." She gave me no hint of whether she approved or disapproved, and she was right not to; it had to be my decision, and mine alone.

Kim had visited us a day after the break-in at our house, and she was still terrified because of the incident. Even though I showed her a van and a car parked across the street and assured her that the FBI was watching over us, she and her husband, a former Special Forces captain, went off to spend the night with friends in Herndon. Barely controlling her fear, Kim said half-jokingly, "If anybody asks, don't tell them you're my sister!"

Back in London, Rob had told me that he would guard my family with a machine gun. Here in this hotel suite, all I had was a Walther PPK and two clips, ten bullets altogether, one of them ready in the chamber. Somehow, though, I didn't feel I needed the pistol or the machine gun; thanks to the tremendous support I had gotten from all the FBI agents who were involved in the "Magic Dragon" operation, I had felt perfectly safe since the day I returned to the United States. They were wonderful to me and my family, not only in the narrow sense of protecting us, but in the sense of camaraderie they projected, seeming to include us as members of their "big family."

I knew the CIA still wasn't happy that I was going ahead with my testimony, thus ending my usefulness to them. Upon my return to Washington, I had gotten word from the office of Admiral Turner, the CIA director, reminding me that even at that late date I could still decide not to testify if I didn't want to. The director would support me if I decided to back out, I was told.

The "option" he offered, plus Rob's obvious discouragement, made me feel that in a sense I had betrayed the CIA, but even that concern was nothing compared to the enormous fear I had when I thought about what might happen to my father. What would they do to him to punish his strayed daughter? How would he feel when the news reached home? I knew that my actions would kill any chances of anyone in the family ever being able to see him or my brother again. My own mother had already blamed me for putting Khoi's life in danger, and for putting my father's "old age in darkness."

I took a small picture of my father out of my wallet, but I couldn't bear to look at it. I couldn't cry, and I tried to shut out my thoughts about what I might be doing to him. But he had said to me, "You are you, and I am me." I had taken that to heart all my life, even when I was young, and I grew up knowing that no one could ever accuse me of the crimes the NLF and the SRV had inflicted on my land. I hoped that the government he worked for would still see me as separate from him, and not hold him responsible for my rebellious acts.

As I lay there wrestling with the pressure, I felt so very alone, as alone as the two spies I had helped put in jail.

I never met Ron Humphrey. The first time I saw him was in the photos in the newspaper, handcuffed and surrounded by FBI agents, some of whom were my friends.

I felt sorry for Humphrey because he had gotten himself into a trap between the Communists in Viet Nam and his Vietnamese girlfriend. I had learned that he was passing documents to David Truong as part of his efforts to get the woman and her children out of Viet Nam; he had met her when he served as a foreign service officer there in 1969. He didn't seem like much of a spy, just a man who had gotten involved in something that was way over his head. I had no other feelings about him, except that for a moment I hoped he would find peace in God's hands, because I knew that only God would be able to save him after I testified in court.

I felt more sorry for David Truong, because I thought it was going to be a terrible waste of a bright, ambitious man for him to have to spend years in prison. He was totally dedicated, and I always admired someone who stuck to principles even if I didn't agree with the principles. He had come from one of the wealthiest families in Sai Gon, a family that had driven the first Mercedes in the city, but now he was so dedicated to his cause that the only good suit he owned had been furnished him by his comrades in Paris so he could blend in on Capitol Hill, where he hung around trying to pick up information.

He was also cold, calculating, and somewhat ruthless. He would stab anyone in the back if it would help him gain the confidence and trust of the leaders of the SRV. He was even cold to his own parents, who wrote to him begging him to ask his superiors to allow them to leave Viet Nam for medical reasons. David refused, explaining his decision to me: "What would they [SRV officials] think of me if I put in a request for my parents to leave Viet Nam? The country is liberated, so a patriotic Vietnamese must remain there to help build the country."

I had suggested he think it over, and offered to pass the word to Phan Thanh Nam if he wanted me to, but he insisted that no one should know about his parents' request except me, him, and his family. His credibility and "face" in the organization were far more important to him than the freedom of his parents. Still, I respected his perseverance and his strength. I realized, however, that this man who never hesitated to use people was about to be used — and used up — by the same people he had been trying so hard to impress.

So many people were involved in the decision I had to make — my own family whom I loved, a sad figure of an American who had been willing to trade his country's secrets for a woman, an ambitious man who would do anything and sacrifice anyone for the cause he followed. So many people, but only one who could decide.

Foolish thoughts ran through my mind as I lay there on the bed. I got up again and looked into my handbag. I found forty-five dollars, seventy-five

French francs, a handful of British coins, and an American Express card. How far could I go if I did want to run? I couldn't take the Thunderbird we were using, because it was a rental car and they would find it in minutes. I could take a taxi to Vienna, Virginia, and check into the Wolf Trap motel where no one could find me, but it would take my whole forty-five dollars for taxi fare. Maybe I could check into another room in this same hotel, using my own credit card; no one would know I was here, since John and I were officially "Mr. and Mrs. John Hopkins" on the hotel registry.

On a sudden impulse I took out an overnight bag and started throwing things into it — shoes, underwear, my dresses. In the middle of this flurry of activity, there was a series of knocks on the door: five raps, a pause, then two more. I knew it was my husband, using our "code." He had come to join me for lunch.

I opened the door and John came in and looked at the suitcase on the bed. "What are you doing?" he asked in surprise.

"Unpacking," I lied.

"Oh," he said, never suspecting the attack of nerves he had just saved me from. "Well, get dressed, lady. Let's go down to have a drink."

I gave the overnight bag a long, dirty look and went into the bathroom to start getting dressed. I thought about the man I had married.

Some people wear a good-luck charm, others carry a rabbit's foot to shield them from evil and bad luck. I married a man who gave me more luck, more protection, and more support than all the rabbit's feet and good-luck charms in the world. I realized there was no way I could have gotten through this alone. John had been there when I needed a strong shoulder to lean on, and he had given me the freedom to be alone when I had to make a decision by myself.

I was ashamed to tell him what I had been doing when he walked into the hotel room that afternoon. I looked forward to the day when the trial would be over, when I would be able to laugh at my foolishness and smile at our accomplishments, and tell him about how he had rescued me from that last traumatic day before I went off to court and testified "in the spirit of an American."

Afterword

Although I served in the Justice Department under Attorney General Griffin Bell, I had no personal involvement in Magic Dragon or the prosecution of Ronald Humphrey and David Truong. It was some time after my retirement that a friend called and asked if I would represent Yung in her then largely unsuccessful effort to get the CIA to declassify her manuscript. My friend commented that she was being very badly treated by the agency, and needed help desperately. Both of those comments were true.

The effort to get enough of the manuscript declassified to permit publication took an exceedingly long time and involved obstacles that no one should have to confront. As it is, the story told by Mrs. Krall in this book is the truth, but it is by no means the whole story. The CIA continues to classify a good deal of information that could be divulged with no harm to our nation's security.

Before briefly recounting the effort to get the manuscript declassified, let me recall my reaction when I finished reading it for the first time. I had three questions. What has happened to these people since 1978? What kind of person is Yung Krall, and how important, and how successful, was her work? How does the Truong-Humphrey case fit in to the history of espionage against America?

After a lengthy trial, in the course of which Mrs. Krall was the principal government witness and was subjected to extensive, grueling cross-examination, the jury convicted Ronald Humphrey and David Truong of espionage on July 8, 1978. Each was sentenced to fifteen years' imprisonment. After serving his time, David Truong and his wife are living abroad — not in Viet Nam. I do not know what has become of Ronald Humphrey since his release from prison.

Mrs. Krall's father, Dang Quang Minh, remained in the Foreign Service of the Socialist Republic of Vietnam until he suffered a stroke and died in 1986. Her brother, Dang Van Khoi, escaped from Viet Nam that same year, and lives in the United States. Mrs. Krall, her husband, son, and mother are living in the Atlanta area, where Yung devotes herself to helping refugees from Communist and war-ravaged countries.

Judge Bell practices law in Atlanta, and continues to serve America in various capacities. John Martin still oversees all espionage investigations and prosecutions for the Department of Justice. Bill Fleshman retired from the FBI and then served as chief investigator for the House Armed Services Committee. The CIA refused to provide me with any information about Rob Hall, so I was unable to obtain his thoughts about this case.

From the information I have been able to acquire, I have concluded that Mrs. Krall's work in the operation directed against the Vietnamese Communists, here and abroad — most of which is *not* detailed in this book — was both important and successful. The details of that part of her story will probably never see the light of day. We do know that it was exceedingly dangerous work. Bill Fleshman told me that he was always torn as to how far to let Mrs. Krall go operationally, because of the great personal danger she regularly faced. In that same vein, John Martin calls her a genuine hero, and describes her willingness to take the witness stand and testify truthfully in this case an act of unbelievable courage.

John Martin also told me that the harm to this country that Ronald Humphrey was in a position to do, given his top secret clearance and extensive access to critical national security information, was incalculable. The potential harm was so great, in the eyes of the FBI and Justice Department, that the espionage operation absolutely had to be shut down, even if it meant the end of Mrs. Krall's work as a CIA agent. The CIA felt so strongly to the contrary that it took Judge Bell, personally, to get it resolved. He saw the importance of prosecuting this case, and did what it took to make it happen.

Given the fact of a lengthy public trial, why has it taken so long, and been so difficult, for this story to be told? The answer lies in the CIA's obsessive attachment to secrecy for its own sake, even when that secrecy borders on the irrational. Every word of the manuscript was initially classified secret. When Mrs. Krall filed a request under the Freedom of Information Act for records pertaining to her work, she was sent a few newspaper clippings about the trial; the agency claimed that every word of every other document was properly classified. Although the CIA's regulations express respect for the First Amendment, and say that the burden of proof on the secrecy issue is on the agency, not the author, the reality is completely opposite.

Only to the extent we could prove, to the agency's reluctant satisfaction, that various basic facts about Mrs. Krall's work had already become public, at the trial or otherwise, would the agency declassify the relevant sections of the manuscript. The public record copy of the exhibits at the trial had disappeared, seemingly after I sought access to it, and the agency refused to share any of its trial materials with me. Statements by members of the prosecution team in the case, that certain information had in fact come out at trial, were not enough. For the most part, unless it was in the portion of the trial record that I was able to locate, the information remains classified, except where the FBI was able to exert a constructive influence.

Former CIA director James Woolsey has said that the agency must find a way to overcome its unvarying tendency to keep everything secret — at a minimum, to enable it to claim credit for its successes. The shameful way Yung Krall was treated in this case suggests that it has not even begun to go down that path. The American people, not just Mrs. Krall, deserve much better treatment, and deserve to know more about what the CIA does in their names.

I know that Yung has no regrets over the great risks she ran in her service to our country, and I share the deep respect and affection that Judge Bell, John Martin, and Bill Fleshman have for this remarkable woman, daughter, wife, and mother. I, too, have come to view her as a genuine *American* hero.

Quinlan J. Shea, Jr.
Columbia, Maryland
April 1995

Quinlan J. Shea, Jr., retired in 1986 after a long and distinguished career in government. He served in the Army and the Department of Justice, with extensive work in law enforcement and intelligence.